**Hossein Bidgoli**

# INFORMATION SYSTEMS LITERACY AND SOFTWARE PRODUCTIVITY TOOLS

## IBM Structured BASIC

Macmillan Publishing Company
New York

Maxwell Macmillan Canada
Toronto

Maxwell Macmillan International
New York   Oxford   Singapore   Sydney

**To so many fine memories of my brother, Mohsen,
for his uncompromising belief in the power of education.**

Cover photo by Jack McWilliams. The Walk-Through Computer is a permanent exhibit of The Computer Museum, Boston, MA.

Editor: Vernon R. Anthony
Production Editor: Rex Davidson
Art Coordinator: Ruth A. Kimpel
Photo Editor: Gail Meese
Text Designer: Anne Daly
Cover Designer: Russ Maselli
Production Buyer: Pamela D. Bennett

This book was set in Baskerville and Helvetica.

Macmillan Publishing Company
866 Third Avenue, New York, New York 10022

Maxwell Macmillan Canada, Inc.
1200 Eglington Avenue East, Suite 200
Don Mills, Ontario M3C 3N1

GW-BASIC® and Microsoft® are registered trademarks of Microsoft Corporation.

Library of Congress Cataloging-in-Publication Data
Bidgoli, Hossein.
    Information systems literacy and software productivity tools/Hossein Bidgoli.
        p.   cm.
    Includes index.
    Contents:   bk. 1. Introductory concepts—bk. 2. DOS—bk. 3. WordPerfect 5.1—bk. 4. dBASE III PLUS—bk. 5. WordStar 5.5—bk. 6. Quattro—bk. 7. GoldSpread—bk. 8. IBM Structured BASIC—bk. 9. DOS, WordPerfect 5.1, Lotus 1-2-3, and dBASE III PLUS—bk. 10. DOS, Wordstar 5.5, Lotus 1-2-3, and dBASE III PLUS.
    ISBN 0-02-3094656 (bk. 8.)
    1. Electronic data processing.    2. Computer software.   I. Title.
QA76.B488   1991                                                    90-20366
005.369—dc20                                                        CIP

Printing: 1  2  3  4  5  6  7  8  9    Year: 1  2  3  4

# Preface

*Information Systems Literacy and Software Productivity Tools: IBM Structured BASIC* is a component of a modular series of textbooks developed for use in introductory computing coursework. This BASIC text is written for first courses in programming, or for use in conjunction with texts in any course where a programming tutorial is required.

The programming tutorials in this book are designed to give the student comprehensive training and reference, all broken down into manageably sized chapters. This approach gives the instructor a choice as to which and how many topics to cover, and gives the student a valuable reference to use long after the class is completed. Advanced topics not covered in many texts are included here, as a growing number of students are coming into introductory courses with some software literacy; this book allows students to go further in their studies.

The programming chapters are pedagogically designed with the student in mind. Features include:

- Introductory sections that explain, in basic terms, what BASIC is, why it was developed, and how it is used. Too many books "jump right in" without giving the student a sense of context.
- Numerous, real-life examples. This book teaches the use of commands by example so the command is clear and in context.
- Frequent use of computer screen illustrations to augment written instruction.
- Each chapter ends with 15–25 review questions, 5–8 hands-on experience assignments, and 10 multiple choice and 10 true/false questions.
- Each chapter includes a complete summary of key terms and key BASIC commands.

In any hands-on computer lab, having an accurate text makes managing the lab far easier. The best way to make a text accurate is to use it. In the four years that I took developing this text I have received corrections and suggestions that make this book one you should find both easy to use and reliable.

Chapters 11 and 12 provide numerous, comprehensive real-life applications. These applications highlight the versatility of BASIC and prepare students for application development using BASIC.

Appendix A explores BASIC's advanced features. This presentation should serve as a guideline for students interested in advanced topics. Answers to selected review questions can be found in Appendix D to assist the students in their studies.

Appendix B, The World of Microcomputers, takes a comprehensive look at microcomputer hardware, software, and their application. This appendix provides a thorough discussion of the types of application software used today and provides the foundation for the hands-on section of the text.

Appendix C provides a quick review of MS/PC DOS. This presentation should assist the readers to use their PC and BASIC program more effectively.

This text puts a heavy emphasis on structured design methodology. By using this methodology, students become familiar with "good" programming practices

The text is accompanied by a complete instructor's manual with lecture outlines, answers to review questions/exercises, and additional projects. Data diskettes with which students can access all the programs and exercises are included in this manual.

## Acknowledgments

Several colleagues reviewed different versions of this manuscript and made constructive suggestions. Without their help the manuscript could not have been refined. The help and comments of the following reviewers are greatly appreciated: Roger Angevine, Houston Baptist University; Cindy Belcher, Western Wyoming College; Doug Myers, DMACC; Charles McDonald, East Texas State University; and Beverly Oswalt, University of Central Arkansas.

Many different groups assisted me in completing this project. I am grateful to over four thousand students who attended by executive seminars and various classes in information systems and software productivity tools. They helped me fine-tune the manuscript during its various stages. My friend Bahram Ahanin helped me to improve many concepts of hardware/software and put them in a non-technical and easy-to-understand format. My colleague and friend Dr. Reza Azarmsa provided support and encouragement. I am grateful for all of his encouragement. My colleague Andrew Prestage assisted me in numerous trouble-spots by running and debugging many of the screens presented in the book. My colleague Robert Grossberg tested the manuscript in several of his classes and assisted me in developing numerous test questions.

My friend Dr. Lois Holloway deserves special recognition. She spent countless hours testing and running all the programs presented here. Her assistance is greatly appreciated.

I am indebted to Jacki Lawson, who typed and retyped various versions of this manuscript. Her thoroughness and patience made it easier to complete this project. She deserves special recognition for all this work. David Koeth designed the majority of the charts presented in the first phase of the text development. His help and thoroughness is appreciated.

A team of professionals from Macmillan Publishing Company assisted me from the very beginning of this venture. Charles Stewart had faith in this project's potential from the onset, for which I thank him. The assistance of Vern Anthony, my executive editor, in guiding me throughout the project is greatly appreciated. Rex Davidson, Jo Anna Arnott, Gail Meese, Ruth Kimple, Teresa George, and Michelle Byron, all from Macmillan, assisted me in completing this project. I am grateful and appreciate their work.

Finally, I want to thank my family for their support and encouragement throughout my life. My two sisters, Azam and Akram, deserve my very special thanks and recognition.

# Contents

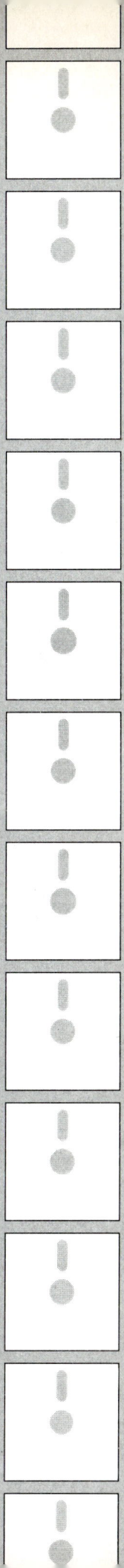

**DR. HOSSEIN BIDGOLI** is professor of Management Information Systems at California State University, Bakersfield. He holds a Ph.D. degree in systems science from Portland State University with a specialization in design and implementation of MIS. His master's degree is in MIS from Colorado State University. Dr. Bidgoli's background includes experience as a systems analyst, information systems consultant, financial analyst, and he was the director of the Microcomputer Center at Portland State University.

Dr. Bidgoli, a two-time winner of the MPPP (Meritorious Performance and Professional Promise) award for outstanding performance in teaching, research and university/community service is the author of fifteen texts and numerous professional papers and articles presented and published throughout the United States on the topics of computers and MIS. Dr. Bidgoli has also designed and implemented over twenty executive seminars on all aspects of information systems and decision support systems.

# IBM STRUCTURED BASIC

# Problem Solving Using Computers

**1**

## 1–1

## INTRODUCTION

In this chapter, we review the principles of programming using the BASIC language. We introduce the steps in developing a program, and you learn about structure charts, flowcharts, and pseudocodes as tools for designing program logic. We also discuss modular and structured programming principles.

## 1–2

## THE PROGRAM DEVELOPMENT LIFE CYCLE

In this chapter, we give you a quick overview of programming and the program development life cycle (PDLC). The steps we present apply to any programming language or software program when it is used as a problem-solving tool.

To use BASIC (or any other application software) as a programming language, you should follow the steps presented in figure 1–1.

## 1–2–1

### Problem Definition

The first step, **problem definition,** is the most important phase of the PDLC. Before you can do anything else, you must first define the nature and scope of the problem you intend to use BASIC to solve.

To do this, you may first have to perform an output analysis, which is a clear definition of all the outputs (answers) you intend to receive from your BASIC program. You also need to determine what sort of input data will be required. A clear definition of the problem as well as the input and output specifications may help you to achieve a solution faster.

For example, suppose that you want to use BASIC to solve a payroll problem. You want your program to print accurate monthly, biweekly, and weekly paychecks for your employees. The output of the program will be the paychecks. Naturally, some input data are needed to produce the paychecks. In

**Figure 1–1**

The Steps in the Program Development Life Cycle

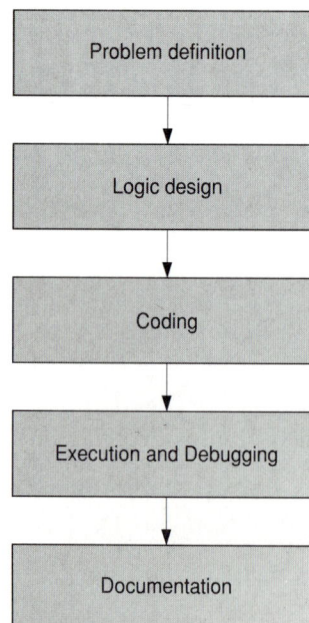

Problem definition

↓

Logic design

↓

Coding

↓

Execution and Debugging

↓

Documentation

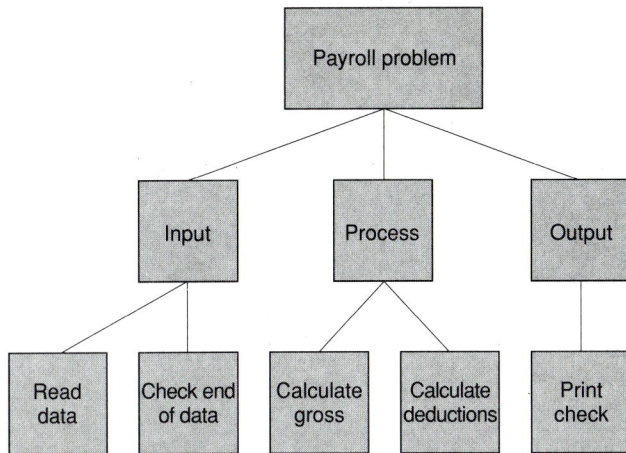

**Figure 1–2**
An Example of a Structure Chart

the simplest case, you need to know the number of hours that each employee has worked, the pay rate, the overtime rate, and the deductions.

## Logic Design                                                                                   1–2–2

The second step in the PDLC is **logic design**. Before you attempt to write a program, you must define how you will reach your solution. In programming, this process is called logic design or algorithm design. An **algorithm** is a series of steps that, when followed properly, lead to the solution of your problem. When you design an algorithm, remember the KISS principle (Keep It Simple Stupid). In other words, try to move the mountain a teaspoonful at a time.

Many tools are available to help clarify your program's logic. Three of the most powerful logic-design tools are flowcharts (the most commonly used tool), structure charts, and pseudocodes. We discuss flowcharts in detail in the next section.

A **structure chart** breaks a problem into its components. Figure 1–2 illustrates a structure chart for a payroll problem.

Table 1–1 presents an example of **pseudocode**. As you can see, pseudocode is very similar to computer code. That is why it is called pseudo ("like") code. Table 1–2 lists some pseudocode keywords.

---

Print Heading
Read the First Time Sheet
Check for the End of Data Marker
IF Hours Is Greater than 40
    THEN
        Calculate Overtime Pay (using overtime
        formula)
    ELSE
        Calculate Regular Pay (using regular
        formula)
Calculate Deductions
Print a Check
Read the Next Time Sheet

---

**Table 1–1**
Pseudocode for a Payroll Problem

**Table 1–2**
Pseudocode Keywords

| Arithmetic | Transfer | Input/Output | Decision | Repetition |
|---|---|---|---|---|
| Add | Move | Read | If Then | Repeat Until |
| Subtract | Store | Input | Else | Perform Until |
| Multiply | Replace | Write | | Do While |
| Divide | Get | Print | | Do Until |
| Compute | Put | Display | | |
| Calculate | | | | |

When you develop pseudocode, you should follow these steps:

1. Conduct an input/output analysis.
2. Break the problem down into several modules (steps).
3. Break each module into smaller steps, repeating this process until the problem is divided into its basic components.
4. Review the proposed solution for possible correction.

You should use these tools to help safeguard your program against logic errors. Logic errors result in erroneous output—your program may run and process the data, but the results are incorrect. Suppose that in your payroll problem, you have the program multiply the pay rate by the number of deductions instead of by the number of hours worked. Your program runs, but you haven't calculated the employee's pay correctly—your program has a logic error.

Logic errors are the hardest to detect. That is why it is important to design your program carefully to begin with. Flowcharts, structure charts, and pseudocode can all help you with your logic design. These tools can also help you avoid syntax errors. These errors include using the wrong keyword (command), using incorrect programming grammar, or even misspelling commands.

After you design your logic and work through it to make sure that it is sound, you are ready to move on to the next step.

## 1–2–3     Coding

After designing your logic and checking it, you are ready to begin **coding** your program. The best approach to coding is the modular approach—entering the program as a series of independent blocks, each performing one particular function. After entering each block, test and document it. When you have it working to your satisfaction, you can begin the next block. We discuss modular programming in more detail later in this chapter.

## 1–2–4     Execution and Debugging

As often happens, your program will probably not run perfectly at first. It may not run at all or it may run completely but generate the wrong answers. The next step in the PDLC is to debug your program. **Debug** means to find the errors in your program.

One method of debugging is to run some test data through your program. If your program produces the expected results, you can be fairly certain that your program is working correctly.

## Documentation

To make your program self-explanatory (and for your own future reference), you should document your program. **Documentation** can be internal or external.

Internal documentation is a series of statements (comments) within your program that explain its function. There are three types of internal documentation:

- Program documentation is a few lines of explanation at the beginning of the program that describe its function.
- Module documentation describes the function of a particular module.
- Line, or segment, documentation explains individual lines or segments of a module.

External documentation may include a flowchart, pseudocode, a structure chart, and a program listing. Comprehensive external documentation can serve as a user manual for future reference.

Both internal and external documentation are important. You should get in the habit of including them with every program you write.

A **flowchart** is a pictorial representation of all the steps involved in a program. A flowchart is similar to a road map. It shows what must be accomplished. The most important reasons for using a flowchart include the following:

- A flowchart makes the logic of a program more understandable to both the programmer and the user of the program.
- A flowchart reduces the complexity of large programs by dividing them into smaller sections.
- A flowchart makes future reference to a program easy.
- A flowchart is a valuable tool for documentation of a program.

There are two different types of flowcharts: program flowcharts and system flowcharts. A system flowchart depicts the entire operation of a computer system. A program flowchart illustrates the operation of a particular program. In this book, we are concerned only with the program flowchart.

## Flowchart Symbols

A series of standard symbols are used for preparing a flowchart. The most commonly used symbols are presented in figure 1–3. Figure 1–4 shows a flowcharting template that contains cutouts of the shapes used when drawing a flowchart.

**Figure 1–3**
Selected Flowcharting Symbols

1.  Terminal
    (e.g., START, END, or STOP)

2.  Process (e.g., X+Y, X*Y, X/Y, ...)

3.  Input/Output (e.g., READ or PRINT)

4.  Decision (e.g., X>Y, X=Y, ...)

5.  Connector (e.g., it connects two
    different parts of a flowchart
    together)

6.  Flowlines (e.g., they connect one
    symbol to another, and show the
    direction of logic)

A connector symbol connects two different parts of a flowchart. Flowlines connect one symbol to another and show the direction of logic.

## 1–3–2          Understanding Flow Direction

All the symbols presented in the flowchart template are connected using straight lines. These lines are called flowlines. Arrowheads indicate the direction of program flow. Usually, when you draw a flowchart, the flow is from left to right and from top to bottom.

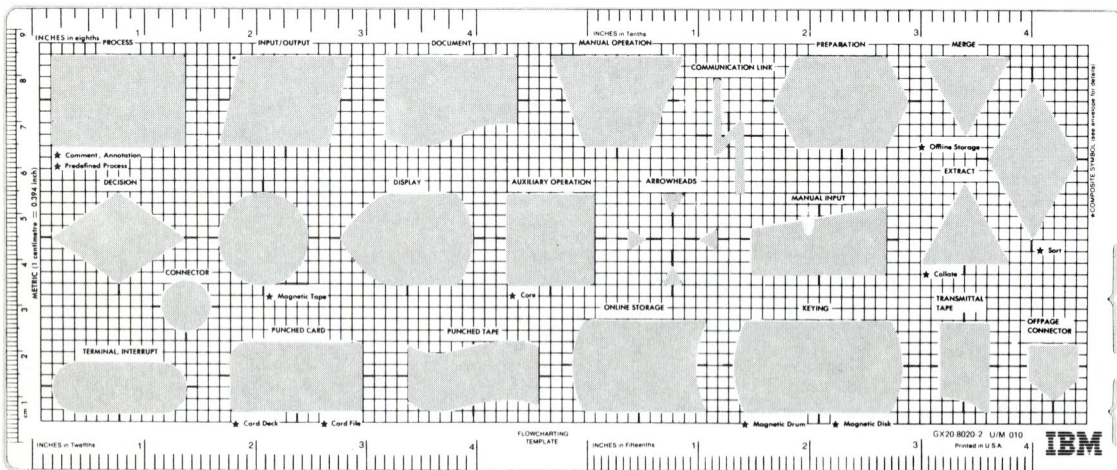

**Figure 1–4**
Flowchart Template (Courtesy of IBM Corporation)

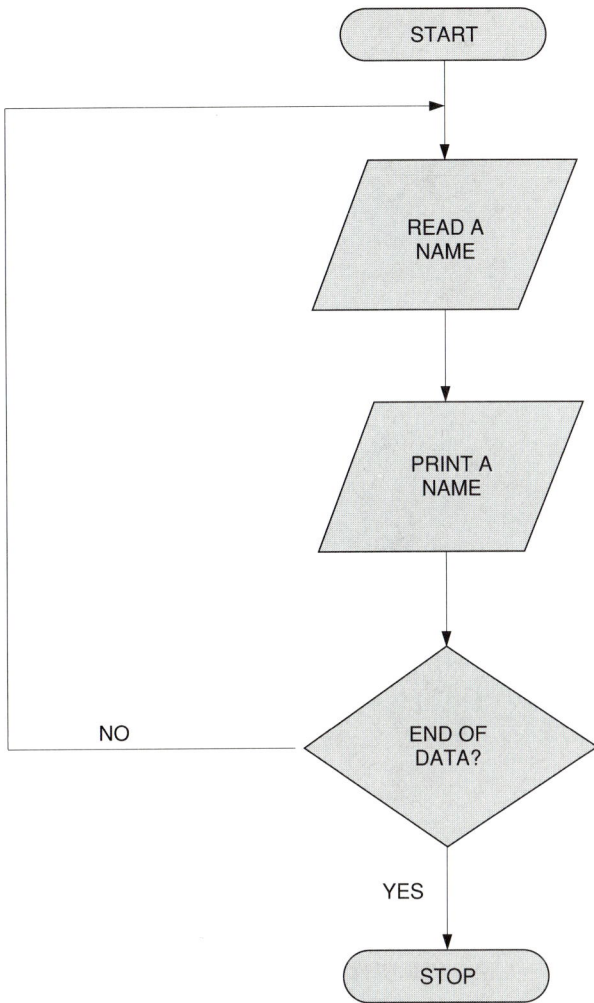

**Figure 1–5**

Flowchart for a Program that Reads Student Names and Prints Them

Figure 1–5 shows a flowchart for a program that reads a group of student names and then prints them. Figure 1–6 shows the pseudocode equivalent of this flowchart.

Figure 1–7 shows a flowchart for a program that reads ten numbers from a data line and prints their average. Figure 1–8 lists the pseudocode equivalent of this flowchart.

In figure 1–9, you can see a flowchart of a program that reads a group of student names and test scores and then prints the names of the students with

```
Start
Repeat the Following:
      READ a Name
      Display the Name
      IF There Are No More Names to Process, Leave This Loop
End of Loop
END
```

**Figure 1–6**

Pseudocode for the Program in Figure 1–5

**Figure 1–7**

Flowchart for a Program that
Reads 10 Numbers and Prints
the Average

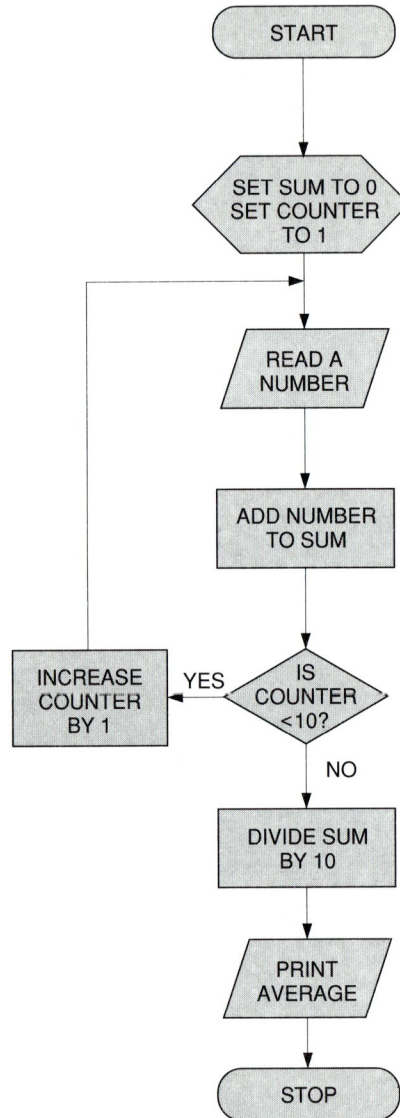

```
            ┌──────────┐
            │  START   │
            └────┬─────┘
                 │
         ┌───────▼────────┐
         │  SET SUM TO 0  │
         │  SET COUNTER   │
         │     TO 1       │
         └───────┬────────┘
                 │
         ┌───────▼────────┐
         │   READ A       │
         │   NUMBER       │
         └───────┬────────┘
                 │
         ┌───────▼────────┐
         │  ADD NUMBER    │
         │   TO SUM       │
         └───────┬────────┘
                 │
  ┌──────────┐   │
  │ INCREASE │YES│   ┌─────────┐
  │ COUNTER  │◄──────│   IS    │
  │  BY 1    │       │ COUNTER │
  └──────────┘       │  <10?   │
                     └────┬────┘
                       NO │
              ┌───────────▼──────┐
              │  DIVIDE SUM      │
              │    BY 10         │
              └───────────┬──────┘
                          │
              ┌───────────▼──────┐
              │   PRINT          │
              │   AVERAGE        │
              └───────────┬──────┘
                          │
                   ┌──────▼─────┐
                   │    STOP    │
                   └────────────┘
```

**Figure 1–8**

Pseudocode for the Program in
Figure 1–7

> Start
> Set the Sum to Zero
> Set the Counter to One
> Repeat the Following:
>       Read a Number
>       Add the Number to the Sum
>       IF the Counter Equals 10, Leave This Loop
>       Add One to the Counter
> End of Loop
> Compute the Average (Sum Divided by 10)
> Display the Average
> END

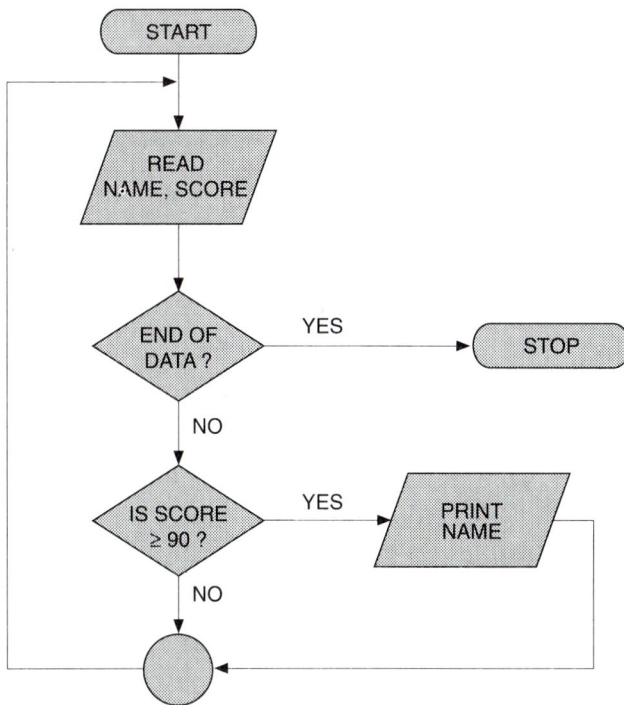

**Figure 1–9**
Flowchart for a Program that
Reads Student Names and Test
Scores, and Prints the Names of
Students with a Test Score of 90
or More

a test score of 90 or above. The pseudocode equivalent of this flowchart is shown
in figure 1–10.

## 1–4
## MODULAR PROGRAMMING

The programming problems you encounter are usually large and complex.
Solving the entire problem in one shot is probably not the most efficient way to
tackle the project. **Modular programming** (sometimes called top-down programming) involves breaking a large project into several smaller ones. It is much
easier to code and debug a small module than an entire program. A modular
program is easier to understand, code, debug, document, and modify.

   In BASIC, when you want to implement a particular module, you use a
subroutine. A subroutine is a set of instructions that performs a particular task
(see Chapter 8). You can break down any large task into a series of subroutines.

```
Start
Repeat the Following:
       READ a Student Name and Score
       IF There Is No More Data, THEN Leave This Loop
       IF the Score Is Greater than or Equal to 90, THEN Display
       the Student's Name
End of Loop
END
```

**Figure 1–10**
Pseudocode for the Program in
Figure 1–9

# 1–5
# STRUCTURED PROGRAMMING

Since the early 1970s, programmers have been moving away from GOTO-type programming because GOTO statements can make a program difficult to debug and modify. Instead, the current trend is toward **structured programming**.

The main objectives of structured programming methodology are as follows:

**Figure 1–11**
Programming Structures

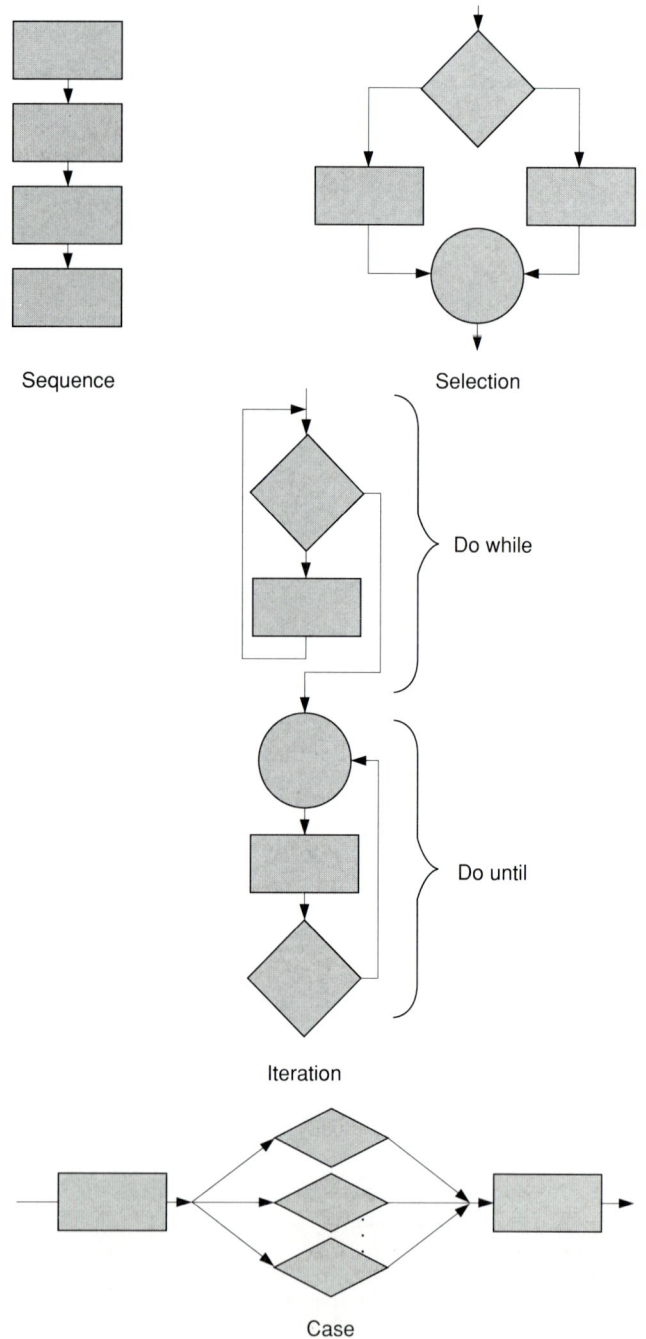

- To produce reliable programs that are error free
- To extend existing code easily to satisfy new users' requirements
- To find and correct bugs easily

In structured programming, four structures are used for performing any task: sequence, selection, iteration, and CASE. Figure 1-11 illustrates these four programming structures, along with specific commands.

In the sequence structure, the program flow goes from step 1 to step 2 to step 3 without looping or branching. The program flow is always from left to right and from top to bottom.

You use the selection structure whenever the program must choose between two options, such as regular and overtime pay, or high and low commission.

The iteration structure is a loop for performing a task a particular number of times, such as printing 100 different checks or calculating the commissions for a group of 200 salespeople.

You use the CASE structure when the program must choose from more than two options, such as choosing one commission formula from nine available formulas.

## SUMMARY

In this chapter, we reviewed the steps in the program development life cycle. We explained structure charts, pseudocode, and flowcharts as tools for designing the logic of a program. We also discussed the advantages of modular programming. In the next chapter, we introduce you to BASIC, the most commonly used programming language for microcomputers.

## REVIEW QUESTIONS

*These questions are answered in Appendix D.

1. What are the steps in the program development life cycle?
*2. Why is problem definition so important? What is an algorithm?
3. Give three examples of problems that can be solved by using a programming language, such as BASIC.
4. What is logic design? What are syntax errors? What are logic errors?
5. What is a structure chart?
6. What is pseudocode?
7. What are flowcharts?
*8. Why do you use flowcharts? Pseudocodes?
9. Compare and contrast structure charts, flowcharts, and pseudocodes.
10. What is documentation?
11. Why is documentation needed?
12. List three flowcharting symbols.
13. What is flow direction?
14. What is modular programming? Why has modular programming become so popular?
15. What is structured programming?
*16. List four types of programming structures.

17. Give an example of each programming structure.

18. What command is used to implement each structure?

---

**HANDS-ON EXPERIENCE**

1. Develop a flowchart for the calculation of the depreciation of an automobile using the straight-line depreciation technique. Use the following data: the price of an automobile is $16,000, the useful life is five years, and the salvage value is $2,000.

2. Consult the Microsoft BASIC manual. What kind of documentation is contained in this manual? Is this documentation easy to read?

3. Draw a flowchart to select an employee from 100 employees for an overseas assignment. The employee must meet the following criteria:

- Must be 35 or older
- Must speak German
- Must hold a masters degree

4. Draw a structure chart for the situation in question 1.

---

**KEY TERMS**

| | | |
|---|---|---|
| Algorithm | Flowchart | Pseudocode |
| Coding | Logic design | Structure chart |
| Debug | Modular programming | Structured programming |
| Documentation | Problem definition | |

---

**ARE YOU READY TO MOVE ON?**

**Multiple Choice**

1. Which of the following is not included in the program development life cycle?
   a. problem definition
   b. logic design
   c. coding
   d. execution and debugging
   e. they are all included

2. In producing comprehensive documentation, you may use all the following except
   a. flowcharts
   b. pseudocode
   c. structure charts
   d. program listing
   e. all of the above may be used

3. Which of the following is not true of modular programs?
   a. they are more difficult to debug
   b. they are easier to develop
   c. they are easier to maintain
   d. they are easier to modify
   e. they are easier to correct

4. Pseudocode is
   a. similar to flowcharts because it uses the same symbols

   **b.** similar to flowcharts because they are both used as logic-design tools

   **c.** not used anymore

   **d.** used only in BASIC

   **e.** none of the above

**5.** The symbol for process in flowchart design is

   **a.** an oval

   **b.** a rhombus

   **c.** a rectangle

   **d.** a circle

   **e.** none of the above

**6.** The connector symbol in flowchart design is

   **a.** a rectangle

   **b.** a rhombus

   **c.** an oval

   **d.** a circle

   **e.** none of the above

**7.** Which of the following structures is not used in structured programming?

   **a.** sequence

   **b.** multiplication

   **c.** selection

   **d.** iteration

   **e.** CASE

**8.** A CASE structure is used when

   **a.** one option is selected from two choices

   **b.** the process continues for 10 repetitions

   **c.** one option is selected from several choices

   **d.** a process continues forever

   **e.** none of the above

**9.** Problem definition in the program development life cycle

   **a.** is the most important step

   **b.** is done as the last step

   **c.** is done when you start debugging

   **d.** is always clear

   **e.** none of the above

**10.** When you write a program you may receive

   **a.** only logic errors

   **b.** only syntax errors

   **c.** either logic errors or syntax errors

   **d.** both logic and syntax errors

   **e.** none of the above

## True/False

**1.** You do the coding before you define the problem.

**2.** Flowcharts are not used as logic-design tools.

**3.** Structure charts are used as logic-design tools.

4. Structured programming principles advocate programs with many GOTO statements.

5. Modular programs are more difficult to develop than non-modular programs.

6. Programs with logic errors may run; however, they may produce incorrect results.

7. Debugging is the process of finding errors and correcting them.

8. Selection and iteration are two of the structures in structured programming.

9. Pseudocode is closer to any programming language than flowcharts.

10. You document your program only after it is completed.

---

**ANSWERS**

| Multiple Choice | True/False |
|---|---|
| 1. c | 1. F |
| 2. e | 2. F |
| 3. a | 3. T |
| 4. b | 4. F |
| 5. c | 5. F |
| 6. d | 6. T |
| 7. b | 7. T |
| 8. c | 8. T |
| 9. a | 9. T |
| 10. d | 10. F |

# Your First Journey with BASIC

**2**

## 2-1

## INTRODUCTION

We begin this chapter with the story of the LOGICAL WAITER, which will help you understand how a computer works. Then we discuss how the keyboard and CRT (Cathode Ray Tube) are used as input and output devices. We introduce the concepts of temporary and permanent storage in a computer system, and we explain several commonly used system commands that will help you manage your computer system. Understanding these commands is essential to BASIC programming.

In this chapter, you also learn about line numbers, and the END and PRINT programming commands. Every programming command in your BASIC program must be preceded by a line number. A system command, such as RUN, does not need a line number. You learn more about these two types of commands in this chapter.

## 2-2

## THE STORY OF THE LOGICAL WAITER

Long ago, there was an emperor who gave rigid commands. Every command he gave had to be carried out with no deviation. The waiters who worked for him lasted for three or four weeks and then were dismissed because they could not follow his instructions precisely. One day, the minister of the imperial court discovered the perfect waiter for the emperor. This person was called LOGICAL WAITER.

LOGICAL WAITER had a very special characteristic. He did exactly as he was commanded, with no deviation at all. The minister of the imperial court hired him immediately, knowing that he was just what the emperor needed.

One hot summer day, several weeks after LOGICAL WAITER had begun his new duties, the emperor went swimming. Before entering the imperial pool, he removed his diamond ring and laid it next to the pool. When the emperor was finished with his imperial swim, he returned to the palace, forgetting to retrieve his ring. It was later in the evening when he remembered that he had not picked up his ring.

He called his loyal and perfect servant LOGICAL WAITER. "What does his majesty wish?" LOGICAL WAITER asked. The emperor commanded LOGICAL WAITER, "Go look for my ring. It is next to the swimming pool." LOGICAL WAITER left to carry out the royal command.

LOGICAL WAITER saw the ring lying next to the pool, but he did not touch it. He returned to the emperor and stood silently at attention.

The emperor asked him, "Did you find the ring?" "Yes," said LOGICAL WAITER. "Did you bring it back with you?" the emperor asked. "No, I didn't," LOGICAL WAITER said.

The emperor flew into a rage and began shouting and shaking his fists at the servant. LOGICAL WAITER calmly interrupted the emperor and said, "Your majesty, you told me, 'Go and look for the ring.' That is exactly what I did. If you wanted me to bring it back as well, you should have said, 'LOGICAL WAITER, go look for my ring and, if you find it, bring it to me.'"

Your computer is like LOGICAL WAITER, it can do only exactly what you instruct it to do. A computer never makes any assumption. As the programmer, it is your job to give the computer a complete, accurate, and precise command; otherwise, the ring will stay at the swimming pool forever!

Now that you have an idea of the principle behind computer programming, you are ready to go on to the next sections of this chapter, which introduce you to the parts of your computer and its basic functions. If you have no experience with microcomputers, please read Appendixes A and B. Appendix A is an overview of microcomputers. Appendix B provides a quick review of DOS (disk operating system).

## THE KEYBOARD AND CRT

In this book, you use your keyboard to enter data into your computer. Your computer displays the data on the **CRT** (cathode ray tube), also known as the **monitor**. Your computer can also display the data on a printer, if you have one. You, the user, enter data through the keyboard (the **input device**) and receive data on either the CRT or the printer (the **output devices**) (see fig. 2–1).

There are several different types of keyboards with different configurations. Figures 2–2 and 2–3 show the two most popular types: an original IBM keyboard and an enhanced keyboard.

On the original IBM keyboard there are three areas. On the left are the function keys, F1 through F10. In BASIC each function key performs a specific task. In the middle of the keyboard are the familiar character keys, similar to those of a typewriter. On the right are the arrow (cursor-movement) keys. This area can also serve as a numeric keypad when the Num Lock key has been pressed. On the enhanced keyboard, the function keys are located across the top of the keyboard.

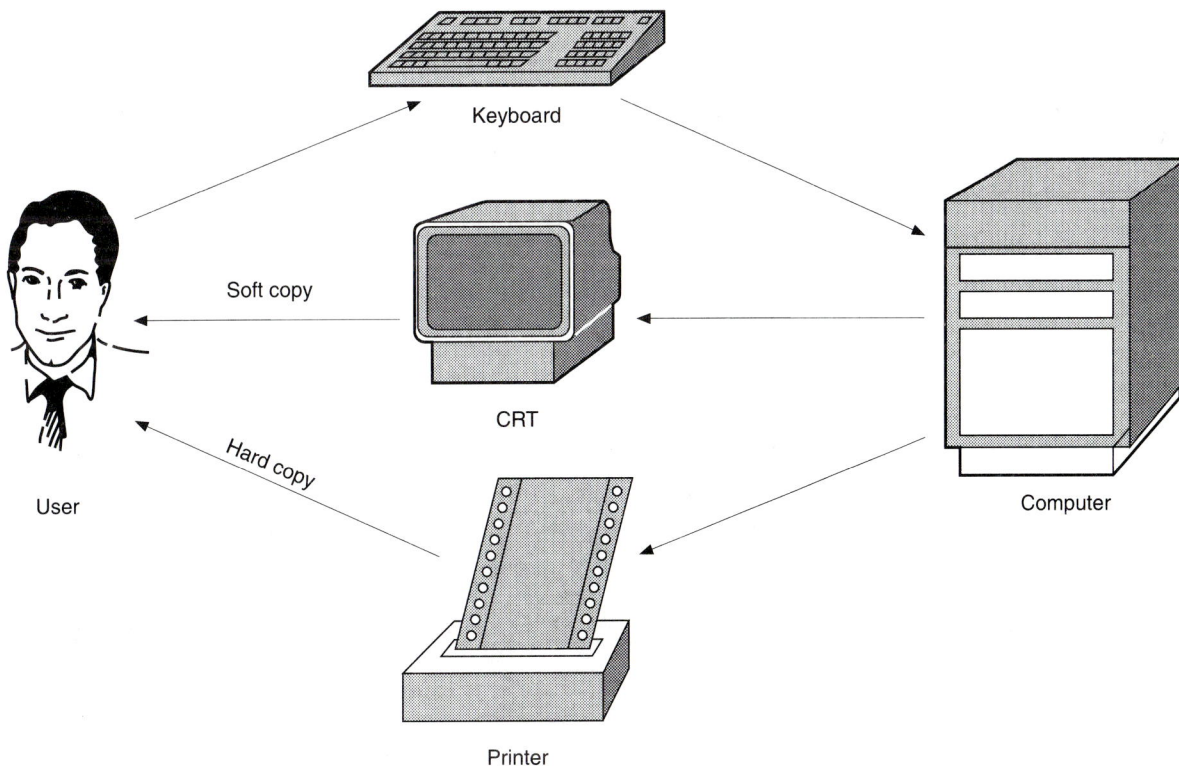

Keyboard

Soft copy

CRT

Hard copy

User

Printer

Computer

**Figure 2–1**
A User and a Computer

| 1 | Function keys | 4 | Shift key | 7 | Print Screen (PrtSc) key |
|---|---|---|---|---|---|
| 2 | Escape key | 5 | Alt key | 8 | Number Lock (Num Lock) key |
| 3 | Control (Ctrl) key | 6 | Shift key | 9 | Scroll Lock (Break) key |

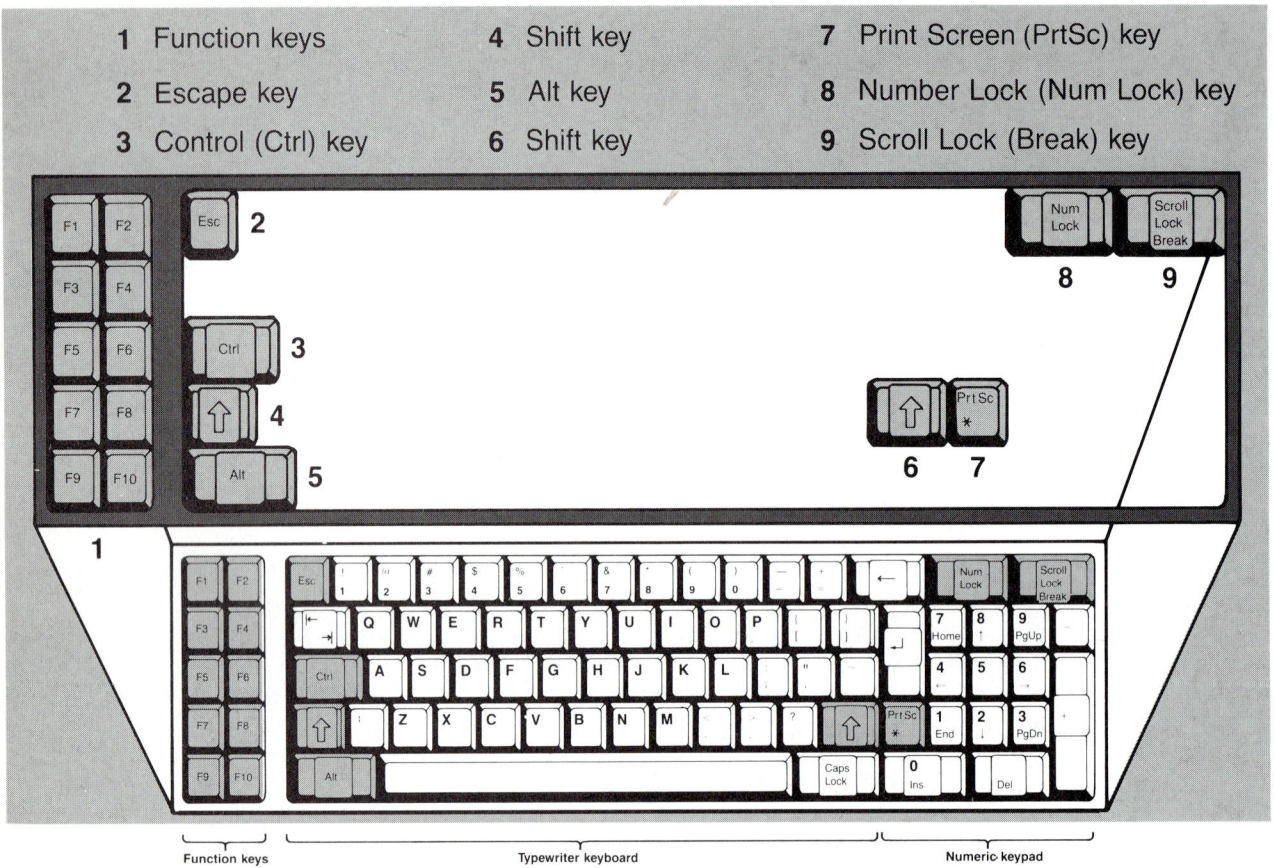

**Figure 2–2**
An Original IBM Keyboard

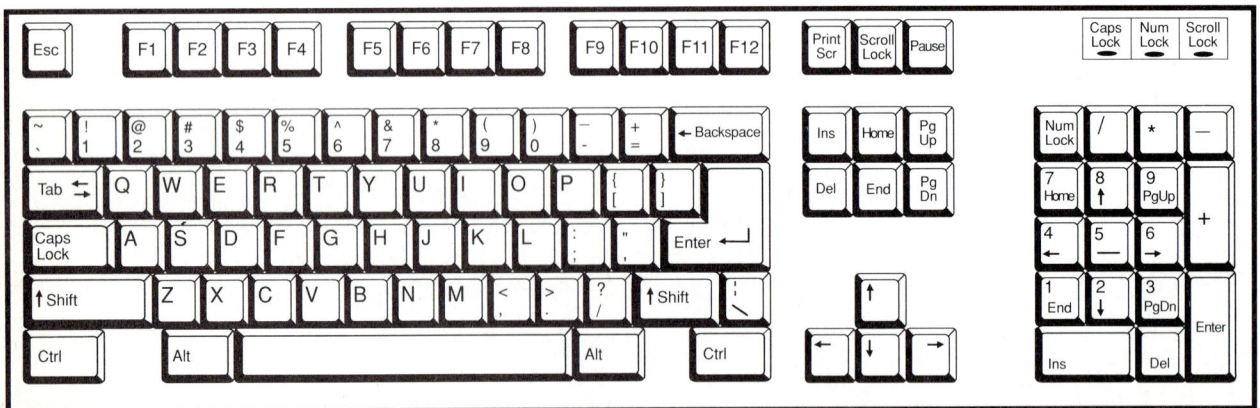

**Figure 2–3**
An Enhanced IBM Keyboard

20

## TWO DISTINCT AREAS OF A COMPUTER SYSTEM

After starting your computer, you can access two different memory areas: the working area and the permanent area. The working area of memory, **RAM** (random access memory), provides you with a temporary location in which to work. When you turn your computer off, everything in this area is erased.

The permanent memory area (also called secondary storage) is your hard or floppy **disk**. The files you store on disk are available for future access until you erase them.

Figure 2–4 shows these two areas of a computer system.

## DEFINING A FILE

In this book, we refer to any computer program or any part of a program as a **file**. A file can be temporary or permanent. The file in the working area is a temporary file. When you transfer the temporary file in RAM to disk, you have generated a permanent file. At any time, you can have many permanent files (depending upon the size of the storage device), but you can have only one temporary file at a time.

## USING BASIC AS A POWERFUL CALCULATOR

Arithmetic operations in BASIC are performed using special symbols. Table 2–1 lists these special symbols.

You can translate any algebraic statement into BASIC by using these special symbols.

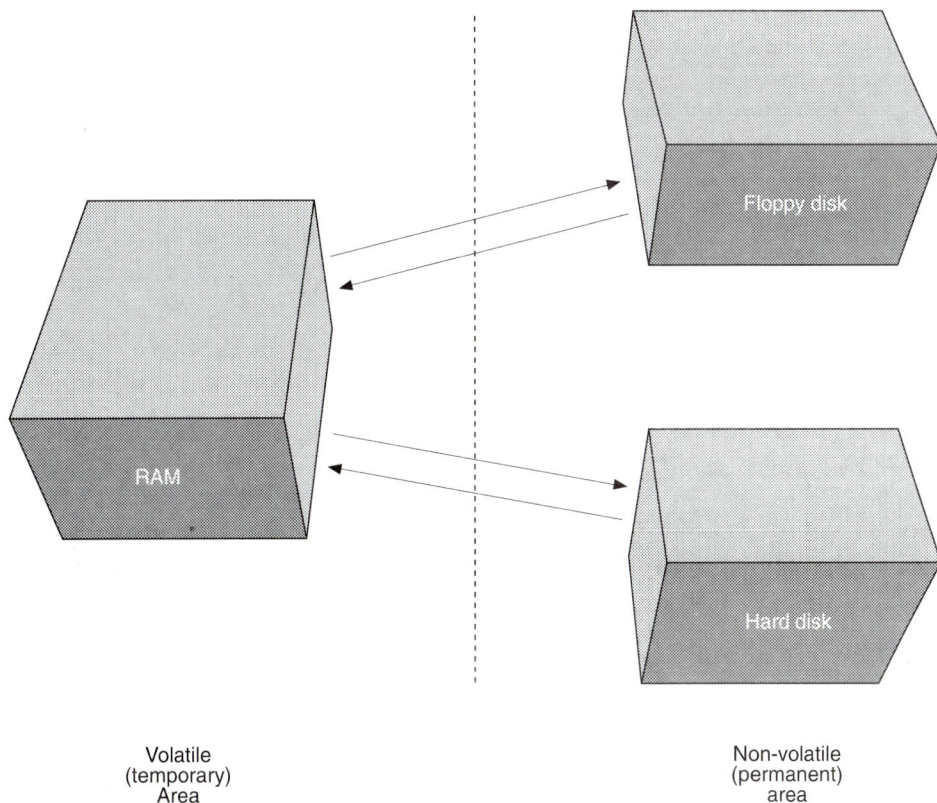

**Figure 2–4**
The Two Memory Areas of a Computer System

Volatile
(temporary)
Area

Non-volatile
(permanent)
area

| Table 2–1 | Symbol | Operation |
|---|---|---|
| Arithmetic Symbols | + | Addition |
| | / (slash) | Division |
| | ˆ (caret) | Exponentiation |
| | * (asterisk) | Multiplication |
| | — | Subtraction |

## 2–7

## UNDERSTANDING ORDER OF PRECEDENCE

When performing algebraic operations, BASIC performs the operations in the following order:

- Statements in parentheses
- Exponentiation (raising to a power)
- Division and multiplication
- Addition and subtraction

Operations with the same priority are performed from left to right.

The following examples demonstrate the order of precedence. You can use as many parentheses as needed to clarify the process, but be sure that every left parenthesis has a matching right parenthesis.

To determine the result of the expression

8*2ˆ6+12/4

BASIC performs the arithmetic operations in the following order:

| Operation | Result |
|---|---|
| 2ˆ6 | 64 |
| 8*64 | 512 |
| 12/4 | 3 |
| 512+3 | 515 |

To determine the result of the expression

8*2ˆ(6+12/4)

(which matches the first expression except that it contains parentheses to direct the flow of calculation), BASIC performs the arithmetic operations in the following order:

| Operation | Result |
|---|---|
| 12/4 | 3 |
| 6+3 | 9 |
| 2ˆ9 | 512 |
| 8*512 | 4096 |

As you can see, this answer is quite different from the first answer.

To load BASIC into your computer's memory, from the A> prompt, place the disk that contains BASIC into drive A, type *BASIC,* and press Enter. (If your computer displays the message

## 2-8
## LOADING BASIC

```
bad command or file name
```

try typing *GWBASIC* followed by Enter.)

     This command loads BASIC. To exit back to DOS, type *SYSTEM* and press Enter. (For an overview of DOS, see Appendix B.) When BASIC is loaded into memory, you should see a screen similar to that shown in figure 2–5.

     At the top of the screen you see the copyright information and the amount of RAM memory that is available (free). You also see the OK prompt, which is the BASIC prompt. At the bottom of the screen you see a listing of ten function keys. You can use these keys as shortcuts for performing tasks in BASIC. For example, to execute the LIST command, you can either type *LIST* and press Enter or press the F1 function key and Enter. If you don't want to see this display at the bottom of the screen, type *KEY OFF* and press Enter. To redisplay the function key list, type *KEY ON* and press Enter.

## 2-9
## LINE NUMBERS IN A BASIC PROGRAM

Any BASIC program must have line numbers. The line numbers tell the computer the sequence in which the BASIC program should be executed. Each line number must be unique. It is best to number your program lines in

```
GW-BASIC 3.20
(C) Copyright Microsoft 1983,1984,1985,1986
60332 Bytes free
Ok




















1LIST   2RUN   3LOAD"  4SAVE"  5CONT  6,"LPT1 7TRON  8TROFF 9KEY    0SCREEN
```

**Figure 2–5**
The BASIC Screen

increments of 5, 10, or 15 to allow room for you to insert more program lines later.

The range of line numbers differs from system to system. In GW-BASIC or Microsoft BASIC, a range between 1 and 65,529 inclusive is acceptable.

## 2–10

## THE END STATEMENT

Every BASIC program should include the END statement, which should be the last statement in the program and should have the highest line number. The END statement terminates a BASIC program. Although it is possible to have line numbers that are higher than the line number of the END statement (in subroutines, for example—see Chapter 8), the generally accepted programming practice is to give the END statement the highest line number. Of course, once the END statement has been executed, no more lines will be processed, no matter what the line number.

## 2–11

## THE RUN COMMAND

RUN is the **system command** that tells your computer to execute your program. When you type *RUN*, BASIC begins executing your program starting with the first line. Provided that your program doesn't contain any errors, your computer will do whatever it has been asked. After the program has been executed, you see the prompt

```
OK
```

This prompt means that your program has been executed and BASIC is waiting for the next command. System commands do not have to be preceded by line numbers.

## 2–12

## THE REM STATEMENT

The REM (remark) statement is also called a non-executable statement. You use REM statements to document your program and explain what is happening in it. You can also use REM statements to separate the different parts of a program. The following program shows how you can use REM statements:

```
10 REM This program was written by H. Bidgoli.
20 REM It was written on July 21, 1990. A good program
30 REM must include many REM statements. This will
40 REM help the user of the program to understand
50 REM the purpose of it.
60 REM
70 REM **********************************************
80 REM **********************************************
90 END
```

## 2–13

## THE PRINT COMMAND

The PRINT command enables a programmer to receive output from the computer. You can use the PRINT command in several ways. You can use the PRINT command to print numeric constants, as follows:

```
10 REM The first application of the PRINT statement.
20 PRINT 2
30 PRINT 4
40 PRINT 2+4
50 END
```

When you type *RUN*, your computer displays the following:

```
2
4
6
```

You can use the PRINT command to have BASIC print anything you want—you only have to enclose the data to be printed inside quotation marks. The following program uses the PRINT command for printing titles:

```
10 REM The second application of the PRINT statement.
20 PRINT "THIS IS PROGRAM NO 2"
30 PRINT "This is a payroll report"
40 PRINT "I ENJOY MY COMPUTER CLASS!"
50 END
```

When you type *RUN*, your computer displays the following output on-screen:

```
THIS IS PROGRAM NO 2
This is a payroll report
I ENJOY MY COMPUTER CLASS!
```

If you use the PRINT command followed by nothing, it prints a blank line. This is called an empty print.

You can use the LPRINT command to direct the output to your printer instead of your screen.

If you are using GW-BASIC, you can split one line of text and have it printed on several lines by using a colon. For example, instead of typing

```
10 PRINT "BASIC"
20 PRINT "COMPUTER"
30 END
```

you can use the command

```
10 PRINT "BASIC" : PRINT "COMPUTER"
```

GW-BASIC also gives you the option of using a ? in place of the PRINT command. For example:

```
10 ? "BASIC"
20 ? "COMPUTER"
30 END
```

When you generate a listing of this program, every ? will be replaced by the word PRINT automatically.

## 2–14

### FORMATTING THE OUTPUT

In each line on-screen, BASIC defines five print zones. Each zone is 14 characters long. In a PRINT statement, you can use a comma (,) or a semicolon (;) to have data items printed in these zones.

The semicolon increases the number of zones in a line. The number of zones you can print depends on the lengths of your data items. The longer the items, the fewer the print zones that will fit on a line. Using the semicolon as a delimiter provides more compact output than the comma.

The following program shows the difference between using commas and using semicolons as delimiters:

```
10 REM A semicolon provides more compact output than a
20 REM comma.
30 PRINT 2,2,2,2,2
40 PRINT 2;2;2;2;2
50 END
```

When you type *RUN,* you see the following output:

```
2     2     2     2     2
2 2 2 2 2
```

## 2–15

### THE AUTO COMMAND

You can use the AUTO command to generate line numbers automatically. To see this command in action, type *AUTO* and press Enter. BASIC displays a 10 for the first line number. Type your BASIC statement and press Enter. BASIC moves the cursor to the next line and automatically displays the next line number, 20. BASIC continues to display a new line number (with the default increment of 10) each time you press Enter. To terminate the AUTO mode, press Ctrl-Break (press the Ctrl and Break keys together) or press Ctrl-C.

You can use the AUTO command to generate line numbers with any increment. For example, the command AUTO 1000 generates line numbers in increments of 10 beginning with 1000, as follows:

```
1000
1010
1020
1030
```

The command *AUTO 5000,50* generates line numbers in increments of 50 beginning with 5000, as follows:

```
5000
5050
5100
5150
```

## 2–16

### THE LIST COMMAND

You can use the LIST command in several ways. If you type *LIST* (or press F1) and press Enter, you will see a listing of your current file on-screen. For example:

```
5000 REM THIS IS A SIMPLE PROGRAM.
5050 PRINT "WE ARE LEARNING BASIC"
5100 PRINT "BASIC IS EASY"
5150 END
```

You can generate a listing of one line or a series of lines on-screen by specifying the lines you want to see. If you type *LIST 5050,* you see the following line:

```
5050 PRINT "WE ARE LEARNING BASIC"
```

If you type *LIST 5050,5150,* you see lines 5050 and 5150. The command *LIST 5000-5100* gives you a listing on-screen of all the lines between the two numbers specified, inclusive. The command *LIST 5000-* generates a listing of lines 5000 to the end of the program. The command *LIST -5100* lists all the lines up to line 5100.

You can use the LLIST command to print your listing on the printer instead of on-screen.

## 2–17
## THE DELETE AND NEW COMMANDS

If you want to delete one line of your program, you have two options. You can type the line number and press Enter, or you can use the DELETE command followed by the number of the line you want deleted.

You can also use the DELETE command to delete a series of lines. The command *DELETE 500-2000* will delete lines 500 to 2000, inclusive. If you use *DELETE* by itself, you will erase the entire current file. The options you can use with DELETE are the same options you can use with LIST.

The NEW command erases any existing file from RAM and makes room for a new file. To use the NEW command, just type *NEW* and press Enter.

## 2–18
## THE SAVE AND LOAD COMMANDS

To transfer a file from RAM to disk for permanent storage, you must save it using the SAVE command.

For example, to save the current file to a disk in drive A, type

SAVE "A:JACK

(or press F4 and type *A:JACK*). BASIC saves your file to the disk as JACK.BAS. The BAS extension is automatically created by BASIC during the SAVE operation. It is used to identify all your BASIC files. JACK.BAS is now a permanent file residing on the disk in drive A. The file will stay there until you erase it. File names can be up to eight characters long.

You can also save your file as an ASCII file. ASCII (American Standard Code for Information Interchange) is a data format generated and accepted by many application software programs. An ASCII file, or simply a "print image" file, is a file in standard keyboard characters without any special or formatting codes.

To save JACK as an ASCII file, type

SAVE "A:JACK",A

You can merge this ASCII file with a file in RAM using the MERGE command. If you type

MERGE "A:JACK

and press Enter, the file JACK is appended to the end of the file in RAM.

To retrieve a file from disk, type *LOAD"*, then the drive and the file name. For example,

LOAD"A:JACK

You can also press F3 and then type *A:JACK* followed by Enter. When the computer displays OK, your program has been loaded into RAM memory successfully. To see a listing of this program, type *LIST* or press F1 followed by Enter. You should see your program listing. For example,

```
10 REM THIS IS A SIMPLE PROGRAM.
20 PRINT "WE ARE LEARNING BASIC"
30 PRINT "BASIC IS EASY"
40 END
```

As mentioned before, in most computer systems, a file name can be any name of up to eight characters. You should not use special characters, such as @, #, $, and %, or spaces in your file names.

## 2–19
## THE KILL COMMAND

To delete a permanent file (a file on your disk), you must use the KILL command. For example, to erase the file JACK.BAS from the disk in drive A, type

KILL "A:JACK.BAS

and press Enter. You must use the file extension (.BAS) with the KILL command.

## 2–20
## THE RENUM COMMAND

You use the RENUM command to change the line numbering in your program. Suppose that you have entered the following program:

```
1000 PRINT "COMPUTER"
1010 PRINT "BASIC"
1020 PRINT "SYSTEM"
1030 PRINT "MICROCOMPUTER"
1040 END
```

If you type *RENUM*, press Enter, and then LIST your program, it will look like the following:

```
10 PRINT "COMPUTER"
20 PRINT "BASIC"
30 PRINT "SYSTEM"
40 PRINT "MICROCOMPUTER"
50 END
```

BASIC has renumbered your program, replacing the first line number with the default value of 10 and using the default increment of 10. You can use the RENUM command to renumber your program starting with any line number and using any increment. Suppose that you use the command *RENUM 2000,30,5*. When you LIST your program, you see the following:

```
10 PRINT "COMPUTER"
20 PRINT "BASIC"
2000 PRINT "SYSTEM"
2005 PRINT "MICROCOMPUTER"
2010 END
```

BASIC has renumbered your program in increments of 5, starting from the old line 30 and replacing 30 with 2000. The old lines 10 and 20 remain the same.

---

**2–21**

**THE FILES COMMAND**

To see a listing of all the files on a disk, you must use the FILES command. To see a listing of all the files on the disk in drive B, for example, type *FILES "B:* and press Enter. Using the FILES command by itself generates a listing of the contents of your default drive—the drive or directory from which you started BASIC.

---

**2–22**

**THE NAME COMMAND**

You can change the name of a program on disk with the NAME command. For example, to rename the file PROG1 as PROG2, you would type

NAME "PROG1.BAS" AS "PROG2.BAS"

followed by Enter to perform the RENAME operation.

---

**2–23**

**MORE ON THE BASIC SCREEN**

You can erase the screen either by typing CLS (clear screen) followed by Enter or by pressing Ctrl-Home.

If you make a typing mistake when you are entering a program line, you can use the Backspace key to erase the incorrect characters. If you have already pressed Enter at the end of the program line, you can either retype the line or edit it.

To edit a program line, move the cursor to the location of the mistake and press the Ins (Insert) key to put BASIC into insert mode. Use the Del key to erase the incorrect characters and then type the new characters. Existing characters are moved to the right. When you are finished, press Enter to finalize your changes.

To display a line for editing purposes, you can use the EDIT command. For example, if you type *EDIT 2000* and press Enter, BASIC displays line 2000 ready for editing. Remember to press Enter to finalize any changes you make to the line.

---

**2–24**

**A SIMPLE BASIC PROGRAM**

In this section, you create a simple BASIC program. Load BASIC and enter the following program. Practice manipulating this program using as many commands as you can:

```
10 REM This is the first programming exercise.
20 REM I want to write a computer program to print my
```

```
30 REM name, major, and Social Security number.
40 PRINT "My name is Tom Brown"
50 PRINT
60 PRINT "My major is computer science"
70 PRINT
80 PRINT "My Social Security number is 524-73-1491"
90 PRINT
100 PRINT "That is enough for today"
110 PRINT "Thank you, LOGICAL WAITER"
120 PRINT "Have a nice day!"
130 END
```

When you run this program by typing *RUN* followed by Enter, you should see the following output:

```
My name is Tom Brown

My major is computer science

My Social Security number is 524-73-1491

That is enough for today
Thank you, LOGICAL WAITER
Have a nice day!
OK
```

## SUMMARY

In this chapter, we presented the story of the LOGICAL WAITER. An understanding of this story will help you understand the overall concept of programming.

We also introduced the keyboard and CRT as input and output devices, and explained the difference between temporary and permanent memory. You learned the rules for naming files. We presented several system and programming commands. These commands will be used throughout the book. An understanding of these commands will help you manage your computer system more effectively. Finally, we presented a simple computer program for you to practice.

## REVIEW QUESTIONS

*These questions are answered in Appendix D.

1. What device do you use to communicate with a computer system?

*2. What is the difference between temporary and permanent areas in a computer system?

3. How many permanent and temporary files can you have at a given time?

4. What is a file?

*5. Some of the following are not valid file names. Circle the invalid ones.

   a. HISTORY

   b. Robertinia

   c. ABC 11

   d. A1Bc111

   e. A—B11

6. How many different ways can you use the LIST command? What does LLIST do?

*7. What is the difference between the DELETE and NEW commands?

8. What is the difference between DELETE and KILL?

9. What is the function of the SAVE command? How do you save a file as an ASCII file?

*10. What command do you use to display a listing of all the files you have saved on a disk?

*11. What command do you use to stop the execution of a program?

12. How do you retrieve a permanent file?

*13. What happens when you retrieve a permanent file? Is the permanent file still on the disk?

14. How do you merge a file on disk with a file in RAM?

15. How do you display a specific line for editing?

16. How do you erase the contents of RAM?

---

1. Load BASIC. At the OK prompt, use the AUTO command and type the following program:

**HANDS-ON EXPERIENCE**

```
10 PRINT "BASIC"
20 PRINT "GW-BASIC"
30 PRINT "MICROSOFT"
40 PRINT "IBM-BASIC"
50 END
```

Do the following:

a. Display a listing of the program on the screen.

b. Run the program.

c. Clear the screen.

d. Display a listing of the program again.

e. Save the program on your default drive as EXERCISE.

f. Erase RAM.

g. Retrieve the program.

h. Save the program as EX1.

i. Display a listing of your directory.

j. Erase the EX1 program from disk.

2. Clear the screen and retrieve EXERCISE from disk. Do the following:

a. Renumber the program starting at 1000.

b. Display the new program.

c. Renumber the program starting at 2000 in increments of 100.

d. Display the new program.

e. Save the program as an ASCII file as EX2.

f. Merge EX2 with the program in RAM.

g. Display a listing of the new file. (It should be 10 lines long.)

3. Clear the screen. Write a program that displays the message

IT IS SO EXCITING TO LEARN BASIC

Save the program on disk as EX3.

---

| CRT | Input device | RAM | **KEY TERMS** |
|-----|--------------|-----|---------------|
| Disk | Monitor | System command | |
| File | Output device | | |

| **KEY COMMANDS** | AUTO | Automatically generates line numbers |
|---|---|---|
| | Ctrl-Break or Ctrl-C | Stops the AUTO command; stops program execution |
| | DELETE | Erases the entire program or portions of it from RAM |
| | END | Marks the end of the program |
| | FILES | Displays the directory listing |
| | KILL | Removes a program from disk |
| | LIST | Displays the listing of the program on-screen |
| | LLIST | Sends the program listing to the printer |
| | MERGE | Merges a disk file with a file in RAM |
| | NAME | Renames a file on disk |
| | NEW | Erases RAM |
| | PRINT | Prints messages and the results of calculations |
| | REM | Used for documentation |
| | RUN | Executes the program |
| | SAVE | Saves a program to disk |
| | SAVE,A | Saves a program as an ASCII file |

## ARE YOU READY TO MOVE ON?

### Multiple Choice

1. What command is used to delete a permanent file?
   a. AUTO
   b. NEW
   c. KILL
   d. FILES
   e. BREAK

2. What command is used to change the sequence of line numbers?
   a. AUTO
   b. NEW
   c. RELEASE
   d. RENUM
   e. BREAK

3. What command do you use to get a listing of all the files you have saved on a disk?
   a. LOG
   b. LIST
   c. FILES
   d. AUTO
   e. NEW

4. Which of the following are true about a file?
   a. A file is a series of related records
   b. Files can be both temporary and permanent
   c. Files can only be temporary
   d. both a and b
   e. both a and c

5. What system command automatically generates line numbers?
   a. NUMBER

    **b.** AUTO

    **c.** SAVE

    **d.** NUM

    **e.** none of the above

**6.** What is the command to generate line numbers beginning with 50 and incremented by 10?

    **a.** NUMBER 50,10

    **b.** NUM 50,10

    **c.** AUTO 50

    **d.** AUTO 50,5

    **e.** both c and d are correct

**7.** What is the system command used to delete one line?

    **a.** DELETE, the line number, and Enter

    **b.** NEW followed by the line number

    **c.** You cannot delete one line of a program

    **d.** DELETE line 1

    **e.** none of the above

**8.** What is the command to transfer a temporary file to disk?

    **a.** TRANSFER followed by the file name

    **b.** MEMORY followed by the file name

    **c.** SAVE followed by the file name in quotation marks

    **d.** none of the above

    **e.** LOAD

**9.** Which of the following are invalid file names?

    **a.** JOHN99-1

    **b.** F15-36S

    **c.** SALLY

    **d.** all of the above are valid file names

    **e.** none of the above is a valid file name

**10.** Assuming that a program includes lines 10 to 1000 inclusive, what is the command to erase this program from RAM (the equivalent of NEW)?

    **a.** DELETE 10-1000

    **b.** DELETE 10, 1000

    **c.** DELETE 10-

    **d.** DELETE 1000-

    **e.** either a or c

## True/False

**1.** A system command must have a line number.

**2.** At any time, the computer can maintain many temporary files, depending on the memory size.

**3.** RENUM is the system command that changes the sequence of line numbers.

**4.** In most systems, a file name can have a maximum of eight characters.

**5.** The programmer must give the computer complete instructions because the computer makes no assumptions.

**6.** The NEW command is capable of deleting segments of a program as well as the entire program.

7. The LIST command provides a listing of all the files you have saved on your disk.

8. To exit AUTO mode, you must press Ctrl-Break or Ctrl-C.

9. The AUTO command automatically generates line numbers.

10. The LIST command can only display the entire program.

---

**ANSWERS**

| Multiple Choice | True/False |
|---|---|
| 1. c | 1. F |
| 2. d | 2. F |
| 3. c | 3. T |
| 4. d | 4. T |
| 5. b | 5. T |
| 6. c | 6. F |
| 7. a | 7. F |
| 8. c | 8. T |
| 9. d | 9. T |
| 10. e | 10. F |

# Sending Data to the Computer

**3**

## 3–1
## INTRODUCTION

In this chapter, we explain the difference between numeric and non-numeric (string) variables. We introduce the LET, READ/DATA, and INPUT commands for entering information into the computer.

We examine the RESTORE statement, a command for reading the same data more than once.

Several short programs demonstrate particular applications of various commands. We conclude the chapter with a discussion of the types of numbers and their accuracy, including integer, single-precision, and double-precision.

## 3–2
## NUMERIC VARIABLES

The word *variable* means "subject to change in value." A computer **variable** is a named memory area that holds a value (number) or a string (text). The variable A, for example, can hold several different values during program execution, depending on what has been assigned to it.

A numeric variable, as its name implies, is used to hold numbers. For example, you might use the variable TOTAL-90 to hold the total amount of the gasoline bills you paid in 1990. The name of a numeric variable can contain any letter of the alphabet and any number. The variable name can be up to 10 characters long. The variable name must begin with an alphabetic character, and you cannot use embedded spaces. Try to give your variables meaningful names, such as COMMISSION, CHECK, ACCOUNT-91, and so on. A numeric variable has a value of zero before it is assigned a value.

## 3–3
## NUMERIC CONSTANTS

A numeric **constant** has one fixed value throughout a program. A numeric constant can be positive or negative. For large numbers, you must use scientific notation (explained in the next section). The following are some examples of numeric constants:

| Valid Constants | Invalid Constants |
|---|---|
| 223 | 199,76 (commas must be omitted) |
| −22 | $10^2$ (scientific notation must |
| −22.35 | be used) |
| +18.11 (for positive numbers, the sign is not required) | |
| 5E5 | |
| 196E−3 | |

## 3–4
## SCIENTIFIC NOTATION

Usually, very large or very small numbers are presented in **scientific notation** (also known as E or D notation). Most computers output very large numbers in scientific notation. The following are some examples of E notation:

| Number | E notation equivalent |
|---|---|
| 2,987 | 2.987E3 or 29.87E2 |
| 0.00223466899 | 0.223466899E−2 |
| 10,000,000,000 | 1.0E10 or 10000.0E6 |
| 2,000 | 2.0E3 or 20.0E2 |
| 0.0002 | 2.0E−4 or 20.0E−5 |

## 3–5
## STRING VARIABLES

Not all variables used in BASIC programs are numeric. For example, in a payroll program, numeric variables may include the number of hours, the pay rate, and the tax rate. The employee's name and address, however, are not numeric. These are called non-numeric, or string, variables. To distinguish between a numeric and a non-numeric variable, you place a dollar sign ($) at the end of the name of a non-numeric variable. All other rules for numeric variable names are observed.

COMMISSION$, CHECK$, and ACCOUNT$ are some examples of string variables. Whenever you assign non-numeric data (text) to a string variable, the text must begin with a single or double quotation mark (the closing quotation mark is optional if the non-numeric data item is just one word, as in the second example). The following are valid string variable assignments:

ADDRESS$="2109 South Broadway"
SEX$="FEMALE"

We present several programs using these types of variables later in the chapter. A string variable has a default value of blank before a data item is assigned to it. A string variable that has no value (is blank) is called a "null string."

## 3–6
## THE LET STATEMENT

The LET statement is one way of assigning a value to a variable (in GW-BASIC, however, you don't need to use LET in the assignment statement). To assign the value of 50 to variable A, for example, you can use the following command:

LET A=50

Understanding this simple statement is very important. It means that you have generated a location inside the computer. The address of this location is A, and you have assigned the value 50 to this address. A particular address can hold only one value at a time. Figure 3–1 shows how the computer understands the assignment statement. The program shown in figure 3–2 illustrates how the LET statement works.

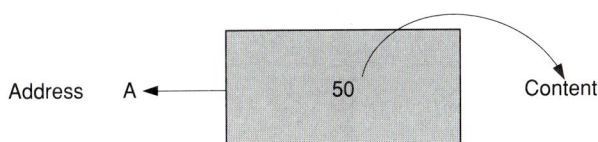

**Figure 3–1**
The LET Statement

Address   A ◄—————   50   ————► Content

**Figure 3-2**

An Example of the LET Statement

```
100     REM SOME EXAMPLES OF THE ASSIGNMENT STATEMENT.
110     REM
120     REM ****** VARIABLE TABLE
130     REM            NUM1 = INPUT VARIABLE
140     REM            NUM2 = INPUT VARIABLE AND TOTAL
150     REM
160     REM ****** INITIALIZATION SECTION
170     LET NUM1 = 10
180     LET NUM2 = 10
190     LET NUM1 = 25
200     REM
210     REM ****** PROCESS SECTION
220     LET NUM2 = NUM1 + NUM2
230     REM
240     REM ****** OUTPUT SECTION
250     PRINT "THE FINAL VALUE OF NUM2 IS =";NUM2
260     END
Ok
RUN
THE FINAL VALUE OF NUM2 IS = 35
Ok
```

In line 170, the value of NUM1 is equal to 10. In line 190, this value is replaced by 25. In line 220, the values of NUM1 and NUM2 are added and the result is stored in variable NUM2. Figure 3-3 shows this process.

In algebra, the statements A=A+1 and B=B+20 don't make sense. A variable cannot equal itself plus 1, nor can a variable equal itself plus 20. In computer programming, however, these statements mean something quite different.

In figure 3-4, line 200 uses the LET statement as an accumulator. This statement tells the computer to take the old value of A, which is 10, add 1 to it, and store the result in the same address (A). Line 210 tells the computer to take the old value of B, which is 20, add 20 to it, and store the result (40) in address B.

Suppose that you have 10 nickels, 25 dimes, 5 quarters, and 3 half dollars. Write a BASIC program to compute the total amount of money in dollars. Figure 3-5 shows a program that calculates the answer to this problem.

Whenever you use a LET statement, there can be only one variable on the left side of the equal sign. On the right side of the equal sign, you can have as many variables as space permits. The following are some examples of valid LET statements:

```
LET M=M+3
LET A=B+C+D
LET PROFIT=INCOME-COST
LET TOTAL=A/B+(A+C)
```

**Figure 3-3**

A Graphic Version of the Program in Figure 3-2

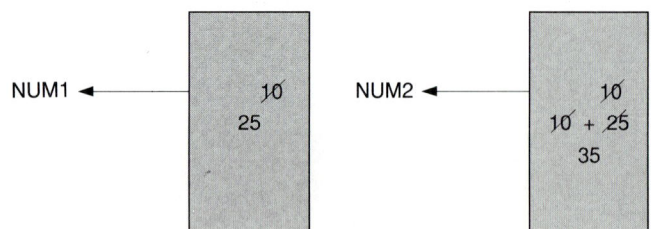

```
100    REM THIS PROGRAM SHOWS THE APPLICATION OF THE LET
110    REM STATEMENT AS AN ACCUMULATOR.
120    REM
130    REM ****** VARIABLE TABLE
140    REM           A = INPUT VARIABLE AND ACCUMULATOR
150    REM           B = INPUT VARIABLE AND ACCUMULATOR
160    REM
170    REM ****** INITIALIZATION SECTION
180    LET A = 10
190    LET B = 20
200    LET A = A + 1
210    LET B = B + 20
220    REM
230    REM ****** OUTPUT SECTION
240    PRINT "THE NEW VALUES OF A AND B ARE = ",A,B
250    END
Ok
RUN
THE NEW VALUES OF A AND B ARE =            11              40
Ok
```

**Figure 3-4**
Using the LET Statement as an
Accumulator

As an exercise, draw a flowchart and write a program to perform the four basic arithmetic operations on the variables NUM1 and NUM2 (see fig. 3-6). Figure 3-7 shows the flowchart for this program.

The following data is related to Sally, one of the employees at UTRR Company. Draw a flowchart and write a program using LET statements to enter her data into the computer (see fig. 3-8). Generate an output of this data.

| Name | Sally |
|---|---|
| Address | S. W. Broadway |
| Employee Number | 1922 |
| Paycheck | $620 |

```
100    REM THIS PROGRAM CALCULATES JOHNNY'S TOTAL MONEY.
110    REM
120    REM ****** VARIABLE TABLE
130    REM           NICKELS = THE NUMBER OF NICKELS
140    REM           DIMES = THE NUMBER OF DIMES
150    REM           QUARTERS = THE NUMBER OF QUARTERS
160    REM           FIFTY = THE NUMBER OF FIFTY-CENT COINS
170    REM           TOTAL = IS THE TOTAL
180    REM
190    REM ****** INITIALIZATION SECTION
200    LET NICKELS = 10
210    LET DIMES = 25
220    LET QUARTERS = 5
230    LET FIFTY = 3
240    REM
250    REM ****** PROCESS SECTION
260    LET TOTAL = NICKELS*5+DIMES*10+QUARTERS*25+FIFTY*50
270    LET TOTAL = TOTAL/100
280    REM
290    REM ****** OUTPUT SECTION
300    PRINT "JOHNNY'S TOTAL MONEY IN DOLLARS IS = ";TOTAL
310    END
JOHNNY'S TOTAL MONEY IN DOLLARS IS =  5.75
```

**Figure 3-5**
Using the LET Statement

**Figure 3–6**
Arithmetic Operations

```
100     REM THIS IS ANOTHER EXAMPLE OF THE PRINT STATEMENT.
110     REM
120     REM ****** VARIABLE TABLE
130     REM            NUM1, NUM2 = INPUT VARIABLES
140     REM            MULT = PRODUCT OF NUM1 AND NUM2
150     REM            DIV = RESULT OF NUM1 DIVIDED BY NUM2
160     REM            SUBT = RESULT OF NUM1 MINUS NUM2
170     REM            ADD = RESULT OF NUM1 PLUS NUM2
180     REM
190     REM ****** INITIALIZATION SECTION
200     LET NUM1 = 10
210     LET NUM2 = 5
220     REM
230     REM ****** PROCESS SECTION
240     LET MULT = NUM1*NUM2
250     LET DIV = NUM1/NUM2
260     LET SUBT = NUM1-NUM2
270     LET ADD = NUM1+NUM2
280     REM
290     REM ****** OUTPUT SECTION
300     PRINT "**************** RESULTS ****************"
310     PRINT "THE MULTIPLICATION OF NUM1 BY NUM2 IS = ";MULT
320     PRINT "THE DIVISION OF NUM1 BY NUM2 IS = ";DIV
330     PRINT "THE SUBTRACTION OF NUM2 FROM NUM1 IS = ";SUBT
340     PRINT "THE ADDITION OF NUM1 AND NUM2 IS = ";ADD
350     PRINT "*****************************************"
360     END
Ok
RUN
**************** RESULTS ****************
THE MULTIPLICATION OF NUM1 BY NUM2 IS =  50
THE DIVISION OF NUM1 BY NUM2 IS =  2
THE SUBTRACTION OF NUM2 FROM NUM1 IS =  5
THE ADDITION OF NUM1 AND NUM2 IS =  15
*****************************************
Ok
```

In the program shown in figure 3–8, whatever is inside quotation marks is called a constant or a string constant. The variable on the left side of the equal sign is called a string variable. Figure 3–9 shows the flowchart for this exercise. Figure 3–10 illustrates another example of using string variables.

# 3–7

## THE READ AND DATA STATEMENTS

Usually, LET statements are used to enter a small amount of data into a program. For larger amounts of data, you can use the READ and DATA statements. These two statements must be used together as follows:

```
10 READ A,B,C
20 DATA 10,14,33
```

The DATA statement supplies the information to be read into the addresses (variables) specified in the READ statement. In the example, the computer places the first value in the DATA statement, 10, into the first variable address, A. Figure 3–11 illustrates this process.

Figure 3–12 illustrates an example of using the READ and DATA statements. You can place the DATA statements anywhere in your program.

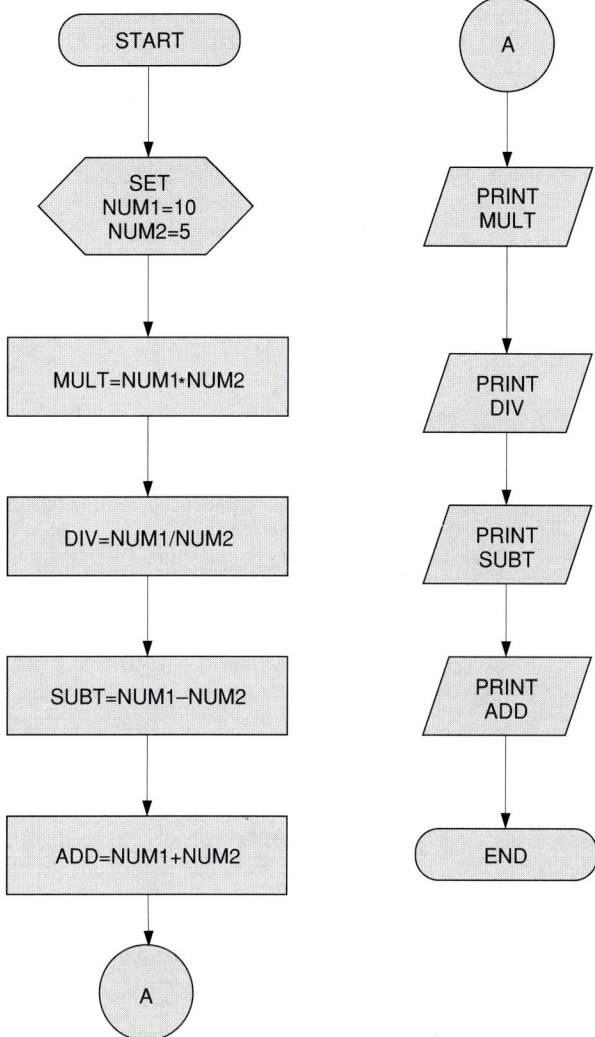

```
START

SET
NUM1=10
NUM2=5

MULT=NUM1*NUM2

DIV=NUM1/NUM2

SUBT=NUM1−NUM2

ADD=NUM1+NUM2

A
```

```
A

PRINT
MULT

PRINT
DIV

PRINT
SUBT

PRINT
ADD

END
```

**Figure 3−8**
Using LET Statements and
String Variables

```
100    REM THIS SIMPLE PROGRAM SHOWS THE APPLICATION OF STRING
110    REM VARIABLES.
120    REM
130    REM ******* VARIABLE TABLE
140    REM          EMP.NAME$ = THE EMPLOYEE'S NAME
150    REM          EMP.ADDRESS$ = THE EMPLOYEE'S ADDRESS
160    REM          EMP.NUMBER = THE EMPLOYEE'S NUMBER
170    REM          PAYCHECK = THE EMPLOYEE'S PAYCHECK
180    REM
190    REM ******* INITIALIZATION SECTION
200    LET EMP.NAME$ = "SALLY"
210    LET EMP.ADDRESS$ = "S. W. BROADWAY"
220    LET EMP.NUMBER = 1922
230    LET PAYCHECK = 620
240    REM
250    REM ******* OUTPUT SECTION
260    PRINT "EMPLOYEE INFORMATION"
270    PRINT EMP.NAME$, EMP.ADDRESS$, EMP.NUMBER, PAYCHECK
280    END
EMPLOYEE INFORMATION
SALLY          S. W. BROADWAY                  1922          620
```

**Figure 3–9**
The Flowchart for the Program
in Figure 3–8

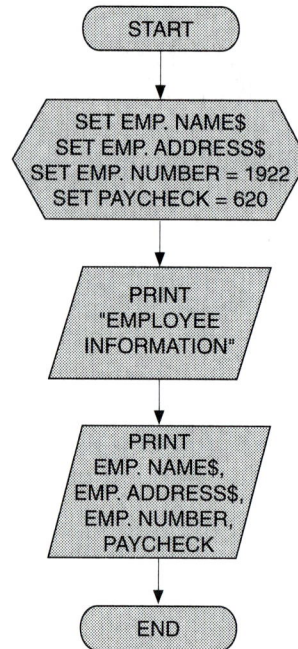

Experienced programmers usually place their DATA statements at the top or at the bottom of the program (before the END statement), which makes it easier to locate the DATA statements for future modifications. In modular programs, DATA statements are placed at the end of each module (if there are any).

```
100     REM THIS PROGRAM SHOWS DIFFERENT TYPES OF STRING
110     REM VARIABLES.   STUDENTS SHOULD BE CAREFUL ABOUT THE
120     REM USE OF QUOTATIONS.
130     REM
140     REM ******* VARIABLE TABLE
150     REM           WORDS.1$ = INPUT STRING VARIABLE
160     REM           WORDS.2$ = INPUT STRING VARIABLE
170     REM           WORDS.3$ = CONVERSION STRING VARIABLE
180     REM
190     REM ******* INITIALIZATION SECTION
200     LET WORDS.1$ = "ORDER ENTRY FOR"
210     LET WORDS.2$ = "OLIVE OIL FACTORY"
220     LET WORDS.3$ = WORDS.1$
230     REM
240     REM ******* OUTPUT SECTION
250     PRINT "THE FOLLOWING ARE SOME EXAMPLES OF STRING CONSTANTS."
260     PRINT WORDS.3$,WORDS.2$
270     END
THE FOLLOWING ARE SOME EXAMPLES OF STRING CONSTANTS.
ORDER ENTRY FOR              OLIVE OIL FACTORY
```

**Figure 3–10**
Using String Variables

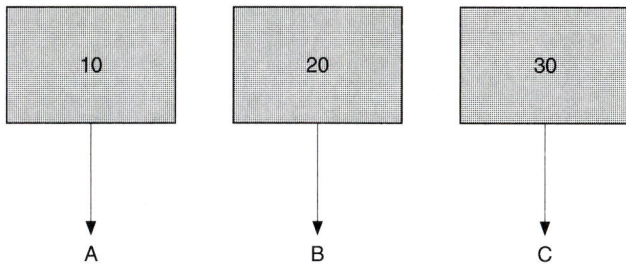

**Figure 3–11**
A Graphic Presentation of the
READ and DATA Statements

The following four programs all generate the same output:

```
10 READ A,B,C            10 READ A,B,C
20 PRINT A,B,C           20 PRINT A,B,C
30 DATA 10,20,30         30 DATA 10,20
40 END                   40 DATA 30
                         50 END


10 READ A,B,C            10 DATA 10,20,30
20 PRINT A,B,C           20 READ A,B,C
30 DATA 10               30 PRINT A,B,C
40 DATA 20               40 END
50 DATA 30
60 END
```

If you specify four variables in the READ line but your DATA lines
provide fewer than four values, your computer will display the following error
message:

```
OUT OF DATA IN xx
```

```
100    REM THIS PROGRAM CALCULATES THE AVERAGE OF 4 NUMBERS.
110    REM
120    REM ****** VARIABLE TABLE
130    REM          NUM1 = VARIABLE 1
140    REM          NUM2 = VARIABLE 2
150    REM          NUM3 = VARIABLE 3
160    REM          NUM4 = VARIABLE 4
170    REM          SUM = THE SUM OF THE NUMBERS
180    REM          AVERAGE = THE AVERAGE OF THE NUMBERS
190    REM
200    REM ****** INITIALIZATION SECTION
210    READ NUM1, NUM2, NUM3, NUM4
220    REM
230    REM ****** PROCESS SECTION
240    LET SUM = NUM1+NUM2+NUM3+NUM4
250    LET AVERAGE = SUM/4
260    REM
270    REM ****** OUTPUT SECTION
280    PRINT "THE AVERAGE OF THE 4 NUMBERS IS =";AVERAGE
290    REM
300    REM ****** DATA SECTION
310    DATA 100, 200, 50, 250
320    END
THE AVERAGE OF THE 4 NUMBERS IS = 150
```

**Figure 3–12**
An Example of READ and DATA

The xx indicates the line number of the READ statement, not the DATA line. If the DATA line provides more values than are required by the READ statement, the computer ignores the extra data. Figures 3–13 through 3–17 show this process.

## 3–8

### THE RESTORE STATEMENT

Sometimes you may want to read the same data more than once. The RESTORE statement enables you to do this. Figure 3–18 shows the way in which this command works.

**Figure 3–13**
An Example of READ and DATA

```
100     REM THIS PROGRAM READS AND THEN PRINTS FOUR NUMBERS
110     REM
120     REM ****** VARIABLE TABLE
130     REM          NUM1 = INPUT VARIABLE 1
140     REM          NUM2 = INPUT VARIABLE 2
150     REM          NUM3 = INPUT VARIABLE 3
160     REM          NUM4 = INPUT VARIABLE 4
170     REM
180     REM ****** INITIALIZATION SECTION
190     READ NUM1, NUM2, NUM3, NUM4
200     REM
210     REM ****** OUTPUT SECTION
220     PRINT NUM1, NUM2, NUM3, NUM4
230     REM
240     REM ****** DATA SECTION
250     DATA 10, 20, 30, 40
260     END
Ok
RUN
 10             20              30              40
Ok
```

**Figure 3–14**
An Example of Extra Data

```
100     REM THIS PROGRAM READS AND THEN PRINTS FOUR NUMBERS.
110     REM THIS IS AN EXAMPLE OF EXTRA DATA.
120     REM
130     REM ****** VARIABLE TABLE
140     REM          NUM1 = INPUT VARIABLE 1
150     REM          NUM2 = INPUT VARIABLE 2
160     REM          NUM3 = INPUT VARIABLE 3
170     REM          NUM4 = INPUT VARIABLE 4
180     REM
190     REM ****** INITIALIZATION SECTION
200     READ NUM1, NUM2, NUM3, NUM4
210     REM
220     REM ****** OUTPUT SECTION
230     PRINT NUM1, NUM2, NUM3, NUM4
240     REM
250     REM ****** DATA SECTION
260     DATA 10, 20, 30, 40, 50
270     END
Ok
RUN
 10             20              30              40
Ok
```

```
100     REM THIS PROGRAM WILL ATTEMPT TO READ FOUR NUMBERS FROM
110     REM A DATA LINE THAT CONTAINS ONLY THREE DATA ITEMS.
120     REM THE EXPECTED RESULT WILL BE AN ERROR MESSAGE.
130     REM
140     REM ****** VARIABLE TABLE
150     REM           NUM1 = INPUT VARIABLE 1
160     REM           NUM2 = INPUT VARIABLE 2
170     REM           NUM3 = INPUT VARIABLE 3
180     REM           NUM4 = INPUT VARIABLE 4
190     REM
200     REM ****** INITIALIZATION SECTION
210     READ NUM1, NUM2, NUM3, NUM4
220     REM
230     REM ****** OUTPUT SECTION
240     PRINT NUM1, NUM2, NUM3, NUM4
250     REM
260     REM ****** DATA SECTION
270     DATA 10, 20, 30
280     END
Ok
RUN
Out of DATA in 210
Ok
```

**Figure 3–15**
An Example of Insufficient Data

When your program reads a data item, the computer's internal data pointer, which keeps track of the current item, moves to the next data item. If you attempt to read the data again, BASIC detects that the data has already been read and will not read it again. The RESTORE command resets the internal data pointer to the beginning of the DATA statements so that you can reuse the data. Figure 3–18 demonstrates this process.

```
100     REM THIS PROGRAM READS AND THEN PRINTS FOUR NUMBERS.
110     REM IN THIS EXAMPLE WE USE 4 READ COMMANDS.
120     REM
130     REM ****** VARIABLE TABLE
140     REM           NUM1 = INPUT VARIABLE 1
150     REM           NUM2 = INPUT VARIABLE 2
160     REM           NUM3 = INPUT VARIABLE 3
170     REM           NUM4 = INPUT VARIABLE 4
180     REM
190     REM ****** INITIALIZATION SECTION
200     READ NUM1
210     READ NUM2
220     READ NUM3
230     READ NUM4
240     REM
250     REM ****** DATA SECTION
260     DATA 10, 20, 30, 40
270     REM
280     REM ****** OUTPUT SECTION
290     PRINT NUM1, NUM2, NUM3, NUM4
300     END
Ok
RUN
 10           20           30           40
Ok
```

**Figure 3–16**
An Example of READ and DATA

**Figure 3–17**
An Example of READ and DATA

```
100     REM THIS PROGRAM READS THEN PRINTS THREE NUMBERS.
110     REM THE NUMBERS ARE NEGATIVE.
120     REM
130     REM ****** VARIABLE TABLE
140     REM          NUM1 = INPUT VARIABLE 1
150     REM          NUM2 = INPUT VARIABLE 2
160     REM          NUMBER = INPUT VARIABLE 3
170     REM
180     REM ****** INITIALIZATION SECTION
190     READ NUM1, NUM2, NUMBER
200     REM
210     REM ****** OUTPUT SECTION
220     PRINT NUM1, NUM2, NUMBER
230     REM
240     REM ****** DATA SECTION
250     DATA -15, -40, -60
260     END
Ok
RUN
-15                -40                -60
Ok
```

## 3–9

## THE INPUT STATEMENT

A third method of entering data into your program is with the INPUT statement. INPUT enables you to use the program in an interactive mode, which means that data will be accepted from the keyboard. This method is useful for running the same program with different data or whenever the data part of a program does not need to be included in the program.

When you run the program, a ? appears on the screen and the program waits for you to type something. You must enter the requested data. If three data items are asked for, you must supply the three data items separated by commas. Figures 3–19 and 3–20 show this process.

You can include a message as part of the INPUT statement. For example, the statement

```
INPUT "TELL ME A NUMBER",X
```

displays the message

```
TELL ME A NUMBER
```

without a question mark. When you type the requested data and press Enter, the program continues. If a semicolon was used at the end of the statement rather than a comma, a question mark would appear at the end of the prompt when the program was run. Use of the comma suppresses the display of the question mark.

## 3–10

## TYPES OF NUMBERS

GW-BASIC recognizes three types of numbers: integer, single-precision, and double-precision.

An integer can be any whole number between −32768 and +32767.

A single-precision constant is any numeric constant that has seven or fewer digits (22.6, for example), exponential form using E (−5.19E−07, for

```
100     REM THIS PROGRAM SHOWS ONE APPLICATION OF THE RESTORE
110     REM STATEMENT.  THREE NUMBERS ARE BEING READ.  THE
120     REM FIRST TIME THEIR SUM IS BEING COMPUTED.  THE SECOND
130     REM TIME THE SUM OF THEIR SQUARES IS BEING COMPUTED.
140     REM AND THE LAST TIME THE SUM OF THEIR CUBES IS BEING
150     REM COMPUTED.  EACH TIME THESE NUMBERS ARE ASSIGNED
160     REM TO DIFFERENT VARIABLES.  THIS IS THE MAJOR POINT.
170     REM
180     REM ****** VARIABLE TABLE
190     REM         NUM1, NUM2, NUM3 = INPUT VARIABLES
200     REM         NUM4, NUM5, NUM6 = INPUT VARIABLES
210     REM         NUM7, NUM8, NUM9 = INPUT VARIABLES
220     REM         SUM1 = SUM OF THE THREE NUMBERS
230     REM         SUM2 = SUM OF THE SQUARES OF THE NUMBERS
240     REM         SUM3 = SUM OF THE CUBES OF THE NUMBERS
250     REM
260     REM ****** PROCESS SECTION
270     REM THIS SECTION WILL CALCULATE AND DISPLAY THE SUM OF THE NUMBERS
280     READ NUM1, NUM2, NUM3
290        LET SUM1 = NUM1+NUM2+NUM3
300        PRINT "THE SUM OF THE THREE NUMBERS IS =";SUM1
310     RESTORE
320     REM
330     REM THIS SECTION WILL CALCULATE AND DISPLAY THE SUM OF THE SQUARES
340     READ NUM4, NUM5, NUM6
350        LET SUM2 = NUM4^2+NUM5^2+NUM6^2
360        PRINT "THE SUM OF THE SQUARES OF THE THREE NUMBERS IS = ";SUM2
370     RESTORE
380     REM
390     REM THIS SECTION WILL CALCULATE AND DISPLAY THE SUM OF THE CUBES
400     READ NUM7, NUM8, NUM9
410        LET SUM3 = NUM7^3+NUM8^3+NUM9^3
420        PRINT "THE SUM OF THE CUBES OF THE THREE NUMBERS IS = ";SUM3
430     REM
440     REM ****** DATA SECTION
450     DATA 2, 4, 6
460     END
Ok
RUN
THE SUM OF THE THREE NUMBERS IS = 12
THE SUM OF THE SQUARES OF THE THREE NUMBERS IS =  56
THE SUM OF THE CUBES OF THE THREE NUMBERS IS =  288
Ok
```

**Figure 3–18**
The RESTORE Statement

example), or a trailing exclamation point (2.478637!, for example). The exclamation point tells the computer that the number is single-precision. You can define a variable as single-precision by using a LET statement as follows:

```
LET X!=?
```

where the ? represents any number or numeric variable. BASIC stores a single-precision number with seven digits of precision and prints the number with up to seven decimal digits (although only six digits may be accurate).

A double-precision constant is any numeric constant that has eight or more digits (383656852, for example), exponential form using D (3.38238D−03, for example), or a trailing pound sign (2.478637#, for example).

```
100     REM THIS PROGRAM ACCEPTS 3 NUMBERS FROM THE KEYBOARD
110     REM AND COMPUTES THEIR SUM.
120     REM
130     REM ****** VARIABLE TABLE
140     REM          NUM1, NUM2, NUM3 = INPUT VARIABLES
150     REM          SUM = SUM OF THE THREE INPUT VARIABLES
160     REM
170     REM ****** INITIALIZATION SECTION
180     PRINT "YOU TELL ME ANY 3 NUMBERS, AND I WILL TELL YOU THEIR SUM."
190     PRINT "THE 3 NUMBERS MUST BE SEPARATED BY COMMAS."
200     INPUT NUM1, NUM2, NUM3
210     REM
220     REM ****** PROCESS SECTION
230     LET SUM = NUM1+NUM2+NUM3
240     REM
250     REM ****** OUTPUT SECTION
260     PRINT "THE SUM OF THE THREE NUMBERS IS = ";SUM
270     END
Ok
RUN
YOU TELL ME ANY 3 NUMBERS, AND I WILL TELL YOU THEIR SUM.
THE 3 NUMBERS MUST BE SEPARATED BY COMMAS.
? 10,20,30
THE SUM OF THE THREE NUMBERS IS =   60
Ok
```

**Figure 3–19**
An Application of the INPUT Statement

```
100     REM THIS PROGRAM ACCEPTS THE RADIUS OF A CIRCLE FROM
110     REM THE KEYBOARD AND COMPUTES ITS AREA.
120     REM
130     REM ****** VARIABLE TABLE
140     REM          PI = VALUE OF PI (3.1416)
150     REM          RADIUS = INPUT VARIABLE (RADIUS OF A CIRCLE)
160     REM          AREA = AREA OF THE CIRCLE
170     REM
180     REM ****** INITIALIZATION SECTION
190     LET PI = 3.1416
200     PRINT "WHAT IS THE RADIUS OF THE CIRCLE"
210     INPUT RADIUS
220     REM
230     REM ****** PROCESS SECTION
240     LET AREA = PI*RADIUS*RADIUS
250     REM
260     REM ****** OUTPUT SECTION
270     PRINT "THE AREA OF THE CIRCLE IS =";AREA
280     END
Ok
RUN
WHAT IS THE RADIUS OF THE CIRCLE
? 5
THE AREA OF THE CIRCLE IS = 78.54
Ok
```

**Figure 3–20**
Another Application of the INPUT Statement

The pound sign tells the computer that the number is double-precision. You can define a variable as double-precision by using a LET statement as follows:

```
LET X#=?
```

where the ? represents any number or numeric variable. BASIC stores a double-precision number with 17 digits of precision and prints the number with up to 16 decimal digits.

---

**SUMMARY**

In this chapter, we explained numeric and string variables and constants. We discussed how you use E notation for presenting very small and very large numbers. We also discussed using the LET, READ and DATA, and INPUT statements to enter data into your program, and you learned about using the RESTORE command to reset the internal data pointers. Finally, we reviewed integer, single-precision, and double-precision numbers.

---

**REVIEW QUESTIONS**

*These questions are answered in Appendix D.

1. What will be printed when you run the following program?

```
10 A=10
20 B=30
30 A=A+1
40 B=A
50 END
```

*2. What is wrong with the following programs?

```
a. 10 READ X+Y
   20 PRINT X, Y
   30 DATA 2,3
   40 END
b. 10 READ Q,W
   20 PRINT Q*W
   30 END
c. 10 LET A=15
   20 LET B=35
   30 LET B+C=X
   40 PRINT X
   50 END
d. 10 READ A,B,C
   20 D=A+B+C
   30 DATA 15,25
   40 PRINT D
   50 END
```

3. What command is used for interactive programming?

4. Correct the following program:

```
10 X$="JACKY"
20 B$=X$
```

```
30 C$=COMPUTER
40 A+B=X
50 PRINT X, X$, C$
50 END
```

5. Convert the following regular notations to E notations.
   a. 16.234561
   b. .00004512
   c. 4000000.
   d. 99.998821

*6. Assign the following three names to three string variables and print their values:

     JACKI
     MARY
     CATHY

7. What is the effect of extra data on a program?

8. What is the effect of insufficient data on a program?

9. What are some of the advantages and disadvantages of the three methods of sending data to the computer?

10. List two applications of the RESTORE statement.

*11. What do we mean by interactive programming?

*12. What are some examples of non-numeric variables?

13. What are some examples of numeric constants?

*14. What is the output of the following programs?
```
a. 10 READ B
   20 PRINT C
   30 DATA 64
   40 END
```
```
b. 10 READ A,B,C
   20 PRINT C, B, A
   30 DATA 5,10,15
   40 END
```

15. Jack's Social Security number is 524-13-9091. Is this numeric or non-numeric data?

---

## HANDS-ON EXPERIENCE

1. Write a program to read values for variables A, B, and C from a data line and calculate their sum and product.

2. Write a program to read the base and height of a triangle and calculate its area.

3. Using the RESTORE command, read one data item into three variables and calculate the average of these variables.

4. Use the three methods of sending data to the computer to compute the average of the following test scores: 89, 61, 70, and 80. Which method is easiest?

5. Using the INPUT command, write a program that accepts the number of hours worked and the pay rate from the keyboard, and then calculates the gross pay.

---

## KEY TERMS

| | | |
|---|---|---|
| Constant | Single precision | Scientific notation |
| Double precision | String variable | Variable |

---

| | |
|---|---|
| LET | Assigns a value to a variable, e.g., LET A = 10 |
| INPUT | Assigns a value to a variable, e.g., INPUT A |
| READ/DATA | Assigns a value to a variable, e.g., READ A, DATA 10 |
| RESTORE | Allows you to read a data item more than once |

---

## Multiple Choice

1. The assignment statement

   **a.** assigns a value to a variable

   **b.** is the only method used to send numeric data to the computer

   **c.** generates a location inside the computer

   **d.** is useful in a program that contains a constant parameter

   **e.** a, c, and d

2. Which is not a valid numeric constant?

   **a.** 223

   **b.** +223

   **c.** −223

   **d.** 22.3

   **e.** 2,233

3. The READ and DATA statements

   **a.** generate an address inside the computer and assign values to that address

   **b.** move values from the data statement to variables

   **c.** should be used when large amounts of data need to be sent to the computer

   **d.** all of the above

   **e.** none of the above

4. The following program produces a result of

```
10 A=10
20 B=A
30 A=20
40 PRINT A; B
50 END
```

   **a.** 20 10

   **b.** 20 0

   **c.** 20 30

   **d.** this program will not run

   **e.** none of the above

5. The following program produces a result of

```
10 A$="JACK"
20 B$=MARY
30 PRINT A$, B$
40 END
```

   **a.** JACK MARY

   **b.** A$ B$

    **c.** 0 0

    **d.** this program will produce an error

    **e.** none of the above

  **6.** The following program produces a result of

```
10 READ A,B,C
20 PRINT A; B; C
30 DATA 10,20,30
40 A=B+C
50 END
```

    **a.** 10 20 30

    **b.** 50 20 30

    **c.** an error message

    **d.** none of the above

    **e.** 30 20 10

  **7.** The following program produces a result of

```
10 READ A$,B,C
20 PRINT A$
30 RESTORE
40 READ A$,B,C
50 PRINT A$; B; C
60 DATA JACK,10,20,90
70 DATA SUE,40,50
80 END
```

    **a.** JACK
       SUE 40 50

    **b.** JACK
       JACK 10 20

    **c.** JACK
       JACK 40 50

    **d.** none of the above

    **e.** JACK
       JACK

  **8.** The following program produces a result of

```
10 READ A,B,C,D,E
20 DATA 20,30,40,50
30 PRINT A; B; C; E
40 END
```

    **a.** 20 30 40 50

    **b.** OUT OF DATA IN 20

    **c.** OUT OF DATA IN 10

    **d.** 20 30 40 50 0

    **e.** none of the above

  **9.** The following program produces a result of

```
10 READ A,B,C
20 RESTORE
```

```
30 READ B,D,A
40 PRINT A; D; B
50 DATA 50,75,25
60 END
```

    **a.** 50 25 75

    **b.** 25 75 50

    **c.** 50 75 25

    **d.** 75 25 50

    **e.** 25 50 75

**10.** The following program produces a result of

```
10 READ A,B,C
20 D=B+C
30 RESTORE
40 READ B,C,A
50 PRINT D
60 DATA 2,4,6
70 END
```

    **a.** 0

    **b.** 6

    **c.** 10

    **d.** 8

    **e.** none of the above

## True/False

**1.** The assignment statement is the best method to use when sending a large amount of data to the computer.

**2.** There is no difference between numeric and string variables in BASIC.

**3.** The INPUT statement enables the user to use different data every time the program runs.

**4.** A variable name can be up to 40 characters long.

**5.** The READ and DATA statements are used for interactive programming.

**6.** The DATA statement can be anywhere in a program as long as it is before the END statement.

**7.** An address in the computer can hold only one value at a time.

**8.** A person's name is an example of string data.

**9.** The RESTORE statement allows the programmer to read the same data exactly twice.

**10.** If the DATA statement contains more items than the READ statement, the computer displays an error message.

---

| **Multiple Choice** | **True/False** | **ANSWERS** |
|---|---|---|
| **1.** e | **1.** F | |
| **2.** e | **2.** F | |
| **3.** d | **3.** T | |
| **4.** a | **4.** T | |
| **5.** d | **5.** F | |

| | | | |
|---|---|---|---|
| **6.** a | | **6.** T | |
| **7.** b | | **7.** T | |
| **8.** c | | **8.** T | |
| **9.** b | | **9.** F | |
| **10.** c | | **10.** F | |

# Branching and Looping

4

## 4–1

## INTRODUCTION

In this chapter, we discuss several interesting features of programming in BASIC. You learn about logical operations, one of the strongest functions of a computer. Using this feature you can use a computer as a decision-making tool. We also explain unconditional branching using the GOTO command and conditional branching using the IF-GOTO, IF-THEN, IF-THEN-ELSE, and ON-GOTO commands. You learn about using the WHILE-WEND loop for performing a series of steps based on a condition and using the FOR-NEXT loop to perform operations a fixed number of times. We also discuss the STOP command for terminating a program.

## 4–2

## LOGICAL OPERATIONS

One of the advantages of using computers is the amazing speed with which computers make comparisons. Table 4–1 shows the symbols (**logical operators**) a computer uses for comparisons. Logical operations are the key element in using computers as decision-making tools. In this chapter and in future chapters, we illustrate several applications of these types of comparisons.

## 4–3

## THE GOTO STATEMENT

Whenever you want to change the normal sequence of a program unconditionally (unconditional branching) you use the GOTO command. Using the GOTO command, for example, you can change the normal program execution sequence from line 200 to line 280. The programs shown in figures 4–1 and 4–2 illustrate this process.

When you run the program shown in figure 4–1, nothing is printed. Program control is transferred from line 210 to line 230; line 220 is never considered as part of the program. In this case the PRINT command in line 220 is ignored.

In the program shown in figure 4–2, we have created an endless **loop** using the GOTO command. BASIC executes line 190, printing JACK. Then line 200 sends program control back to line 190, and the process continues. To stop the endless loop, you must press the Ctrl and Break keys together or press Ctrl-C.

For practice, write a program that uses a GOTO statement to read a variable from a data line and print its contents. An example of this type of program is shown in figure 4–3.

In the program shown in figure 4–3, line 170 reads one variable and line 180 prints its contents. Line 190 sends control back to line 170, where

**Table 4–1**
Logical Operations Symbols

| Math Symbol | Meaning | Logical Operator | Example |
|---|---|---|---|
| = | equal to | = | A+B=C+D |
| < | less than | < | A+B<C+D |
| > | greater than | > | A+B>C+D |
| ≦ | less than or equal to | <= | X+W<=Q+R |
| ≧ | greater than or equal to | >= | X+W>=Q+R |
| ≠ | not equal to | <> | M+N<>Q+R |

```
100    REM THIS PROGRAM SHOWS THE WAY IN WHICH THE GOTO STATEMENT
110    REM WORKS.  IT SIMPLY CHANGES THE NORMAL SEQUENCE OF THE
120    REM PROGRAM.
130    REM
140    REM ****** VARIABLE TABLE
150    REM          NUM1 = INPUT VARIABLE
160    REM
170    REM ****** INITIALIZATION SECTION
180    LET NUM1 = 5
190    REM
200    REM ****** OUTPUT SECTION
210    GOTO 230
220    PRINT NUM1
230    END
Ok
RUN
Ok
```

**Figure 4-1**
Using the GOTO Statement

```
100    REM THIS PROGRAM GENERATES AN ENDLESS LOOP.
110    REM
120    REM ****** VARIABLE TABLE
130    REM          WORD1$ = INPUT STRING VARIABLE
140    REM
150    REM ****** INITIALIZATION SECTION
160    LET WORD1$ = "JACK"
170    REM
180    REM ****** OUTPUT SECTION
190    PRINT WORD1$
200    GOTO 190
210    END
JACK
JACK
JACK
JACK
JACK
JACK
JACK
JACK
JACK
JACK
JACK
JACK
JACK
JACK
JACK
JACK
JACK
JACK
JACK
^C
Break in 190
Ok
```

**Figure 4-2**
Another Use of the GOTO Statement

```
100     REM THIS PROGRAM READS A DATA ITEM FROM A DATA LINE AND
110     REM PRINTS IT.
120     REM
130     REM ****** VARIABLE TABLE
140     REM          NUM1 = INPUT VARIABLE
150     REM
160     REM ****** OUTPUT SECTION
170     READ NUM1
180     PRINT NUM1
190     GOTO 170
200     REM
210     REM ****** DATA SECTION
220     DATA 5, 10, 15
230     END
Ok
RUN
 5
 10
 15
Out of DATA in 170
Ok
```

**Figure 4–3**
Printing with the GOTO Statement

another data item will be read. When BASIC attempts to read a fourth data item, you receive the error message

```
OUT OF DATA IN 170
```

## 4–4

### THE IF-GOTO, IF-THEN, AND IF-THEN-ELSE STATEMENTS

The IF-GOTO, IF-THEN, and IF-THEN-ELSE statements cause your program to branch to another line based on a condition. This is called **conditional branching**. One use of conditional branching is checking a customer's credit limit. If the credit limit is positive, then you have the program branch to one area; if the credit limit is negative, you have the program branch to another area. Figure 4–4 shows a program that chooses the smallest number from three given numbers.

The program reads NUM1, NUM2, and NUM3. In line 190, if NUM1 is smaller than NUM2, program control is transferred to line 230. There, NUM1 is compared with NUM3. If NUM1 is smaller than NUM3, program control is transferred to line 250. Line 250 prints the message and the smallest number, NUM1.

If in line 200, NUM2 is smaller than NUM3, program control is transferred to line 270. Line 270 prints the message and the smallest number, NUM2.

If neither line 190 nor line 200 is true, program execution moves to line 210, which prints the message and the smallest number, NUM3.

Figure 4–5 shows a program that reads five students' names and their G.P.A.s from a data line and prints the name of every student with a G.P.A. of 3.50 or more.

In line 210, the check for

```
GPA=-1
```

is called **flagging**. You should always put a fictitious data item at the end of the data lines so that when the program reads this item, you know you have reached

```
100     REM THIS PROGRAM SELECTS THE SMALLEST NUMBER AMONG THREE.
110     REM
120     REM ****** VARIABLE TABLE
130     REM          NUM1, NUM2, NUM3 = INPUT VARIABLES
140     REM
150     REM ****** INITIALIZATION SECTION
160     READ NUM1,NUM2,NUM3
170     REM
180     REM ****** PROCESS SECTION
190     IF NUM1<NUM2 THEN GOTO 230
200     IF NUM2<NUM3 THEN GOTO 270
210     PRINT "THE SMALLEST NUMBER AMONG 5, 10 AND 15 =";NUM3
220     GOTO 310
230     IF NUM1<NUM3 THEN GOTO 250
240     GOTO 210
250     PRINT "THE SMALLEST NUMBER AMONG 5, 10 AND 15 =";NUM1
260     GOTO 310
270     PRINT "THE SMALLEST NUMBER AMONG 5, 10 AND 15 =";NUM2
280     REM
290     REM ****** DATA SECTION
300     DATA 15, 10, 5
310     END
Ok
RUN
THE SMALLEST NUMBER AMONG 5, 10 AND 15 = 5
Ok
```

**Figure 4-4**

Selection of the Smallest Number

```
100     REM THIS PROGRAM PRINTS THE NAME OF THE STUDENTS WITH A
110     REM GPA OF 3.5 OR BETTER.
120     REM
130     REM ****** VARIABLE TABLE
140     REM          GPA = GRADE POINT AVERAGE
150     REM          STUDENT$ = STUDENT NAME
160     REM
170     REM ****** INITIALIZATION SECTION
180     READ GPA, STUDENT$
190     REM
200     REM ****** PROCESS SECTION
210        IF GPA = -1 THEN GOTO 360
220        IF GPA >= 3.5 THEN GOTO 260
230     GOTO 180
240     REM
250     REM ****** OUTPUT SECTION
260     PRINT STUDENT$;" HAS A GPA OF";GPA
270     GOTO 180
280     REM
290     REM ****** DATA SECTION
300     DATA 3.00, JACK
310     DATA 3.60, SUE
320     DATA 3.90, PAT
330     DATA 1.80, DENISE
340     DATA 2.20, CHARLES
350     DATA -1, FLAG
360     END
Ok
RUN
SUE HAS A GPA OF 3.6
PAT HAS A GPA OF 3.9
Ok
```

**Figure 4-5**

Using IF-THEN Statements

the end of the data. The flag can be any data item, but it is a good practice to make it unusual. In this case, because the program is reading a pair of data items each time, we put two data flags at the end of the data lines (−1 and FLAG).

Line 220 checks whether the G.P.A. is greater than or equal to 3.50. If so, the program branches to line 260, which prints the name and G.P.A. of the student. Then the program branches to line 180 to read more data. If the G.P.A. is not greater than or equal to 3.50, line 230 sends program control to line 180 to read more data.

You can use the IF-THEN-ELSE command to replace lines 220 and 230 as follows:

```
IF GPA>=3.50 THEN 260 ELSE 180
```

IF-THEN and IF-GOTO perform the same function. You can use either of these methods, depending on your personal preference.

As an exercise, draw a flowchart and write an interactive program that uses the IF-THEN statement to INPUT a number and print out whether the number is positive, negative, or zero. Figure 4−6 shows such a program, and figure 4−7 shows the flowchart for this program.

In lines 410 and 420 of this program we have used two commands that you have not seen before: OR and AND. The OR command means that if one condition among several conditions is correct, the test is passed. The AND command means that all conditions must be met in order to pass the test.

## 4−5

## THE ON-GOTO STATEMENT

The ON-GOTO statement is another command for conditional branching. The general format of this statement is as follows:

ON X GOTO L1,L2,L3, . . .

where X is any numerical expression or variable, and L1,L2,L3, . . . are line numbers. During the execution of the program, the integer value of X will be computed. Based on the value of X, the program will branch to one of the line numbers. If X=1, the program continues from line number L1; if X=2, program execution continues from line number L2, and so on.

You can include as many line numbers as will fit on one line. If the value of X is less than 1 or is greater than the number of program lines specified, you will see the error message

```
INVALID COMPUTED GOTO IN LN
```

where LN is the line number of the ON-GOTO statement.

Figure 4−8 shows one application of the ON-GOTO statement in an interactive program. Figure 4−9 shows another example of the ON-GOTO statement, and the WHILE-WEND command.

## 4−6

## THE WHILE-WEND LOOP

The WHILE-WEND loop is used for performing a series of steps based on a given condition. Figure 4−9 shows one example of this command.

```
100    REM THIS PROGRAM IS AN EXAMPLE OF INTERACTIVE PROGRAMMING.
110    REM YOU CAN INPUT ANY NUMBER FROM THE KEYBOARD, AND THE
120    REM COMPUTER WILL TELL YOU WHETHER YOUR NUMBER IS NEGATIVE,
130    REM ZERO OR POSITIVE.
140    REM
150    REM ****** VARIABLE TABLE
160    REM          NUMBER = INPUT VARIABLE
170    REM          ANSWER$ = REPEAT PROGRAM STRING VARIABLE
180    REM
190    REM ****** INITIALIZATION SECTION
200    PRINT "YOU TELL ME A NUMBER, I WILL TELL YOU"
210    PRINT "WHETHER IT IS ZERO, NEGATIVE, OR POSITIVE."
220    PRINT
230    INPUT "WHAT IS YOUR NUMBER";NUMBER
240    PRINT
250    REM
260    REM ****** PROCESS SECTION
270    IF NUMBER < 0 THEN 320
280    IF NUMBER = 0 THEN 340
290    GOTO 360
300    REM
310    REM ****** OUTPUT SECTION
320    PRINT "THE NUMBER YOU ENTERED IS NEGATIVE."
330    GOTO 400
340    PRINT "THE NUMBER YOU ENTERED IS ZERO."
350    GOTO 400
360    PRINT "THE NUMBER YOU ENTERED IS POSITIVE."
370    PRINT
380    REM
390    REM ****** TERMINATION SECTION
400    INPUT "WOULD YOU LIKE TO TRY AGAIN?  ANSWER WITH Y OR N";ANSWER$
410    IF ANSWER$ = "Y" OR ANSWER$ = "y" THEN GOTO 230
420    IF ANSWER$ <> "N" AND ANSWER$ <> "n" THEN GOTO 400
430    END
Ok
RUN
YOU TELL ME A NUMBER, I WILL TELL YOU
WHETHER IT IS ZERO, NEGATIVE, OR POSITIVE.

WHAT IS YOUR NUMBER? -7

THE NUMBER YOU ENTERED IS NEGATIVE.
WOULD YOU LIKE TO TRY AGAIN?  ANSWER WITH Y OR N? Y
WHAT IS YOUR NUMBER? 5

THE NUMBER YOU ENTERED IS POSITIVE.

WOULD YOU LIKE TO TRY AGAIN?  ANSWER WITH Y OR N? Y
WHAT IS YOUR NUMBER? 0

THE NUMBER YOU ENTERED IS ZERO.
WOULD YOU LIKE TO TRY AGAIN?  ANSWER WITH Y OR N? N
Ok
```

**Figure 4–6**
Finding the Sign of a Number

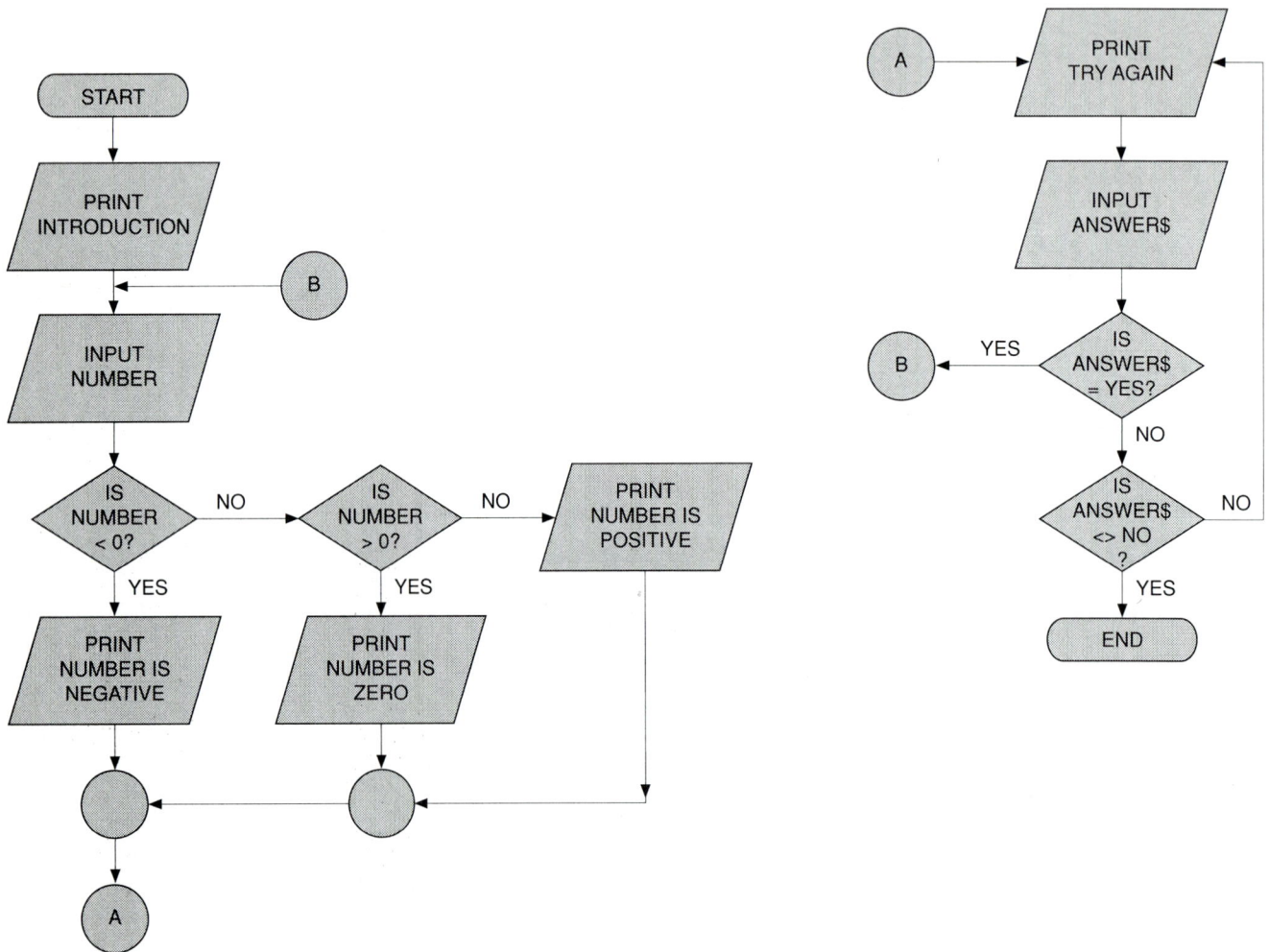

**Figure 4–7**
The Flowchart for the Program Shown in Figure 4–6

Line 180 reads NUM1 and NUM2. At the end of the data items, we included two zeros as flags. The WHILE-WEND command is used as a loop for performing a series of steps as long as the end of data has not been reached. Based on the calculated values of NUM1 and NUM2, program control will be transferred to line 230, 250, 270, or 290.

Figure 4–10 illustrates another example of the WHILE-WEND command.

## 4–7

## THE FOR-NEXT LOOP

The FOR-NEXT command is used to perform an operation or a series of operations a fixed number of times. Figures 4–11 through 4–13 show this process.

As you see in these programs, the FOR-NEXT loop is used to perform a set of operations a fixed number of times. In figure 4–11, lines 210 through

```
100     REM BASED UPON THE VALUE OF A NUMBER, THE
110     REM COMPUTER WILL PRINT ONE OF FOUR DIFFERENT NAMES.
120     REM
130     REM ****** VARIABLE TABLE
140     REM          NUMBER = INPUT VARIABLE
150     REM          ANSWER$ = REPEAT PROGRAM STRING VARIABLE
160     REM
170     REM ****** INITIALIZATION SECTION
180     PRINT "WHICH NAME DO YOU WANT TO BE PRINTED?"
190     PRINT "     IF 1 IS ENTERED, THE COMPUTER WILL PRINT 'SUSAN'."
200     PRINT "     IF 2 IS ENTERED, THE COMPUTER WILL PRINT 'CARLA'."
210     PRINT "     IF 3 IS ENTERED, THE COMPUTER WILL PRINT 'JACKI'."
220     PRINT "     IF 4 IS ENTERED, THE COMPUTER WILL PRINT 'MARTHA'."
230     PRINT
240     PRINT "PLEASE ENTER A NUMBER BETWEEN 1 AND 4."
250     INPUT "I WILL PRINT A NAME FOR YOU. ",NUMBER
260     REM
270     REM ****** PROCESS SECTION
280     ON NUMBER GOTO 320,340,360,380
290     GOTO 450
300     REM
310     REM ****** OUTPUT SECTION
320     PRINT "YOU ENTERED 1, WHICH = SUSAN."
330     GOTO 410
340     PRINT "YOU ENTERED 2, WHICH = CARLA."
350     GOTO 410
360     PRINT "YOU ENTERED 3, WHICH = JACKI."
370     GOTO 410
380     PRINT "YOU ENTERED 4, WHICH = MARTHA."
390     REM
400     REM ****** TERMINATION SECTION
410     INPUT "DO YOU WANT TO TRY ANOTHER?  ANSWER WITH Y OR N";ANSWER$
420     IF ANSWER$ = "Y" OR ANSWER$ = "y" THEN GOTO 240
430     IF ANSWER$ <> "N" AND ANSWER$ <> "n" THEN GOTO 410
440     GOTO 460
450     PRINT "THE NUMBER MUST BE 1, 2, 3 OR 4.  TRY AGAIN." : GOTO 250
460     END
Ok
RUN
WHICH NAME DO YOU WANT TO BE PRINTED?
     IF 1 IS ENTERED, THE COMPUTER WILL PRINT 'SUSAN'.
     IF 2 IS ENTERED, THE COMPUTER WILL PRINT 'CARLA'.
     IF 3 IS ENTERED, THE COMPUTER WILL PRINT 'JACKI'.
     IF 4 IS ENTERED, THE COMPUTER WILL PRINT 'MARTHA'.

PLEASE ENTER A NUMBER BETWEEN 1 AND 4.
I WILL PRINT A NAME FOR YOU. 2
YOU ENTERED 2, WHICH = CARLA.
DO YOU WANT TO TRY ANOTHER?  ANSWER WITH Y OR N? Y
PLEASE ENTER A NUMBER BETWEEN 1 AND 4.
I WILL PRINT A NAME FOR YOU. 4
YOU ENTERED 4, WHICH = MARTHA.
DO YOU WANT TO TRY ANOTHER?  ANSWER WITH Y OR N? Y
PLEASE ENTER A NUMBER BETWEEN 1 AND 4.
I WILL PRINT A NAME FOR YOU. 5
THE NUMBER MUST BE 1, 2, 3 OR 4.  TRY AGAIN.
I WILL PRINT A NAME FOR YOU. 3
YOU ENTERED 3, WHICH = JACKI.
DO YOU WANT TO TRY ANOTHER?  ANSWER WITH Y OR N? N
Ok
```

**Figure 4–8**
The ON-GOTO Statement

```
100    REM THIS PROGRAM WILL READ TWO NUMBERS FROM A DATA STATEMENT"
110    REM AND THEN ADD THE TWO NUMBERS TOGETHER.  IT WILL REPEAT"
120    REM THIS PROCESS THREE TIMES.
130    REM
140    REM ****** VARIABLE TABLE
150    REM           NUM1, NUM2 = INPUT VARIABLES
160    REM
170    REM ****** INITIALIZATION SECTION
180    READ NUM1, NUM2
190    REM
200    REM ****** PROCESS SECTION
210    WHILE NUM1 <> 0
220       ON NUM1+NUM2 GOTO 230,250,270,290
230       PRINT "THE SUM OF THE TWO NUMBERS =";NUM1+NUM2
240       GOTO 300
250       PRINT "THE SUM OF THE TWO NUMBERS =";NUM1+NUM2
260       GOTO 300
270       PRINT "THE SUM OF THE TWO NUMBERS =";NUM1+NUM2
280       GOTO 300
290       PRINT "THE SUM OF THE TWO NUMBERS =";NUM1+NUM2
300       READ NUM1, NUM2
310    WEND
320    REM
330    REM ****** DATA SECTION
340    DATA .50,.50,.70,1.30,-2,3,-5,9,0,0
350    END
Ok
RUN
THE SUM OF THE TWO NUMBERS = 1
THE SUM OF THE TWO NUMBERS = 2
THE SUM OF THE TWO NUMBERS = 1
THE SUM OF THE TWO NUMBERS = 4
Ok
```

**Figure 4–9**
Another Example of the ON-GOTO Statement, and the WHILE-WEND Command

**Figure 4–10**
Another Example of the WHILE-WEND Command

```
100    REM THIS PROGRAM ILLUSTRATES THE WHILE-WEND COMMAND.
110    REM
120    REM ****** VARIABLE TABLE
130    REM           COUNTER = WHILE-WEND LOOP COUNTER VARIABLE
140    REM
150    COUNTER=1
160    WHILE COUNTER<10
170       PRINT "BASIC"
180       COUNTER=COUNTER+2
190    WEND
200    PRINT "FORTRAN"
210    END
Ok
RUN
BASIC
BASIC
BASIC
BASIC
BASIC
FORTRAN
Ok
```

```
100     REM THIS PROGRAM WILL PRINT THE NAME "JACK" IN FIVE
110     REM DIFFERENT PRINT ZONES USING THE FOR-NEXT LOOP STRUCTURE.
120     REM
130     REM ****** VARIABLE TABLE
140     REM          NAM$ = STRING VARIABLE (JACK)
150     REM          COUNTER = FOR-NEXT LOOP COUNTER VARIABLE
160     REM
170     REM ****** INITIALIZATION SECTION
180     LET NAM$ = "JACK"
190     REM
200     REM ****** PROCESS SECTION
210     FOR COUNTER = 1 TO 5
220        PRINT NAM$,
230     NEXT COUNTER
240     END
Ok
RUN
JACK           JACK           JACK           JACK           JACK
Ok
```

**Figure 4-11**
One Application of the FOR-NEXT Loop

230 constitute the FOR-NEXT loop. When the process has been repeated five times, the loop is terminated and line 240, which is the end of the program, is encountered. This program prints the word "JACK" five times. COUNTER assumes values of 1, 2, 3, 4, and 5.

In figure 4-12, line 180 prints the square of the value of COUNTER. In succession, COUNTER's value becomes 1, 2, 3, 4, and then 5.

In figure 4-13 the values of COUNTER are accumulated in the address TOTAL. After the loop is terminated, the final value of TOTAL, 55, is printed. At the beginning of the program, TOTAL is equal to 0. In the first round it becomes 1 (TOTAL=0+1=1). In the second round, it becomes 3 (TOTAL=1+2=3), and so forth.

In a FOR-NEXT loop, you can use a STEP value. This STEP value can be any numeric value or a formula (as long as the value of the formula is defined when it is needed). The starting, ending, and STEP values of a loop can be any numbers, positive or negative (however, STEP 0 will generate an endless loop, so

```
100     REM THIS PROGRAM WILL PRINT THE SQUARES OF THE NUMBERS
110     REM 1 THROUGH 5 USING THE FOR-NEXT LOOP STRUCTURE.
120     REM
130     REM ****** VARIABLE TABLE
140     REM          COUNTER = FOR-NEXT LOOP COUNTER VARIABLE
150     REM
160     REM ****** PROCESS SECTION
170     FOR COUNTER = 1 TO 5
180        PRINT COUNTER^2,
190     NEXT COUNTER
200     END
Ok
RUN
 1             4             9             16            25
Ok
```

**Figure 4-12**
Another Application of the FOR-NEXT Loop

```
100     REM THIS PROGRAM PRINTS THE SUM OF NUMBERS 1 THROUGH 10
110     REM INCLUSIVE.
120     REM
130     REM ****** VARIABLE TABLE
140     REM           TOTAL = SUM OF ALL THE NUMBERS
150     REM           COUNTER = FOR-NEXT LOOP COUNTER VARIABLE
160     REM
170     REM ****** INITIALIZATION SECTION
180     LET TOTAL = 0
190     REM
200     REM ****** PROCESS SECTION
210     FOR COUNTER = 1 TO 10
220        LET TOTAL = TOTAL + COUNTER
230     NEXT COUNTER
240     REM
250     REM ****** OUTPUT SECTION
260     PRINT "THE SUM OF THE NUMBERS 1 THROUGH 10 =";TOTAL
270     END
Ok
RUN
THE SUM OF THE NUMBERS 1 THROUGH 10 = 55
Ok
```

**Figure 4–13**
Another Application of the FOR-NEXT Loop

it is pointless to use this value). Figures 4–14 and 4–15 show more applications for the FOR-NEXT loop.

The first loop in figure 4–15 extends from line 180 through line 200. COUNTER1 assumes the following values:

$$1$$
$$(1+.5)=1.5$$
$$(1.5+.5)=2$$

```
100     REM THIS PROGRAM USES THE FOR-NEXT LOOP STRUCTURE FOR
110     REM PRINTING A SERIES OF NUMBERS, THEIR SQUARES AND
120     REM THEIR CUBES.
130     REM
140     REM ****** VARIABLE TABLE
150     REM           COUNTER = FOR-NEXT LOOP COUNTER VARIABLE
160     REM           SQUARE = SQUARE OF COUNTER
170     REM           CUBE = CUBE OF COUNTER
180     REM
190     REM ****** PROCESS SECTION
200     PRINT "NUMBER", "SQUARE", "CUBE"
210     FOR COUNTER = 1 TO 6
220        PRINT COUNTER, COUNTER^2, COUNTER^3
230     NEXT COUNTER
240     END
NUMBER          SQUARE          CUBE
 1               1               1
 2               4               8
 3               9               27
 4               16              64
 5               25              125
 6               36              216
```

**Figure 4–14**
Another Application of the FOR-NEXT Loop

```
100    REM THERE ARE 3 LOOPS IN THIS PROGRAM.    CAN YOU FIND THEM?
110    REM
120    REM ****** VARIABLE TABLE
130    REM            COUNTER1 = FOR-NEXT LOOP COUNTER VARIABLE
140    REM            COUNTER2 = FOR-NEXT LOOP COUNTER VARIABLE
150    REM            COUNTER3 = FOR-NEXT LOOP COUNTER VARIABLE
160    REM
170    REM ****** PROCESS SECTION
180    FOR COUNTER1 = 1 TO 2 STEP .5
190       PRINT "A COMPUTER IS AN INTERESTING DEVICE"
200    NEXT COUNTER1
210    REM
220    PRINT
230    FOR COUNTER2 = 6 TO 2 STEP -2
240       PRINT "BASIC IS EASY"
250    NEXT COUNTER2
260    REM
270    PRINT
280    FOR COUNTER3 = -1 TO 7 STEP 2
290       PRINT "LOOP",
300    NEXT COUNTER3
310    END
Ok
RUN
A COMPUTER IS AN INTERESTING DEVICE
A COMPUTER IS AN INTERESTING DEVICE
A COMPUTER IS AN INTERESTING DEVICE

BASIC IS EASY
BASIC IS EASY
BASIC IS EASY

LOOP            LOOP            LOOP            LOOP            LOOP
Ok
```

**Figure 4–15**
FOR-NEXT with STEP


This loop will be executed three times and the message

```
A COMPUTER IS AN INTERESTING DEVICE
```

will be printed three times. The second loop in figure 4–15 is in lines 230 through 250. COUNTER2 assumes the following values:

$$6$$
$$(6-2)=4$$
$$(4-2)=2$$

The loop is executed three times and the message

```
BASIC IS EASY
```

is printed three times.

The third loop is in lines 280 through 300. COUNTER3 assumes the following values:

$$-1$$
$$(-1+2)=1$$

$(1+2)=3$
$(3+2)=5$
$(5+2)=7$

This loop is executed five times and the message

```
LOOP
```

is printed five times on one line. Do you know why the output is printed on one line?

# 4-8

## NESTED LOOPS

There are many occasions for having one loop inside another loop. This is called **nested looping**. Whenever you are using a nested loop, the inner loop must be completely inside the outer loop. Therefore, nested loops cannot cross each other. Each loop should have only one entry and one exit point.

As an exercise, write a program to print a 5-by-15 square of stars using nested loops. Figure 4-16 shows one solution program.

In figure 4-16 the first loop is in lines 170 to 220; the second loop is in lines 180 to 200. This is how this program works:

Row=1 and Column=1

One * is printed and the printer stays on the same line because we have included a semicolon.

Row=1 and Column=2

**Figure 4-16**
An Example of Nested Loops

```
100   REM THIS PROGRAM PRINTS A 5 BY 15 SQUARE OF STARS.
110   REM
120   REM ****** VARIABLE TABLE
130   REM          ROW = FOR-NEXT LOOP COUNTER VARIABLE
140   REM          COLUMN = FOR-NEXT LOOP COUNTER VARIABLE
150   REM
160   REM ****** PROCESS SECTION
170   FOR ROW = 1 TO 5
180      FOR COLUMN = 1 TO 15
190         PRINT "*";
200      NEXT COLUMN
210      PRINT
220   NEXT ROW
230   END
Ok
RUN
***************
***************
***************
***************
***************
Ok
```

```
100    REM THIS PROGRAM USES A TOTAL ACCUMULATOR TO ADD TOGETHER
110    REM THE VALUES OF FOR-NEXT LOOP VARIABLES AT SUCCESSIVE
120    REM POINTS THROUGH THE EXECUTION OF THE PROGRAM, AND
130    REM PROVIDES A RUNNING DISPLAY OF THE TOTAL.
140    REM
150    REM ****** VARIABLE TABLE
160    REM          TOTAL = TOTAL ACCUMULATOR
170    REM          COUNTER1 = FOR-NEXT LOOP COUNTER VARIABLE
180    REM          COUNTER2 = FOR-NEXT LOOP COUNTER VARIABLE
190    REM
200    REM ****** INITIALIZATION SECTION
210    LET TOTAL = 0
220    REM
230    REM ****** PROCESS SECTION
240    FOR COUNTER1 = 1 TO 5 STEP 2
250       FOR COUNTER2 = -6 TO -10 STEP -2
260          LET TOTAL = TOTAL+COUNTER1+COUNTER2
270          PRINT TOTAL
280       NEXT COUNTER2
290    NEXT COUNTER1
300    END
Ok
RUN
-5
-12
-21
-24
-29
-36
-37
-40
-45
Ok
```

**Figure 4–17**
Another Example of Nested Loops

Another * is printed and the printer stays on the same line. This will continue until 15 asterisks are printed. At this time the inner loop is terminated, and BASIC executes line 210, which is an empty PRINT. This empty PRINT moves the printer to the next line. Now ROW=2 and the inner loop is executed again. For each value of ROW, the inner loop is executed 15 times.

In figure 4–17, the values of COUNTER1 and COUNTER2 are accumulated in address TOTAL. To get you started with this idea, look at the following examples:

| Round 1 | Round 2 |
|---|---|
| TOTAL=0 | TOTAL=−5 |
| COUNTER1=1 | COUNTER1=1 |
| COUNTER2=−6 | COUNTER2=−8 |
| TOTAL=0+1−6=−5 | TOTAL=−5+1−8=−12 |

Can you complete all the rounds?

The number of loops within the outside loop can be practically unlimited. Figures 4–18 and 4–19 show examples of valid and invalid nested loops.

**Figure 4-18**
Valid Nested Loops

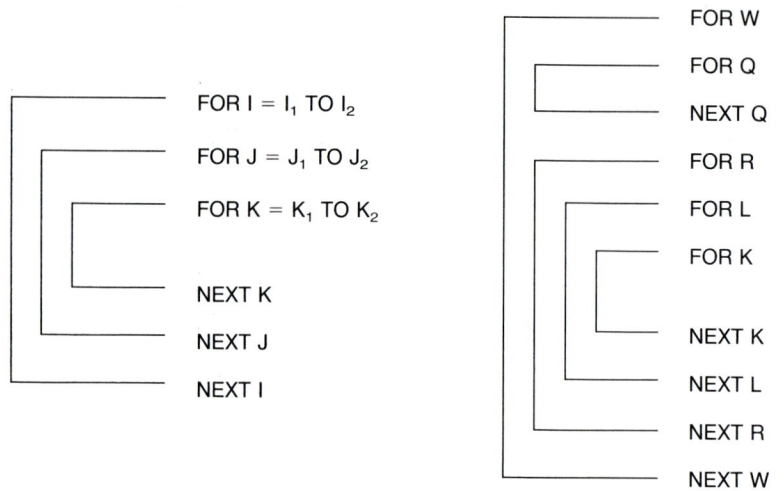

FOR I = $I_1$ TO $I_2$

FOR J = $J_1$ TO $J_2$

FOR K = $K_1$ TO $K_2$

NEXT K

NEXT J

NEXT I

FOR W

FOR Q

NEXT Q

FOR R

FOR L

FOR K

NEXT K

NEXT L

NEXT R

NEXT W

**Figure 4-19**
Invalid Nested Loops

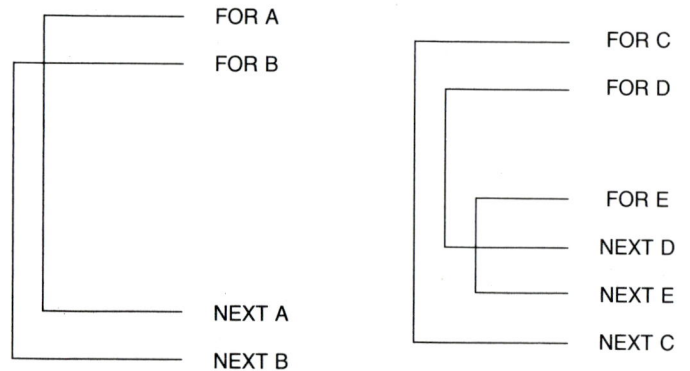

FOR A

FOR B

NEXT A

NEXT B

FOR C

FOR D

FOR E

NEXT D

NEXT E

NEXT C

## 4-9

## THE STOP STATEMENT

The STOP statement terminates a BASIC program. This statement is similar to the END statement, but a BASIC program can have only one END statement, while it can have many STOP statements, and the END statement must be at the end of the program, while the STOP statement can be anywhere.

The STOP statement transfers program control to the last line, the END statement. The following two programs are identical in function.

**Program 1**
```
10 PRINT "ANDREW"
20 STOP
30 PRINT "JACK"
40 END
```

**Program 2**
```
10 PRINT "ANDREW"
20 GOTO 40
30 PRINT "JACK"
40 END
```

When you run the first program you see the following:

```
ANDREW
BREAK IN 20
```

In this chapter, we reviewed several interesting features of programming in BASIC. We discussed the logical operations, one of the strongest functions of computers. You learned about unconditional branching using the GOTO statement and conditional branching using the IF-GOTO, IF-THEN, and IF-THEN-ELSE statements. We also explained how you use the ON-GOTO command for conditional branching.

**SUMMARY**

We discussed program looping, including how to use WHILE-WEND for performing a series of steps based on a condition, and FOR-NEXT for performing a series of operations a fixed number of times. Nested loops and valid and invalid loops were explained. Finally, you learned about the STOP statement as a command for terminating a program.

**REVIEW QUESTIONS**

*These questions are answered in Appendix D.

1. What is the symbol for "not equal to" in BASIC?

*2. What is the output of the following programs?

a.
```
10  A=5
20  GOTO 40
30  PRINT A
40  END
```

b.
```
10  B=10
20  PRINT B
30  GOTO 50
40  PRINT B
50  END
```

c.
```
10  A$="COMPUTER"
20  PRINT A$
30  GOTO 20
40  END
```

d.
```
10  READ A
20  PRINT A
30  GOTO 10
40  DATA 5, 10, 15
50  END
```

3. What is wrong with the following FOR-NEXT loops?

a.
```
10  FOR I=12 TO 6
20      PRINT I
30  NEXT I
40  END
```

b.
```
10  FOR I=-6 TO 6 STEP -6
20      PRINT I
30  NEXT I
40  END
```

4. Correct the following nested loops:

```
10  FOR I=1 TO 5
20      FOR J=1 TO 4
30          PRINT I*J
40      NEXT I
50  NEXT J
60  END
```

**\*5.** To complete the following program, how many data items are required?

```
10 FOR I=2 TO 8 STEP 2
20     FOR J=6 TO 2 STEP -2
30         READ A,B
40     NEXT J
50 NEXT I
60 DATA
70 END
```

**6.** If we run the following program, how many lines of output will be printed?

```
10 FOR I=6 TO 14 STEP 2
20     FOR J=-3 TO 6 STEP 3
30         FOR K=1 TO 3
40     PRINT I*J*K
50         NEXT K
60     NEXT J
70 NEXT I
80 END
```

**7.** What is wrong with the following branching statements?
   **a.** ON W GOTO 100
   **b.** IF W THEN 1000
   **c.** THEN 300 IF W=0
   **d.** IF W>5 THEN W1
   **e.** IF W<150 THEN PRINT W
   **f.** GOTO W1+W2

**8.** What is the output of the following program?

```
10 FOR I=4 TO 16 STEP 12
20     PRINT I^.50
30 NEXT I
40 END
```

**9.** What is the output of the following program?

```
10 FOR I=-12 TO 0 STEP 3
20     FOR J=0 TO 12 STEP 3
30         PRINT "I*J="; I*J
40     NEXT J
50 NEXT I
60 END
```

**\*10.** Correct the following FOR-NEXT loop.

```
10 FOR I=2 TO -6
20 PRINT I
30 NEXT I
40 END
```

**11.** What is wrong with the following program?

```
10 ON 2 GOTO 20,30,40
20 PRINT "S"
30 PRINT "G"
40 GOTO 60
50 PRINT "M"
60 END
```

**HANDS-ON EXPERIENCE**

1. Write a program to read three student names and the students' Social Security numbers from a DATA line and print them. Before reading a new name, the program should check for the end of data.

2. Write a program to calculate the sum of the numbers 1 through 100. You should use the FOR-NEXT loop.

3. Using the FOR-NEXT loop, write a program to display the numbers 2, 5, 8, and 11 and their squares.

4. Using the FOR-NEXT loop, write a program to display the numbers 1 through 10, their squares, and their cubes.

5. Using a FOR-NEXT loop, write a program that prints a 20-by-20 square of plus signs (+).

**KEY TERMS**

| | | |
|---|---|---|
| Conditional branching | Logical operator | Nested looping |
| Flagging | Loop | |

**KEY COMMANDS**

| | |
|---|---|
| FOR-NEXT | Performs a task a specified number of times |
| GOTO n | Branches to line number n |
| IF-GOTO | Branches to a line number based on a condition |
| IF-THEN | Same as IF-GOTO |
| IF-THEN-ELSE | Same as two IF-GOTO or two IF-THEN statements |
| ON x GOTO z | Branches to line number z based on value x |
| STOP | Equivalent to GOTO n, where n is the line number of the END statement, but generates an error message |
| WHILE-WEND | Same as FOR-NEXT |

## Multiple Choice

**ARE YOU READY TO MOVE ON?**

What is the output of the following programs?

1. 
```
10 A=5
20 GOTO 40
30 PRINT "BASIC"
40 PRINT B+A
50 END
```
   **a.** 5
   **b.** BASIC   5

    **c.** BASIC

    **d.** this program will not run

    **e.** none of the above

2. 
```
10  A=5
20  B=32
30  C=A+B
40  PRINT C
50  GOTO 70
60  PRINT A
70  GOTO 40
80  END
```

    **a.** 7

    **b.** 7
       5

    **c.** 5
       7

    **d.** 7
       7

    **e.** an endless loop

3. 
```
10  READ A,B,C
20  PRINT A,B,C
30  GOTO 70
40  DATA 10,20,30
50  READ A,B,C
60  DATA 40,50,60
70  PRINT A;B;C
80  END
```

    **a.** 10  20  30
        40  50  60

    **b.** 10  20  30
        10  20  30

    **c.** OUT OF DATA IN LINE 10

    **d.** none of the above

    **e.** the program will continue running until interrupted

4. 
```
10  A=10
20  B=30
30  IF B>A THEN 50
40  PRINT A
50  PRINT B+A
60  END
```

    **a.** 30

    **b.** 40

    **c.** 10  40

    **d.** this program will not run

    **e.** 40  10

5. 
```
10  A=10
20  B=10
30  C=5
40  IF C<B THEN 60
50  READ C
60  C=B
```

```
70 PRINT C+A
80 DATA 2
90 END
```

a. 20

b. 12

c. 15

d. none of the above

e. the program creates an error message

6.
```
10 FOR J=.1 TO .5 STEP .1
20    PRINT 3;
30 NEXT J
40 END
```

a. 3   3   3

b. 3

c. 3   3   3   3   3

d. nothing

e. none of the above

7.
```
10 A=0
20 FOR I=1 TO 3
30    FOR J=1 TO 2
40       A=A+I+J
50    NEXT J
60 NEXT I
70 PRINT A
80 END
```

a. 7

b. 6

c. 21

d. 0

e. nothing

8.
```
10 READ D,E,F
20 IF D<E THEN 40
30 IF E>F THEN 70
40 K=D+E+F
50 PRINT K
60 DATA 3,7,1
70 END
```

a. nothing

b. 17

c. 8

d. 11

e. none of the above

9.
```
10 E=0
20 FOR N=1 TO 7
30    LET E=E+N
40 NEXT N
50 PRINT E
60 END
```

a. 7

b. 280

      **c.** 14

      **d.** 28

      **e.** none of the above

10. 
```
10 READ A
20 PRINT A;
30 GOTO 50
40 READ C
50 PRINT A
60 DATA 2,3,1
70 END
```

      **a.** 3  2

      **b.** 2  3

      **c.** 2

      **d.** 0

      **e.** 2  2

## True/False

1. Logical operations are the key element in using the computer as a decision-making tool.

2. The GOTO statement is an example of conditional branching.

3. The IF-THEN and IF-GOTO statements perform the same function.

4. The ON-GOTO statement is a command for unconditional branching.

5. The FOR-LAST loop statement is used to perform a series of operations a fixed number of times.

6. Nested looping simply means having one loop inside another loop.

7. The BASIC symbol for greater than or equal to is ">=".

8. The flagging technique signals that the computer has reached the beginning of the data section of the program.

9. The FOR-NEXT statement is used to perform repetitive operations.

10. Nested loops may cross each other under two special circumstances.

---

**ANSWERS**

| **Multiple Choice** | **True/False** |
|---|---|
| **1.** a | **1.** T |
| **2.** e | **2.** F |
| **3.** b | **3.** T |
| **4.** b | **4.** F |
| **5.** a | **5.** F |
| **6.** c | **6.** T |
| **7.** c | **7.** T |
| **8.** d | **8.** F |
| **9.** d | **9.** T |
| **10.** e | **10.** F |

# Formatting

# 5

## 5–1
### INTRODUCTION

In this chapter, we explain how to format your program output using commas and semicolons. We also discuss how to use the TAB function for spacing your program's output. You can format your program's output with PRINT USING statements. We discuss PRINT USING statements for integer, decimal, exponential, alphanumeric, and literal fields.

## 5–2
### FORMATTING PROGRAM OUTPUT

There are five standard **print zones** in each line. Each zone is 14 characters long. To enter the output of a PRINT statement into each of these five zones, you use a comma between data items. Using a semicolon as a **delimiter** provides a more compact output than using a comma.

Figures 5–1 and 5–2 show this process. As you can see in figure 5–2, if you print string variables using semicolons, the string data items "stick" to each other. As you can see in figure 5–1, this is not the case for numeric data.

## 5–3
### USING COMMAS AND SEMICOLONS AFTER VARIABLES

The appearance of a comma or a semicolon after a variable in a PRINT statement keeps the printer at the same line until all the printing zones have been used. Figure 5–3 shows this process.

Because there are five standard zones in each line, you can print up to five variables (if the length of a field does not exceed the length of its zone). Any extra variables are printed on the next line. When you execute the following statement:

```
100 PRINT A,B,C,D,E,F,G
```

```
100     REM A SEMICOLON PROVIDES MORE COMPACT OUTPUT THAN A COMMA.
110     REM
120     REM ****** VARIABLE TABLE
130     REM          NUM1, NUM2, NUM3, NUM4, NUM5 = INPUT VARIABLES
140     REM
150     REM ****** INITIALIZATION SECTION
160     LET NUM1 = 1
170     LET NUM2 = 2
180     LET NUM3 = 3
190     LET NUM4 = 4
200     LET NUM5 = 5
210     REM
220     REM ****** OUTPUT SECTION
230     PRINT NUM1,NUM2,NUM3,NUM4,NUM5
240     PRINT NUM1;NUM2;NUM3;NUM4;NUM5
250     END
Ok
RUN
 1              2              3              4              5
 1  2  3  4  5
Ok
```

**Figure 5–1**
Using Commas and Semicolons as Space Delimiters

```
100    REM THIS IS ANOTHER EXAMPLE OF SEMICOLONS AND
110    REM COMMAS AS DELIMITERS.
120    REM
130    REM ****** VARIABLE TABLE
140    REM          WORD1$, WORD2$, WORD3$ = INPUT STRING VARIABLES
150    REM
160    REM ****** INITIALIZATION SECTION
170    LET WORD1$ = "THIS IS"
180    LET WORD2$ = "A COMPUTER"
190    LET WORD3$ = "CLASS"
200    REM
210    REM ****** OUTPUT SECTION
220    PRINT WORD1$,WORD2$,WORD3$
230    PRINT WORD1$;WORD2$;WORD3$
240    END
Ok
RUN
THIS IS          A COMPUTER      CLASS
THIS ISA COMPUTERCLASS
Ok
```

**Figure 5–2**
Using Commas and Semicolons Between String Variables


the first five values (A, B, C, D, and E) are printed in the five standard zones across the page; values F and G are printed in the first and second zones on the following line.

You can use both comma and semicolon delimiters on the same line. The following statements show this process:

```
PRINT A,B,C;D,E
PRINT A,A,A;A,A
```

```
100    REM THIS EXAMPLE SHOWS THE EFFECT OF A COMMA AFTER A VARIABLE.
110    REM
120    REM ****** VARIABLE TABLE
130    REM          NUM1, NUM2, NUM3 = INPUT VARIABLES
140    REM
150    REM ****** INITIALIZATION SECTION
160    LET NUM1 = 1
170    LET NUM2 = 2
180    LET NUM3 = 3
190    REM
200    REM ****** OUTPUT SECTION
210    PRINT NUM1,
220    PRINT NUM2,
230    PRINT NUM3
240    PRINT NUM1;
250    PRINT NUM2;
260    PRINT NUM3
270    END
Ok
RUN
 1               2               3
 1   2   3
Ok
```

**Figure 5–3**
Using Commas and Semicolons after Variables

```
100     REM THIS PROGRAM SHOWS THE WAY IN WHICH THE TAB FUNCTION WORKS.
110     REM
120     REM ****** VARIABLE TABLE
130     REM         THERE ARE NO VARIABLES IN THIS PROGRAM.
140     REM
150     REM ****** OUTPUT SECTION
160     PRINT TAB(10);"COMPUTERS"
170     PRINT TAB(18);"ARE INTERESTING"
180     END
Ok
RUN
         COMPUTERS
                 ARE INTERESTING
Ok
```

**Figure 5–4**
One Application of the TAB Function

# 5–4
## THE TAB COMMAND

You use the TAB command to space your output within an output line. The general format of this function is as follows:

PRINT TAB(expression);(data to be printed)

TAB causes the next data field to be printed at the column indicated by the value of the expression. Figures 5–4 and 5–5 show this process.

In Figure 5–4, line 160 tells the computer to skip the first nine columns and begin printing at column 10. Therefore, the word COMPUTERS will occupy columns 10 through 18. Line 170 tells the computer to skip the first 17 columns and begin printing at column 18.

Whenever you use the TAB function, you must consider the following two rules:

■ If the value of the expression is less than the current position of the cursor, the TAB function is ignored.

```
100     REM THIS PROGRAM WILL PRINT A HORIZONTAL LINE OF ASTERISKS.
110     REM
120     REM ****** VARIABLE TABLE
130     REM         COUNTER = FOR-NEXT LOOP CONTROL VARIABLE
140     REM
150     REM ****** PROCESS SECTION
160     FOR COUNTER = 1 TO 5
170        PRINT TAB(COUNTER);"*"
180     NEXT COUNTER
190     PRINT "1234567890"
200     END
*
  *
    *
      *
        *
1234567890
```

**Figure 5–5**
Another Application of the TAB Function

```
100     REM THIS PROGRAM DISPLAYS THE USE OF THE TAB FUNCTION.
110     REM
120     REM ****** VARIABLE TABLE
130     REM         SPACES = OPEN SPACES TO BE USED IN THE OUTPUT
140     REM
150     REM ****** INITIALIZATION SECTION
160     LET SPACES = 10
170     REM
180     REM ****** OUTPUT SECTION
190     PRINT TAB(30);"DATA BASE";TAB(2*SPACES+5);"SYSTEM"
200     END
                                DATA BASE
                    SYSTEM
```

**Figure 5–6**
Using Rule 1 in the TAB Function

■ If the value of the expression is greater than the limit of the line, the TAB function is ignored.

Figures 5–6 and 5–7 show these two rules in action.

In Figure 5–6, the first TAB command tells the computer to skip 29 columns and begin printing in column 30—the words DATA BASE will occupy columns 30 to 38. After printing, the cursor is in column 39. The value of the second TAB expression is 25, which is less than 39 (the current cursor position). Therefore, this TAB is ignored, and the word "SYSTEM" is printed in columns 25 to 30 on the next line.

In figure 5–7, the TAB command is ignored because the expression gives a value that is beyond the limit of the print line (which is only 70 columns wide). Therefore, the word MIS is printed in columns 1 to 3 on the next line.

Write and run a BASIC program to draw any rhombus with a width between 5 and 35 (see fig. 5–8).

This program introduces the use of **error traps**, which trap errors that the user might make while entering data in response to an input prompt. For example, refer to lines 500 to 520 in figure 5–8. Line 500 instructs the user to press either Y or N. Pressing Y causes the program to repeat, pressing N causes the program to end.

```
100     REM THIS PROGRAM DISPLAYS THE USE OF THE TAB FUNCTION
110     REM
120     REM ****** VARIABLE TABLE
130     REM         SPACES = OPEN SPACES TO BE USED IN THE OUTPUT
140     REM
150     REM ****** INITIALIZATION SECTION
160     LET SPACES = 26
170     REM
180     REM ****** OUTPUT SECTION
190     PRINT TAB(3*SPACES+2);"MIS"
200     END

MIS
```

**Figure 5–7**
Using Rule 2 in the TAB Function

```
100     REM THIS PROGRAM DRAWS ANY RHOMBUS OF WIDTH 5 TO 35 USING ASTERISKS.
110     REM
120     REM ****** VARIABLE TABLE
130     REM          NUMBER = INPUT VARIABLE (WIDTH OF RHOMBUS)
140     REM          HALF = HALF OF NUMBER (.5 * NUMBER)
150     REM          LOOP.COUNTER1 = LOOP COUNTER CONTROL VARIABLE
160     REM          LOOP.COUNTER2 = LOOP COUNTER CONTROL VARIABLE
170     REM          COUNTER = INCREMENT COUNTER VARIABLE
180     REM          ANSWER$ = REPEAT PROGRAM TEST STRING VARIABLE
190     REM
200     REM ****** INITIALIZATION SECTION
210     PRINT "PLEASE ENTER THE WIDTH OF THE RHOMBUS."
220     INPUT "SELECT AN ODD NUMBER BETWEEN 5 AND 35, INCLUSIVE: ",NUMBER
230     IF NUMBER >= 5 AND NUMBER <= 35 THEN GOTO 250
240        PRINT "YOUR NUMBER MUST BE FROM 5 TO 35.  TRY AGAIN.":GOTO 220
250     IF NUMBER/2 <> INT(NUMBER/2) THEN GOTO 270
260        PRINT "YOUR MUST SELECT AN ODD NUMBER.  TRY AGAIN.":GOTO 220
270     REM
280     REM ****** PROCESS SECTION
290     REM DRAW THE TOP HALF OF THE RHOMBUS
300     LET HALF = NUMBER/2+.5
310     LET COUNTER = 0
320     FOR LOOP.COUNTER1 = 1 TO NUMBER STEP 2
330        LET COUNTER = COUNTER + 1
340        FOR LOOP.COUNTER2 = 1 TO LOOP.COUNTER1
350           PRINT TAB(HALF-COUNTER+LOOP.COUNTER2);"*";
360        NEXT LOOP.COUNTER2
370        PRINT
380     NEXT LOOP.COUNTER1
390     REM
400     REM DRAW THE BOTTOM HALF OF THE RHOMBUS
410     FOR LOOP.COUNTER1 = (NUMBER-2) TO 1 STEP -2
420        LET COUNTER = COUNTER - 1
430        FOR LOOP.COUNTER2 = 1 TO LOOP.COUNTER1
440           PRINT TAB(HALF-COUNTER+LOOP.COUNTER2);"*";
450        NEXT LOOP.COUNTER2
460        PRINT
470     NEXT LOOP.COUNTER1
480     REM
490     REM ****** TERMINATION SECTION
500     INPUT "DO YOU WANT TO TRY ANOTHER ONE (Y OR N): ",ANSWER$
510     IF ANSWER$ = "Y" OR ANSWER$ = "y" THEN GOTO 210
520     IF ANSWER$ <> "N" AND ANSWER$ <> "n" THEN GOTO 500
530     END
Ok
RUN
PLEASE ENTER THE WIDTH OF THE RHOMBUS.
SELECT AN ODD NUMBER BETWEEN 5 AND 35, INCLUSIVE: 5
   *
  ***
 *****
  ***
   *
DO YOU WANT TO TRY ANOTHER ONE (Y OR N): N
Ok
```

**Figure 5–8**
Drawing a Rhombus

Assume that line 500 is executed by the computer. You see the message

DO YOU WANT TO TRY ANOTHER ONE (Y OR N):

If the user presses Y and Enter, program control is transferred to line 210. If the response is not Y, line 520 checks to see whether ANSWER$ is equal to N or n. If it isn't, program control is transferred to line 500, and the user is prompted to enter another response. If ANSWER$ is equal to N or n, program control is transferred to line 530, where the program ends.

Some error traps include messages that tell users what they might have done wrong, or that provide more information about the type of response expected. Also, in line 250 we used the INT (integer) function, which extracts the integer portion of a number. BASIC functions are discussed in Chapter 10.

## 5–5
## THE PRINT USING STATEMENT

You use a PRINT USING statement to format a line using a script or map of how the output should appear. With PRINT USING statements, you can produce accurately placed output. You can use a PRINT USING statement with integer, decimal, exponential, alphanumeric, and literal fields. The following sections explain each of these field types.

## Integer Fields
### 5–5–1

When you use a PRINT USING statement for integer numbers, each digit of an integer field is indicated by a pound sign (#). You also need to indicate the sign (positive or negative) with a pound sign. The number of pound signs must be equal to the width of the field (see fig. 5–9).

When the program is executed, the specified values are printed in a right-justified format. Because this format is only for integer fields, the decimal part of any number is rounded. In the program shown in figure 5–9, the number 5267 is printed in columns 1 to 4. The number 918.99 is rounded to 919 and is printed in columns 9 to 11. The number 5011.44 is rounded to 5011 and is printed in columns 15 to 18. Columns 5, 6, 7, 12, 13, and 14 are blank because we included the blanks in the format line.

```
100     REM THIS PROGRAM WILL PRINT THREE NUMBERS
110     REM USING THE PRINT USING STATEMENT.
120     REM
130     REM ****** VARIABLE TABLE
140     REM         NUM1, NUM2, NUM3 = INPUT VARIABLES
150     REM
160     REM ****** INITIALIZATION SECTION
170     LET NUM1 = 5267
180     LET NUM2 = 918.99
190     LET NUM3 = 5011.44
200     REM
210     REM ****** OUTPUT SECTION
220     PRINT USING "####    ####    ####";NUM1,NUM2,NUM3
230     END
Ok
RUN
5267    919    5011
Ok
```

Figure 5–9
PRINT USING with Integer Fields

**Figure 5–10**

Insufficient Format Width in the
Integer Field

```
100      REM THIS PROGRAM WILL PRINT TWO NUMBERS
110      REM USING THE PRINT USING STATEMENT.
120      REM
130      REM ****** VARIABLE TABLE
140      REM           NUM1, NUM2 = INPUT VARIABLES
150      REM
160      REM ****** INITIALIZATION SECTION
170      LET NUM1 = 9999
180      LET NUM2 = 9999
190      REM
200      REM ****** OUTPUT SECTION
210      PRINT USING "#### ###";NUM1,NUM2
220      END
Ok
RUN
9999 %9999
Ok
```

When you have not specified enough space for the number, BASIC displays a percent sign as part of the output. In figure 5–10, we specified only three spaces (using three pound signs) for NUM2.

To include a dollar sign as part of the output, you must include a $ within the format line (see fig. 5–11). If you include two $, as we did in figure 5–11, BASIC "floats" the dollar sign, moving it to the immediate left of the number. You can also separate every three digits with a comma by specifying commas in your format line. For example, the statement:

```
PRINT USING "#,### #,###";A,B
```

will produce output with commas.

## 5–5–2    Decimal Fields

The decimal field format is very similar to the integer field format. The only difference is that a decimal point separates the integer part from the decimal part of the number (see fig. 5–12).

**Figure 5–11**

Including a Dollar Sign as Part
of the Output

```
100      REM THIS PROGRAM WILL PRINT TWO NUMBERS USING
110      REM THE PRINT USING STATEMENT WITH CURRENCY FORMAT.
120      REM
130      REM ****** VARIABLE TABLE
140      REM           NUM1, NUM2 = INPUT VARIABLES
150      REM
160      REM ****** INITIALIZATION SECTION
170      LET NUM1 = 9999
180      LET NUM2 = 9999
190      REM
200      REM ****** OUTPUT SECTION
210      PRINT USING "$$#### $$####";NUM1,NUM2
220      END
Ok
RUN
 $9999   $9999
Ok
```

```
100     REM THIS PROGRAM WILL PRINT FOUR NUMBERS USING THE PRINT
110     REM USING STATEMENT CARRYING THE DECIMAL TO DIFFERENT LENGTHS.
120     REM
130     REM ****** VARIABLE TABLE
140     REM        NUM1, NUM2, NUM3, NUM4 = INPUT VARIABLES
150     REM
160     REM ****** INITIALIZATION SECTION
170     LET NUM1 = -999.99
180     LET NUM2 = -300.43
190     LET NUM3 = -11.019
200     LET NUM4 = 999.99
210     REM
220     REM ****** OUTPUT SECTION
230     PRINT USING "####.## ####.#### ###.## ###.####";NUM1,NUM2,NUM3,NUM4
240     END
Ok
RUN
-999.99 -300.4300 -11.02 999.9900
Ok
```

**Figure 5–12**
PRINT USING with Decimal Fields

## Exponential Fields                                                    5–5–3

The exponential field is similar to the decimal field, but the format statement includes four carets (^^^^). These carets provide the spaces required for the exponent (see fig. 5–13).

## Alphanumeric Fields                                                   5–5–4

Figure 5–14 illustrates an example of an alphanumeric field. A value is left-justified within the field, and the rest of the field is filled with blank spaces. As you see in this figure, you must start with a quotation mark (″) and a back

```
100 REM THIS PROGRAM WILL PRINT FOUR NUMBERS USING
110 REM THE PRINT USING STATEMENT WITH EXPONENTIAL FORMAT.
120 REM
130 REM ****** VARIABLE TABLE
140 REM NUM1, NUM2, NUM3, NUM4=INPUT VARIABLES
150 REM
160 REM ****** INITIALIZATION SECTION
170   NUM1=1296540!
180   NUM2=.0000489
190   NUM3=-764692!
200   NUM4=11.96721
210 REM
220 REM ****** OUTPUT SECTION
230   PRINT USING "##.##^^^^   ##.###^^^^   ##.##^^^^   #.##^^^^";NUM1,NUM2,NUM3,
NUM4
290 END
Ok
RUN
 1.30E+06    4.890E-05    -7.65E+05    0.12E+02
Ok
```

**Figure 5–13**
PRINT USING with Exponential Fields

**Figure 5–14**
PRINT USING with Alphanumeric Fields

```
100    REM THIS PROGRAM WILL PRINT STRING DATA USING
110    REM THE PRINT USING STATEMENT.
120    REM
130    REM ****** VARIABLE TABLE
140    REM        WORD1$ = STRING VARIABLE
150    REM        WORD2$ = STRING VARIABLE
160    REM
170    REM ****** INITIALIZATION SECTION
180    LET WORD1$ = "BASIC"
190    LET WORD2$ = "ABCDEWELL"
200    REM
210    REM ****** OUTPUT SECTION
220    PRINT USING "\                \";WORD1$,WORD2$
230    END
Ok
RUN
BASIC           ABCDEWELL
Ok
```

slash (\). You include as much space as needed, and then you close with a back slash and a quotation mark. You follow this with a semicolon and then you specify your variables. If the string is longer than the specified format, the output will be truncated.

## 5–5–5        Literal Fields

A literal field is composed of characters. When the program is executed, the field is printed exactly as specified in the PRINT USING format. You cannot include control characters, such as ', #, or ˆ (see fig. 5–15).

## 5–6

### A PROGRAMMING EXERCISE

Suppose that Alpha Company uses a computer to print employee paychecks. Each employee receives a base salary of $400 per week plus the following commissions:

- 5 percent commission on total sales of product 1
- 4 percent commission on total sales of product 2
- 6 percent commission on total sales of product 3

```
100    REM THIS PROGRAM WILL DISPLAY SOME DATA USING THE PRINT
110    REM STATEMENT AND THE PRINT USING STATEMENT.
120    REM
130    REM ****** VARIABLE TABLE
140    REM        WORD$ = INPUT STRING VARIABLE
150    REM
160    REM ****** INITIALIZATION SECTION
170    LET WORD$ = "COBOL"
180    REM
190    REM ****** OUTPUT SECTION
200    PRINT "Common Business Oriented Language is";
210    PRINT TAB(38);
220    PRINT USING "\      \";WORD$
230    END
Common Business Oriented Language is COBOL
```

**Figure 5–15**
PRINT USING with Literal Fields

Ten percent of the total salary and commissions is deducted for tax and social security.

Draw a flowchart and write a BASIC program to calculate each employee's paycheck. The output should look like the following:

**ALPHA COMPANY**

| NAME | S.S.N. | GROSS SALARY | NET SALARY |
|------|--------|--------------|------------|
| xxx | xxx | $xxx | $xxx |

```
100     REM THIS PROGRAM PRINTS THE PAYCHECK OF THE EMPLOYEES
110     REM OF THE ALPHA COMPANY
120     REM
130     REM ****** VARIABLE TABLE
140     REM         BASE = EMPLOYEES BASE SALARY
150     REM         NAM$ = EMPLOYEE NAME
160     REM         SSN$ = EMPLOYEES SOCIAL SECURITY NUMBER
170     REM         PROD1 = TOTAL SALES OF PRODUCT 1
180     REM         PROD2 = TOTAL SALES OF PRODUCT 2
190     REM         PROD3 = TOTAL SALES OF PRODUCT 3
200     REM         COMM = TOTAL COMMISSION
210     REM         GROSS = EMPLOYEES GROSS SALARY
220     REM         NET = EMPLOYEES NET SALARY
230     REM         COUNTER = FOR-NEXT CONTROL VARIABLE
240     REM
250     REM ****** INITIALIZATION SECTION
260     PRINT TAB(24);"ALPHA COMPANY"
270     PRINT
280     PRINT "NAME";TAB(21);"S.S.N.";TAB(36);"GROSS SALARY";TAB(52);"NET SALARY"
290     LET BASE = 400
300     REM
310     REM ****** PROCESS SECTION
320     FOR COUNTER = 1 TO 3
330        READ NAM$, SSN$, PROD1, PROD2, PROD3
340        COMM = .05*PROD1+.04*PROD2+.06*PROD3
350        GROSS = COMM+BASE
360        NET = GROSS-.1*GROSS
370        PRINT NAM$;TAB(18);SSN$;TAB(38);
380        PRINT USING "$$####";GROSS;
390        PRINT TAB(53);
400        PRINT USING "$$####";NET
410     NEXT COUNTER
420     REM
430     REM ****** DATA SECTION
440     DATA KATHY FISHLER,"524-13-8021",3000,2000,500
450     DATA BECKY SHOEMAKER,"524-14-8080",4000,1000,2000
460     DATA CHARLES THOMSON,"524-90-8025",3000,3000,4000
470     END
                        ALPHA COMPANY

NAME                 S.S.N.          GROSS SALARY      NET SALARY
KATHY FISHLER        524-13-8021         $660            $594
BECKY SHOEMAKER      524-14-8080         $760            $684
CHARLES THOMSON      524-90-8025         $910            $819
```

**Figure 5–16**
A Sample Payroll Program

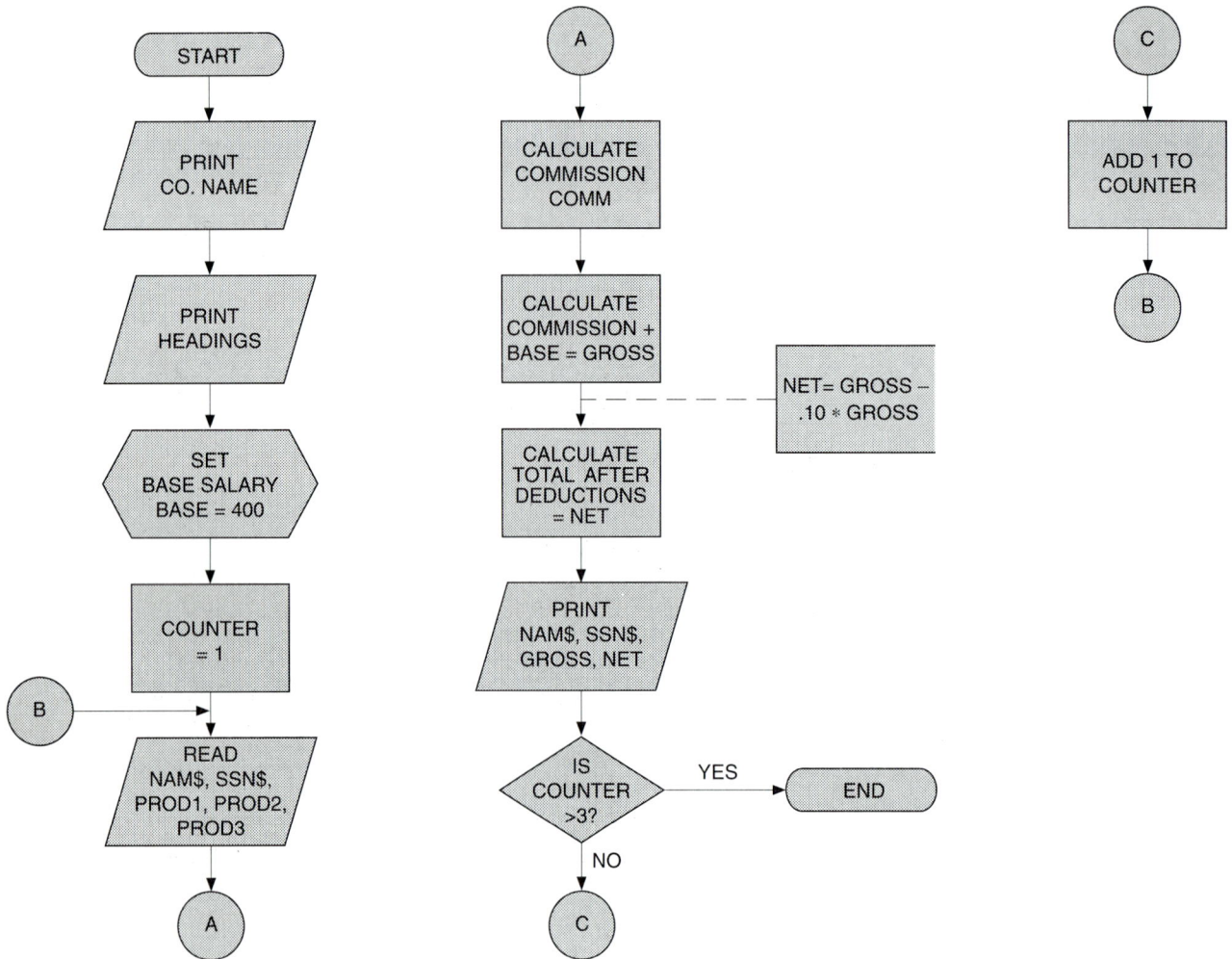

**Figure 5–17**
The Flowchart for the Program Shown in Figure 5–16

Use the following sample data, consisting of each employee's name, Social Security number, and total sales of products 1, 2, and 3:

Kathy Fishler, 524-13-0821, 3000, 2000, 500
Becky Shoemaker, 524-14-8080, 4000, 1000, 2000
Charles Thomson, 524-90-8025, 3000, 3000, 4000

Figure 5–16 shows a program that performs this calculation. Figure 5–17 shows the flowchart for this program.

**SUMMARY**

In this chapter, we discussed several different commands for dressing up the output of a computer program. We examined the uses of the comma and semicolon, and we discussed using the TAB function for spacing within a line. We also discussed how to use PRINT USING statements for formatting output. These commands are helpful in generating professional-looking output from your programs.

*These questions are answered in Appendix D.     **REVIEW QUESTIONS**

  **\*1.** What command(s) will produce two empty lines in the output of a program?

  **\*2.** What is the output of the following program?

```
10 A=5
20 PRINT USING "# ### #";A,A,A
30 END
```

  **3.** What is the output of the following program?

```
10 PRINT TAB(10);"BASIC"
20 PRINT TAB(5);"BASIC"
30 PRINT TAB(75);"BASIC"
40 PRINT TAB(-20);"BASIC"
50 END
```

  **4.** What is the output of the following program?

```
10 PRINT TAB(22);"PAYROLL";TAB(24);"ALPHA COMPANY"
20 PRINT TAB(16);"COMPUTER"
30 END
```

  **5.** Complete the following programs, using appropriate PRINT USING statements.

```
10 X=-99.60
20 Y=78.20
30 PRINT USING
40 END
```

```
10 X=629872000
20 Y=-187972110
30 PRINT USING
40 END
```

```
10 X$="SCHOOL OF BUSINESS"
20 Y$="DEPT. OF MGMT."
30 PRINT USING
40 END
```

```
10 X=642
20 X$="NO OF COMPUTERS ARE"
30 PRINT USING
40 END
```

**1.** Using the TAB function, write a program to print a plus sign of asterisks as follows:     **HANDS-ON EXPERIENCE**

```
        *
        *
        *
**********
        *
        *
        *
```

**2.** Write a program to generate the following output:

```
***B.B. COMPANY***
*PAYROLL REPORT*

LOIS HOLLOWAY      524-18-1912    $624.19
SUSAN SHANTA       524-80-8080    $187.62
FAY THOMAS         524-90-9180    $246.91
```

For input data, your program should read the name, Social Security number, hourly pay, and overtime pay. Calculate the gross pay.

**3.** Using PRINT USING statements, write a program to print the results of the following calculations:

```
A=625.7*7
B=(−11.80)/2.42
C=(62000)*1251
```

---

**KEY TERMS**

| Delimiter | Error trap | Print zone |
|---|---|---|

---

**KEY COMMANDS**

| | |
|---|---|
| PRINT USING "### ###";X,Y | Prints integer fields |
| PRINT USING "##.## ##.##";X,Y | Prints integer fields with decimals |
| PRINT USING "##.##^^^^ ##.##^^^^";X,Y | Prints exponential fields |
| PRINT USING "\\";A$,B$ | Prints alphanumeric fields |
| PRINT USING "$####.##";X | Prints a currency field |
| PRINT USING "$$####.##";X | Prints a floating currency field |
| PRINT USING "#,###.##";X | Prints a comma field |

---

**ARE YOU READY TO MOVE ON?**

## Multiple Choice

What is the output of the following programs?

```
1. 10 B=30
   20 READ A
   30 PRINT A;B
   40 PRINT B;A
   50 DATA 25,15
   60 END
```

   **a.** 30   30
       30   30

   **b.** 25   30

       30   25

   **c.** 25   30
       30   30

   **d.** 25   30
       30   25

   **e.** 25   30   30   25

2. ```
   10 READ A,B
   20 PRINT A;
   30 REM
   40 PRINT B
   50 DATA 35,50
   60 END
   ```
   **a.** 35   50

   **b.** 35

   **c.** 35
      50

   **d.** 50   35

   **e.** none of the above

3. ```
   10 PRINT TAB(2);"Computers"
   20 PRINT TAB(1);"are useful."
   30 END
   ```
   **a.** Computers are useful.

   **b.** Computersare useful.

   **c.**    Computers
      are useful.

   **d.** Computers
                  are useful.

   **e.** none of the above

4. ```
   10 PRINT "List of";TAB(5);"inventory"
   20 END
   ```
   **a.** List of inventory

   **b.** List ofinventory

   **c.** List of
            inventory

   **d.** List of
      inventory

   **e.** none of the above

5. ```
   10 A$="STRING VARIABLE"
   20 PRINT USING "\      \";A$
   30 END
   ```
   **a.** ^$

   **b.** STRING VARIABLE

   **c.** "STRING VARIABLE"

   **d.** \STRING VARIABLE\

   **e.** none of the above

6. ```
   10 X=472.08
   20 Y=394.79
   30 PRINT USING "#### ####";X,Y
   40 END
   ```
   **a.** 473   394

   **b.** 394   472

   **c.** 473   395

   **d.** an error message

   **e.** 472   395
   ```

**7.**
```
10 READ A,B
20 PRINT A,
30 PRINT
40 PRINT B
50 DATA 7,8
60 END
```
  **a.** 7   8

  **b.** 7
       8

  **c.** 8
       7

  **d.** 8
       8

  **e.** 8   7

**8.** The REM statement

  **a.** is a nonexecutable statement

  **b.** can be used to print a blank line of output

  **c.** can be used to dress up a program

  **d.** is used for documentation

  **e.** a, c, and d

**9.** The TAB function

  **a.** can be used with the PRINT statement

  **b.** can be used with the INPUT statement

  **c.** prints the data in the column stated in the expression

  **d.** both a and c

  **e.** all of the above

**10.** The PRINT USING statement uses

  **a.** # to print integer numbers

  **b.** ^^^^ following a decimal field to print an exponential field

  **c.** $ to print a $ in an integer field

  **d.** all of the above

  **e.** both a and c

## True/False

**1.** The PRINT USING statement cannot be used for exponential fields.

**2.** The computer will right-justify a literal field when using the PRINT USING statement.

**3.** The computer will left-justify a numeric field when using the PRINT USING statement.

**4.** A PRINT statement followed by nothing causes the printer to skip five character spaces before printing the next item.

**5.** A good program has many documentation lines to explain what is happening.

**6.** The argument of a TAB function can be any numeric variable or constant, or it can be a formula.

**7.** The PRINT USING statement is very helpful in producing exact output.

**8.** The PRINT USING statement can be used only for integer and alphanumeric fields.

**9.** When using the PRINT USING statement for an integer field, the number of pound signs (#) can be less than the width of the field.

**10.** If the value of the TAB expression is less than the current position of the carriage, the output will be printed on the next line.

---

| Multiple Choice | True/False | ANSWERS |
|---|---|---|
| **1.** d | **1.** F | |
| **2.** a | **2.** F | |
| **3.** c | **3.** F | |
| **4.** c | **4.** F | |
| **5.** b | **5.** T | |
| **6.** e | **6.** T | |
| **7.** b | **7.** T | |
| **8.** e | **8.** F | |
| **9.** d | **9.** F | |
| **10.** d | **10.** T | |

# One-Dimensional Arrays

**6**

## 6–1
## INTRODUCTION

In Chapter 3, we talked about simple numeric variables. In this chapter, we introduce subscripted variables. Several example programs demonstrate the different aspects of working with subscripted variables. We explain the DIMENSION (DIM) statement, which is used for defining the size of an array (a place holder that stores data items). At the end of this chapter, we introduce a bubble-sort routine for sorting numeric and non-numeric data.

## 6–2
## SUBSCRIPTED VARIABLES

Using **subscripted variables**, you can increase the number of variables available to a program to an almost infinite number. The general form of a subscripted variable is as follows:

A(I)
B(J)
W9(T)
SALES(100)

In these examples, A, B, W9, and SALES are called subscripted variables or **arrays**. An array stands for a family of variables, all of which are referred to by the same name (A, B, W9, or SALES) but which have different subscripts (I, J, T, and 100). I, for example, can be any positive integer from 1 to 100,000 or more. You need to remember that A, A1, and A(1) are three different variables. A and A1 are both simple numeric variables. A(1) is a subscripted variable. The starting element in an array has address zero. The statement

```
DIM YEAR(365)
```

generates 366 locations. The first location is YEAR(0) and the last location is YEAR(365). If you would rather begin your array with address 1, use the following statement at the beginning of your program:

```
OPTION BASE 1
```

## 6–3
## THE DIMENSION STATEMENT

Before using an array, you must define the size of the array using a DIM statement. In most systems, an array with up to 10 addresses (or 11 if the BASE is 0) does not need to be dimensioned. It is, however, a good practice to dimension all arrays no matter what the size.

The following program segment shows two types of DIM statements:

```
10 DIM A(100),B(50)
20 DIM A$(70),B$(40)
```

In line 10, we have reserved 101 spaces in array A and 51 spaces in array B. These spaces are place holders for numeric data. In line 20, we have reserved 71 spaces in the string array A$ and 41 spaces in the string array B$. These spaces are place holders for non-numeric (string) data.

To illustrate the idea of place holder, the statement

DIM A(10)

dimensions an array as follows:

A(0)   ----- 0 -----
A(1)   ----- 0 -----
A(2)   ----- 0 -----
A(3)   ----- 0 -----
A(4)   ----- 0 -----
A(5)   ----- 0 -----
A(6)   ----- 0 -----
A(7)   ----- 0 -----
A(8)   ----- 0 -----
A(9)   ----- 0 -----
A(10)  ----- 0 -----

There are 11 addresses—A(0) through A(10)—and these addresses contain zeros (no data has been stored there yet).

## 6–4
## STORING DATA IN AN ARRAY

You can use READ/DATA, LET, and INPUT statements to fill an array. The following programs show this process.

The program shown in figure 6–1 uses READ and DATA statements to fill an array of five addresses with the values 10, 20, 30, 40, and 50.

The program shown in figure 6–2 enters the same numeric data into an array using LET statements.

The program shown in figure 6–3 uses an INPUT statement to accomplish the same data entry.

## 6–5
## RETRIEVING THE CONTENTS OF AN ARRAY

When an array is filled, you can use the PRINT statement to retrieve its contents. The following programs demonstrate this process.

In figure 6–4, the program fills an array of 11 addresses with the numbers 2, 4, 6, 8, 10, 12, 14, 16, 18, 20, and 22, and then it retrieves the data.

The program shown in figure 6–5 uses READ and DATA statements to fill an array, and then it prints the average of the numbers.

**Figure 6–1**

Using READ and DATA Statements to Fill an Array

```
100     REM THIS PROGRAM FILLS AN ARRAY OF SIZE 5
110     REM BY USING THE READ AND DATA STATEMENT COMBINATION.
120     REM
130     REM ****** VARIABLE TABLE
140     REM          COUNTER = FOR-NEXT LOOP CONTROL VARIABLE
150     REM
160     REM ****** ARRAY TABLE
170     REM          A(5) = A FIVE-ELEMENT INPUT DATA ARRAY
180     REM
190     REM ****** INITIALIZATION SECTION
200     DIM A(5)
210     REM
220     REM ****** PROCESS SECTION
230     FOR COUNTER = 1 TO 5
240        READ A(COUNTER)
250     NEXT COUNTER
260     REM
270     REM ****** DATA SECTION
280     DATA 10,20,30,40,50
290     END
Ok
RUN
Ok
```

You can accomplish the same task without using an array, as shown in figure 6–6.

The program shown in figure 6–7 reads ten numbers from a DATA line into an array, reverses the order of the array, and prints the contents of the original array and its reverse.

In figure 6–8, the program reads ten values from a DATA line into array ARRAY1; stores these values, their squares, and their cubes in arrays ARRAY2, ARRAY3, and ARRAY4; and then prints the contents of these three arrays.

As another example, suppose that Beta Company has two branches—A and B. You want to read the total sales of branch A into array COMPANY1 and the total sales of branch B into array COMPANY2. Then you want to add the

```
100     REM THIS PROGRAM FILLS AN ARRAY OF SIZE 5 BY THE ASSIGN-
110     REM MENT STATEMENT.
120     REM
130     REM ****** VARIABLE TABLE
140     REM          THERE ARE NO VARIABLES IN THIS PROGRAM.
150     REM
160     REM ****** ARRAY TABLE
170     REM          A(5) = A FIVE-ELEMENT INPUT DATA ARRAY.
180     REM
190     REM ****** INITIALIZATION SECTION
200     DIM A(5)
210     LET A(1) = 10
220     LET A(2) = 20
230     LET A(3) = 30
240     LET A(4) = 40
250     LET A(5) = 50
260     END
Ok
RUN
Ok
```

**Figure 6–2**

Using LET Statements to Fill an Array

```
100     REM THIS PROGRAM FILLS AN 5-ELEMENT ARRAY CALLED SALES
110     REM USING AN INPUT STATEMENT WITHIN A FOR-NEXT LOOP STRUCTURE.
120     REM
130     REM ****** VARIABLE TABLE
140     REM           COUNTER = FOR-NEXT LOOP CONTROL VARIABLE
150     REM
160     REM ****** ARRAY TABLE
170     REM           SALES(5) = A FIVE-ELEMENT INPUT DATA ARRAY
180     REM
190     REM ****** INITIALIZATION SECTION
200     DIM SALES(5)
210     REM
220     REM ****** PROCESS SECTION
230     FOR COUNTER = 1 TO 5
240        INPUT SALES(COUNTER)
250     NEXT COUNTER
260     END
Ok
RUN
? 1
? 2
? 3
? 4
? 5
Ok
```

**Figure 6–3**

Using an INPUT Statement to Fill an Array

```
100     REM THIS PROGRAM FILLS AN 11-ELEMENT ARRAY CALLED ROOM
110     REM AND DISPLAYS ITS CONTENTS.
120     REM
130     REM ****** VARIABLE TABLE
140     REM           COUNTER1 = FOR-NEXT LOOP CONTROL VARIABLE
150     REM           COUNTER2 = FOR-NEXT LOOP CONTROL VARIABLE
160     REM
170     REM ****** ARRAY TABLE
180     REM           ROOM(11) = AN 11-ELEMENT INPUT DATA ARRAY
190     REM
200     REM ****** INITIALIZATION SECTION
210     OPTION BASE 1
220     DIM ROOM(11)
230     REM
240     REM ****** PROCESS SECTION
250     FOR COUNTER1 = 1 TO 11
260        READ ROOM(COUNTER1)
270     NEXT COUNTER1
280     REM
290     REM ****** OUTPUT SECTION
300     REM THIS PART OF THE PROGRAM RETRIEVES THE ARRAY'S CONTENTS.
310     FOR COUNTER2 = 1 TO 11
320        PRINT ROOM(COUNTER2);
330     NEXT COUNTER2
340     REM
350     REM ****** DATA SECTION
360     DATA 2,4,6,8,10,12,14,16,18,20,22
370     END
Ok
RUN
 2   4   6   8   10   12   14   16   18   20   22
Ok
```

**Figure 6–4**

Filling and Retrieving an Array

```
100    REM THIS PROGRAM READS 5 NUMBERS FROM A DATA LINE
110    REM AND PRINTS THEIR AVERAGE.  HERE WE ARE USING AN ARRAY.
120    REM
130    REM ****** VARIABLE TABLE
140    REM          COUNTER1 = FOR-NEXT LOOP CONTROL VARIABLE
150    REM          COUNTER2 = FOR-NEXT LOOP CONTROL VARIABLE
160    REM          TOTAL    = SUM OF THE NUMBERS IN THE ARRAY
170    REM          AVERAGE  = AVERAGE OF THE NUMBERS IN THE ARRAY
180    REM
190    REM ****** ARRAY TABLE
200    REM          ZOOM(5) = A 5-ELEMENT INPUT DATA ARRAY
210    REM
220    REM ****** INITIALIZATION SECTION
230    DIM ZOOM(5)
240    LET TOTAL = 0
250    REM
260    REM ****** PROCESS SECTION
270    REM THE NEXT SECTION WILL LOAD THE ARRAY.
280    FOR COUNTER1 = 1 TO 5
290       READ ZOOM(COUNTER1)
300    NEXT COUNTER1
310    REM
320    REM THE NEXT SECTION WILL SUM THE NUMBERS.
330    FOR COUNTER2 = 1 TO 5
340       LET TOTAL = TOTAL+ZOOM(COUNTER2)
350    NEXT COUNTER2
360    LET AVERAGE = TOTAL/5
370    REM
380    REM ****** OUTPUT SECTION
390    PRINT "THE AVERAGE OF THE 5 NUMBERS IS =";AVERAGE
400    REM
410    REM ****** DATA SECTION
420    DATA 5,10,15,20,30
430    END
Ok
RUN
THE AVERAGE OF THE 5 NUMBERS IS = 16
Ok
```

**Figure 6-5**
Using READ and DATA to Fill an Array and Then Retrieve It

total sales and store the result in array TOT.COMPANY. Next you want to generate an output of the total sales for each branch and for the company as a whole over the past 12 months. Use the following data as the total sales over the past 12 months:

| Branch A | Branch B |
|---|---|
| 2000 | 3000 |
| 3000 | 1000 |
| 5000 | 6000 |
| 6000 | 7000 |
| 2000 | 3000 |
| 4500 | 2000 |
| 8000 | 7000 |
| 7000 | 8000 |
| 5000 | 6000 |
| 9000 | 8000 |
| 6000 | 5000 |
| 5000 | 7000 |

```
100   REM THIS PROGRAM CALCULATES THE AVERAGE OF 5 NUMBERS.
110   REM
120   REM ****** VARIABLE TABLE
130   REM          SUM = SUM OF THE INPUT NUMBERS
140   REM          AVERAGE = AVERAGE OF THE INPUT NUMBERS
150   REM          COUNTER = FOR-NEXT LOOP CONTROL VARIABLE
160   REM          NUMBER = INPUT VARIABLE
170   REM
180   REM ****** INITIALIZATION SECTION
190   LET SUM = 0
200   REM
210   REM ****** PROCESS SECTION
220   FOR COUNTER = 1 TO 5
230      READ NUMBER
240      LET SUM = SUM+NUMBER
250   NEXT COUNTER
260   REM
270   REM THE NEXT SECTION COMPUTES THE AVERAGE OF THE NUMBERS
280   LET AVERAGE = SUM/5
290   REM
300   REM ****** OUTPUT SECTION
310   PRINT "THE AVERAGE OF THE 5 NUMBERS =";AVERAGE
320   REM
330   REM ****** DATA SECTION
340   DATA 5,10,15,20,30
350   END
THE AVERAGE OF THE 5 NUMBERS = 16
```

**Figure 6–6**
Using Simple Numeric Variables to Find the Average

Figure 6–9 shows a program that performs these functions.

You can perform many different kinds of operations with arrays. There is no difference between a simple numeric variable and a subscripted variable except in appearance.

## 6–6
## SELECTING THE LARGEST MEMBER OF AN ARRAY

Often you are interested in knowing the value of a particular member of an array. In an array of student G.P.A.s, for example, you might be interested in knowing the highest G.P.A. Or in an array of total sales for different regions, you may want to know the region with the highest total sales or the region with the lowest total sales.

The program shown in figure 6–10 is an algorithm for selecting the largest member of an array. Suppose that ABC Company has stored the total sales of its 13 branches in array ROOM. Write and run a program to print the number of the branch that has generated the highest total sales. Use the following sample data:

    24000
    42000
    64000
    82000
    16000
    99000
    80000

32000
15000
29000
57000
62000
50000

In line 290, we dimension the array ROOM, which can hold 202 data items. Line 340 checks for the end of data. If the end of data has been reached, the program branches to line 380.

```
100    REM THIS PROGRAM READS 10 VALUES FROM A DATA LINE
110    REM INTO AN ARRAY.  IT THEN REVERSES THE ORDER OF THE
120    REM ARRAY AND PRINTS THE ORIGINAL ARRAY AND ITS REVERSE.
130    REM
140    REM ******* VARIABLE TABLE
150    REM          COUNTER1 = FOR-NEXT LOOP CONTROL VARIABLE
160    REM          COUNTER2 = FOR-NEXT LOOP CONTROL VARIABLE
170    REM          COUNTER3 = FOR-NEXT LOOP CONTROL VARIABLE
180    REM
190    REM ******* ARRAY TABLE
200    REM          ARRAY1 = A 10-ELEMENT INPUT DATA ARRAY
210    REM          ARRAY2 = A 10-ELEMENT REVERSE OF ARRAY1
220    REM
230    REM ******* INITIALIZATION SECTION
240    DIM ARRAY1(10), ARRAY2(10)
250    REM
260    REM ******* PROCESS SECTION
270    REM THE NEXT SECTION WILL LOAD THE ARRAY
280    FOR COUNTER1 = 1 TO 10
290        READ ARRAY1(COUNTER1)
300    NEXT COUNTER1
310    REM
320    REM THE NEXT SECTION WILL REVERSE THE ORDER OF THE ARRAY
330    FOR COUNTER2 = 1 TO 10
340        LET ARRAY2(COUNTER2) = ARRAY1(11-COUNTER2)
350    NEXT COUNTER2
360    REM
370    REM ******* OUTPUT SECTION
380    PRINT "****THE OUTPUT****"
390    FOR COUNTER3 = 1 TO 10
400        PRINT ARRAY1(COUNTER3), ARRAY2(COUNTER3)
410    NEXT COUNTER3
420    REM
430    REM ******* DATA SECTION
440    DATA 5,10,15,20,25,30,35,40,45,50
450    END
****THE OUTPUT****
 5              50
10              45
15              40
20              35
25              30
30              25
35              20
40              15
45              10
50               5
```

**Figure 6-7**

Another Example of an Array

```
100    REM THIS PROGRAM READS 10 VALUES FROM A DATA LINE AND
110    REM STORES THESE VALUES, THEIR SQUARES AND THEIR CUBES
120    REM INTO ARRAYS.  AT THE END IT PRINTS OUT THE CONTENTS
130    REM OF THE ARRAYS.
140    REM
150    REM ****** VARIABLE TABLE
160    REM          COUNTER1 = FOR-NEXT LOOP CONTROL VARIABLE
170    REM          COUNTER2 = FOR-NEXT LOOP CONTROL VARIABLE
180    REM          COUNTER3 = FOR-NEXT LOOP CONTROL VARIABLE
190    REM
200    REM ****** ARRAY TABLE
210    REM          ARRAY1(10) = A 10-ELEMENT INPUT DATA ARRAY
220    REM          ARRAY2(10) = A 10-ELEMENT COPY OF ARRAY1
230    REM          ARRAY3(10) = A 10-ELEMENT ARRAY (SQUARES OF ARRAY1)
240    REM          ARRAY4(10) = A 10-ELEMENT ARRAY (CUBES OF ARRAY1)
250    REM
260    REM ****** INITIALIZATION SECTION
270    DIM ARRAY1(10), ARRAY2(10), ARRAY3(10), ARRAY4(10)
280    REM
290    REM ****** PROCESS SECTION
300    REM THE NEXT SECTION LOAD THE ORIGINAL ARRAY
310    FOR COUNTER1 = 1 TO 10
320        READ ARRAY1(COUNTER1)
330    NEXT COUNTER1
340    REM
350    REM THE NEXT SECTION FILLS THE REMAINING ARRAYS
360    FOR COUNTER2 = 1 TO 10
370        LET ARRAY2(COUNTER2) = ARRAY1(COUNTER2)
380        LET ARRAY3(COUNTER2) = ARRAY1(COUNTER2)^2
390        LET ARRAY4(COUNTER2) = ARRAY1(COUNTER2)^3
400    NEXT COUNTER2
410    REM
420    REM ****** OUTPUT SECTION
430    PRINT "ORIGINAL", "SQUARE", "CUBE"
440    PRINT
450    FOR COUNTER3 = 1 TO 10
460        PRINT ARRAY2(COUNTER3),ARRAY3(COUNTER3),ARRAY4(COUNTER3)
470    NEXT COUNTER3
480    REM
490    REM ****** DATA SECTION
500    DATA 1,2,3,4,5,6,7,8,9,10
510    END
ORIGINAL        SQUARE          CUBE

1               1               1
2               4               8
3               9               27
4               16              64
5               25              125
6               36              216
7               49              343
8               64              512
9               81              729
10              100             1000
```

**Figure 6–8**
Simple Operations with Arrays

In line 380, we subtract 1 from the total number of data items that have been read because all the data items plus the flag data item have been stored in the array. By subtracting 1 from the total, the flag data item is ignored.

In line 390, we assume that the first member of the array—ROOM(1)—is the largest member. It has the first address. We store the value of

```
100    REM THIS PROGRAM READS THE TOTAL SALES FOR THE PAST
110    REM 12 MONTHS FOR BRANCHES A AND B INTO ARRAYS.
120    REM THE SUM OF BOTH ARRAYS ARE STORED IN A SEPARATE
130    REM ARRAY.  THE PROGRAM ALSO DISPLAYS THE TOTAL SALES
140    REM FOR EACH BRANCH AND THE COMPANY AS A WHOLE.
150    REM
160    REM ****** VARIABLE TABLE
170    REM          COUNTER1 = FOR-NEXT LOOP CONTROL VARIABLE
180    REM          COUNTER2 = FOR-NEXT LOOP CONTROL VARIABLE
190    REM
200    REM ****** ARRAY TABLE
210    REM          COMPANY1(12) = A 12-ELEMENT COMPANY NUMBER 1 SALES ARRAY
220    REM          COMPANY2(12) = A 12-ELEMENT COMPANY NUMBER 2 SALES ARRAY
230    REM          TOT.COMPANY(12) = A 12-ELEMENT TOTAL COMPANY SALES ARRAY
240    REM
250    REM ****** INITIALIZATION SECTION
260    DIM COMPANY1(12), COMPANY2(12), TOT.COMPANY(12)
270    REM
280    REM ****** PROCESS SECTION
290    FOR COUNTER1 = 1 TO 12
300       READ COMPANY1(COUNTER1), COMPANY2(COUNTER1)
310       LET TOT.COMPANY(COUNTER1) = COMPANY1(COUNTER1)+COMPANY2(COUNTER1)
320    NEXT COUNTER1
330    REM
340    REM ****** OUTPUT SECTION
350    PRINT "THE SALES REPORT OF BETA COMPANY"
360    PRINT
370    PRINT "BRANCH A", "BRANCH B", "COMPANY TOTAL"
380    FOR COUNTER2 = 1 TO 12
390       PRINT COMPANY1(COUNTER2), COMPANY2(COUNTER2), TOT.COMPANY(COUNTER2)
400    NEXT COUNTER2
410    REM
420    REM ****** DATA SECTION
430    DATA 2000,3000,3000,1000,5000,6000,6000,7000,2000,3000,4500,2000
440    DATA 8000,7000,7000,8000,5000,6000,9000,8000,6000,5000,5000,7000
450    END
THE SALES REPORT OF BETA COMPANY

BRANCH A        BRANCH B        COMPANY TOTAL
 2000            3000            5000
 3000            1000            4000
 5000            6000           11000
 6000            7000           13000
 2000            3000            5000
 4500            2000            6500
 8000            7000           15000
 7000            8000           15000
 5000            6000           11000
 9000            8000           17000
 6000            5000           11000
 5000            7000           12000
```

**Figure 6-9**
Sales Analysis Using an Array

ROOM(1) in the address LARGE, and we store its position in the address INDEX.

In line 430, we compare all the other members of the array against this member. When we find a number larger than the one in ROOM(1), we replace the value of ROOM(1) in the address LARGE with the new number (lines 450 and 460). The process continues until all the members are compared.

```
100     REM THIS PROGRAM IS AN ALGORITHM FOR THE SELECTION OF
110     REM THE LARGEST MEMBER OF AN ARRAY.   THE NUMBER OF THE
120     REM MEMBERS OF THIS ARRAY CAN BE UP TO 200.   BEYOND THIS
130     REM LIMIT THE DIM STATEMENT MUST BE REDEFINED.
140     REM THEREFORE WE MUST ALWAYS CHECK FOR THE END OF DATA,
150     REM AND IF WE PASS THIS LIMIT A MESSAGE SHOULD BE PRINTED.
160     REM OTHERWISE THE PROGRAM SHOULD FOLLOW ITS NORMAL SEQUENCE.
170     REM
180     REM ****** VARIABLE TABLE
190     REM          COUNT1 = FOR-NEXT LOOP CONTROL VARIABLE
200     REM          COUNT2 = FOR-NEXT LOOP CONTROL VARIABLE
210     REM          LARGE = THE LARGEST ELEMENT IN THE ARRAY
220     REM          INDEX = THE INDEX FOR THE LARGEST ARRAY ELEMENT
230     REM          SIZE = THE SIZE OF THE ARRAY
240     REM
250     REM ****** ARRAY TABLE
260     REM          ROOM(201) = A 201-ELEMENT INPUT DATA ARRAY
270     REM
280     REM ****** INITIALIZATION SECTION
290     DIM ROOM(201)
300     REM
310     REM ****** PROCESS SECTION
320     FOR COUNT1 = 1 TO 201
330        READ ROOM(COUNT1)
340        IF ROOM(COUNT1) = -999 THEN GOTO 380
350     NEXT COUNT1
360     PRINT "SORRY YOU PASSED THE LIMIT!" : GOTO 580
370     REM
380     LET SIZE = COUNT1-1
390     LET LARGE = ROOM(1)
400     LET INDEX = 1
410     REM
420     FOR COUNT2 = 2 TO SIZE
430        IF ROOM(COUNT2)>LARGE THEN GOTO 450
440        GOTO 470
450        LET LARGE = ROOM(COUNT2)
460        LET INDEX = COUNT2
470     NEXT COUNT2
480     REM
490     REM ****** OUTPUT SECTION
500     PRINT "*****************************************************"
510     PRINT "********** SELECTION OF THE LARGEST MEMBER ***********"
520     PRINT "** BRANCH NO";INDEX"HAS THE LARGEST TOTAL SALES OF $";LARGE;"**"
530     PRINT "*****************************************************"
540     REM
550     REM ****** DATA SECTION
560     DATA 24000,42000,64000,82000,16000,99000,80000,32000,15000,
570     DATA 29000,57000,62000,50000,-999
580     END
Ok
RUN
*****************************************************
********** SELECTION OF THE LARGEST MEMBER ***********
** BRANCH NO 6 HAS THE LARGEST TOTAL SALES OF $ 99000 **
*****************************************************
Ok
```

**Figure 6–10**

Using an Array for Finding the Highest Sales

If two or more quantities tie for largest, the computer prints only the first one encountered.

This program can easily be changed to select the smallest member of the array by changing line 430 to

```
IF ROOM(COUNT2) <LARGE THEN GOTO 450
```

## 6–7

## SEQUENTIAL SEARCH

Sometimes you are interested in the value of one particular member of an array regardless of its relation to the other members of the array. You can use a **sequential search** algorithm to find the particular member (see fig. 6–11). In this algorithm, you compare all the members of the array until you find the desired value.

Suppose that the G.P.A.s of 11 students in a computer class have been stored in array GPA. As a matter of curiosity, we want to search this array to see whether any of these students has a G.P.A. of 2.2. Write and run a program to do this job. Use the following sample data:

```
2.90
3.60
2.88
3.60
4.00
1.50
1.75
3.20
2.20
4.00
3.75
```

If there is more than one person with a G.P.A. of 2.20, the computer prints the first one encountered.

You can change the size of the array to store any number of data items.

Suppose that Oriental Rug Company has stored the names of all its salespeople in array NAM$ and the total sales for the past two years in array TOT. The president of the company wants to know the names of all the salespeople who have generated total sales of $25,000 or more. Write and run a program to do this job (see fig. 6–12). Use the following sample data:

| Martha | 25000 |
|--------|-------|
| Maggie | 18000 |
| Murray | 17000 |
| Sally | 31000 |
| Charles | 10000 |
| Kathy | 16000 |
| Laura | 20500 |
| Terry | 21000 |
| Fred | 29000 |

## 6–8

## SORTING

There are many applications of sorting procedures. You can sort numeric or non-numeric data in ascending or descending order. Sorting is always per-

```
100    REM THIS IS AN ALGORITHM FOR SEQUENTIAL SEARCH.
110    REM
120    REM ****** VARIABLE TABLE
130    REM          COUNT = FOR-NEXT LOOP CONTROL VARIABLE
140    REM
150    REM ****** ARRAY TABLE
160    REM          GPA(11) = AN 11-ELEMENT ARRAY CONTAINING ARRAY VALUES
170    REM
180    REM ****** INITIALIZATION SECTION
190    PRINT "****** G.P.A.   REPORT ******"
200    DIM GPA(11)
210    REM
220    REM ****** PROCESS SECTION
230    FOR COUNT = 1 TO 11
240       READ GPA(COUNT)
250       IF GPA(COUNT) = 2.2 THEN GOTO 300
260    NEXT COUNT
270    REM
280    REM ****** OUTPUT SECTION
290    PRINT "THERE IS NOBODY WITH A GPA OF 2.20!   SORRY" : GOTO 340
300    PRINT "STUDENT NO";COUNT;"HAS A GPA OF 2.20."
310    REM
320    REM ****** DATA SECTION
330    DATA 2.90,3.60,2.88,3.60,4.00,1.50,1.75,3.20,2.20,4.00,3.75
340    END
Ok
RUN
****** G.P.A.   REPORT ******
STUDENT NO 9 HAS A GPA OF 2.20.
Ok
```

**Figure 6–11**

Using an Array for Sequential Search

```
100    REM THIS PROGRAM SEARCHES FOR HIGH PERFORMANCE SALES PERSONS.
110    REM
120    REM ****** VARIABLE TABLE
130    REM          COUNT = FOR-NEXT CONTROL VARIABLE
140    REM
150    REM ****** ARRAY TABLE
160    REM          NAM$(9) = A 9-ELEMENT SALESPERSON NAME ARRAY
170    REM          TOT(9) = A 9-ELEMENT SALESPERSON SALES AMOUNT ARRAY
180    REM
190    REM ****** INITIALIZATION SECTION
200    DIM NAM$(9), TOT(9)
210    REM
220    REM ****** PROCESS SECTION
230    FOR COUNT = 1 TO 9
240       READ NAM$(COUNT), TOT(COUNT)
250       IF TOT(COUNT) < 25000 THEN GOTO 270
260       PRINT NAM$(COUNT);" HAD SALES IN THE AMOUNT OF";TOT(COUNT)
270    NEXT COUNT
280    REM
290    REM ****** DATA SECTION
300    DATA MARTHA, 25000, MAGGIE, 18000, MURRAY, 17000, SALLY
310    DATA 310000, CHARLES, 10000, KATHY, 16000, LAURA, 20500
320    DATA TERRY, 21000, FRED, 29000
330    END
MARTHA HAD SALES IN THE AMOUNT OF 25000
SALLY HAD SALES IN THE AMOUNT OF 310000
FRED HAD SALES IN THE AMOUNT OF 29000
```

**Figure 6–12**

Another Example of Search Operations Using Arrays

formed based on key values, such as G.P.A.s, last names, or Social Security numbers. You could sort the names of salespeople in a department store based on sales performance.

There are several different sorting routines. The one discussed in this section is called **bubble sort**. In a bubble sort, when the program is completed, the smallest or the largest number has "bubbled" to the top. The bubble sort routine is a relatively slow procedure, but it is probably the easiest. Figure 6–13 presents a general algorithm for a bubble sort routine.

In GW-BASIC, you can replace lines 240, 250, and 260 with the SWAP command `SWAP X(K),X(J)`. The process presented here, however, helps you to better understand the array operations.

Write and run a program to sort the numbers 18, 40, 31, 25, and 10 in ascending order (see fig. 6–14).

Lines 340 to 410 are the sorting part of this program. Before the sorting routine begins, the data in array ARRAY appear as follows:

ARRAY(1)=18
ARRAY(2)=40
ARRAY(3)=31
ARRAY(4)=25
ARRAY(5)=10

The following list shows the procedure that the program goes through on the first iteration:

| COUNT2=1 | COUNT3=2 | TEMP=18 | ARRAY(1)=10 |
| | COUNT3=3 | | ARRAY(5)=18 |
| | COUNT3=4 | | |
| | COUNT3=5 | | |

After the array is filled, the program continues from line 340. The starting value of COUNT2 is 1, and the starting value of COUNT3 is 2. The variable TEMP is a temporary location. When the inner loop of this program has

```
100 REM THIS PROGRAM PERFORMS A BUBBLE SORT IN ASCENDING ORDER.
110 REM N IS THE SIZE OF THE ARRAY. X IS THE NAME OF THE ARRAY AND
120 REM T IS A TEMPORARY ADDRESS.
130 REM
140 REM******* VARIABLE TABLE
150 REM          K, J = FOR-NEXT LOOP COUNTER VARIABLE
160 REM          T = TEMPORARY LOCATION
170 REM
180 REM******* ARRAY TABLE
190 REM          X(I) = AN INPUT DATA ARRAY
200 REM
210 FOR K=1 TO N-1
220    FOR J=K+1 TO N
230       IF X(K)<=X(J) THEN 280
240       T=X(K)
250       X(K)=X(J)
260       X(J)=T
270    NEXT J
280 NEXT K
290 END
```

**Figure 6–13**

A General Algorithm for a Bubble Sort Routine

```
100     REM THIS PROGRAM SORTS 5 NUMBERS INTO ASCENDING ORDER.
110     REM
120     REM ****** VARIABLE TABLE
130     REM          COUNT1 = FOR-NEXT LOOP CONTROL VARIABLE
140     REM          COUNT2 = FOR-NEXT LOOP CONTROL VARIABLE
150     REM          COUNT3 = FOR-NEXT LOOP CONTROL VARIABLE
160     REM          COUNT4 = FOR-NEXT LOOP CONTROL VARIABLE
170     REM
180     REM ****** ARRAY TABLE
190     REM          ARRAY(5) = A 5-ELEMENT INPUT DATA ARRAY
200     REM
210     REM ****** INITIALIZATION SECTION
220     DIM ARRAY(5)
230     REM
240     REM ****** PROCESS SECTION
250     FOR COUNT1 = 1 TO 5
260        READ ARRAY(COUNT1)
270     NEXT COUNT1
280     REM
290     REM ****** DATA SECTION
300     DATA 18,40,31,25,10
310     REM
320     REM THE SORTING ROUTINE BEGINS.
330     PRINT "THE FOLLOWING NUMBERS ARE SORTED IN AN ASCENDING ORDER"
340     FOR COUNT2 = 1 TO 4
350        FOR COUNT3 = COUNT2+1 TO 5
360           IF ARRAY(COUNT2)<=ARRAY(COUNT3) THEN GOTO 400
370           LET TEMP = ARRAY(COUNT2)
380           ARRAY(COUNT2) = ARRAY(COUNT3)
390           ARRAY(COUNT3) = TEMP
400        NEXT COUNT3
410     NEXT COUNT2
420     REM ****** OUTPUT SECTION
430     REM THIS SEGMENT OF THE PROGRAM PRINTS THE SORTED ARRAY.
440     FOR COUNT4 = 1 TO 5
450        PRINT TAB(25);ARRAY(COUNT4)
460     NEXT COUNT4
470     END
Ok
RUN
THE FOLLOWING NUMBERS ARE SORTED IN AN ASCENDING ORDER
                         10
                         18
                         25
                         31
                         40
Ok
```

**Figure 6–14**
An Example of a Bubble Sort

finished executing, COUNT3 has assumed the values 3, 4, and then 5. During the sort process, only addresses 1 and 5 of the array were affected.

When the program has finished with the first iteration, the value 10 has bubbled to the top and is now located in address ARRAY(1). The array appears as follows:

ARRAY(1)=10
ARRAY(2)=40
ARRAY(3)=31
ARRAY(4)=25
ARRAY(5)=18

On the second time through the sort, the process is as follows:

| COUNT2=2 | COUNT3=3 | TEMP=40 | ARRAY(2)=31 |
| | | | ARRAY(3)=40 |
| | | | ARRAY(2)=25 |
| | | | ARRAY(4)=31 |
| | COUNT3=4 | TEMP=31 | ARRAY(2)=18 |
| | COUNT3=5 | TEMP=25 | ARRAY(5)=25 |

When the second iteration is finished, the second smallest number is in the second position from the top. The value 18 is now stored in address ARRAY(2). The array is as follows:

ARRAY(1) 10
ARRAY(2) 18
ARRAY(3) 40
ARRAY(4) 31
ARRAY(5) 25

On the third time through the sort, the process is as follows:

| COUNT2=3 | COUNT3=4 | TEMP=40 | ARRAY(3)=31 |
| | | | ARRAY(4)=40 |
| | | | ARRAY(3)=25 |
| | COUNT3=5 | TEMP=31 | ARRAY(5)=31 |

When the third iteration is finished, the third smallest number is in the third position from the top. The value 25 is now stored in address ARRAY(3). The array is as follows:

ARRAY(1)=10
ARRAY(2)=18
ARRAY(3)=25
ARRAY(4)=40
ARRAY(5)=31

On the fourth time through the sort, the process is as follows:

| COUNT2=4 | COUNT3=5 | TEMP=40 | ARRAY(4)=31 |
| | | | ARRAY(5)=40 |

When the fourth iteration is finished, the fourth smallest number is in the fourth position from the top. The value 31 is now stored in address ARRAY(4). The array is as follows:

ARRAY(1)=10
ARRAY(2)=18
ARRAY(3)=25
ARRAY(4)=31
ARRAY(5)=40

After this iteration, the largest number is in ARRAY(5) and the sorting routine is over. In a bubble sort, the number of iterations is $N-1$, where N is the size of the array.

Let's look at another program example. Suppose that Oriental Rug Company wants to sort the names of their salespeople based on performance in descending order. Draw a flowchart and write a program to do this job (see figs. 6–15 and 6–16).

Lines 430 to 450 swap the names in NAM$ associated with the total sales whenever two total sales figures are swapped in SALES.

Suppose that you want to sort the salespeople's names in ascending order. Generate an output from the sorted array and total sales (see fig. 6–17).

**Figure 6–15**
Another Example of Sort Operations

```
100    REM THIS PROGRAM SORTS THE TOTAL SALES OF THE ORIENTAL
110    REM RUG COMPANY IN DESCENDING ORDER.  ALSO EACH SALES
120    REM PERSON WILL BE ASSOCIATED WITH HIS OR HER TOTAL SALES.
130    REM
140    REM ****** VARIABLE TABLE
150    REM          COUNT1 = FOR-NEXT LOOP CONTROL VARIABLE
160    REM          COUNT2 = FOR-NEXT LOOP CONTROL VARIABLE
170    REM          TEMP = TEMPORARY ARRAY ELEMENT HOLDER VARIABLE
180    REM          TEMP$ = TEMPORARY ARRAY ELEMENT HOLDER VARIABLE
190    REM
200    REM ****** ARRAY TABLE
210    REM          NAM$(9) = A 9-ELEMENT SALESPERSON NAME ARRAY
220    REM          SALES(9) = A 9-ELEMENT SALESPERSON SALES ARRAY
230    REM
240    REM ****** INITIALIZATION SECTION
250    DIM NAM$(9), SALES(9)
260    REM
270    REM ****** PROCESS SECTION
280    PRINT "THE ORIGINAL LISTING OF THE TOTAL SALES AND SALES PEOPLE"
290    REM FILL UP THE TWO ARRAYS.
300    FOR COUNT1 = 1 TO 9
310       READ NAM$(COUNT1), SALES(COUNT1)
320       PRINT , SALES(COUNT1), NAM$(COUNT1)
330    NEXT COUNT1
340    REM
350    PRINT "THE SORTED LISTING OF THE TOTAL SALES AND SALES PEOPLE"
360    REM THE SORT ROUTINE STARTS HERE.
370    FOR COUNT1 = 1 TO 8
380       FOR COUNT2 = COUNT1+1 TO 9
390          IF SALES(COUNT1)>=SALES(COUNT2) THEN GOTO 460
400          LET TEMP = SALES(COUNT1)
410          LET SALES(COUNT1) = SALES(COUNT2)
420          LET SALES(COUNT2) = TEMP
430          LET TEMP$ = NAM$(COUNT1)
440          LET NAM$(COUNT1) = NAM$(COUNT2)
450          LET NAM$(COUNT2) = TEMP$
460       NEXT COUNT2
470    NEXT COUNT1
480    REM
490    REM ****** OUTPUT SECTION
500    FOR COUNT1 = 1 TO 9
510       PRINT , SALES(COUNT1), NAM$(COUNT1)
520    NEXT COUNT1
530    REM
540    REM ****** DATA SECTION
550    DATA MARTHA, 25000,MAGGIE, 18000, MURRAY, 17000, SALLY, 31000
560    DATA CHARLES, 10000, KATHY, 16000, LAURA, 20500, TERRY, 21000
570    DATA FRED,29000
580    END
THE ORIGINAL LISTING OF THE TOTAL SALES AND SALES PEOPLE
                  25000          MARTHA
                  18000          MAGGIE
```

```
               17000         MURRAY
               31000         SALLY
               10000         CHARLES
               16000         KATHY
               20500         LAURA
               21000         TERRY
               29000         FRED
THE SORTED LISTING OF THE TOTAL SALES AND SALES PEOPLE


               31000         SALLY
               29000         FRED
               25000         MARTHA
               21000         TERRY
               20500         LAURA
               18000         MAGGIE
               17000         MURRAY
               16000         KATHY
               10000         CHARLES
```

**Figure 6–15** (Continued)

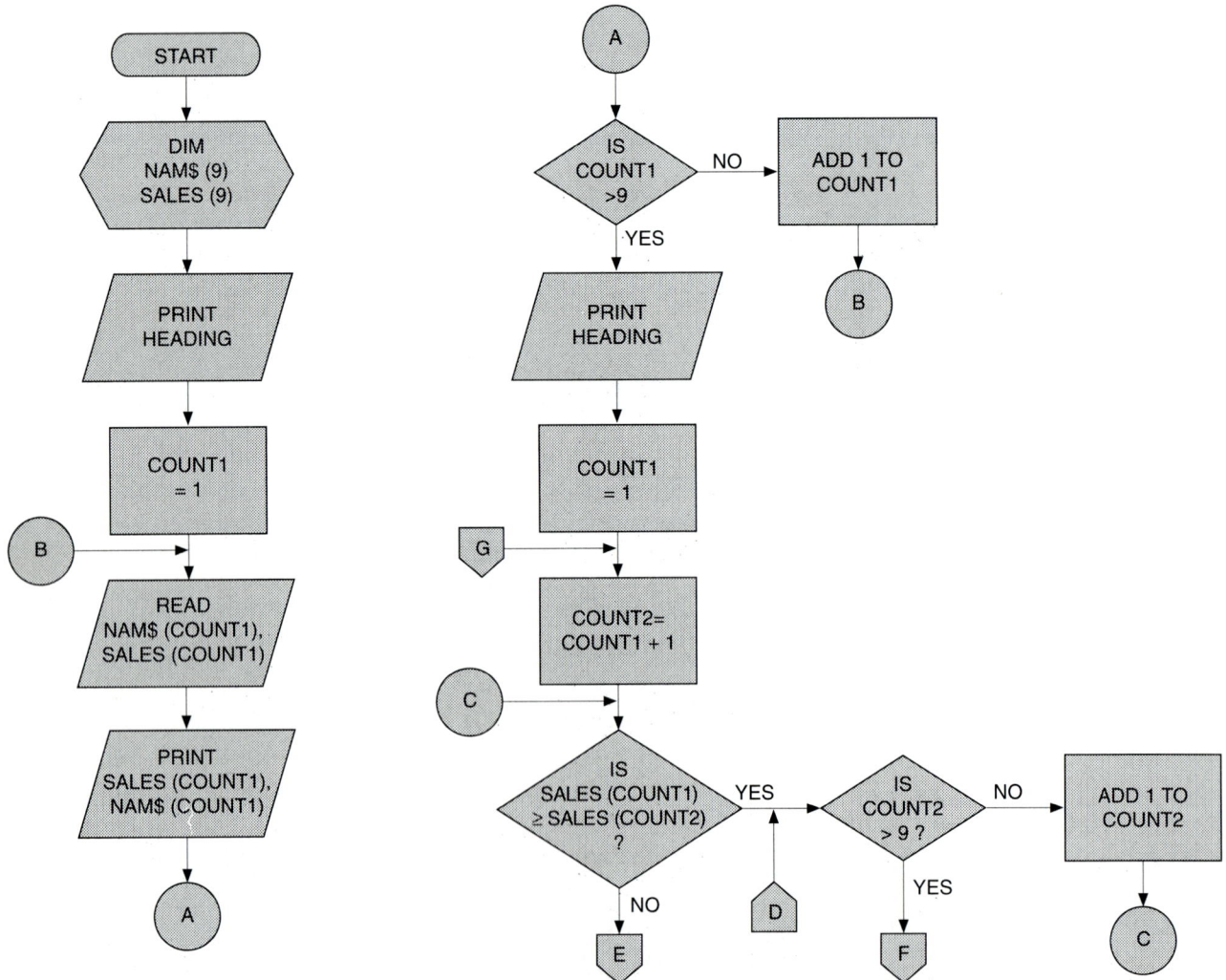

**Figure 6–16**
The Flowchart for the Program in Figure 6–15

**Flowchart (continued):**

E → TEMP = SALES (COUNT1) → SALES (COUNT1) = SALES (COUNT2) → SALES (COUNT2) = TEMP → TEMP$ = NAM$ (COUNT1) → NAM$ (COUNT1) = NAM$ (COUNT2) → H

H → NAM$ (COUNT2) = TEMP$ → D

F → IS COUNT1 > 8? — YES → I
IS COUNT1 > 8? — NO → ADD 1 TO COUNT1 → G

I → COUNT1 = 1 → PRINT SALES (COUNT1), NAM$ (COUNT1) → IS COUNT1 > 9? — NO → ADD 1 TO COUNT1 → (back to PRINT)
IS COUNT1 > 9? — YES → END

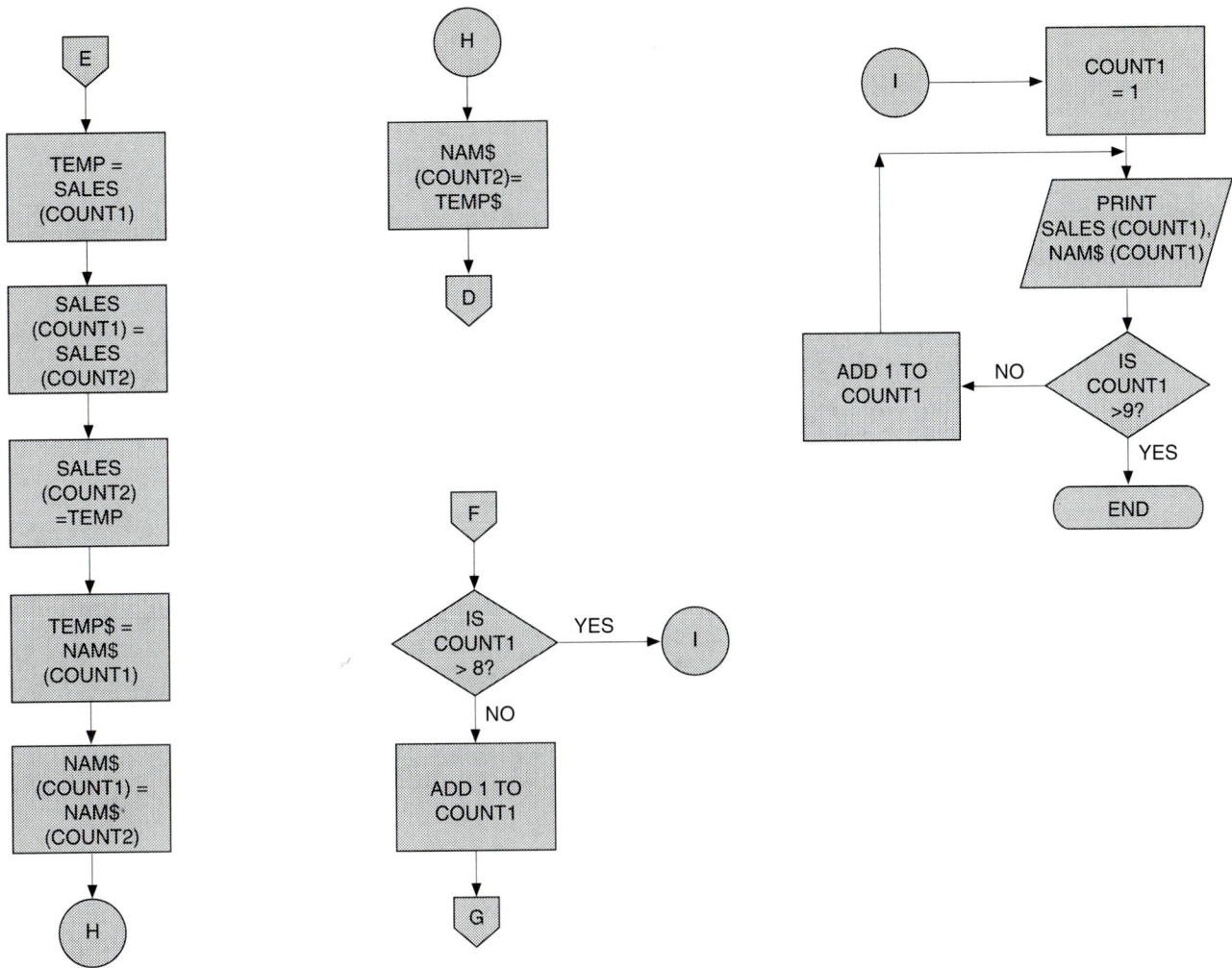

```
100    REM THIS PROGRAM SORTS THE TOTAL SALES OF THE ORIENTAL
110    REM RUG COMPANY IN DESCENDING ORDER.  ALSO EACH SALES
120    REM PERSON WILL BE ASSOCIATED WITH HIS OR HER TOTAL SALES.
130    REM
140    REM ****** VARIABLE TABLE
150    REM          COUNT1 = FOR-NEXT LOOP CONTROL VARIABLE
160    REM          COUNT2 = FOR-NEXT LOOP CONTROL VARIABLE
170    REM          TEMP = TEMPORARY ARRAY ELEMENT HOLDER VARIABLE
180    REM          TEMP$ = TEMPORARY ARRAY ELEMENT HOLDER VARIABLE
190    REM
200    REM ****** ARRAY TABLE
210    REM          NAM$(9) = A 9-ELEMENT SALESPERSON NAME ARRAY
220    REM          SALES(9) = A 9-ELEMENT SALESPERSON SALES ARRAY
230    REM
240    REM ****** INITIALIZATION SECTION
250    DIM NAM$(9), SALES(9)
260    REM
270    REM ****** PROCESS SECTION
280    PRINT "THE ORIGINAL LISTING OF THE TOTAL SALES AND SALES PEOPLE"
290    REM FILL UP THE TWO ARRAYS.
300    FOR COUNT1 = 1 TO 9
310       READ NAM$(COUNT1), SALES(COUNT1)
320       PRINT , NAM$(COUNT1), SALES(COUNT1)
```

**Figure 6–17**
Another Example of Sort Operations

```
330    NEXT COUNT1
340    REM
350    PRINT "THE SORTED LISTING OF THE TOTAL SALES AND SALES PEOPLE"
360    REM THE SORT ROUTINE STARTS HERE.
370    FOR COUNT1 = 1 TO 8
380       FOR COUNT2 = COUNT1+1 TO 9
390          IF NAM$(COUNT1)<=NAM$(COUNT2) THEN GOTO 460
400          LET TEMP$ = NAM$(COUNT1)
410          LET NAM$(COUNT1) = NAM$(COUNT2)
420          LET NAM$(COUNT2) = TEMP$
430          LET TEMP = SALES(COUNT1)
440          LET SALES(COUNT1) = SALES(COUNT2)
450          LET SALES(COUNT2) = TEMP
460       NEXT COUNT2
470    NEXT COUNT1
480    REM
490    REM ******* OUTPUT SECTION
500    FOR COUNT1 = 1 TO 9
510       PRINT , NAM$(COUNT1), SALES(COUNT1)
520    NEXT COUNT1
530    REM
540    REM ******* DATA SECTION
550    DATA MARTHA, 25000,MAGGIE, 18000, MURRAY, 17000, SALLY, 31000
560    DATA CHARLES, 10000, KATHY, 16000, LAURA, 20500, TERRY, 21000
570    DATA FRED,29000
580    END
THE ORIGINAL LISTING OF THE TOTAL SALES AND SALES PEOPLE
               MARTHA          25000
               MAGGIE          18000
               MURRAY          17000
               SALLY           31000
               CHARLES         10000
               KATHY           16000
               LAURA           20500
               TERRY           21000
               FRED            29000
THE SORTED LISTING OF THE TOTAL SALES AND SALES PEOPLE


               CHARLES         10000
               FRED            29000
               KATHY           16000
               LAURA           20500
               MAGGIE          18000
               MARTHA          25000
               MURRAY          17000
               SALLY           31000
               TERRY           21000
```

**Figure 6–17**   *(Continued)*

## SUMMARY

In this chapter, we introduced subscripted variables, which enable you to use as many variables as needed in a program. We explained how you use the DIM statement as a command for defining the size of an array. We discussed how you store data in an array and retrieve the data. You also learned how to perform some special operations with an array, such as selecting the largest and smallest members of the array, sequential search, and bubble sort.

---

*These questions are answered in Appendix D.

**\*1.** Circle the valid subscripted variables in BASIC:

    **a.** A1        **e.** W1(2*A+11)

    **b.** A(1)     **f.** W5(2*A−10)

    **c.** A         **g.** A1(25)

    **d.** A(WW)   **h.** A1($1)

**2.** How many spaces are reserved by the following DIM statements?

```
10 DIM A(100),B(25)
20 DIM W(220),C(125)
```

**\*3.** What is printed when you run the following program?

```
10 DIM A(11)
20 FOR I=1 TO 11
30    READ A(I)
40    IF A(I)>=0 THEN 60
50    GOTO 70
60    PRINT A(I);
70 NEXT I
80 DATA -6,11,12,18,-9,0,-7,-11,22,40,-33
90 END
```

**4.** What is the output of the following program?

```
10 DIM A(10)
20 FOR I=1 TO 10
30    READ A(I)
40    IF A(I)>0 THEN 60
50    GOTO 70
60    A(I)=0
70 NEXT I
80 FOR W=1 TO 10
90     PRINT A(W)
100 NEXT W
110 DATA 5,-6,-11,0,7,22,-13,19,-1,60
120 END
```

**5.** What is the output of the following program?

```
10 DIM X(11)
20 FOR I=1 TO 11
30    READ X(I)
40 NEXT I
50 FOR W=11 TO 1 STEP -2
60    PRINT X(W)
70 NEXT W
80 DATA 5,10,15,20,25,30,35,40,45,50,55
90 END
```

**HANDS-ON EXPERIENCE**

1. Write a program to store the numbers 1 to 50 in array W and print their average.
2. The following numbers have been stored in array Q; write and run a program to print the smallest number in the array:

    15
    11
    9
    6
    8
    4
    29
    3

3. Write a program to sort the names of all the students in your computer class in alphabetical order by last name.
4. Store the numbers 1 to 20 in array Q and, using a FOR/NEXT loop, print only the numbers 1, 5, 9, 13, and 17.
5. Store the numbers 1 to 5 in array X, the numbers 6 to 10 in array Y, and the numbers 11 to 15 in array Z. Add all the numbers and store the result in array W. Generate an output from the arrays X, Y, Z, and W.

---

**KEY TERMS**

| | | |
|---|---|---|
| Array | Sequential search | Subscripted variable |
| Bubble sort | | |

---

**KEY COMMANDS**

| | |
|---|---|
| DIM | Defines the size of an array |
| OPTION BASE | Defines the beginning address of an array (0 or 1) |

---

**ARE YOU READY TO MOVE ON?**

**Multiple Choice**

What is the output of the following programs?

1.
```
10 DIM L(5)
20 READ N
30 PRINT L(N),
40 DATA 2,3,4,5,6
50 END
```
   a. 2    3    4    5    6
   b. 2    0    0    0    0
   c. 2    6    3
   d. 2
   e. none of the above

2.
```
5 OPTION BASE 1
10 DIM R(10)
20 READ S
30 FOR K=1 TO 5 STEP .5
40    READ R(K)
```

```
50      S=S+R(K)
60 NEXT K
70 PRINT S
80 DATA 0,1,2,3,4,5,6,7,8,9,10
90 END
```

   **a.** 15

   **b.** 45

   **c.** 33

   **d.** 10

   **e.** none of the above

**3.**
```
5 OPTION BASE 1
10 DIM A(10)
20 FOR J=1 TO 3
30     READ A(J)
40     PRINT A(J);
50     PRINT
60 NEXT J
70 DATA 5,10,15,20,25
80 END
```

   **a.** 5 10 15

   **b.** 5
     10
     15

   **c.** 5 10 15 20 25

   **d.** 1 2 3

   **e.** none of the above

**4.**
```
10 DIM A(12)
20 FOR J=12 TO 1 STEP -1
30     READ A(J)
40     IF A(J)>=9 THEN 60
50     GOTO 70
60     PRINT A(J);
70 NEXT J
80 DATA 7,3,10,-4,22,9,17,0,8,12,2,31
90 END
```

   **a.** 31 12 17 9 22 10

   **b.** 7 3 10 −4 17 0 8
     12 2 31

   **c.** 10 22 9 17 12 31

   **d.** an error message

   **e.** none of the above

**5.**
```
10 DIM B(4),C(4)
20 FOR J=1 TO 4
30     READ B(J)
40 NEXT J
50 FOR I=1 TO 4
60     C(I)=B(I)+12
70     PRINT C(I);
80 NEXT I
90 DATA 1,2,3,4,5,6,7,8
100 END
```

a. 13 14 15 16

b. 5 6 7 8

c. 12 13 14 15

d. 4 3 2 1

e. none of the above

6.
```
10 DIM K(8)
20 FOR L=1 TO 7
30     READ K(L)
40     IF K(L)=5 THEN 60
50     GOTO 70
60     PRINT "YES";
70 NEXT L
80 PRINT K(L)
90 DATA 1,2,3,4,5,6,7
100 END
```

a. 1 2 3 4 YES 6 7

b. YES

c. YES 6 7

d. 1 2 3 4 5
   6 7

e. YES 0

7. To fill an array

a. the DIM statement must be used regardless of the size of the array

b. a FOR/NEXT loop must be used

c. READ/DATA must be used

d. READ/DATA, INPUT, or LET statements can be used

e. none of the above

8. An array

a. can use negative subscripts

b. can be retrieved with the PRINT ARRAY command

c. does not need a DIM statement unless 100 or more spaces are needed

d. can increase the number of variables to a very large number

e. none of the above

What is the output of the following programs?

9.
```
10 DIM A(20)
20 FOR I=1 TO 4
30     PRINT A(I);
40 NEXT I
50 DATA 10,20,30,40
60 END
```

a. 10 20 30 40

b. 10
   20
   30
   40

c. 0 0 0 0

d. this program will not run

e. none of the above

```
10. 10 DIM A(5)
    20 FOR I=1 TO 5
    30     READ A(I)
    40 NEXT I
    50 PRINT A(I)
    60 DATA 1,2,3,4,5
    70 END
```

    **a.** 1    2    3    4

    **b.** 1    2    3    4    5

    **c.** 5

    **d.** 4

    **e.** this program will not run

## True/False

  **1.** The use of one-dimensional arrays increases the total number of variables significantly.

  **2.** A sequential search program compares a particular value with all the members of an array.

  **3.** The READ/DATA, INPUT, and LET statements can be used to fill arrays.

  **4.** A1 and A(1) are the same variable.

  **5.** READ/DATA is the only method of filling an array.

  **6.** The PRINT statement can be used to retrieve an array element.

  **7.** When running a program that selects the smallest member of an array, if there is more than one smallest member, the computer prints the last smallest member encountered.

  **8.** To find a particular member of an array and its address, you can use the sequential search method.

  **9.** Non-numeric data stored in an array cannot be sorted in alphabetical order.

**10.** The bubble sort is one of the fastest methods for sorting data.

| Multiple Choice | True/False | ANSWERS |
|---|---|---|
| **1.** e | **1.** T | |
| **2.** b | **2.** T | |
| **3.** b | **3.** T | |
| **4.** c | **4.** F | |
| **5.** a | **5.** F | |
| **6.** e | **6.** T | |
| **7.** d | **7.** F | |
| **8.** d | **8.** T | |
| **9.** c | **9.** F | |
| **10.** e | **10.** F | |

# Two-Dimensional Arrays

**7**

## 7–1
## INTRODUCTION

In Chapter 6, we discussed one-dimensional arrays, also called lists or **vectors**. A one-dimensional array has either rows or columns. In this chapter, we discuss two-dimensional arrays. A two-dimensional array is sometimes called a table or **matrix**. A two-dimensional array has both rows and columns. You learn ways in which a two-dimensional array can be filled and retrieved. Several examples highlight the applications of two-dimensional arrays.

## 7–2
## DEFINING A TABLE

A table or a two-dimensional array is a group of memory locations like a grid of boxes arranged in rows and columns, as shown in figure 7–1.

As with one-dimensional arrays, the size of a table must be defined in a DIM statement. The DIM statement always defines the number of rows and the number of columns. For example, the statement

```
DIM A(5,3), D(4,2)
```

defines two tables. Table A has 5 rows and 3 columns, table D has 4 rows and 2 columns. In the DIM statement, the first number enclosed in parentheses refers to the number of rows, and the second number refers to the number of columns.

There are many applications of tables in the real world. A shoe company, for example, may record its inventory in a table. The rows of the table are the different sizes of the shoes, and the columns are the different colors of the shoes. For example, row 1, column 1 may indicate the number of shoes of size 7 in the color white. Row 12, column 5 may indicate the number of shoes of size 9 in the color brown, and so on.

A college might maintain students' records in a table. The rows of the table are the students' names and the columns are the students' ages, majors, and G.P.A.s. Row 1 may be all the information related to John Brown; column 10 may list all the G.P.A.s of the students.

## 7–3
## THE ELEMENTS OF A TABLE

As you already know, the DIM statement defines the size of a table. Each **element** of a table is referred to by its unique address in the table. For example, the statement

**Figure 7–1**
A Two-Dimensional Array

Figure 7–2
Identification of Cells in a Table

```
DIM X(4,5)
```

defines a 4-by-5 table, as shown in figure 7–2.

Keep in mind that these are just addresses in the computer; these addresses contain zeros.

## 7–4
## FILLING AND RETRIEVING A TABLE

The three common methods of sending data to the computer (READ/DATA, LET, and INPUT statements) can be used to fill a table. However, nested loops and READ/DATA statements are probably the most efficient method of filling a table. You can use PRINT statements to retrieve the contents of a table.

Suppose that Fan-Fan Company has three branches that are active in four different regions. Each of the following data lines shows the total sales of one branch in each of the four different regions.

```
Branch 1,  15000,  20000,  18000,  22000
Branch 2,  17000,  14000,  13000,  15000
Branch 3,  14000,  17000,  22000,  11000
```

Read the data into table SALES and print the contents of this table (see fig. 7–3).

In line 200, we have dimensioned the table SALES. In many systems, a table up to 10 by 10 does not need to be dimensioned. However, it is a good programming practice to dimension all tables regardless of size.

Lines 250 through 290 fill the table row by row. Therefore, the first line of data fills the first row, the second line of data fills the second row, and so on.

Lines 330 through 380 retrieve the table in a row by row sequence. In line 350, we have placed a semicolon after the variable to keep the carriage on the line on which its value is being printed. The empty PRINT statement in line 370 moves the carriage to the next line.

When this program is executed, table SALES will look like figure 7–4. The addresses and their contents are arrayed as follows:

| | | |
|---|---|---|
| SALES(1,1) = 15000 | SALES(2,1) = 17000 | SALES(3,1) = 14000 |
| SALES(1,2) = 20000 | SALES(2,2) = 14000 | SALES(3,2) = 17000 |
| SALES(1,3) = 18000 | SALES(2,3) = 13000 | SALES(3,3) = 22000 |
| SALES(1,4) = 22000 | SALES(2,4) = 15000 | SALES(3,4) = 11000 |

```
100   REM THIS PROGRAM GENERATES A 3 BY 4 TABLE OF SALES INFORMATION.
110   REM
120   REM ****** VARIABLE TABLE
130   REM          COUNT1 = FOR-NEXT LOOP CONTROL VARIABLE
140   REM          COUNT2 = FOR-NEXT LOOP CONTROL VARIABLE
150   REM
160   REM ****** ARRAY TABLE
170   REM          SALES(3,4) = A 3x4 SALES DATA ARRAY
180   REM
190   REM ****** INITIALIZATION SECTION
200   DIM SALES(3,4)
210   PRINT "SALES INFORMATION FOR FAN-FAN COMPANY"
220   REM
230   REM ****** PROCESS SECTION
240   REM THIS SECTION FILLS THE SALES ARRAY.
250   FOR COUNT1 = 1 TO 3
260     FOR COUNT2 = 1 TO 4
270       READ SALES(COUNT1,COUNT2)
280     NEXT COUNT2
290   NEXT COUNT1
300   REM
310   REM ****** OUTPUT SECTION
320   REM THIS SECTION DISPLAYS THE CONTENTS OF THE SALES ARRAY.
330   FOR COUNT1 = 1 TO 3
340     FOR COUNT2 = 1 TO 4
350       PRINT "   ";SALES(COUNT1,COUNT2);
360     NEXT COUNT2
370     PRINT
380   NEXT COUNT1
390   REM
400   REM ****** DATA SECTION
410   DATA 15000,20000,18000,22000
420   DATA 17000,14000,13000,15000
430   DATA 14000,17000,22000,11000
440   END
Ok
RUN
SALES INFORMATION FOR FAN-FAN COMPANY
    15000     20000     18000     22000
    17000     14000     13000     15000
    14000     17000     22000     11000
Ok
```

**Figure 7–3**

An Example of a Two-Dimensional Array

## 7–5

## SIMPLE OPERATIONS WITH TABLES

Once a table is filled, you can perform several operations with its values. For example, you can compute the sum of each row or column, you can compute the average of each row or column, and so on. These types of computations have many applications in market analysis. For example, you can find out which region is below sales goals or which branch is doing the best or the worst.

Suppose that the president of Fan-Fan Company has asked the following questions:

- How much is the total sales for the past 12 months for the entire company?
- How much is the total sales for each branch?
- How much is the total sales for each region?

SALES (3,4)

| 15000 | 20000 | 18000 | 22000 |
|-------|-------|-------|-------|
| 17000 | 14000 | 13000 | 15000 |
| 14000 | 17000 | 22000 | 11000 |

**Figure 7–4**

The Final Contents of the SALES
Table from Figure 7–3

Draw a flowchart, and then write and run a BASIC program to answer
the above three questions (see figs. 7–5 and 7–6).

In figure 7–5 we have dimensioned one two-dimensional array and two
one-dimensional arrays as follows:

SALES(3,4)
ROW(3)
COL(4)

**Figure 7–5**

Another Example of a Two-Dimensional Array

```
100    REM THIS PROGRAM PERFORMS SIMPLE OPERATIONS WITH TABLE SALES.
110    REM
120    REM ****** VARIABLE TABLE
130    REM          COUNT1 = FOR-NEXT LOOP CONTROL VARIABLE
140    REM          COUNT2 = FOR-NEXT LOOP CONTROL VARIABLE
150    REM          TOTAL = TOTAL SALES FOR THE COMPANY
160    REM
170    REM ****** ARRAY TABLE
180    REM          SALES(3,4) = A 3-BY-4 COMPANY SALES DATA ARRAY
190    REM          ROW(3) = A 3-ELEMENT ROW COPY OF SALES
200    REM          COL(4) = A 4-ELEMENT COLUMN COPY OF SALES
210    REM
220    REM ****** INITIALIZATION SECTION
230    DIM SALES(3,4), ROW(3), COL(4)
240    REM
250    REM ****** PROCESS SECTION
260    REM THIS PART OF THE PROGRAM FILLS TABLE SALES.
270    FOR COUNT1 = 1 TO 3
280      FOR COUNT2 = 1 TO 4
290        READ SALES(COUNT1,COUNT2)
300      NEXT COUNT2
310    NEXT COUNT1
320    REM
330    REM THIS PART OF THE PROGRAM COMPUTES THE TOTAL SALES.
340    PRINT "SALES REPORT FOR FAN-FAN COMPANY"
350    LET TOTAL = 0
360    FOR COUNT1 = 1 TO 3
370      FOR COUNT2 = 1 TO 4
380        LET TOTAL = TOTAL+SALES(COUNT1,COUNT2)
390      NEXT COUNT2
400    NEXT COUNT1
410    REM
420    PRINT "THE SUM OF THE TOTAL SALES FOR THE PAST 12 MONTHS =";TOTAL
430    REM
440    REM THIS PART OF THE PROGRAM COMPUTES
```

```
450    REM THE TOTAL SALES FOR EACH BRANCH.
460    LET TOTAL = 0
470    FOR COUNT1 = 1 TO 3
480      FOR COUNT2 = 1 TO 4
490        LET TOTAL = TOTAL+SALES(COUNT1,COUNT2)
500      NEXT COUNT2
510      LET ROW(COUNT1) = TOTAL
520      LET TOTAL = 0
530    NEXT COUNT1
540    PRINT
550    PRINT "THE SUM OF THE TOTAL SALES FOR BRANCH #1 =";ROW(1)
560    PRINT "THE SUM OF THE TOTAL SALES FOR BRANCH #2 =";ROW(2)
570    PRINT "THE SUM OF THE TOTAL SALES FOR BRANCH #3 =";ROW(3)
580    REM
590    REM THIS PART OF THE PROGRAM COMPUTES THE TOTAL SALES
600    REM FOR EACH REGION.
610    LET TOTAL = 0
620    FOR COUNT1 = 1 TO 4
630      FOR COUNT2 = 1 TO 3
640        LET TOTAL = TOTAL+SALES(COUNT2,COUNT1)
650      NEXT COUNT2
660      LET COL(COUNT1) = TOTAL
670      LET TOTAL = 0
680    NEXT COUNT1
690    PRINT
700    PRINT "THE SUM OF THE TOTAL SALES FOR REGION #1 =";COL(1)
710    PRINT "THE SUM OF THE TOTAL SALES FOR REGION #2 =";COL(2)
720    PRINT "THE SUM OF THE TOTAL SALES FOR REGION #3 =";COL(3)
730    PRINT "THE SUM OF THE TOTAL SALES FOR REGION #4 =";COL(4)
740    REM
750    REM ****** DATA SECTION
760    DATA 15000,20000,18000,22000
770    DATA 17000,14000,13000,15000
780    DATA 14000,17000,22000,11000
790    END
Ok
RUN
SALES REPORT FOR FAN-FAN COMPANY
THE SUM OF THE TOTAL SALES FOR THE PAST 12 MONTHS = 198000

THE SUM OF THE TOTAL SALES FOR BRANCH #1 = 75000
THE SUM OF THE TOTAL SALES FOR BRANCH #2 = 59000
THE SUM OF THE TOTAL SALES FOR BRANCH #3 = 64000

THE SUM OF THE TOTAL SALES FOR REGION #1 = 46000
THE SUM OF THE TOTAL SALES FOR REGION #2 = 51000
THE SUM OF THE TOTAL SALES FOR REGION #3 = 53000
THE SUM OF THE TOTAL SALES FOR REGION #4 = 48000
Ok
```

**Figure 7-5**  *(Continued)*

126

Lines 270 through 310 fill the SALES table. In line 350, we have initialized TOTAL to 0. The loop in lines 360 to 400 accumulates the SALES table in TOTAL. Line 420 prints the total sales for the company.

In line 460, TOTAL is reset to 0. Lines 470 to 530 add the sales table row by row. When the program is finished with one row, the result is stored in array ROW (line 510). Line 520 resets TOTAL to 0, and the loop continues. Lines 550 to 570 print the total of each row.

The loop in lines 620 to 680 adds the SALES table column by column. The total of each column is stored in TOTAL (line 640); the result is stored in array COL (line 660). TOTAL is reset to 0 (line 670), and the process continues. Lines 700 to 730 print the total of each column.

Suppose that The Olive Oil Factory records its total sales in a table. These sales have been generated by different salespersons in different regions. The head of the marketing department asks the following two questions:

- Which salesperson has generated the highest total sales in the past six months?
- Which region has generated the lowest total sales in the past six months?

Write and run a BASIC program to answer these questions using the following sample data:

| Connie | 2000 | 3000 | 7000 | 6000 | 11000 |
|--------|------|------|------|------|-------|
| Sue    | 3000 | 4000 | 4000 | 7000 | 9000  |
| Bernie | 7000 | 6000 | 9000 | 5000 | 3000  |
| Fred   | 7000 | 4000 | 9000 | 6000 | 2000  |
| Doug   | 8000 | 2000 | 5000 | 5000 | 9000  |

The sales have been generated in Portland, Beaverton, Lake Oswego, Pendleton, and Gresham, respectively. Figure 7−7 illustrates this table graphically. Figure 7−8 shows the program that performs these tasks.

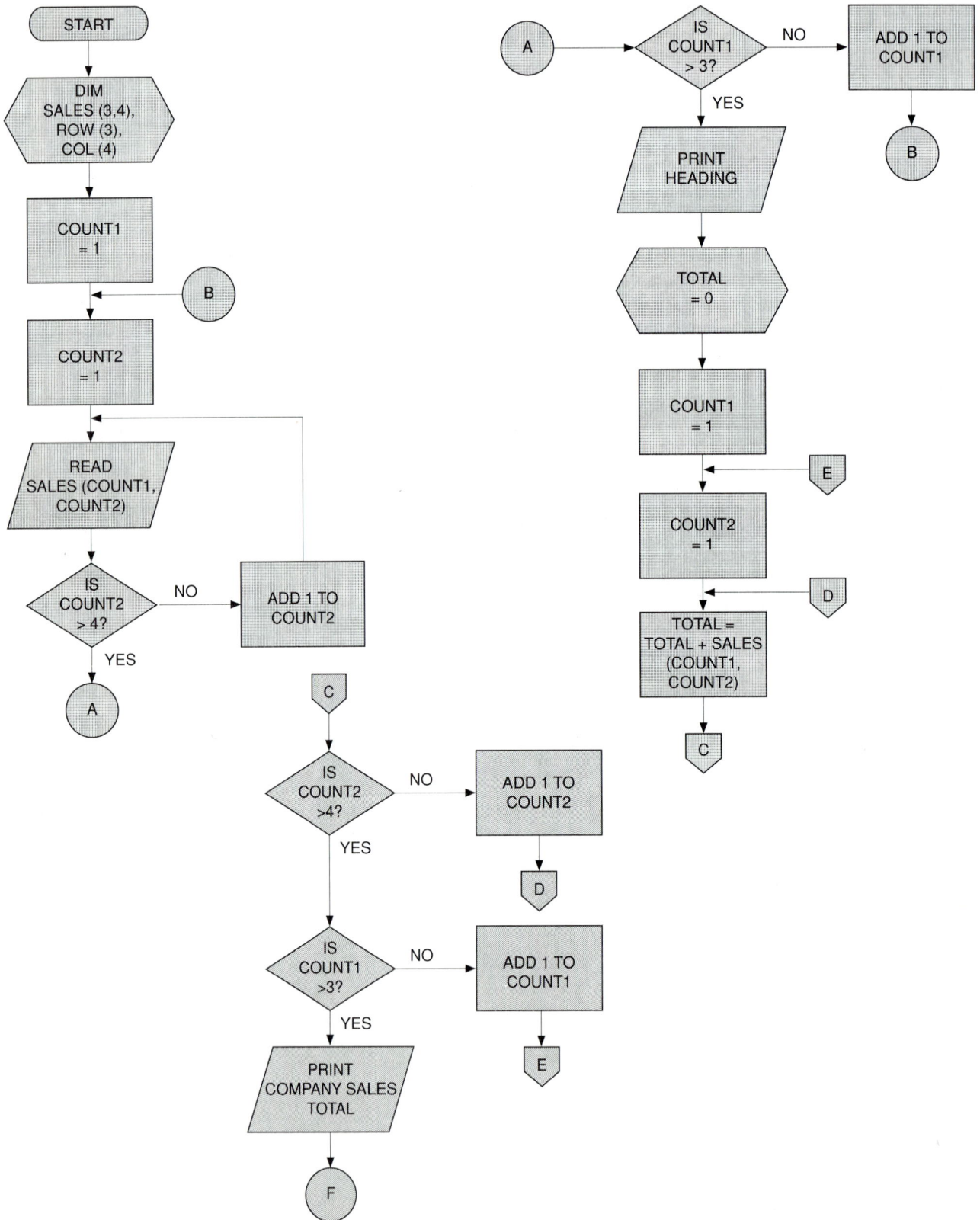

**Figure 7–6**
The Flowchart for the Program in Figure 7–5

128

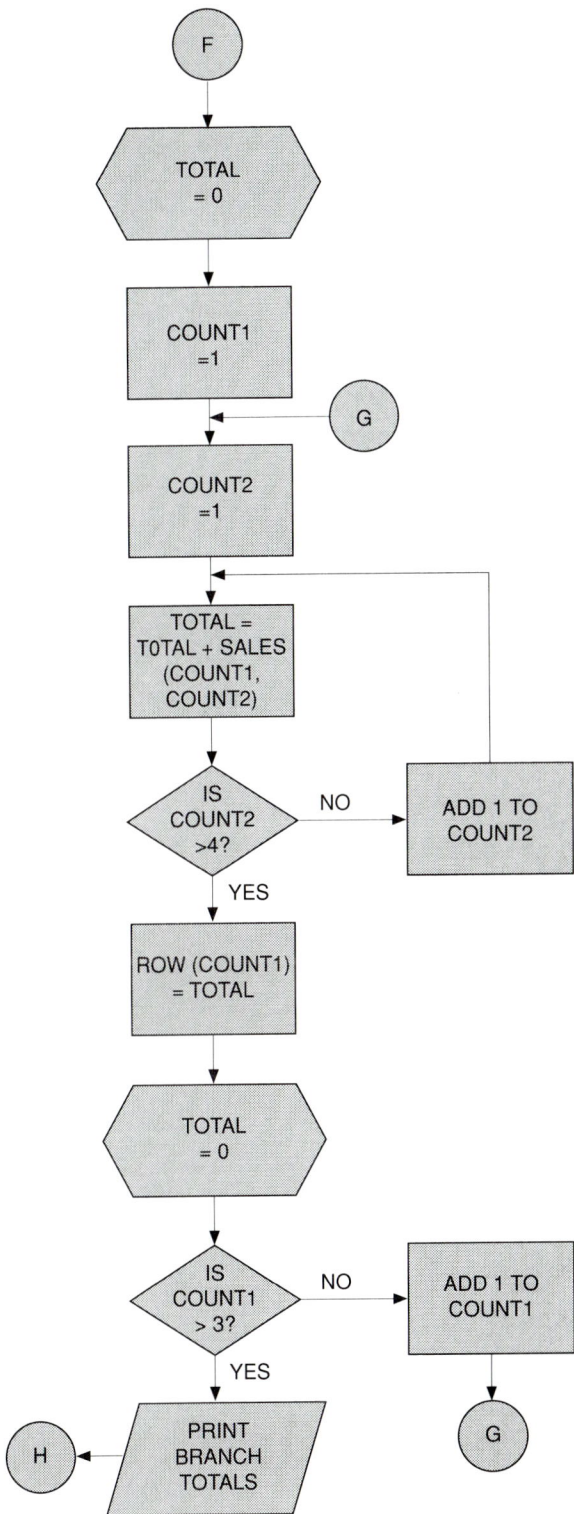

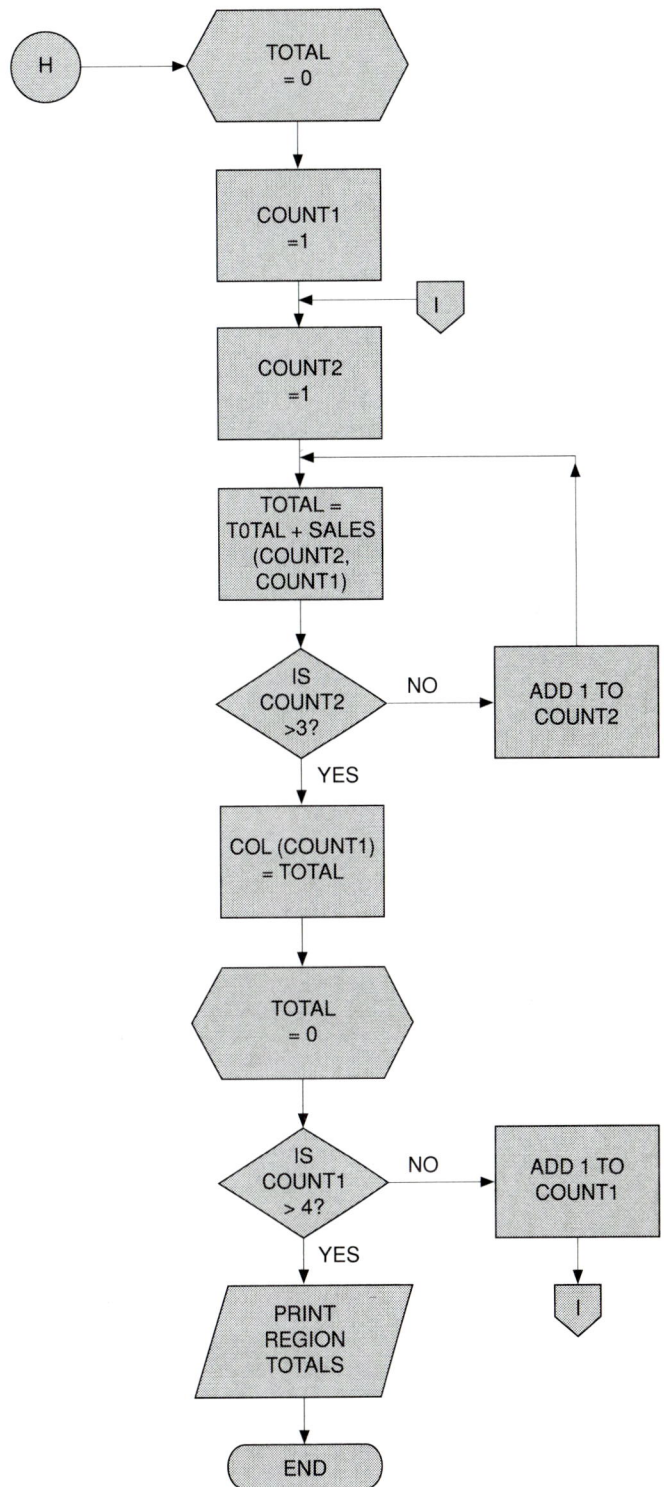

**Figure 7-6** *(Continued)*

**Figure 7–7**

Sales Data for The Olive Oil
Factory

| | Portland | Beaverton | Lake Oswego | Pendleton | Gresham |
|---|---|---|---|---|---|
| Connie | 2000 | 3000 | 7000 | 6000 | 11000 |
| Sue | 3000 | 4000 | 4000 | 7000 | 9000 |
| Bernie | 7000 | 6000 | 9000 | 5000 | 3000 |
| Fred | 7000 | 4000 | 9000 | 6000 | 2000 |
| Doug | 8000 | 2000 | 5000 | 5000 | 9000 |

**Figure 7–8**

Another Example of Two-Dimensional Arrays

```
100    REM THIS PROGRAM SEARCHES FOR THE SALESPERSON WHO HAS
110    REM GENERATED THE HIGHEST TOTAL SALES.   IT ALSO SEARCHES
120    REM FOR THE REGION WHICH HAS GENERATED THE LOWEST TOTAL
130    REM SALES.
140    REM
150    REM ****** VARIABLE TABLE
160    REM        COUNT1 = FOR-NEXT LOOP CONTROL VARIABLE
170    REM        COUNT2 = FOR-NEXT LOOP CONTROL VARIABLE
180    REM        TOTAL = TOTAL SALES FOR A SALESPERSON
190    REM        HIGH = HIGHEST TOTAL SALES AMOUNT
200    REM        TEMPNAM$ = SALESPERSON WITH HIGHEST TOTAL SALES
210    REM        TEMPLOC$ = REGION WITH THE LOWEST TOTAL SALES
220    REM        LOW = LOWEST TOTAL SALES AMOUNT
230    REM
240    REM ****** ARRAY TABLE
250    REM        SALES(5,5) = 5-PERSON TOTAL SALES ARRAY
260    REM        NAM$(5) = SALESPERSON NAME ARRAY
270    REM        ROW(5) = A 5-ELEMENT ROW COPY OF SALES
280    REM        COL(5) = A 5-ELEMENT COLUMN COPY OF SALES
290    REM        REGION$(5) = A 5-ELEMENT ARRAY OF REGIONS
300    REM
310    REM ****** INITIALIZATION SECTION
320    DIM SALES(5,5), NAM$(5), ROW(5), COL(5), REGION$(5)
330    REM
340    REM ****** PROCESS SECTION
350    REM THIS PART OF THE PROGRAM FILLS THE SALES, NAME AND REGION ARRAYS.
360    FOR COUNT1 = 1 TO 5
370      READ NAM$(COUNT1), REGION$(COUNT1)
380    NEXT COUNT1
390    REM
400    FOR COUNT1 = 1 TO 5
410      FOR COUNT2 = 1 TO 5
420        READ SALES(COUNT1,COUNT2)
430      NEXT COUNT2
440    NEXT COUNT1
450    REM
460    REM THIS PART OF THE PROGRAM COMPUTES THE
470    REM TOTAL SALES FOR EACH SALESPERSON.
480    LET TOTAL = 0
490    FOR COUNT1 = 1 TO 5
500      FOR COUNT2 = 1 TO 5
510        LET TOTAL = TOTAL+SALES(COUNT1,COUNT2)
520      NEXT COUNT2
530      LET ROW(COUNT1) = TOTAL
540      LET TOTAL = 0
550    NEXT COUNT1
560    REM
570    REM THIS PART OF THE PROGRAM COMPUTES THE
580    REM TOTAL SALES FOR EACH REGION.
590    LET TOTAL = 0
```

**130**

```
600    FOR COUNT1 = 1 TO 5
610      FOR COUNT2 = 1 TO 5
620        LET TOTAL = TOTAL+SALES(COUNT2,COUNT1)
630      NEXT COUNT2
640      LET COL(COUNT1) = TOTAL
650      LET TOTAL = 0
660    NEXT COUNT1
670    REM
680    REM AT THIS POINT TWO NEW ARRAYS HAVE BEEN GENERATED.
690    REM THESE TWO ARE ROW(5) AND COL(5).  THE ROW ARRAY STORES
700    REM THE TOTAL SALES FOR EACH SALESPERSON IN DIFFERENT
710    REM REGIONS.  THE COL ARRAY STORES THE TOTAL SALES OF
720    REM EACH REGION BY DIFFERENT SALESPERSONS.
730    REM
740    REM THIS PART OF THE PROGRAM SEARCHES FOR THE SALES-
750    REM PERSON WITH THE HIGHEST TOTAL SALES.
760    LET TEMPNAM$ = "CONNIE"
770    LET HIGH = ROW(1)
780    REM HERE YOU ARE ASSUMING THAT THE FIRST SALESPERSON
790    REM HAS GENERATED THE HIGHEST TOTAL SALES.  AFTER
800    REM THIS YOU COMPARE THIS PERSON'S PERFORMANCE
810    REM WITH OTHERS TO SEE IF THIS IS STILL THE BEST.
820    REM IF THIS NO LONGER IS TRUE, THE CONTENTS
830    REM OF TEMPNAM$ AND HIGH ARE REPLACED WITH NEW VALUES.
840    REM
850    FOR COUNT1 = 2 TO 5
860      IF ROW(COUNT1)>HIGH THEN 880
870      GOTO 900
880      LET TEMPNAM$ = NAM$(COUNT1)
890      LET HIGH = ROW(COUNT1)
900    NEXT COUNT1
910    REM
920    PRINT TEMPNAM$;" HAS GENERATED THE HIGHEST TOTAL SALES WHICH IS =";HIGH
930    PRINT
940    REM THIS PART OF THE PROGRAM SEARCHES FOR THE REGION WHICH
950    REM HAS GENERATED THE LOWEST TOTAL SALES.
960    REM
970    LET TEMPLOC$ = "PORTLAND"
980    LET LOW = COL(1)
990    FOR COUNT1 = 2 TO 5
1000     IF COL(COUNT1) < LOW THEN 1020
1010     GOTO 1040
1020     LET TEMPLOC$ = REGION$(COUNT1)
1030     LET LOW = COL(COUNT1)
1040   NEXT COUNT1
1050   PRINT TEMPLOC$;" HAS GENERATED THE LOWEST TOTAL SALES WHICH IS =";LOW
1060   REM
1070   REM ****** DATA SECTION
1080   DATA CONNIE, PORTLAND
1090   DATA SUE, BEAVERTON
1100   DATA BERNIE, LAKE OSWEGO
1110   DATA FRED, PENDLETON
1120   DATA DOUG, GRESHAM
1130   DATA 2000,3000,7000,6000,11000
1140   DATA 3000,4000,4000,7000,9000
1150   DATA 7000,6000,9000,5000,3000
1160   DATA 7000,4000,9000,6000,2000
1170   DATA 8000,2000,5000,5000,9000
1180   END
Ok
RUN
BERNIE HAS GENERATED THE HIGHEST TOTAL SALES WHICH IS = 30000

BEAVERTON HAS GENERATED THE LOWEST TOTAL SALES WHICH IS = 19000
Ok
```

**Figure 7–8**  (Continued)

---

**SUMMARY**

In this chapter, we introduced you to two-dimensional arrays. You learned how to fill and retrieve a table, and we introduced several simple operations with tables.

---

**REVIEW QUESTIONS**

*These questions are answered in Appendix D.

*1. What is wrong with the following program?

```
10 DIM A(20,35)
20 A(21,22)=64
30 END
```

*2. How many data items are required to fill the following two matrices?

```
DIM A(20,30),B(18,40),C$(55)
```

---

**HANDS-ON EXPERIENCE**

1. Store 100 four-digit numbers in a one-dimensional array and again in a 10-by-10 matrix. Provide a listing of the array and the matrix.

2. Following is a listing of some of the students in a BASIC class. Use the sample data below to write a program that:

   a. generates a listing of students and their grades on each test.

   b. generates a listing of the average score of each student.

   c. generates a listing of the average score for each test.

   d. generates a sorted list of all the students based upon their averages on the four tests (in descending order).

   | Name | Test 1 | Test 2 | Test 3 | Test 4 |
   |---|---|---|---|---|
   | Melanie | 99 | 96 | 93 | 100 |
   | Pat | 98 | 100 | 97 | 92 |
   | Tom | 100 | 98 | 98 | 93 |
   | Sue | 67 | 63 | 80 | 71 |
   | Sharon | 99 | 93 | 96 | 95 |
   | Jim | 65 | 52 | 68 | 58 |
   | Leslie | 78 | 69 | 52 | 70 |
   | Mary | 70 | 60 | 65 | 58 |
   | Denise | 90 | 88 | 92 | 94 |
   | Lisa | 62 | 92 | 93 | 98 |
   | Edward | 90 | 68 | 40 | 80 |
   | Eddy | 82 | 68 | 72 | 90 |
   | Jack | 80 | 68 | 52 | 92 |

3. Northwest Regional Textile Company has begun to analyze its customers. The head of the marketing department has requested:

   a. a listing of all the customers who have purchased more than $15,000 worth of goods in the past 12 months.

   b. a listing of all the customers who have purchased more than $15,000 worth of goods and who have not exceeded their credit limit.

   c. a listing of all the customers who have purchased more than $15,000 worth of goods, who have not exceeded their credit limit, and who have accepted back orders. Use the following data:

   | | | | |
   |---|---|---|---|
   | 100 | 2000 | 2500 | 1 |
   | 110 | 3600 | 3000 | 1 |
   | 120 | 7000 | 6500 | 1 |

| 130 | 2700 | 3000 | 1 |
| 140 | 14000 | 15000 | 1 |
| 150 | 22000 | 30000 | 0 |
| 160 | 11500 | 12000 | 0 |
| 170 | 17750 | 18000 | 1 |
| 180 | 31000 | 35000 | 1 |
| 190 | 41000 | 35000 | 0 |

Each line of data consists of the customer number, the total purchase, the credit limit, and the acceptance (1) or rejection (2) of back orders.

Write and run a BASIC program that provides the answers to the questions.

4. Write a program to generate a 10-by-10 table using a FOR-NEXT loop. Your table should be filled with 0s except for the diagonal, which should be filled with 1s.

5. Write a program that generates the transposition of a 10-by-5 table.

---

| Element | Matrix | Vector | **KEY TERMS** |

---

## Multiple Choice

1. What is the output of the following program?

```
10 DIM B(3,4)
20 FOR I=1 TO 3
30    FOR J=1 TO 4
40       READ B(I,J)
50    NEXT J
60 NEXT I
70 PRINT B(I,J)
80 DATA 2,4,6,8,10,12,14,16,18,20,24,28,30
90 END
```

a. 28

b. 30

c. 24

d. nothing

e. an error message

2. How many data items are needed to fill the following matrices?

```
10 FOR I=1 TO 4
20    FOR J=1 TO 6
30       READ A(I,J), B(I,J)
40    NEXT J
50 NEXT I
60 DATA
70 END
```

a. 24

b. 10

c. 20

d. 48

e. none of the above

**ARE YOU READY TO MOVE ON?**

What is the output of the following programs?

```
3. 10 FOR I=1 TO 2
   20     FOR J=1 TO 3
   30         READ B(I,J)
   40         PRINT B(I,J);
   50     NEXT J
   60 PRINT
   70 NEXT I
   80 DATA 2,4,6,8,10,12
   90 END
```

   a. 2  4  6  8  10  12

   b. 2    4    6
      8   10   12

   c. 2    4    6

      8   10   12

   d. 2  6  10
      4  8  12

   e. 12  8  4
      10  6  2

```
4. 10 FOR I=1 TO 5
   20     FOR J=1 TO 2
   30         READ K(I,J)
   40         X=X+K(I,J)
   50     NEXT J
   60 NEXT I
   70 A=X/10
   80 PRINT A
   90 DATA 1,2,3,4,5,6,7,8,9,10
   100 END
```

   a. 5.5

   b. 27.5

   c. 2

   d. 55

   e. an error message

```
5. 10 FOR J=1 TO 3
   20     FOR I=1 TO 4
   30         READ W(I,J)
   40     NEXT I
   50 NEXT J
   60 FOR K=1 TO 4
   70     B=B+W(K,2)
   80 NEXT K
   90 PRINT B
   100 DATA 1,2,3,4,2,3,1,2,3,4,2,3
   110 END
```

   a. 6

   b. 5

   c. 8

   d. 9

   e. none of the above

```
6. 10 DIM A(5,5)
   20 FOR I=1 TO 5 STEP 2
```

```
30      FOR J=1 TO 5 STEP 3
40         READ A(I,J)
50      NEXT J
60 NEXT I
70 DATA 2,4,6,1,2,3,8,10,5,7,9,15,20,30,12,18,17,35,25,3,5,11,20,25,14
80 PRINT A(1,4),A(5,2),A(4,1),A(3,1)
90 END
```

**a.** 4   4   1   6

**b.** 1   10   18   9

**c.** 4   0   0   6

**d.** none of the above

**e.** an error message

7.
```
10 DIM A(3,4)
20 FOR I=1 TO 3
30      FOR J=1 TO 4
40         READ A(I,J)
50      NEXT J
60 NEXT I
70 PRINT A(I,J)
80 DATA 1,2,3,4,5,6,7
90 END
```

**a.** 3   7

**b.** 7   3

**c.** 4   0

**d.** 5

**e.** an error message

8.
```
10 DIM A(2,3)
20 FOR I=1 TO 2
30      FOR J=1 TO 3
40         READ A(I,J)
50         PRINT A(I,J)
60      NEXT J
70 NEXT I
80 DATA 1,2,3,4,5,6
90 END
```

**a.** 1   2   3
    4   5   6

**b.** 1   2   3   4   5   6

**c.** 1
    2
    3
    4
    5
    6

**d.** 1   4
    2   5
    3   6

**e.** none of the above

9. How many data items are needed in line 80 to fill the array?

```
5 OPTION BASE 1
10 DIM A(12,12)
20 FOR I=1 TO 12
30      FOR J=1 TO 12
```

```
40        READ A(I,J)
50     NEXT J
60 NEXT I
70 PRINT A(I,J)
80 DATA
90 END
```

  a. 24
  b. 24
  c. 100
  d. 12
  e. 144

10. Not counting address 0,0, the statement DIM A(5,5),B(5,5)
  a. reserves space for two arrays, both of which contain five rows
  b. reserves space for two arrays, both of which contain five columns and five rows
  c. tells the computer that 30 spaces will be needed for a 5-by-5 matrix
  d. none of the above
  e. reserves 106 spaces

## True/False

1. Two-dimensional arrays are also called matrices or tables.
2. In the DIM statement, the number of columns comes first and the number of rows second.
3. The LET statement is the most efficient way of filling a table.
4. You cannot use the INPUT command to fill a table.
5. The READ/DATA commands are probably the most efficient method to fill a table.
6. Not counting address 0,0, to fill table X(10,20), you need 200 data items.
7. DIM X(30,10) specifies a table with 10 rows and 30 columns.
8. The data from the DATA line is inserted into a table in column order. This means that the first DATA line fills the first column, the second DATA line fills the second column, and so forth.
9. Using FOR-NEXT statements, you cannot set all the values in an array to 0.
10. Using FOR-NEXT statements, you can calculate the sum of a table.

## ANSWERS

**Multiple Choice**

1. e
2. d
3. b
4. a
5. c
6. c
7. e
8. c
9. e
10. b

**True/False**

1. T
2. F
3. F
4. F
5. T
6. T
7. F
8. F
9. F
10. T

# Subroutines: An Introduction to Modular Programming

**8**

## 8-1

### INTRODUCTION

In this chapter, we introduce the subroutine and the advantages of modular programming using subroutines. We introduce the commands for entering and exiting a subroutine. You learn how to use nested subroutines and subroutines with multiple RETURN statements.

## 8-2

### DEFINING A SUBROUTINE

A **subroutine** is a series of instructions in a BASIC program. A subroutine can be called from anywhere in the program and as many times as needed.

Using subroutines saves you writing time. Whenever a portion of a program must be used more than once, you can write it once and call it as many times as you want. Large programs can be divided into several small **modules**, and each module can be written as a subroutine. Modular programs are easier to write, run, and debug than non-modular programs.

## 8-3

### ENTERING AND EXITING A SUBROUTINE

You use the GOSUB command to enter a subroutine. When the requested task is done, the RETURN command exits from the subroutine and returns you to the line following the GOSUB command. The GOSUB command is very similar to the GOTO command as an unconditional branching technique. However, GOSUB always transfers program control to a subroutine.

## 8-4

### PROGRAM AND SUBROUTINE FORMAT

A program with subroutines is divided into two major sections: the main program and the subroutine section. Figure 8-1 shows this configuration.

In Figure 8-1, lines 10 to 1995 are the main program; lines 2000 to 3000 are the subroutine section of this program. The statements in this program are executed in the following order:

        10-150
        2000-3000
        160-300

**Figure 8-1**
A General Configuration of a Main Program and Subroutine

```
10 REM Program with subroutine
20
.
150 GOSUB 2000
160
.
300 GOSUB 2000
310
.
600 GOSUB 2000
610
.
1995 GOTO 9999
2000 PRINT "SUBROUTINE STARTS HERE"
.
3000 RETURN
9999 END
```

2000–3000
310–600
2000–3000
610–1995
9999

Using a subroutine, write a program to calculate the average of three numbers, the average of their squares, and the average of their cubes (see fig. 8–2). This program can be written without using the subroutine, but lines 330 to 400 must be repeated three times.

```
100    REM THIS PROGRAM READS 3 NUMBERS FROM A DATA LINE AND
110    REM COMPUTES THEIR AVERAGE, THE AVERAGE OF THEIR
120    REM SQUARES, AND THE AVERAGE OF THEIR CUBES.
130    REM
140    REM ****** VARIABLE TABLE
150    REM          NUM1, NUM2, NUM3 = INPUT VARIABLES
160    REM          AVERAGE1 = AVERAGE OF NUM1, NUM2 AND NUM3
170    REM          AVERAGE2 = AVERAGE OF THE SQUARES OF NUM1, NUM2, NUM3
180    REM          AVERAGE3 = AVERAGE OF THE CUBES OF NUM1, NUM2, NUM3
190    REM
200    REM ****** INITIALIZATION SECTION
210    READ NUM1, NUM2, NUM3
220    REM
230    REM ****** DATA SECTION
240    DATA 1,2,3,4,5,6,7,8,9
250    REM
260    REM ****** PROCESS SECTION
270    GOSUB 330
280    READ NUM1, NUM2, NUM3
290    GOSUB 330
300    READ NUM1, NUM2, NUM3
310    GOSUB 330
320    GOTO 430
330    LET AVERAGE1 = (NUM1+NUM2+NUM3)/3
340    LET AVERAGE2 = (NUM1^2+NUM2^2+NUM3^2)/3
350    LET AVERAGE3 = (NUM1^3+NUM2^3+NUM3^3)/3
360    REM
370    REM ****** OUTPUT SECTION
380    PRINT "THE AVERAGE OF THE 3 NUMBERS =";AVERAGE1
390    PRINT "THE AVERAGE OF THEIR SQUARES =";AVERAGE2
400    PRINT "THE AVERAGE OF THEIR CUBES   =";AVERAGE3
410    PRINT
420    RETURN
430    END
Ok
RUN
THE AVERAGE OF THE 3 NUMBERS = 2
THE AVERAGE OF THEIR SQUARES = 4.666667
THE AVERAGE OF THEIR CUBES   = 12

THE AVERAGE OF THE 3 NUMBERS = 5
THE AVERAGE OF THEIR SQUARES = 25.66667
THE AVERAGE OF THEIR CUBES   = 135

THE AVERAGE OF THE 3 NUMBERS = 8
THE AVERAGE OF THEIR SQUARES = 64.66666
THE AVERAGE OF THEIR CUBES   = 528

Ok
```

**Figure 8–2**

An Example of a Subroutine

## 8–5

### MULTIPLE RETURN STATEMENTS

A subroutine can be called from several different points within a program. When the subroutine is finished executing, the RETURN statement sends program control to the line following the GOSUB statement that called the subroutine. A subroutine can include more than one RETURN statement as in Figure 8–3.

Figure 8–3 shows a program that reads three numbers from a DATA line and computes their squares. If the square of any of these numbers is greater than 100, that set of three numbers is printed. If the square of any of these numbers is not greater than 100, that set is ignored.

## 8–6

### NESTED SUBROUTINES

In the last two programs, only the main program has called a subroutine. It is possible to have a subroutine call another subroutine. These subroutines within subroutines are known as **nested subroutines**. When you use nested subroutines, the inner subroutine must be contained completely inside the calling subroutine.

Figure 8–4 shows an example of nested subroutines. This program reads two numbers from a DATA line, calls one subroutine to compute their sum, and calls another subroutine to compute their difference.

If you have trouble following the sequence of program execution, you can use the TRON command. This command tells you in what sequence your program is being executed, and it is useful for debugging purposes. To use the TRON command, press F7 and type *RUN*. To turn off the facility, press F8 (TROFF). Figure 8–5 shows the program execution sequence for the program in figure 8–4.

## 8–7

### MODULAR PROGRAMMING

A large program can always be divided into small segments called modules. Writing, running, and debugging modular programs is easier than working with large programs. The modules are usually independent of each other. Modifying a modular program is an easy task. Figure 8–6 shows an example of modular programming, and figure 8–7 shows the flowchart for this program.

In this example, Teliteck Company is using a computer to print its employees' paychecks. In the main program, each employee's record is read from a DATA line. The main program calls three subroutines. The first subroutine calculates the gross pay, the second subroutine calculates the income tax and net pay, and the third subroutine prints the employee's take-home pay, using the following data:

| Lisa | 524-90-1438 | 5.20 | 43 |
| Kim | 189-91-1824 | 8.20 | 18 |
| Andy | 519-24-4218 | 7.40 | 48 |
| Flag | −999 | −99 | −99 |

Each record consists of the employee's name, Social Security number, and hourly pay rate, and the total number of hours the employee worked in a given week. Overtime hours (hours above 40) are paid at 1.5 times the regular rate. The income tax is calculated as follows:

| Income less than $150 | 5 percent |
| Income between $150 and $250 | 12 percent |
| Income above $250 | 18 percent |

```
100    REM THIS PROGRAM READS 3 NUMBERS FROM A DATA LINE,
110    REM COMPUTES THEIR SQUARES, AND IF THE SQUARE OF ANY
120    REM OF THESE NUMBERS IS GREATER THAN 100, THAT SET
130    REM WILL BE PRINTED.  OTHERWISE THAT SET IS IGNORED.
140    REM
150    REM ****** VARIABLE TABLE
160    REM          DATASETS = NUMBER OF DATA SETS TRIED
170    REM          DATAPASS = NUMBER OF DATA SETS PASSED
180    REM          NUM1, NUM2, NUM3 = INPUT VARIABLES
190    REM          SQNUM1 = SQUARE OF NUM1
200    REM          SQNUM2 = SQUARE OF NUM2
210    REM          SQNUM3 = SQUARE OF NUM3
220    REM
230    REM ****** INITIALIZATION SECTION
240    LET DATASETS = 0
250    LET DATAPASS = 0
260    READ NUM1, NUM2, NUM3
270    REM
280    REM ****** DATA SECTION
290    DATA 5,8,9,10,7,6,7,9,4,12,20,6
300    REM
310    REM ****** PROCESS SECTION
320    LET DATASETS = DATASETS+1
330    GOSUB 500
340    READ NUM1, NUM2, NUM3
350    LET DATASETS = DATASETS+1
360    GOSUB 500
370    READ NUM1, NUM2, NUM3
380    LET DATASETS = DATASETS+1
390    GOSUB 500
400    READ NUM1, NUM2, NUM3
410    LET DATASETS = DATASETS+1
420    GOSUB 500
430    REM
440    REM ****** OUTPUT SECTION
450    PRINT "OUT OF";DATASETS;"DATA SETS ONLY";DATAPASS;"SETS ";
460    PRINT "ARE ACCEPTABLE."
470    GOTO 600
480    REM
490    REM SUBROUTINE STARTS ON LINE 1000
500    LET SQNUM1 = NUM1^2
510    LET SQNUM2 = NUM2^2
520    LET SQNUM3 = NUM3^2
530    IF SQNUM1 >= 100 THEN 570
540    IF SQNUM2 >= 100 THEN 570
550    IF SQNUM3 >= 100 THEN 570
560    RETURN
570    PRINT "THIS IS AN ACCEPTABLE SET------->";NUM1;NUM2;NUM3
580    LET DATAPASS = DATAPASS+1
590    RETURN
600    END
Ok
RUN
THIS IS AN ACCEPTABLE SET-------> 10  7  6
THIS IS AN ACCEPTABLE SET-------> 12  20  6
OUT OF 4 DATA SETS ONLY 2 SETS ARE ACCEPTABLE.
Ok
```

**Figure 8–3**

A Subroutine with Multiple RETURN Statements

```
100     REM THIS PROGRAM READS TWO NUMBERS FROM A DATA LINE,
110     REM CALLS A SUBROUTINE AND COMPUTES THEIR SUM.  THIS
120     REM SUBROUTINE WILL CALL ANOTHER SUBROUTINE TO COMPUTE
130     REM THEIR DIFFERENCES.
140     REM
150     REM ****** VARIABLE TABLE
160     REM          NUM1, NUM2 = INPUT VARIABLES
170     REM          SUM = SUM OF NUM1 AND NUM2
180     REM          DIFF = REMAINDER OF NUM1 MINUS NUM2
190     REM
200     REM ****** DATA SECTION
210     DATA 50,200,150,200,250,400,350,700,750,900
220     REM
230     REM ****** PROCESS SECTION
240     READ NUM1,NUM2
250     GOSUB 370
260     READ NUM1,NUM2
270     GOSUB 370
280     READ NUM1,NUM2
290     GOSUB 370
300     READ NUM1,NUM2
310     GOSUB 370
320     READ NUM1,NUM2
330     GOSUB 370
340     GOTO 450
350     REM
360     REM SUBROUTINE STARTS ON LINE 370.
370     LET SUM = NUM1+NUM2
380     PRINT "THE SUM OF";NUM1;"AND";NUM2,"------------------->";SUM
390     GOSUB 420
400     RETURN
410     REM THE SECOND SUBROUTINE STARTS ON LINE 420.
420     LET DIFF = NUM1-NUM2
430     PRINT "THE DIFFERENCE OF";NUM1;"AND";NUM2,"-----> ";DIFF
440     RETURN
450     END
Ok
RUN
THE SUM OF 50 AND 200                -------------------> 250
THE DIFFERENCE OF 50 AND 200                   -----> -150
THE SUM OF 150 AND 200               -------------------> 350
THE DIFFERENCE OF 150 AND 200                  -----> -50
THE SUM OF 250 AND 400               -------------------> 650
THE DIFFERENCE OF 250 AND 400                  -----> -150
THE SUM OF 350 AND 700               -------------------> 1050
THE DIFFERENCE OF 350 AND 700                  -----> -350
THE SUM OF 750 AND 900               -------------------> 1650
THE DIFFERENCE OF 750 AND 900                  -----> -150
Ok
```

**Figure 8-4**

An Example of Nested Subroutines

```
Ok
TRON
Ok
RUN
[100][110][120][130][140][150][160][170][180][190][200][210][220][230][240][250]
[370][380]THE SUM OF 50 AND 200              -------------------> 250
[390][420][430]THE DIFFERENCE OF 50 AND 200            -----> -150
[440][400][260][270][370][380]THE SUM OF 150 AND 200    ------------------->
 350
[390][420][430]THE DIFFERENCE OF 150 AND 200           -----> -50
[440][400][280][290][370][380]THE SUM OF 250 AND 400    ------------------->
 650
[390][420][430]THE DIFFERENCE OF 250 AND 400           -----> -150
[440][400][300][310][370][380]THE SUM OF 350 AND 700    ------------------->
 1050
[390][420][430]THE DIFFERENCE OF 350 AND 700           -----> -350
[440][400][320][330][370][380]THE SUM OF 750 AND 900    ------------------->
 1650
[390][420][430]THE DIFFERENCE OF 750 AND 900           -----> -150
[440][400][340][450]
Ok
```

**Figure 8–5**
The Sequence of Execution for Figure 8–4

The output looks like the following:

**TELITECK COMPANY**
**PAYROLL REPORT**

| NAME | SSN | GROSS PAY | NET PAY |
|------|-----|-----------|---------|
| XXXX | XXXX | XXXXXX | XXXXXX |

This is just one example of modular programming. Many more modules can be added to this program. As you can see, each module is independent of the others. This is a great advantage of modular programs. The modules can be tested, modified, or even replaced independently.

**Figure 8–6**
A Payroll Example Using Subroutines

```
100    REM THIS PROGRAM COMPUTES THE PAYCHECKS OF THE
110    REM EMPLOYEES OF TELITECK COMPANY.  IN THIS PROGRAM,
120    REM 3 SUBROUTINES ARE BEING CALLED.
130    REM
140    REM
150    REM ****** VARIABLE TABLE
160    REM        NAM$ = EMPLOYEE NAME
170    REM        SSN$ = EMPLOYEE SOCIAL SECURITY NUMBER
180    REM        RATE = EMPLOYEE HOURLY RATE
190    REM        HOURS = NUMBER OF HOURS WORKED
200    REM        GROSS = GROSS PAY
210    REM        TAX = TAX WITHHELD
220    REM        NET = NET PAY
230    REM
240    REM ****** DATA SECTION
250    DATA LISA, "524-90-1438", 5.20, 43
260    DATA KIM, "189-91-1824", 8.20, 18
270    DATA ANDY, "519-24-4218", 7.40, 48
280    DATA FLAG, "-999",-99, -99
290    REM
```

```
300     REM ****** INITIALIZATION SECTION
310     PRINT TAB(28); "TELITECK COMPANY"
320     PRINT TAB(29); "PAYROLL REPORT"
330     PRINT "    NAME";TAB(23);"SSN";TAB(37);"GROSS PAY";TAB(59);"NET PAY"
340     REM
350     READ NAM$, SSN$, RATE, HOURS
360     REM
370     REM ****** PROCESS SECTION
380     IF SSN$ = "-999" THEN 700
390     GOSUB 450
400     GOSUB 520
410     GOSUB 670
420     GOTO 350
430     REM
440     REM SUBROUTINE TO COMPUTE GROSS PAY.
450     IF HOURS > 40 THEN 480
460     LET GROSS = RATE*HOURS
470     GOTO 490
480     LET GROSS = RATE*40 + 1.5*RATE*(HOURS-40)
490     RETURN
500     REM
510     SUBROUTINE TO COMPUTE THE INCOME TAX AND NET INCOME.
520     IF GROSS < 150 THEN 550
530     IF GROSS < 250 THEN GOTO 580
540     GOTO 610
550     LET TAX = GROSS*.05
560     LET NET = GROSS-TAX
570     RETURN
580     LET TAX = GROSS*.12
590     LET NET = GROSS-TAX
600     RETURN
610     LET TAX = GROSS*.18
620     LET NET = GROSS-TAX
630     RETURN
640     REM
650     REM ****** OUTPUT SECTION
660     REM SUBROUTINE TO PRINT EMPLOYEE'S TAKE HOME PAYCHECK.
670     PRINT TAB(4);NAM$;TAB(19);SSN$;TAB(36);
680     PRINT USING "$$####.##            $$####.##";GROSS,NET
690     RETURN
700     END
Ok
RUN
                      TELITECK COMPANY
                      PAYROLL REPORT
        NAME              SSN          GROSS PAY            NET PAY
        LISA          524-90-1438       $231.40            $203.63
        KIM           189-91-1824       $147.60            $140.22
        ANDY          519-24-4218       $384.80            $315.54
Ok
```

**Figure 8–6** *(Continued)*

**Figure 8–7**
The Flowchart for the Program Shown in Figure 8–6

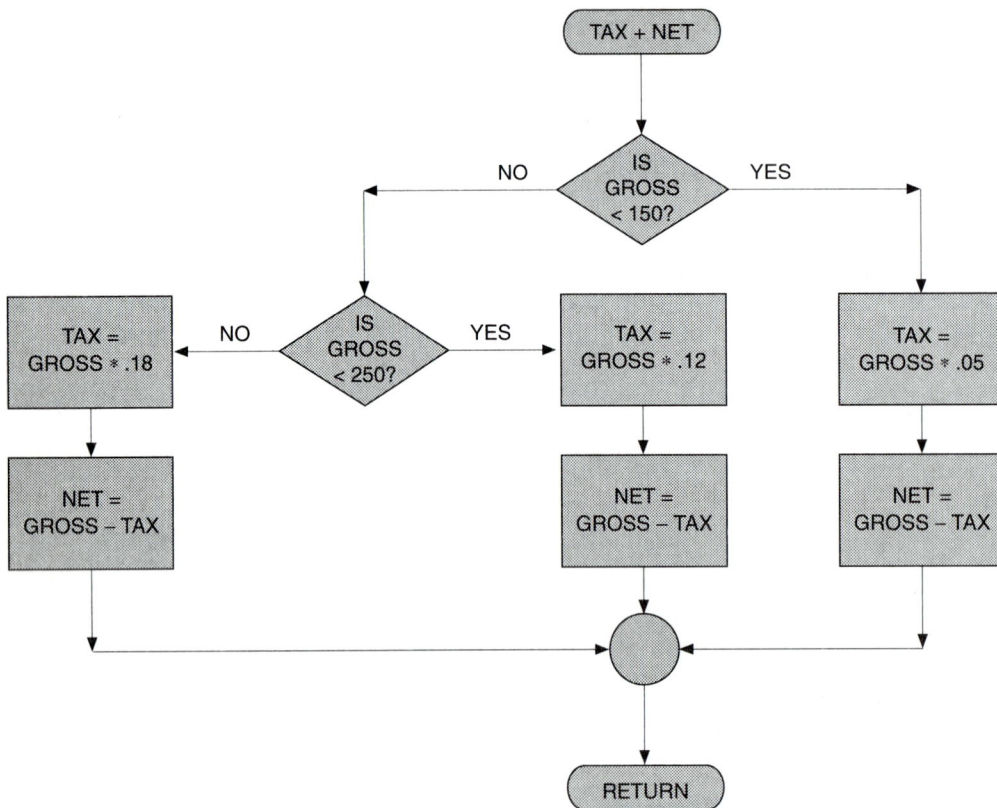

**Figure 8–7**   *(Continued)*

## SUMMARY

In this chapter, we discussed using a subroutine as an independent segment of a program. We explained using the GOSUB command to enter a subroutine and using the RETURN command to exit from it. We introduced the subroutine as a tool for modular programming. We also examined using nested subroutines and subroutines with multiple RETURN statements.

## REVIEW QUESTIONS

*These questions are answered in Appendix D.

1. What is the difference between GOTO and GOSUB as unconditional branching commands?

2. Show the sequence of the operations in the following program:

```
10 DATA 15,5,20,4,80,20,-999,-999
20 READ A,B
30 IF A=-999 THEN 9999
40 GOSUB 500
50 GOTO 20
60 GOTO 9999
```

```
490 REM *** SUBROUTINE ***
500 M=A*B
510 PRINT "The product of the two numbers is ";M
520 GOSUB 1000
530 RETURN
990 REM **********
1000 D=A/B
1010 PRINT "THE DIVISION OF TWO NUMBERS IS ";D
1020 RETURN
9999 END
```

*3. What is wrong with the following programs?

a.
```
10 READ A, B
20 IF A=-999 THEN 900
30 GOSUB 500
40 GOTO 10
500 E=A-B
600 F=A/B
700 C=A+B
800 RETURN
900 END
```

b.
```
10 READ C,D
20 DATA 5,10,15,20,30,35,-999,-999
30 IF C=-999 THEN 999
40 GOSUB 500
50 GOTO 10
60 GOTO 999
500 PRINT "TITLE"
510 X=C^2+D^2
520 PRINT X
999 END
```

c.
```
10 READ C,D
20 DATA 5,10,15,20,30,35,-999,-999
30 IF C=-999 THEN 999
40 IF (C+D)>20 THEN 510
50 PRINT C,D
60 GOSUB 500
70 GOTO 10
80 GOTO 999
490 REM SUBROUTINE STARTS ON LINE 500
500 PRINT C^2, D^2
510 PRINT C^3, D^3
520 RETURN
999 END
```

d.
```
10 READ A,B
20 DATA 10,20,30,40,50,60,-99,-99
30 IF A=-99 THEN 999
40 GOSUB 500
50 GOTO 10
60 GOTO 999
500 REM SUBROUTINE
510 PRINT (A+B)/2
520 GOTO 50
530 RETURN
999 END
```

**HANDS-ON EXPERIENCE**

1. Using subroutines, read a portion of the crime statistics collected from City Hall:

| Year | Crime 1 | Crime 2 | Crime 3 |
|------|---------|---------|---------|
| 1987 | 10 | 99 | 53 |
| 1988 | 18 | 105 | 19 |
| 1989 | 34 | 110 | 160 |
| 1990 | 37 | 194 | 211 |

   Use a second subroutine to sort each crime in descending order. Use a third subroutine to sort each year based on the total number of all crimes in ascending order. Use a fourth subroutine to print the results.

2. Using subroutines, read a series of account numbers, amounts of purchase, and credit limits. Your first subroutine should print the original data. Your second subroutine should print account numbers of those customers with a negative balance. The third subroutine should sort all the customers based on balance in ascending order. Use the following sample data:

| Account Number | Purchase | Credit Limit |
|----------------|----------|--------------|
| 100 | 2,000 | 4,000 |
| 200 | 3,500 | 2,000 |
| 300 | 6,000 | 6,500 |
| 400 | 7,000 | 4,700 |
| 500 | 2,500 | 5,000 |
| 600 | 9,400 | 7,200 |
| 700 | 6,350 | 4,000 |
| 800 | 7,240 | 8,000 |
| 900 | 2,430 | 2,670 |

3. Write a modular program to compute a student's grade for a course. The program should have an input subroutine, a process subroutine, and an output subroutine. The user should be asked to enter five test scores. All test scores must be greater than or equal to zero. After all the data have been entered, the process subroutine should compute the student's grade based on the following grading scale:

   90 to 100 = A
   80 to 89 = B
   70 to 79 = C
   60 to 69 = D
   Less than 60 = F

   Your program's output should consist of an appropriate title, the five test scores, the average test score, and the student's grade. Be sure to use good programming style.

4. Using the formula

$$X = \frac{-B \pm \sqrt{B^2 - 4AC}}{2A}$$

   write a modular program to find both roots (positive and negative) of an equation. The user should enter values for A, B, and C. To avoid division by zero, set an error trap to guarantee that the user doesn't enter inappropriate input data. The output should consist of a descriptive title and values for both roots. Your program should have an input subroutine, a process subroutine, and an output subroutine.

**KEY TERMS**          Module                    Nested subroutines          Subroutine

| | | |
|---|---|---|
| GOSUB | Transfers control to a subroutine | **KEY COMMANDS** |
| RETURN | Returns control to the line following the GOSUB command | |
| TROFF (F8) | Turns off the trace feature | |
| TRON (F7) | Turns on the trace feature | |

## Multiple Choice

**ARE YOU READY TO MOVE ON?**

What is the output of the following programs?

1.
```
10 B=7
20 L=7
30 IF L<>B THEN 50
40 GOSUB 90
50 GOSUB 70
60 GOTO 110
70 PRINT "YES"
80 RETURN
90 PRINT "BASIC"
100 RETURN
110 END
```

a. YES
   BASIC

b. BASIC
   YES

c. BASIC
   BASIC

d. BASIC

e. none of the above

2.
```
10 READ X,Y,Z
20 DATA 9,49,26
30 GOSUB 60
40 GOSUB 90
50 GOTO 110
60 PRINT X^2;
70 PRINT Y^.5;
80 RETURN
90 PRINT Z
100 RETURN
110 END
```

a. 81   9   1

b. 9    7   25

c. 81   7   26

d. 81   9   1

e. none of the above

3.
```
10 READ D,E
20 GOSUB 40
30 GOTO 80
40 A=D/E+2
50 PRINT A
60 RETURN
70 DATA 12,3
80 END
```

**a.** 17

**b.** 0

**c.** 6

**d.** an error message

**e.** none of the above

4. 
```
 10 READ B
 20 C=B+3
 30 GOSUB 100
 40 READ B
 50 C=B+C
 60 GOSUB 100
 70 GOTO 140
100 PRINT C;
110 RESTORE
120 RETURN
130 DATA 2,7
140 END
```

**a.** 5   7

**b.** 2   9

**c.** 5   7

**d.** an error message

**e.** none of the above

5. 
```
 10 READ B,D,E
 20 GOSUB 50
 30 GOSUB 90
 40 GOTO 130
 50 K=B+D
 60 X=K/E
 70 PRINT X;
 80 RETURN
 90 I=X+D
100 PRINT I
110 RETURN
120 DATA 6,12,2
130 END
```

**a.** 0

**b.** 72   48

**c.** 7    19

**d.** 9   21

**e.** none of the above

6. 
```
 10 READ A,B
 20 DATA 2,4,6,8
 30 GOSUB 100
 40 READ A,B
 50 GOSUB 100
 60 GOTO 140
100 C=A+B
110 PRINT C;
120 RETURN
130 PRINT
140 END
```

**a.** 6   14

**b.** 8    12

**c.** 6
    14

**d.** 14

**e.** none of the above

7.
```
10 READ X,Y
20 IF Y>Z THEN 40
30 GOTO 240
40 GOSUB 100
50 PRINT X,Y
100 X=X*3
110 IF X >= 6 THEN 130
120 RETURN
130 GOSUB 200
140 GOTO 220
200 Y=Y+3
210 RETURN
220 RETURN
230 DATA 3,3
240 END
```

**a.** 3    3

**b.** 9    6

**c.** 9    3

**d.** 3    9

**e.** none of the above

8.
```
10 READ A,B,C
20 DATA 1,2,3,4,5,6
30 GOSUB 500
40 GOTO 530
50 READ A,B,C
60 GOSUB 500
70 STOP
500 Z=A^2+B^2+C^2
510 PRINT Z,
520 RETURN
530 END
```

**a.** 14    77

**b.** 14

**c.** 12

**d.** none of the above

**e.** 36

9.
```
10 READ X,Y,Z
20 IF Y > X THEN 40
30 GOSUB 110
40 GOTO 150
100 W=X+Y+Z/3
110 M=X*Y*Z
120 PRINT X,M
130 RETURN
140 DATA 10,5,15
150 END
```

**a.** 18    750

**b.** 10    750

    **c.** the program will not run

    **d.** none of the above

    **e.** 0   750

10. ```
    10 READ E,F,G
    20 IF E=1 THEN 50
    30 GOSUB 100
    40 GOTO 10
    50 GOTO 140
    100 X=(E+F+G)/3
    110 PRINT X
    120 RETURN
    130 DATA 3,6,9,1,2,3
    140 END
    ```

    **a.** 6
       9

    **b.** 6
       2

    **c.** the program will not run

    **d.** none of the above

    **e.** 6

## True/False

1. Subroutines can be placed only at the end of a program.

2. Using subroutines to reduce the complexity of a program is called modular programming.

3. The GOSUB and GOTO statements can be used interchangeably.

4. You can reduce the number of coding lines in a program by using subroutines.

5. Modular programs are easier to write and debug than non-modular programs.

6. There is always a one-to-one relationship between the number of GOSUB and RETURN statements.

7. A subroutine can call another subroutine.

8. When using nested subroutines, one subroutine must be completely inside the other subroutine.

9. The GOSUB command is used to exit a subroutine.

10. The GOTO statement must be used to exit a subroutine.

---

**ANSWERS**

| Multiple Choice | True/False |
|---|---|
| **1.** b | **1.** F |
| **2.** c | **2.** T |
| **3.** c | **3.** F |
| **4.** a | **4.** T |
| **5.** d | **5.** T |
| **6.** a | **6.** F |
| **7.** e | **7.** T |
| **8.** b | **8.** T |
| **9.** b | **9.** F |
| **10.** e | **10.** F |
    ```

# File Processing

9

## 9–1
## INTRODUCTION

In this chapter, you learn about file processing in BASIC. So far, you have learned that READ statements receive the necessary data from DATA lines. In this chapter, we present a new option: data files. You learn how to read data from a file and print data to a file. We also explain reading data from a file into a table and writing data from a table into a data file. We also present simple operations with data files.

## 9–2
## DATA FILES

Often, data items are used by more than one program or application. To enable several programs to have access to this data, the data can be stored in a **data file**. Data stored in a data file are practically independent of a particular program.

There are three types of data file processing: sequential, random, and indexed sequential.

To reach a particular item of data in a **sequential data file**, all the previous data items must be read. This process is similar to selecting a song on a cassette tape. To listen to a song in the middle of the cassette, you must either listen to all the previous songs or fast forward through them to reach the song you want.

In a **random data file**, data items are located by record number and can be addressed by record number. This process is similar to selecting a song on a phonograph record. You can position the needle on a particular song, bypassing the previous selections.

To search an **indexed sequential file**, you must first search an index file (organized in a particular order) and then the index file will tell you where to look for a particular record. This process is similar to using a card catalog system in a library. You first go to the card catalog, and then it tells you where to look for the desired book.

In this chapter, we present operations that can be performed with sequential data files. Appendix A presents several examples of random files.

## 9–3
## FILE PROCESSING COMMANDS

To create a sequential file in BASIC, you should know the following commands:

OPEN
WRITE
CLOSE

The general formats of these commands are as follows:

OPEN "filename" FOR INPUT AS # file designator
OPEN "filename" FOR OUTPUT AS # file designator
OPEN "filename" FOR APPEND AS # file designator

WRITE file designator, variable list

CLOSE file designator

The file designator tells you which file you are working with. The variable list includes all your variables.

```
100     REM THIS PROGRAM PRODUCES THE FILE CH9-1X.TXT.
110     REM
120     REM ****** VARIABLE TABLE
130     REM           COUNT = FOR-NEXT LOOP CONTROL VARIABLE
140     REM           WORD1$, WORD2$ = INPUT STRING VARIABLES
150     REM           NUM = INPUT NUMERIC VARIABLE
160     REM
170     REM ****** INITIALIZATION SECTION
180     OPEN "A:CH9-1X.TXT" FOR OUTPUT AS #1
190     REM
200     REM ****** PROCESS SECTION
210     FOR COUNT = 1 TO 3
220       READ WORD1$, WORD2$, NUM
230       WRITE #1, WORD1$, WORD2$, NUM
240     NEXT COUNT
250     REM
260     REM ****** OUTPUT SECTION
270     PRINT "THE END"
280     REM
290     REM ****** DATA SECTION
300     DATA SUSAN SHAY, BUSINESS, 3.85
310     DATA KIM BROWN, COMPUTER, 2.60
320     DATA ED STRONG, MATH., 4.00
330     REM
340     REM ****** TERMINATION SECTION
350     CLOSE #1
360     END
Ok
RUN
THE END
Ok
```

**Figure 9–1**

The Program that Creates CH9-1X.TXT

To generate a listing of a sequential file, you must exit BASIC to DOS using the SYSTEM command. Then you use the TYPE command to create a file listing.

## 9–4
## READING FROM A FILE

To read data from a file, you must specify the file name before starting the operation. Suppose that the file CH9-1X.TXT has been generated with the following data items:

Susan Shay, Business, 3.85
Kim Brown, Computer, 2.60
Ed Strong, Math, 4.00

This file can be created in several ways. You can use a line editor, a word processor, or the BASIC file facility. Figure 9–1 displays the program that generates this file, and figure 9–2 displays a listing of this file.

```
A:\>TYPE CH9-1X.TXT
"SUSAN SHAY","BUSINESS",3.85
"KIM BROWN","COMPUTER",2.6
"ED STRONG","MATH.",4

A:\>
```

**Figure 9–2**

A Listing of CH9-1X.TXT

The OPEN statement instructs BASIC to go out and find the indicated file. If the file is found, then the file contents can be accessed for further processing. If the file is not found GW-BASIC responds with the error message

```
FILE NOT FOUND IN LINE #
```

where # indicates the line number of the OPEN statement.

When a file is opened for output, BASIC determines whether there is enough room on the destination disk to hold another file. If there is enough room, the file is created and processing begins. If there is not enough room, you receive an error message. If you open a file for output and the file already exists, the contents of the file will be overwritten. No error message is displayed; therefore, you should exercise care when naming output files.

If you use the APPEND command to add data to an existing file, the file pointer is moved to the end of the data and the new data are added to the file.

Suppose that you want to write a program to read the data from the permanent file CH9-1X.TXT and print the contents. This program is shown in figure 9−3.

As you see in this program, the permanent file CH9-1X.TXT includes three lines of data (data elements must be separated by commas). In line 190, the file CH9-1X.TXT has been opened as the first file for input. Line 210 has the following general format:

INPUT # file designator, input list

The file designator identifies a particular file to be read. The input list identifies variables to be read from the specified file. To read from a data file, there must be a one-to-one correspondence between the input list and the data items in the file.

Figure 9−4 shows a program to read files CH9-1X.TXT and CH9-2X.TXT and print their contents. Figure 9−5 creates CH9-2X.TXT. Figure 9−6 displays a listing of CH9-2X.TXT.

**Figure 9−3**

A Program to Read from a File and Print the Contents

```
100     REM THIS PROGRAM READS A SERIES OF DATA ITEMS
110     REM FROM A PERMANENT FILE AND PRINTS THE CONTENTS.
120     REM
130     REM ****** VARIABLE TABLE
140     REM          COUNT1 = FOR-NEXT LOOP CONTROL VARIABLE
150     REM          WORD1$, WORD2$ = INPUT STRING VARIABLES
160     REM          NUMBER = INPUT VARIABLE
170     REM
180     REM ****** PROCESS SECTION
190     OPEN "A:CH9-1X.TXT" FOR INPUT AS #1
200     FOR COUNT1 = 1 TO 3
210        INPUT #1, WORD1$, WORD2$, NUMBER
220        PRINT "" , WORD1$, WORD2$, NUMBER
230     NEXT COUNT1
240     REM
250     REM ****** TERMINATION SECTION
260     CLOSE #1
270     PRINT "END OF FILE"
280     END
Ok
RUN
                SUSAN SHAY      BUSINESS         3.85
                KIM BROWN       COMPUTER         2.6
                ED STRONG       MATH.            4
END OF FILE
Ok
```

```
100    REM THIS PROGRAM READS FROM PERMANENT FILES
110    REM CH9-1X.TXT AND CH9-2X.TXT AND PRINTS THEIR CONTENTS.
120    REM
130    REM ****** VARIABLE TABLE
140    REM          COUNT = FOR-NEXT LOOP CONTROL VARIABLE
150    REM          NAM$ = STUDENT NAME
160    REM          MAJOR$ = STUDENT MAJOR
170    REM          GPA = GRADE POINT AVERAGE
180    REM          LOCATION$ = SCHOOL LOCATION
190    REM
200    REM ****** INITIALIZATION SECTION
210    OPEN "A:CH9-1X.TXT" FOR INPUT AS #1
220    OPEN "A:CH9-2X.TXT" FOR INPUT AS #2
230    REM
240    REM ****** PROCESS SECTION
250    FOR COUNT = 1 TO 3
260      INPUT #1,NAM$,MAJOR$,GPA
270      INPUT #2,LOCATION$
280      PRINT NAM$,MAJOR$,GPA,LOCATION$
290    NEXT COUNT
300    REM
310    REM ****** TERMINATION SECTION
320    CLOSE #1
330    CLOSE #2
340    PRINT "END OF PROGRAM"
350    END
Ok
RUN
SUSAN SHAY     BUSINESS        3.85       PORTLAND
KIM BROWN      COMPUTER        2.6        BEAVERTON
ED STRONG      MATH.           4          PENDLETON
END OF PROGRAM
Ok
```

**Figure 9-4**

A Program to Read from Two Files and Print the Contents

```
100    REM TO CREATE FILE CH9-2X.TXT.
110    REM
120    REM ****** VARIABLE TABLE
130    REM          COUNT = FOR-NEXT LOOP CONTROL VARIABLE
140    REM          DESTINATION$ = CITY OF DESTINATION
150    REM
160    REM ****** INITIALIZATION SECTION
170    OPEN "A:CH9-2X.TXT" FOR OUTPUT AS #2
180    REM
190    REM ****** PROCESS SECTION
200    FOR COUNT = 1 TO 3
210      READ DESTINATION$
220      WRITE #2, DESTINATION$
230    NEXT COUNT
240    REM
250    REM ****** TERMINATION SECTION
260    CLOSE #2
270    REM
280    REM ****** OUTPUT SECTION
290    PRINT "END"
300    DATA PORTLAND
310    DATA BEAVERTON
320    DATA PENDLETON
330    END
Ok
RUN
END
Ok
```

**Figure 9-5**

A Program that Creates CH9-2X.TXT

**Figure 9—6**
A Listing of CH9-2X.TXT

```
A:\>TYPE CH9-2X.TXT
"PORTLAND"
"BEAVERTON"
"PENDLETON"

A:\>
```

Figure 9—7 shows a program that reads files CH9-3X.TXT and CH9-3Y.TXT and prints their contents. Figure 9—8 creates CH9-3X.TXT, and figure 9—9 displays a listing of CH9-3X.TXT. Figure 9—10 creates CH9-3Y.TXT, and figure 9—11 displays a listing of CH9-3Y.TXT.

## 9—5
## CREATING A PERMANENT FILE

You use the WRITE # command to generate a data file on disk. Figure 9—12 shows a program that reads data from CH9-1X.TXT and generates the new file CH9-4X.TXT.

```
100    REM THIS PROGRAM READS FROM PERMANENT FILES CH9-3X.TXT
110    REM AND CH9-3Y.TXT AND PRINTS THEIR CONTENTS.
120    REM
130    REM ****** VARIABLE TABLE
140    REM         COUNT = FOR-NEXT LOOP CONTROL VARIABLE
150    REM         NUM1, NUM2, NUM3 = INPUT VARIABLES
160    REM         WORD1$, WORD2$, WORD3$ = INPUT STRING VARIABLES
170    REM
180    REM ****** INITIALIZATION SECTION
190    OPEN "A:CH9-3X.TXT" FOR INPUT AS #1
200    OPEN "A:CH9-3Y.TXT" FOR INPUT AS #2
210    PRINT "THE CONTENTS OF CH9-3X.TXT"
220    REM
230    REM ****** PROCESS SECTION
240    FOR COUNT = 1 TO 3
250      INPUT #1,NUM1,NUM2,NUM3
260      PRINT NUM1,NUM2,NUM3
270    NEXT COUNT
280    REM
290    PRINT "THE CONTENTS OF CH9-3Y.TXT"
300    FOR COUNT = 1 TO 3
310      INPUT #2,WORD1$,WORD2$,WORD3$,NUM1
320      PRINT WORD1$,WORD2$,WORD3$,NUM1
330    NEXT COUNT
340    REM ****** TERMINATION SECTION
350    CLOSE #1
360    CLOSE #2
370    END
Ok
RUN
THE CONTENTS OF CH9-3X.TXT
 10500          600            700
 20600          700            800
 30700          800            900
THE CONTENTS OF CH9-3Y.TXT
RTI            LONDON         T.V.           1000
MRY            PARIS          REFRIGERATOR   2000
RTN            DENVER         CALCULATOR     2500
Ok
```

**Figure 9—7**
A Program that Reads Files CH9-3X.TXT and CH9-3Y.TXT and Prints Their Contents

```
100    REM  ** THIS PROGRAM PRODUCES FILE CH9-3X.TXT. **
110    REM
120    REM ****** VARIABLE TABLE
130    REM           COUNT = FOR-NEXT LOOP CONTROL VARIABLE
140    REM           NUM1, NUM2, NUM3 = INPUT NUMERIC VARIABLES
150    REM
160    REM ****** INITIALIZATION SECTION
170    OPEN "A:CH9-3X.TXT" FOR OUTPUT AS #1
180    REM
190    REM ****** PROCESS SECTION
200    FOR COUNT = 1 TO 3
210      READ NUM1, NUM2, NUM3
220      WRITE #1, NUM1, NUM2, NUM3
230    NEXT COUNT
240    REM
250    REM ****** OUTPUT SECTION
260    PRINT "THE END"
270    REM
280    REM ****** DATA SECTION
290    DATA 10500, 600, 700
300    DATA 20600, 700, 800
310    DATA 30700, 800, 900
320    REM
330    REM ****** TERMINATION SECTION
340    CLOSE #1
350    END
Ok
RUN
THE END
Ok
```

**Figure 9–8**
A Program that Creates CH9-3X.TXT

When you run this program, nothing is printed, because you wrote the data to the file CH9-4X.TXT. To see the contents of CH9-4X.TXT, exit BASIC by typing *SYSTEM*, and then type

*TYPE A:CH9-4X.TXT*

You will see the following listing:

"SUSAN SHAY", "BUSINESS", 3.85
"KIM BROWN", "COMPUTER", 2.6
"ED STRONG", "MATH", 4

## 9–6
## READING A FILE MORE THAN ONCE

After a file is read, you must use the CLOSE # command to position the data pointer at the beginning of the file. This allows the file to be read again.

```
A:\>TYPE CH9-3X.TXT
10500,600,700
20600,700,800
30700,800,900

A:\>
```

**Figure 9–9**
A Listing of CH9-3X.TXT

```
100     REM   ** THIS PROGRAM PRODUCES FILE CH9-3Y.TXT **
110     REM
120     REM ****** VARIABLE TABLE
130     REM          COUNT = FOR-NEXT LOOP CONTROL VARIABLE
140     REM          WORD1$, WORD2$, WORD3$ = INPUT STRING VARIABLES
150     REM          NUM = INPUT NUMERIC VARIABLE
160     REM
170     REM ****** INITIALIZATION SECTION
180     OPEN "A:CH9-3Y.TXT" FOR OUTPUT AS #1
190     REM
200     REM ****** PROCESS SECTION
210     FOR COUNT = 1 TO 3
220       READ WORD1$,WORD2$, WORD3$,NUM
230       WRITE #1, WORD1$,WORD2$,WORD3$,NUM
240     NEXT COUNT
250     REM
260     REM ****** OUTPUT SECTION
270     PRINT "THE END"
280     REM
290     REM ****** DATA SECTION
300     DATA RTI, LONDON, T.V., 1000
310     DATA MRY, PARIS, REFRIGERATOR, 2000
320     DATA RTN, DENVER, CALCULATOR, 2500
330     REM
340     REM ****** TERMINATION SECTION
350     CLOSE #1
360     END
Ok
RUN
THE END
Ok
```

**Figure 9–10**
A Program that Creates CH9-3Y.TXT

The program shown in figure 9–13 shows this process. The program reads the data from CH9-1X.TXT twice. The first time, the program creates a new file called CH9-5X.TXT. The second time, the program reads the same data and creates a new file called CH9-5Z.TXT.

## 9–7

## FORMATTING A DATA FILE

To format data written to a data file, you can use the PRINT # USING command. The general format of this command is as follows:

PRINT # file designator, USING FORMAT, output list

**Figure 9–11**
A Listing of CH9-3Y.TXT

```
A:\>TYPE CH9-3Y.TXT
"RTI","LONDON","T.V.",1000
"MRY","PARIS","REFRIGERATOR",2000
"RTN","DENVER","CALCULATOR",2500

A:\>
```

```
100     REM THIS PROGRAM READS FROM PERMANENT FILE CH9-1X.TXT
110     REM AND GENERATES A NEW CH9-1X.TXT WHICH WILL BE
120     REM CALLED CH9-4X.TXT.
130     REM
140     REM ****** VARIABLE TABLE
150     REM           COUNT = FOR-NEXT LOOP CONTROL VARIABLE
160     REM           WORD1$, WORD2$ = STRING VARIABLES
170     REM           NUM = NUMERIC VARIABLE
180     REM
190     REM ****** INITIALIZATION SECTION
200     OPEN "A:CH9-1X.TXT" FOR INPUT AS #1
210     OPEN "A:CH9-4X.TXT" FOR OUTPUT AS #2
220     REM
230     REM ****** PROCESS SECTION
240     FOR COUNT = 1 TO 3
250       INPUT #1,WORD1$,WORD2$,NUM
260       WRITE #2,WORD1$,WORD2$,NUM
270     NEXT COUNT
280     REM
290     REM ****** TERMINATION SECTION
300     CLOSE ALL
310     END
Ok
RUN
Ok


A:\>TYPE CH9-4X.TXT
"SUSAN SHAY","BUSINESS",3.85
"KIM BROWN","COMPUTER",2.6
"ED STRONG","MATH.",4

A:\>
```

**Figure 9–12**

A Program to Read from a File and Create Another File

where file designator is the number of a particular file, format is the image of the format line, and output list is a list of the variables to be printed in sequential order and separated by commas.

The general rules for PRINT USING statements apply. (See Chapter 5 for more information on PRINT USING statements.)

Figure 9–14 shows a program that writes examples of all types of PRINT USING statements into file CH9-6X.TXT.

## 9–8

## USING DATA FILES AND TABLES

To exchange data between tables and data files you don't need to learn any new commands. Figures 9–15 and 9–16 show programs that illustrate these operations.

The program shown in figure 9–15 reads data items from the data file CH9-7X.TXT into tables DATA1 and DATA2. The program shown in figure 9–16 reads data from tables DATA1 and DATA2 (CH9-7X.TXT) and writes the contents of these tables into data file CH9-8X.TXT.

The program shown in figure 9–17 creates CH9-7X.TXT. Figure 9–18 displays a listing of CH9-7X.TXT.

Figure 9–19 shows a program that fills table DATA3 from data file CH9-7X.TXT and writes the contents of this table into data file CH9-9X.TXT.

```
100     REM THIS PROGRAM READS FROM THE PERMANENT FILE CH9-1X.TXT
110     REM AND GENERATES A NEW FILE CALLED CH9-5X.TXT.
120     REM THE SECOND TIME, THE SAME FILE WILL BE READ
130     REM AND A NEW FILE WILL BE GENERATED WHICH WILL
140     REM BE CALLED CH9-5Z.TXT.
150     REM
160     REM ****** VARIABLE TABLE
170     REM          COUNT = FOR-NEXT LOOP CONTROL VARIABLE
180     REM          WORD1$, WORD2$ = STRING VARIABLES
190     REM          NUM = NUMERIC VARIABLE
200     REM
210     REM ****** INITIALIZATION SECTION
220     OPEN "A:CH9-1X.TXT" FOR INPUT AS #1
230     OPEN "A:CH9-5X.TXT" FOR OUTPUT AS #2
240     REM
250     REM ****** PROCESS SECTION
260     FOR COUNT = 1 TO 3
270        INPUT #1,WORD1$,WORD2$,NUM
280        WRITE #2,WORD1$,WORD2$,NUM
290     NEXT COUNT
300     CLOSE #1
310     REM
320     OPEN "A:CH9-1X.TXT" FOR INPUT AS #1
330     OPEN "A:CH9-5Z.TXT" FOR OUTPUT AS #3
340     FOR COUNT = 1 TO 3
350        INPUT #1,WORD1$,WORD2$,NUM
360        WRITE #3,WORD1$,WORD2$,NUM
370     NEXT COUNT
380     REM
390     REM ****** TE
400     CLOSE ALL
410     END


A:\>TYPE CH9-5X.TXT
"SUSAN SHAY","BUSINESS",3.85
"KIM BROWN","COMPUTER",2.6
"ED STRONG","MATH.",4
A:\>TYPE CH9-5Z.TXT
"SUSAN SHAY","BUSINESS",3.85
"KIM BROWN","COMPUTER",2.6
"ED STRONG","MATH.",4

A:\>
```

**Figure 9–13**
A Program that Reads from a File Twice

```
100     REM THIS PROGRAM GENERATES A FORMATTED FILE CALLED CH9-6X.TXT.
110     REM
120     REM ****** VARIABLE TABLE
130     REM           NUM1, NUM2, NUM3 = INPUT VARIABLES
140     REM           WORD1$, WORD2$ = INPUT STRING VARIABLES
150     REM
160     REM ****** INITIALIZATION SECTION
170     OPEN "A:CH9-6X.TXT" FOR OUTPUT AS #1
180     LET NUM1 = 5267
190     LET NUM2 = -999.99
200     LET NUM3 = 1296540!
210     LET WORD1$ = "BASIC"
220     LET WORD2$ = "BIDGOLI-LOIS"
230     REM
240     REM ****** PROCESS SECTION
250     PRINT #1, "INTEGER   ";
260     PRINT #1, USING "#######,";NUM1
270     PRINT #1, "DECIMAL   ";
280     PRINT #1, USING "####.##";NUM2
290     PRINT #1, "EXPONENTIAL  ";
300     PRINT #1, USING "##.##^^^^";NUM3
310     PRINT #1, "ALPHANUMERIC   ";
320     PRINT #1, WORD1$
330     PRINT #1, "LITERAL   ";
340     PRINT #1, USING "\            \";WORD2$
350     REM
360     REM ****** TERMINATION SECTION
370     CLOSE #1
380     PRINT "END"
390     END
Ok
RUN
END
Ok


A:\>TYPE CH9-6X.TXT
 INTEGER     5,267
 DECIMAL   -999.99
 EXPONENTIAL   1.30E+06
 ALPHANUMERIC   BASIC
 LITERAL   BIDGOLI-LOIS

A:\>
```

**Figure 9–14**

Generating a Formatted File

**Figure 9–15**

Reading from a Data File into a Matrix

```
100    REM THIS PROGRAM READS DATA FROM THE DATA FILE
110    REM CH9-7X.TXT INTO MATRIX DATA1 AND DATA2.
120    REM
130    REM ****** VARIABLE TABLE
140    REM           COUNT1 = FOR-NEXT LOOP CONTROL VARIABLE
150    REM           COUNT2 = FOR-NEXT LOOP CONTROL VARIABLE
160    REM
170    REM ****** MATRIX TABLE
180    REM           DATA1(11,2) = FILE OUTPUT DATA MATRIX
190    REM           DATA2(3,3) = FILE OUTPUT DATA MATRIX
200    REM
210    REM ****** INITIALIZATION SECTION
220    DIM DATA1(11,2), DATA2(3,3)
230    OPEN "A:CH9-7X.TXT" FOR INPUT AS #1
240    REM
250    REM           PROCESS SECTION
260    FOR COUNT1 = 1 TO 11
270      FOR COUNT2 = 1 TO 2
280        INPUT #1,DATA1(COUNT1,COUNT2)
290      NEXT COUNT2
300    NEXT COUNT1
310    REM
320    PRINT "THE CONTENTS OF THE FIRST MATRIX [DATA1(11,2)]:"
330    FOR COUNT1 = 1 TO 11
340      PRINT DATA1(COUNT1,1),DATA1(COUNT1,2)
350    NEXT COUNT1
360    REM
370    FOR COUNT1 = 1 TO 3
380      FOR COUNT2 = 1 TO 3
390        INPUT #1,DATA2(COUNT1,COUNT2)
400      NEXT COUNT2
410    NEXT COUNT1
420    PRINT "THE CONTENTS OF THE SECOND MATRIX [DATA2(3,3)]:"
430    FOR COUNT1 = 1 TO 3
440      PRINT DATA2(COUNT1,1),DATA2(COUNT1,2),DATA2(COUNT1,3)
450    NEXT COUNT1
460    REM
470    REM ****** TERMINATION SECTION
480    PRINT "END OF PROGRAM"
490    CLOSE #1
500    END
Ok
RUN
THE CONTENTS OF THE FIRST MATRIX [DATA1(11,2)]:
 5              10
 15             20
 25             30
 35             40
 45             50
 55             60
 65             70
 75             80
 85             90
 95             96
 97             98
THE CONTENTS OF THE SECOND MATRIX [DATA2(3,3)]:
 99            100            101
 102           103            104
 105           106            107
END OF PROGRAM
```

```
100     REM THIS PROGRAM COPIES THE CONTENTS OF TABLES DATA1 AND
110     REM DATA2 TO DATA FILE CH9-8X.TXT.
120     REM
130     REM ******* VARIABLE TABLE
140     REM         COUNT1 = FOR-NEXT LOOP CONTROL VARIABLE
150     REM         COUNT2 = FOR-NEXT LOOP CONTROL VARIABLE
160     REM
170     REM ******* MATRIX TABLE
180     REM         DATA1(11,2) = FILE DATA MATRIX
190     REM         DATA2(3,3) = FILE DATA MATRIX
200     REM
210     REM ******* INITIALIZATION SECTION
220     REM INPUT FILE DATA IS IN THE DATA FILE CH9-7X.TXT.
230     DIM DATA1(11,2), DATA2(3,3)
240     OPEN "A:CH9-7X.TXT" FOR INPUT AS #1
250     OPEN "A:CH9-8X.TXT" FOR OUTPUT AS #2
260     REM
270     REM ******* PROCESS SECTION
280     FOR COUNT1 = 1 TO 11
290       FOR COUNT2 = 1 TO 2
300         INPUT #1, DATA1(COUNT1,COUNT2)
310       NEXT COUNT2
320     NEXT COUNT1
330     REM
340     FOR COUNT1 = 1 TO 3
350       FOR COUNT2 = 1 TO 3
360         INPUT #1, DATA2(COUNT1,COUNT2)
370       NEXT COUNT2
380     NEXT COUNT1
390     REM
400     FOR COUNT1 = 1 TO 11
410       WRITE #2,DATA1(COUNT1,1),DATA1(COUNT1,2)
420     NEXT COUNT1
430     REM
440     FOR COUNT1 = 1 TO 3
450       WRITE #2, DATA2(COUNT1,1),DATA2(COUNT1,2),DATA2(COUNT1,3)
460     NEXT COUNT1
470     REM
480     REM ******* TERMINATION SECTION
490     CLOSE #1
500     CLOSE #2
510     PRINT "TABLES WRITTEN"
520     END
Ok
RUN
TABLES WRITTEN
Ok

A:\>TYPE CH9-8X.TXT
5,10
15,20
25,30
35,40
45,50
55,60
65,70
75,80
85,90
95,96
97,98
99,100,101
102,103,104
105,106,107

A:\>
```

**Figure 9-16**
Reading from Tables into a Data File

```
100     REM THIS PROGRAM PRODUCES FILE CH9-7X.TXT.
110     REM
120     REM ****** VARIABLE TABLE
130     REM          COUNT = FOR-NEXT LOOP CONTROL VARIABLE
140     REM          NUM1, NUM2, NUM3, NUM4, NUM5, NUM6 = INPUT VARIABLES
150     REM
160     REM ****** INITIALIZATION SECTION
170     OPEN "A:CH9-7X.TXT" FOR OUTPUT AS #1
180     REM
190     REM ****** PROCESS SECTION
200     FOR COUNT = 1 TO 5
210       REM
220       READ NUM1, NUM2, NUM3, NUM4, NUM5, NUM6
230       WRITE #1, NUM1, NUM2, NUM3, NUM4, NUM5, NUM6
240     NEXT COUNT
250     READ NUM1
260     WRITE #1, NUM1
270     REM
280     REM ****** TERMINATION SECTION
290     CLOSE #1
300     REM
310     REM ****** OUTPUT SECTION
320     PRINT "MATRICES WRITTEN"
330     REM
340     REM ****** DATA SECTION
350     DATA 5, 10, 15, 20, 25,30
360     DATA 35, 40, 45, 50, 55, 60
370     DATA 65, 70, 75, 80, 85, 90
380     DATA 95, 96, 97, 98, 99, 100
390     DATA 101, 102, 103, 104, 105, 106
400     DATA 107
410     END
Ok
RUN
MATRICES WRITTEN
Ok
```

**Figure 9–17**
The Program that Creates CH9-7X.TXT

## 9–9

### ADDING DATA TO AN EXISTING FILE

You use the APPEND # command to add additional data to an existing file. The general format for this command is as follows:

OPEN "file.txt" FOR APPEND AS #

An APPEND # statement places a particular data file into write mode and permits a WRITE # statement to append new data to the data already in

**Figure 9–18**
A Listing of CH9-7X.TXT

```
A:\>TYPE CH9-7X.TXT
5,10,15,20,25,30
35,40,45,50,55,60
65,70,75,80,85,90
95,96,97,98,99,100
101,102,103,104,105,106
107

A:\>
```

```
100     REM THIS PROGRAM FILLS UP TABLE DATA3 FROM DATA
110     REM FILE CH9-7X.TXT, THEN COPIES THE CONTENTS OF
120     REM THIS TABLE TO DATA FILE CH9-9X.TXT.
130     REM
140     REM ****** VARIABLE TABLE
150     REM          C1, C2 = FOR-NEXT LOOP CONTROL VARIABLES
160     REM
170     REM ****** MATRIX TABLE
180     REM          DATA3(5,5) = FILE DATA MATRIX VARIABLE
190     REM
200     REM ****** INITIALIZATION SECTION
210     OPEN "A:CH9-7X.TXT" FOR INPUT AS #1
220     OPEN "A:CH9-9X.TXT" FOR OUTPUT AS #2
230     DIM DATA3(5,5)
240     FOR C1 = 1 TO 5
250       FOR C2 = 1 TO 5
260         INPUT #1,DATA3(C1,C2)
270       NEXT C2
280       WRITE #2,DATA3(C1,1),DATA3(C1,2),DATA3(C1,3),DATA3(C1,4),DATA3(C1,5)
290     NEXT C1
300     REM
310     REM ****** TERMINATION SECTION
320     PRINT  "TABLE DATA3 WRITTEN"
330     CLOSE ALL
340     END
Ok
RUN
TABLE DATA3 WRITTEN
Ok


A:\>TYPE CH9-9X.TXT
5,10,15,20,25
30,35,40,45,50
55,60,65,70,75
80,85,90,95,96
97,98,99,100,101

A:\>
```

**Figure 9–19**
Reading a Data File into a Table and Copying the Table into a File

that particular file. After the APPEND # statement is executed, the data pointer
for the designated file is moved past the last data item in the file, and the data file
is placed in write mode so that it can accept more data items.

The program in figure 9–20 shows how the APPEND command works.
This program reads the data for four salespeople and then appends this data to
the permanent file CH9-10X.TXT. The program shown in figure 9–21 creates
CH9-10X.TXT. Figure 9–22 shows a listing of CH9-10X.TXT before the new
data have been appended.

## 9–10
## THE END OF FILE STATEMENT

The purpose of the EOF command is to test for the end of a data file. If the end
of the data file is encountered, program control is transferred to the line
following the WEND statement. The general format for the EOF command is as
follows:

WHILE NOT EOF(#)

```
100    REM THIS PROGRAM APPENDS FOUR MORE SALEPERSON'S INFORMATION
110    REM TO THE PERMANENT FILE CH9-10X.TXT.
120    REM
130    REM ****** VARIABLE TABLE
140    REM           COUNT = FOR-NEXT LOOP CONTROL VARIABLE
150    REM           WORD1$, WORD2$, WORD3$ = STRING DATA TO FILL CH9-10X.TXT
160    REM
170    REM ****** INITIALIZATION SECTION
180    OPEN "A:CH9-10X.TXT" FOR APPEND AS #1
190    REM
200    REM ****** PROCESS SECTION
210    FOR COUNT = 1 TO 4
220      READ  WORD1$, WORD2$, WORD3$
230      WRITE #1, WORD1$, WORD2$, WORD3$
240    NEXT COUNT
250    REM
260    REM ****** TERMINATION SECTION
270    CLOSE #1
280    REM
290    REM ****** DATA SECTION
300    DATA SANDY SMITH, FT. COLLINS, "519-62-1761"
310    DATA CAROL THOMAS, PORTLAND, "191-19-1981"
320    DATA MARY JACKSON, PORTLAND, "215-19-8112"
330    DATA LARRY JOHNSON, FOREST GROVE, "218-11-1715"
340    END
Ok
RUN
Ok


A:\>TYPE CH9-10X.TXT
"JACK JACKLYN","PORTLAND","524-13-1921"
"SUSAN SUSANT","DENVER","524-19-6200"
"ARLYN ARTIST","WASHINGTON","524-24-6211"
"SANDY SMITH","FT. COLLINS","519-62-1761"
"CAROL THOMAS","PORTLAND","191-19-1981"
"MARY JACKSON","PORTLAND","215-19-8112"
"LARRY JOHNSON","FOREST GROVE","218-11-1715"

A:\>
```

**Figure 9–20**
The APPEND Command in Action

.
WEND
or
WHILE EOF(#)=0
.

WEND

The program in figure 9–23 reads from the permanent file CH9-1X.TXT and checks for the end of the data file. When the program reaches the end of the data file, the program prints an appropriate message.

```
100     REM THIS PROGRAM PRODUCES FILE CH9-10X.TXT.
110     REM
120     REM ****** VARIABLE TABLE
130     REM          COUNT = FOR-NEXT LOOP CONTROL VARIABLE
140     REM          WORD1$, WORD2$, WORD3$ = INPUT STRING VARIABLES
150     REM
160     REM ****** INITIALIZATION SECTION
170     OPEN "A:CH9-10X.TXT" FOR OUTPUT AS #1
180     REM
190     REM ****** PROCESS SECTION
200     FOR COUNT = 1 TO 3
210       READ WORD1$, WORD2$, WORD3$
220       WRITE #1, WORD1$, WORD2$, WORD3$
230     NEXT COUNT
240     REM
250     REM ****** TERMINATION SECTION
260     CLOSE #1
270     REM
280     REM ****** OUTPUT SECTION
290     PRINT "END OF CH9-10X.TXT"
300     REM
310     REM ****** DATA SECTION
320     DATA "JACK JACKLYN", "PORTLAND", "524-13-1921"
330     DATA "SUSAN SUSANT", "DENVER", "524-19-6200"
340     DATA "ARLYN ARTIST", "WASHINGTON", "524-24-6211"
350     END
Ok
RUN
END OF CH9-10X.TXT
Ok
```

**Figure 9–21**
The Program that Creates CH9-10X.TXT

## 9–11
## SIMPLE OPERATIONS WITH FILES

You have learned enough about sequential files to perform some applications. When you set up files, you can perform many different operations. You can, for example, add new information to an existing file, delete information from an existing file, modify the contents of an existing file, or merge several files.

Suppose that we have copied a small portion of the customer file of Community National Bank. We call this file CH9-12X.TXT. Figure 9–24 shows the program that generates this file. Figure 9–25 shows a listing of CH9-12X.TXT. Each line of this data file contains a customer name, account number, and address. In the following sections, you perform some simple operations with this file.

```
A:\>TYPE CH9-10X.TXT
"JACK JACKLYN","PORTLAND","524-13-1921"
"SUSAN SUSANT","DENVER","524-19-6200"
"ARLYN ARTIST","WASHINGTON","524-24-6211"

A:\>
```

**Figure 9–22**
A Listing of CH9-10X.TXT Before Appending New Data

```
100     REM THIS PROGRAM READS FROM DATA FILE CH9-1X.TXT AND
110     REM DISPLAYS THE CONTENTS OF THIS FILE.  AFTER REACHING THE
120     REM BOTTOM OF THE FILE, THE PROGRAM WILL DISPLAY AN
130     REM APPROPRIATE MESSAGE.
140     REM
150     REM ****** VARIABLE TABLE
160     REM            WORD1$, WORD2$ = STRING DATA FROM FILE CH9-1X.TXT
170     REM            NUM = NUMERIC DATA FROM FILE CH9-1X.TXT
180     REM
190     REM ****** INITIALIZATION SECTION
200     OPEN "A:CH9-1X.TXT" FOR INPUT AS #1
210     REM
220     REM ****** PROCESS SECTION
230     WHILE EOF(1) = 0
240       INPUT #1, WORD1$, WORD2$, NUM
250       PRINT WORD1$, WORD2$, NUM
260     WEND
270     REM
280     REM ****** TERMINATION SECTION
290     PRINT "SORRY, YOU HAVE REACHED THE BOTTOM OF THE DATA FILE."
300     CLOSE #1
310     END
Ok
RUN
SUSAN SHAY      BUSINESS        3.85
KIM BROWN       COMPUTER        2.6
ED STRONG       MATH.           4
SORRY, YOU HAVE REACHED THE BOTTOM OF THE DATA FILE.
Ok
```

**Figure 9–23**
Checking for the End of a File

## 9–11–1      Adding Information

You can use the APPEND # command to append the new information to an existing file. Another method is to generate a new file and then copy the old file and the new information to this new file.

Suppose that Community National Bank, through an advertising campaign, has attracted three new customers. The information for these customers is as follows:

| Name | Address |
|---|---|
| Bev Bowen | 161921, 911 S.E. March, Portland |
| Kim Addams | 291827, 919 S.W. May, Beaverton |
| Camely Vigen | 691821, 219 S.E. Fun, Forest Grove |

The program shown in figure 9–26 creates the new file CH9-12Y.TXT, which contains the old file CH9-12X.TXT and the new information.

## 9–11–2      Deleting Information

One way of deleting information from an existing file is to create a new file and then copy the information you want from the old file to this new file, skipping the items that you want to delete.

Suppose that Community National Bank has been informed that three of the customers listed in CH9-12X.TXT have moved to another state. These

```
100     REM THIS PROGRAM WILL CONSTRUCT THE FILE CH9-12X.TXT.
110     REM
120     REM ******* VARIABLE TABLE
130     REM             COUNT = FOR-NEXT LOOP CONTROL VARIABLE
140     REM             WORD1$, WORD2$ = INPUT STRING VARIABLES
150     REM             NUM = INPUT NUMERIC VARIABLE
160     REM
170     REM ******* INITIALIZATION SECTION
180     OPEN "A:CH9-12X.TXT" FOR OUTPUT AS #1
190     REM
200     REM ******* PROCESS SECTION
210     FOR COUNT = 1 TO 10
220        READ WORD1$, NUM, WORD2$
230        WRITE #1, WORD1$, NUM, WORD2$
240     NEXT COUNT
250     REM
260     REM
270     REM ******* OUTPUT SECTION
280     PRINT "FILE TRANSFER ACCOMPLISHED."
290     REM
300     REM ******* TERMINATION SECTION
310     CLOSE #1
320     REM
330     REM ******* DATA SECTION
340     DATA JACKSON JAKS, 961187, "163 S. W. PARK, BEAVERTON"
350     DATA SUSAN ATRATY, 761198, "291 N. E. BROADWAY, PORTLAND"
360     DATA JOANN PESON, 911181, "111 N. W. JACKSON, FOREST GROVE"
370     DATA H. BIDGOLI, 156721, "211 S. W. CLAY, PORTLAND"
380     DATA G. BROWN, 911729, "219 S. W. HALL, PORTLAND"
390     DATA CHAR THOMAS, 219721, "921 S. W. 6th, PORTLAND"
400     DATA RID SMART, 621719, "711 S. W. CLAY, BEAVERTON"
410     DATA DOUG HAPPY, 961719, "901 S. W. CIRCLE, LAKE OSWEGO"
420     DATA ROBERT BURN, 191716, "911 S. E. OVAL, BEAVERTON"
430     DATA JACKY HUSTAN, 915511, "620 S. E. CRY, PORTLAND"
440     END
Ok
RUN
FILE TRANSFER ACCOMPLISHED.
Ok
```

**Figure 9–24**
The Program that Generates CH9-12X.TXT

```
A:\>TYPE CH9-12X.TXT
"JACKSON JAKS",961187,"163 S. W. PARK, BEAVERTON"
"SUSAN ATRATY",761198,"291 N. E. BROADWAY, PORTLAND"
"JOANN PESON",911181,"111 N. W. JACKSON, FOREST GROVE"
"H. BIDGOLI",156721,"211 S. W. CLAY, PORTLAND"
"G. BROWN",911729,"219 S. W. HALL, PORTLAND"
"CHAR THOMAS",219721,"921 S. W. 6th, PORTLAND"
"RID SMART",621719,"711 S. W. CLAY, BEAVERTON"
"DOUG HAPPY",961719,"901 S. W. CIRCLE, LAKE OSWEGO"
"ROBERT BURN",191716,"911 S. E. OVAL, BEAVERTON"
"JACKY HUSTAN",915511,"620 S. E. CRY, PORTLAND"

A:\>
```

**Figure 9–25**
A Listing of CH9-12X.TXT

```
100    REM THIS PROGRAM UPDATES THE CUSTOMERS' FILE FOR THE COMMUNITY
110    REM NATIONAL BANK BY ADDING NEW INFORMATION TO THIS FILE.
120    REM
130    REM ****** VARIABLE TABLE
140    REM            WORDFILE1$, WORDFILE2$ = FILE STRING VARIABLES
150    REM            NUMFILE = FILE NUMERIC VARIABLE
160    REM            WORDLINE1$, WORDLINE2$ = DATA LINE STRING VARIABLES
170    REM            NUMLINE = DATA LINE NUMERIC VARIABLE
180    REM
190    REM ****** INITIALIZATION SECTION
200    OPEN "A:CH9-12X.TXT" FOR INPUT AS #1
210    OPEN "A:CH9-12Y.TXT" FOR OUTPUT AS #2
220    REM
230    REM ****** PROCESS SECTION
240    WHILE EOF(1) = 0
250      INPUT #1, WORDFILE1$, NUMFILE, WORDFILE2$
260      WRITE #2, WORDFILE1$, NUMFILE, WORDFILE2$
270    WEND
280    REM
290    READ WORDLINE1$, NUMLINE, WORDLINE2$
300    IF WORDLINE1$ = "FLAG" THEN 350
310    WRITE #2, WORDLINE1$, NUMLINE, WORDLINE2$
320    GOTO 290
330    REM
340    REM ****** TERMINATION SECTION
350    CLOSE #1
360    CLOSE #2
370    REM
380    REM ****** DATA SECTION
390    DATA BEV BOWEN, 161921, "911 S. E. MARCH, PORTLAND"
400    DATA KIM ADDAMS, 291827, "919 S. W. MAY, BEAVERTON"
410    DATA CAMELY VIGEN, 691821, "219 S. E. FUN, FOREST GROVE"
420    DATA FLAG,1234,WHOOPS
430    END
Ok
RUN
Ok


A:\>TYPE CH9-12Y.TXT
"JACKSON JAKS",961187,"163 S. W. PARK, BEAVERTON"
"SUSAN ATRATY",761198,"291 N. E. BROADWAY, PORTLAND"
"JOANN PESON",911181,"111 N. W. JACKSON, FOREST GROVE"
"H. BIDGOLI",156721,"211 S. W. CLAY, PORTLAND"
"G. BROWN",911729,"219 S. W. HALL, PORTLAND"
"CHAR THOMAS",219721,"921 S. W. 6th, PORTLAND"
"RID SMART",621719,"711 S. W. CLAY, BEAVERTON"
"DOUG HAPPY",961719,"901 S. W. CIRCLE, LAKE OSWEGO"
"ROBERT BURN",191716,"911 S. E. OVAL, BEAVERTON"
"JACKY HUSTAN",915511,"620 S. E. CRY, PORTLAND"
"BEV BOWEN",161921,"911 S. E. MARCH, PORTLAND"
"KIM ADDAMS",291827,"919 S. W. MAY, BEAVERTON"
"CAMELY VIGEN",691821,"219 S. E. FUN, FOREST GROVE"

A:\>
```

**Figure 9–26**
Adding More Information to an Existing File

172

customers must be deleted from the existing file. Write a program that performs this task and provides a new file (CH9-13X.TXT) showing the remaining customers. The customers who must be deleted have the following account numbers:

761198
219721
915511

Figure 9–27 shows the program that performs this task.

## Changing Information                                                          9–11–3

To change some of the information in a particular file, you can create a new file and then copy the information from the old file, making the necessary changes.

```
100    REM THIS PROGRAM UPDATES THE CUSTOMERS' FILE FOR THE COMMUNITY
110    REM NATIONAL BANK BY DELETING SOME INFORMATION FROM THE FILE.
120    REM
130    REM ****** VARIABLE TABLE
140    REM         WORD1$, WORD2$ = FILE STRING DATA
150    REM         NUM1 = FILE NUMERIC DATA
160    REM
170    REM ****** INITIALIZATION SECTION
180    OPEN "A:CH9-12X.TXT" FOR INPUT AS #1
190    OPEN "A:CH9-13X.TXT" FOR OUTPUT AS #2
200    REM
210    REM ****** PROCESS SECTION
220    WHILE EOF(1) = 0
230      INPUT #1, WORD1$,NUM1,WORD2$
240      IF NUM1 = 761198! THEN 280
250      IF NUM1 = 219721! THEN 280
260      IF NUM1 = 915511! THEN 280
270      WRITE #2, WORD1$, NUM1, WORD2$
280    WEND
290    REM
300    REM ****** TERMINATION SECTION
310    CLOSE #1
320    CLOSE #2
330    PRINT "JOB FINISHED"
340    END
Ok
RUN
JOB FINISHED
Ok


A:\>TYPE CH9-13X.TXT
"JACKSON JAKS",961187,"163 S. W. PARK, BEAVERTON"
"JOANN PESON",911181,"111 N. W. JACKSON, FOREST GROVE"
"H. BIDGOLI",156721,"211 S. W. CLAY, PORTLAND"
"G. BROWN",911729,"219 S. W. HALL, PORTLAND"
"RID SMART",621719,"711 S. W. CLAY, BEAVERTON"
"DOUG HAPPY",961719,"901 S. W. CIRCLE, LAKE OSWEGO"
"ROBERT BURN",191716,"911 S. E. OVAL, BEAVERTON"

A:\>
```

**Figure 9–27**

Deleting Information from an Existing File

Suppose that three of Community National Bank's customers listed in CH9-12X.TXT have changed their addresses. Write a program that updates the customer file and provides a new file (CH9-14X.TXT). The following customers have changed their addresses:

```
100    REM THIS PROGRAM UPDATES THE CUSTOMERS' FILE FOR THE COMMUNITY
110    REM NATIONAL BANK BY CHANGING SOME INFORMATION ON THE
120    REM EXISTING FILE.
130    REM
140    REM ****** VARIABLE TABLE
150    REM          WORD1$, WORD2$ = BANK FILE STRING DATA VARIABLES
160    REM          NUM1# = BANK FILE NUMERIC DATA VARIABLE
170    REM
180    REM ****** INITIALIZATION SECTION
190    OPEN "A:CH9-12X.TXT" FOR INPUT AS #1
200    OPEN "A:CH9-14X.TXT" FOR OUTPUT AS #2
210    REM
220    REM ****** PROCESS SECTION
230    WHILE EOF(1) = 0
240      INPUT #1, WORD1$, NUM1#, WORD2$
250      IF WORD1$ = "JOANN PESON" THEN 290
260      IF WORD1$ = "RID SMART" THEN 310
270      IF WORD1$ = "JACKY HUSTAN" THEN 330
280      GOTO 340
290      WORD2$ = "555 NORTH PAUL, PORTLAND"
300      GOTO 340
310      WORD2$ = "299 S. W. JACKSON, LAKE OSWEGO"
320      GOTO 340
330      WORD2$ = "279 N. E. GRASHANI, PORTLAND"
340      WRITE #2, WORD1$, NUM1#, WORD2$
350    WEND
360    REM
370    REM ****** TERMINATION SECTION
380    CLOSE #1
390    CLOSE #2
400    PRINT "CHANGES MADE"
410    END
Ok
RUN
CHANGES MADE
Ok


A:\>TYPE CH9-14X.TXT
"JACKSON JAKS",961187,"163 S. W. PARK, BEAVERTON"
"SUSAN ATRATY",761198,"291 N. E. BROADWAY, PORTLAND"
"JOANN PESON",911181,"555 NORTH PAUL, PORTLAND"
"H. BIDGOLI",156721,"211 S. W. CLAY, PORTLAND"
"G. BROWN",911729,"219 S. W. HALL, PORTLAND"
"CHAR THOMAS",219721,"921 S. W. 6th, PORTLAND"
"RID SMART",621719,"299 S. W. JACKSON, LAKE OSWEGO"
"DOUG HAPPY",961719,"901 S. W. CIRCLE, LAKE OSWEGO"
"ROBERT BURN",191716,"911 S. E. OVAL, BEAVERTON"
"JACKY HUSTAN",915511,"279 N. E. GRASHANI, PORTLAND"

A:\>
```

**Figure 9–28**

Changing Information in an Existing File

```
100    REM CONSTRUCT CH9-15X.TXT.
110    REM
120    REM ****** VARIABLE TABLE
130    REM          COUNTER = FOR-NEXT LOOP CONTROL VARIABLE
140    REM          CUSTOMER$ = CUSTOMER NAME
150    REM          ACCNUMBER# = CUSTOMER ACCOUNT NUMBER
160    REM          ADDRESS$ = CUSTOMER ADDRESS
170    REM
180    OPEN "A:CH9-15X.TXT" FOR OUTPUT AS #1
190    FOR COUNTER = 1 TO 5
200      READ CUSTOMER$,ACCNUMBER#,ADDRESS$
210      WRITE #1, CUSTOMER$,ACCNUMBER#,ADDRESS$
220    NEXT COUNTER
230    CLOSE #1
240    DATA ADAM ATTAYAN, 968651, "799 S. W. GILBERT, PORTLAND"
250    DATA SUSAN JONES, 761999, "266 S. W. MARK, BEAVERTON"
260    DATA DEBBIE SHY, 976666, "211 S. W. TARK, LAKE OSWEGO"
270    DATA MARY THOMAS, 961752, "911 S. W. HALL, GRESHAM"
280    DATA KATHY FRIEND, 255666, "777 S. W. COLLEGE, PORTLAND"
290    END
Ok
RUN
Ok
```

**Figure 9–29**
The Program that Creates CH9-15X.TXT

| Name | New Address |
|------|-------------|
| Joann Peson | 555 North Paul, Portland |
| Rid Smart | 299 S.W. Jackson, Lake Oswego |
| Jacky Hustan | 279 N.E. Grashani, Portland |

Figure 9–28 shows the program that performs this task.

## Merging Files                                                                     9–11–4

One way to merge files is to create a new file and then copy all the old files into this new file.

Suppose that Community National Bank is expanding its operations and recently bought two small banks. To update file CH9-12X.TXT, the bank must add the customers of the other two banks to its customer file. Write a program that performs this task and provides the bank with a final listing of its customer file.

The customer list for the first bank has been saved as CH9-15X.TXT. Figure 9–29 shows the program that creates this file. Figure 9–30 is a listing of CH9-15X.TXT.

```
A:\>TYPE CH9-15X.TXT
"ADAM ATTAYAN",968651,"799 S. W. GILBERT, PORTLAND"
"SUSAN JONES",761999,"266 S. W. MARK, BEAVERTON"
"DEBBIE SHY",976666,"211 S. W. TARK, LAKE OSWEGO"
"MARY THOMAS",961752,"911 S. W. HALL, GRESHAM"
"KATHY FRIEND",255666,"777 S. W. COLLEGE, PORTLAND"

A:\>
```

**Figure 9–30**
A Listing of CH9-15X.TXT

**Figure 9–31**
The Program that Creates CH9-15Y.TXT

```
100     REM CONSTRUCT CH9-15Y.TXT.
110     REM
120     REM ****** VARIABLE TABLE
130     REM         COUNTER = FOR-NEXT LOOP CONTROL VARIABLE
140     REM         CUSTOMER$ = CUSTOMER NAME
150     REM         ACCNUMBER = CUSTOMER ACCOUNT NUMBER
160     REM         ADDRESS$ = CUSTOMER ADDRESS
170     REM
180     OPEN "A:CH9-15Y.TXT" FOR OUTPUT AS #1
190     FOR COUNTER= 1 TO 5
200       READ CUSTOMER$, ACCNUMBER, ADDRESS$
210       WRITE #1, CUSTOMER$, ACCNUMBER, ADDRESS$
220     NEXT COUNTER
230     CLOSE #1
240     DATA MAR JACKSON, 791655, "971 S. W. STARK, PORTLAND"
250     DATA JOE HUBBY, 292971, "911 S. W. 66TH, BEAVERTON"
260     DATA JACK FUNTA, 911777, "211 S. W. 76TH, LAKE OSWEGO"
270     DATA SUSAN GRITAN, 551666, "219 N. E. MASON, PORTLAND"
280     DATA KATHY EGAN, 911766, "217 S. E. STARK, PORTLAND"
290     END
Ok
RUN
Ok
```

The customer list for the second bank has been saved as CH9-15Y.TXT. Figure 9–31 displays the program that creates this file, and figure 9–32 shows a listing of CH9-15Y.TXT.

The program shown in figure 9–33 merges these two files with the bank's file, creating the new file CH9-15Z.TXT.

## 9–12
## SORTING FILES

Often, you may want to sort your file in ascending or descending order. To sort a file, you must select a particular key for sorting. You can, for example, sort a customer file alphabetically by first name, or numerically by Social Security number or perhaps by account number.

One way of sorting a file is to read the values of a particular key into an array and then sort that array. Once the array is sorted, you can search a particular file based on the values in the sorted array and then print the matched pairs of data.

Suppose that Community National Bank wants to sort its customer file by customer account number in ascending order. Write a program that sorts the file CH9-12X.TXT and provides a sorted listing of this file (CH9-16X.TXT). Figure 9–34 shows a program that performs this task. Figure 9–35 illustrates the flowchart for this program.

**Figure 9–32**
A Listing of CH9-15Y.TXT

```
A:\>TYPE CH9-15Y.TXT
"MAR JACKSON",791655,"971 S. W. STARK, PORTLAND"
"JOE HUBBY",292971,"911 S. W. 66TH, BEAVERTON"
"JACK FUNTA",911777,"211 S. W. 76TH, LAKE OSWEGO"
"SUSAN GRITAN",551666,"219 N. E. MASON, PORTLAND"
"KATHY EGAN",911766,"217 S. E. STARK, PORTLAND"

A:\>
```

```
100     REM THIS PROGRAM MERGES THREE FILES TOGETHER.
110     REM
120     REM ******* VARIABLE TABLE
130     REM             NAM$ = CUSTOMER NAME
140     REM             NUM1 = CUSTOMER ACCOUNT NUMBER
150     REM             ADDR$ = CUSTOMER ADDRESS
160     REM
170     REM ******* INITIALIZATION SECTION
180     OPEN "A:CH9-12X.TXT" FOR INPUT AS #1
190     OPEN "A:CH9-15X.TXT" FOR INPUT AS #2
200     OPEN "A:CH9-15Z.TXT" FOR OUTPUT AS #3
210     REM
220     REM ******* PROCESS SECTION
230     INPUT #1, NAM$, NUM1, ADDR$
240     WRITE #3, NAM$, NUM1, ADDR$
250     IF EOF(1) THEN 280
260     GOTO 230
270     REM
280     INPUT #2, NAM$, NUM1, ADDR$
290     WRITE #3, NAM$, NUM1, ADDR$
300     IF EOF(2) THEN 330
310     GOTO 280
320     REM
330     CLOSE #1
340     CLOSE #2
350     OPEN "A:CH9-15Y.TXT" FOR INPUT AS #1
360     INPUT #1, NAM$, NUM1, ADDR$
370     WRITE #3, NAM$, NUM1, ADDR$
380     IF EOF(1) THEN 410
390     GOTO 360
400     REM
410     CLOSE #1, #3
420     REM ******* OUTPUT SECTION
430     REM=========================================
440     REM TO PRINT THE MERGED FILE: CH9-15Z.
450     REM=========================================
460     OPEN "A:CH9-15Z.TXT" FOR INPUT AS #1
470     INPUT #1, NAM$, NUM1, ADDR$
480     PRINT NAM$, NUM1, ADDR$
490     IF EOF(1) THEN 530
500     GOTO 470
510     REM
520     REM ******* TERMINATION SECTION
530     CLOSE #1
540     END
Ok
RUN
JACKSON JAKS    961187         163 S.  W.  PARK, BEAVERTON
SUSAN ATRATY    761198         291 N.  E.  BROADWAY, PORTLAND
JOANN PESON     911181         111 N.  W.  JACKSON, FOREST GROVE
H. BIDGOLI      156721         211 S.  W.  CLAY, PORTLAND
G. BROWN        911729         219 S.  W.  HALL, PORTLAND
CHAR THOMAS     219721         921 S.  W.  6th, PORTLAND
RID SMART       621719         711 S.  W.  CLAY, BEAVERTON
DOUG HAPPY      961719         901 S.  W.  CIRCLE, LAKE OSWEGO
ROBERT BURN     191716         911 S.  E.  OVAL, BEAVERTON
JACKY HUSTAN    915511         620 S.  E.  CRY, PORTLAND
ADAM ATTAYAN    968651         799 S.  W.  GILBERT, PORTLAND
SUSAN JONES     761999         266 S.  W.  MARK, BEAVERTON
DEBBIE SHY      976666         211 S.  W.  TARK, LAKE OSWEGO
MARY THOMAS     961752         911 S.  W.  HALL, GRESHAM
KATHY FRIEND    255666         777 S.  W.  COLLEGE, PORTLAND
MAR JACKSON     791655         971 S.  W.  STARK, PORTLAND
```

**Figure 9-33**
Merging Files

```
JOE HUBBY        292971      911 S. W. 66TH, BEAVERTON
JACK FUNTA       911777      211 S. W. 76TH, LAKE OSWEGO
SUSAN GRITAN     551666      219 N. E. MASON, PORTLAND
KATHY EGAN       911766      217 S. E. STARK, PORTLAND
Ok


A:\>TYPE CH9-15Z.TXT
"JACKSON JAKS",961187,"163 S. W. PARK, BEAVERTON"
"SUSAN ATRATY",761198,"291 N. E. BROADWAY, PORTLAND"
"JOANN PESON",911181,"111 N. W. JACKSON, FOREST GROVE"
"H. BIDGOLI",156721,"211 S. W. CLAY, PORTLAND"
"G. BROWN",911729,"219 S. W. HALL, PORTLAND"
"CHAR THOMAS",219721,"921 S. W. 6th, PORTLAND"
"RID SMART",621719,"711 S. W. CLAY, BEAVERTON"
"DOUG HAPPY",961719,"901 S. W. CIRCLE, LAKE OSWEGO"
"ROBERT BURN",191716,"911 S. E. OVAL, BEAVERTON"
"JACKY HUSTAN",915511,"620 S. E. CRY, PORTLAND"
"ADAM ATTAYAN",968651,"799 S. W. GILBERT, PORTLAND"
"SUSAN JONES",761999,"266 S. W. MARK, BEAVERTON"
"DEBBIE SHY",976666,"211 S. W. TARK, LAKE OSWEGO"
"MARY THOMAS",961752,"911 S. W. HALL, GRESHAM"
"KATHY FRIEND",255666,"777 S. W. COLLEGE, PORTLAND"
"MAR JACKSON",791655,"971 S. W. STARK, PORTLAND"
"JOE HUBBY",292971,"911 S. W. 66TH, BEAVERTON"
"JACK FUNTA",911777,"211 S. W. 76TH, LAKE OSWEGO"
"SUSAN GRITAN",551666,"219 N. E. MASON, PORTLAND"
"KATHY EGAN",911766,"217 S. E. STARK, PORTLAND"

A:\>
```

**Figure 9–33**  (Continued)

**Figure 9–34**
Sorting Files

```
100   REM THIS PROGRAM SORTS CH9-12X.TXT FOR THE COMMUNITY NATIONAL BANK.
110   REM THIS PROGRAM CAN HANDLE UP TO 500 CUSTOMERS.  FOR MORE
120   REM THAN 500 THE SIZE OF THE ARRAY MUST BE REDEFINED.
130   REM FIRST WE WILL FILL UP THE ARRAY CUST$ WITH CUSTOMERS' ACCOUNT
140   REM NUMBERS.
150   REM
160   REM ******* VARIABLE TABLE
170   REM        COUNT1, COUNT2, COUNT3 = COUNT CONTROL VARIABLES
180   REM        WORD1$, WORD2$, WORD3$ = FILE STRING DATA
190   REM        TEMP$ = TEMPORARY STRING DATA HOLDER
200   REM
210   REM ******* ARRAY TABLE
220   REM        CUST$(500)
230   REM
240   REM ******* INITIALIZATION SECTION
250   OPEN "A:CH9-12X.TXT" FOR INPUT AS #1
260   OPEN "A:CH9-16X.TXT" FOR OUTPUT AS #2
270   DIM CUST$(500)
280   REM
290   REM ******* PROCESS SECTION
300   LET COUNT1 = 0
310   INPUT #1, WORD1$, WORD2$, WORD3$
320   LET COUNT1 = COUNT1 + 1
330   CUST$(COUNT1) = WORD2$
340   IF EOF(1) THEN 370
350   GOTO 310
360   REM
370   FOR COUNT2 = 1 TO COUNT1 - 1
380     FOR COUNT3 = COUNT2 + 1 TO COUNT1
390       IF CUST$(COUNT2) <= CUST$(COUNT3) THEN 430
400       LET TEMP$ = CUST$(COUNT2)
410       LET CUST$(COUNT2) = CUST$(COUNT3)
```

```
420         LET CUST$(COUNT3) = TEMP$
430       NEXT COUNT3
440     NEXT COUNT2
450     REM
460     REM NOW ARRAY CUST$ CONTAINS THE SORTED ACCOUNT
470     REM NUMBERS OF THE CUSTOMERS.
480     REM
490     CLOSE #1
500     REM
510     OPEN "A:CH9-12X.TXT" FOR INPUT AS #1
520     FOR COUNT2 = 1 TO COUNT1
530       FOR COUNT3 = 1 TO COUNT1
540         INPUT #1, WORD1$, WORD2$, WORD3$
550         IF WORD2$ = CUST$(COUNT2) THEN 570
560       NEXT COUNT3
570       WRITE #2, WORD1$, WORD2$, WORD3$
580       CLOSE #1
590       OPEN "A:CH9-12X.TXT" FOR INPUT AS #1
600     NEXT COUNT2
610     REM
620     CLOSE #1, #2
630     REM
640     REM ****** OUTPUT SECTION
650     REM=============================================
660     REM TO PRINT THE CONTENTS OF CH9-16X.TXT
670     REM=============================================
680     OPEN "A:CH9-16X.TXT" FOR INPUT AS #1
690     INPUT #1, WORD1$, WORD2$, WORD3$
700     PRINT WORD1$, WORD2$, WORD3$
710     IF EOF(1) THEN 750
720     GOTO 690
730     REM
740     REM ****** TERMINATION SECTION
750     CLOSE #1
760     END
Ok
RUN
H. BIDGOLI      156721          211 S. W. CLAY, PORTLAND
ROBERT BURN     191716          911 S. E. OVAL, BEAVERTON
CHAR THOMAS     219721          921 S. W. 6th, PORTLAND
RID SMART       621719          711 S. W. CLAY, BEAVERTON
SUSAN ATRATY    761198          291 N. E. BROADWAY, PORTLAND
JOANN PESON     911181          111 N. W. JACKSON, FOREST GROVE
G. BROWN        911729          219 S. W. HALL, PORTLAND
JACKY HUSTAN    915511          620 S. E. CRY, PORTLAND
JACKSON JAKS    961187          163 S. W. PARK, BEAVERTON
DOUG HAPPY      961719          901 S. W. CIRCLE, LAKE OSWEGO
Ok


A:\>TYPE CH9-16X.TXT
"H. BIDGOLI","156721","211 S. W. CLAY, PORTLAND"
"ROBERT BURN","191716","911 S. E. OVAL, BEAVERTON"
"CHAR THOMAS","219721","921 S. W. 6th, PORTLAND"
"RID SMART","621719","711 S. W. CLAY, BEAVERTON"
"SUSAN ATRATY","761198","291 N. E. BROADWAY, PORTLAND"
"JOANN PESON","911181","111 N. W. JACKSON, FOREST GROVE"
"G. BROWN","911729","219 S. W. HALL, PORTLAND"
"JACKY HUSTAN","915511","620 S. E. CRY, PORTLAND"
"JACKSON JAKS","961187","163 S. W. PARK, BEAVERTON"
"DOUG HAPPY","961719","901 S. W. CIRCLE, LAKE OSWEGO"

A:\>
```

**Figure 9–34** *(Continued)*

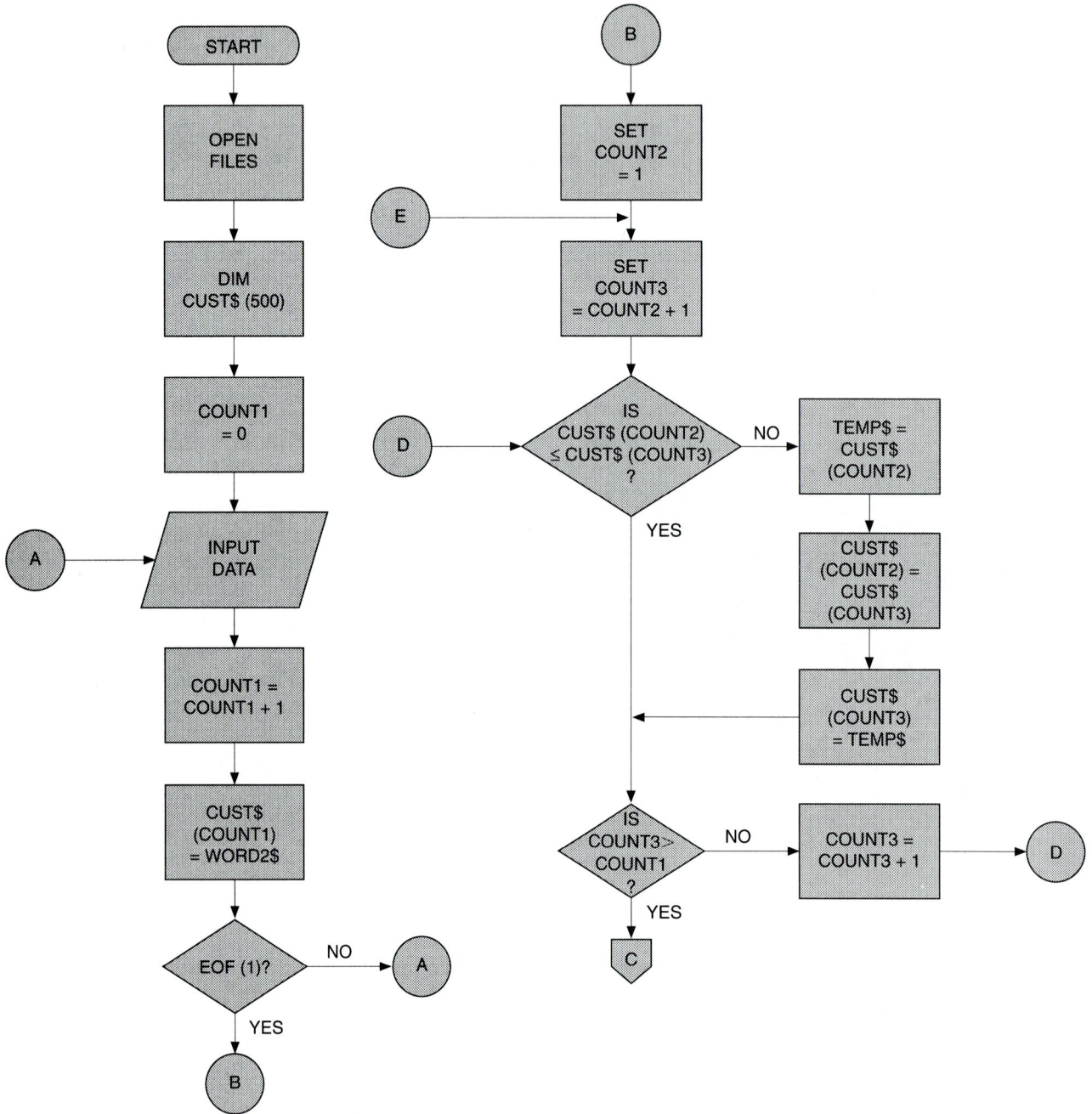

**Figure 9–35**
The Flowchart for the Program Shown in Figure 9–34

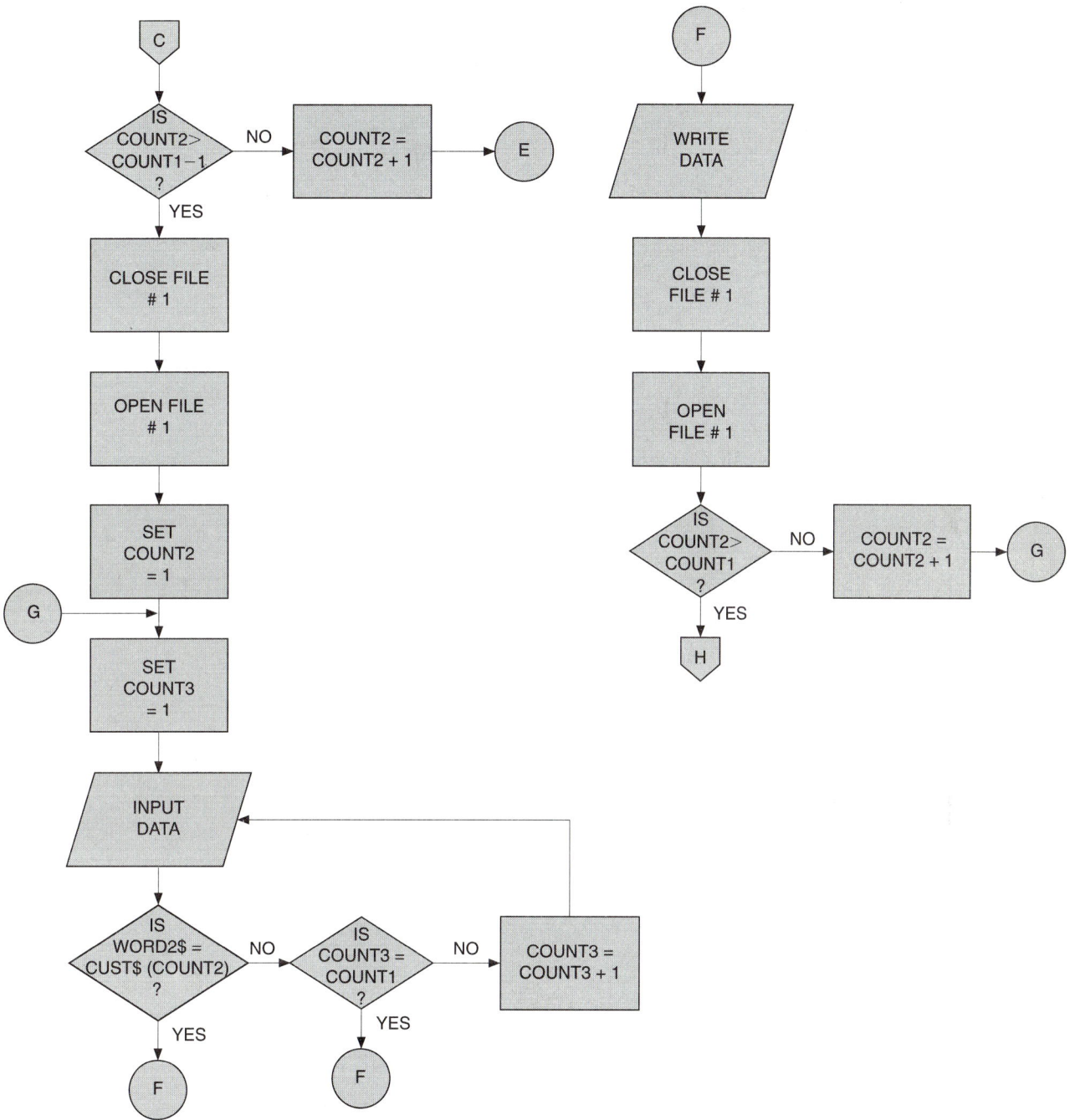

**Figure 9–35** *(Continued)*

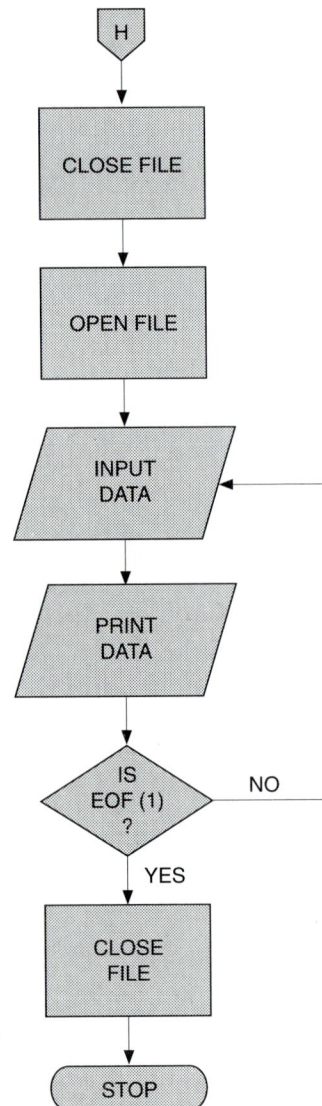

**Figure 9–35**   *(Continued)*

---

**SUMMARY**

In this chapter, we presented a detailed discussion of file processing in BASIC. We explained the advantages of storing data in data files instead of in data lines. We introduced you to the commands used for reading from and writing to a file. You learned how to format a file using the PRINT # USING statement and how to read data to and from a table. You learned how to use the APPEND # command to add information to an existing file. Finally, we presented some simple operations with files.

---

**REVIEW QUESTIONS**

*These questions are answered in Appendix D.

1. What is a sequential file?

2. How is a sequential file created?

*3. What is a random file?

4. Which type of file processing is faster, random or sequential? Discuss.

*5. How do you open a file for input?

6. How do you open a file for output?

7. How do you read a file more than once?

8. How do you read a data file into a table?

9. How do you read a table into a file?

10. What is the difference between the OUTPUT and APPEND commands?

11. What command is used for checking for the end of a file?

12. What are some of the basic operations that can be performed on a sequential file?

*13. Why do you use files?

14. What is the difference between the INPUT # and WRITE # commands?

1. The file STUDENT contains the following list of the students in a programming class as follows:     **HANDS-ON EXPERIENCE**

| Name | Major | G.P.A. | Sex | Age |
|------|-------|--------|-----|-----|
| Simon J. | Business | 2.80 | M | 21 |
| Erickson M. | Psychology | 4.00 | F | 19 |
| Thomas C. | Computer | 3.20 | M | 23 |
| Stowart T. | Computer | 2.90 | M | 22 |
| Stoney C. | Physics | 3.50 | F | 18 |
| Starky K. | Finance | 3.80 | F | 22 |
| Power T. | Accounting | 4.00 | M | 20 |
| Makaby C. | Marketing | 4.00 | M | 19 |
| Acaff R. | Computer | 3.60 | F | 22 |
| Brown Z. | Economics | 2.60 | F | 25 |

a. Write a program to read from STUDENT and generate a new file called STU1 that contains only student names and G.P.A.s.

b. Write a program to extract the students who are under 20 years old.

c. Write a program to sort STUDENT by last name and store the result in file STU2.

d. Write a program to calculate the average G.P.A.

e. Write a program to extract all the students who are computer majors and have a G.P.A. of 3.00 or better.

f. Write a program to read from STUDENT and store the contents of this file in five arrays, three non-numeric and two numeric.

g. Write a program to calculate the average student age.

2. How do you erase the contents of a file that has been generated within your program?

3. Suppose that two of the students in the file STUDENT have changed their majors as follows:

   Erickson M. from Psychology to Computer
   Brown Z. from Economics to Finance

Write a program to reflect these changes and create a new file called STUDENT1.

4. Write a program to add the following students to STUDENT and provide a new listing:

| Name | Major | G.P.A. | Sex | Age |
|------|-------|--------|-----|-----|
| Johny J. | Computer | 3.2 | F | 22 |
| Lyley T. | Math | 4.00 | M | 22 |
| Okata J. | Math | 3.20 | F | 21 |

**5.** Northwest Waterbed Company's accounts receivable are organized in the file ACTSRV. This information must be updated to include the results of the previous month's activities, as follows:

| Name | Address | Amount Due |
|---|---|---|
| Taylor, Susan | Portland | 1218.00 |
| Smith, Paul | Portland | 309.99 |
| Sperry, Meg | Beaverton | 1000.55 |
| Butler, Chris | Wilsonville | 200.00 |
| Clark, Brian | Portland | 1559.95 |
| Heath, Gary | Portland | 1199.00 |
| Ashby, Eric | Beaverton | 435.60 |
| Cook, Tim | Medford | 220.11 |
| Lawson, Karl | Hillsboro | 342.50 |
| Abdie, Troy | Corvallis | 356.88 |

Write a program to do the following (you can create as many files as necessary):

**a.** Update ACTSRV with the following new customer information:

| Name | Address | Amount Due |
|---|---|---|
| Wilson, James | Beaverton | 728.99 |
| Hoover, Cindy | Portland | 199.99 |
| Nixon, Andrew | Tigard | 695.45 |

**b.** The following customers have paid on their accounts. Update the balance due. If the balance is paid in full, delete the customer's information:

| Name | Amount Paid |
|---|---|
| Clark, Brian | 759.95 |
| Abdie, Troy | 156.88 |
| Smith, Paul | 200.00 |
| Sperry, Meg | 1000.55 |
| Taylor, Susan | 518.00 |
| Heath, Gary | 1199.00 |

**c.** Alphabetize the updated file, save it as a new file, and print the new file with the following heading:

Northwest Waterbed Company
Accounts Receivable
June 1, 1991

**d.** From this new file, print only the names of the customers with a balance of less than $200, under the following heading:

Preferred Customers as of June 1, 1991

**KEY TERMS**

| Data file | Random data file | Sequential data file |
|---|---|---|
| Indexed sequential file | | |

**KEY COMMANDS**

| APPEND # | EOF(#) | PRINT # USING |
|---|---|---|
| CLOSE # | INPUT # | WRITE # |

## Multiple Choice

1. Which of the following is not a type of file processing?

   **a.** sequential

   **b.** random

   **c.** index-sequential

   **d.** they all are

   **e.** both a and b

2. Generally speaking,

   **a.** a random file is faster than a sequential file

   **b.** in a random file you can access data in any order

   **c.** a random file is slower than a sequential file

   **d.** a random file is similar to a cassette tape

   **e.** both a and b

3. A permanent file or a disk file used for processing in BASIC can be generated by

   **a.** a line editor

   **b.** a word processor

   **c.** the BASIC language file facility

   **d.** all of the above

   **e.** none of the above

4. The format for opening a file for input is

   **a.** INPUT # File designator, INPUT list

   **b.** INPUT, INPUT list

   **c.** INPUT #, Filename

   **d.** INPUT #, OUTPUT

   **e.** none of the above

5. To display the contents of a sequential file created by BASIC in DOS you must use the command

   **a.** TYPE

   **b.** LIST

   **c.** FILES

   **d.** RUN

   **e.** none of the above

6. The format for the WRITE command is

   **a.** WRITE #

   **b.** WRITE # File designator, OUTPUT list

   **c.** WRITE # OUTPUT list

   **d.** WRITE OUTPUT

   **e.** none of the above

7. To read a file more than once, you can use the

   **a.** INPUT command

   **b.** CLOSE command

   **c.** WRITE command

   **d.** READ command

   **e.** APPEND command

**8.** To write data items into data files using PRINT USING, the general format is
 a. PRINT # USING
 b. PRINT # USING "INTEGER"
 c. PRINT # File designator, "USING FORMAT"; Variable list
 d. PRINT # File designator
 e. none of the above

**9.** To add new data to an existing file without losing the existing data, the command is
 a. WRITE
 b. INPUT
 c. APPEND
 d. OUTPUT
 e. none of the above

**10.** The command to check for the end of a data file is
 a. EOF(INPUT)
 b. EOF(end of file)
 c. EOF(OUTPUT)
 d. END OF DATA
 e. EOF(file designator)

## True/False

**1.** Sequential processing is slower than random processing.
**2.** Using data files, you can make a set of data items available to several programs.
**3.** Using DATA lines in a program provides more flexibility than using data files.
**4.** You can use BASIC file facilities to generate a sequential file.
**5.** To open a file for input or output, you must specify the file designator.
**6.** To generate a listing of a sequential file in DOS, you must use the LIST command.
**7.** You cannot create a permanent file using the WRITE command.
**8.** To make a file available for reading more than once, you can use the CLOSE command.
**9.** When you use the APPEND command, you lose the present contents of a file.
**10.** Using the BASIC sequential file facility, you cannot write data items to a two-dimensional array.

---

**ANSWERS**

| Multiple Choice | True/False |
|---|---|
| **1.** d | **1.** T |
| **2.** e | **2.** T |
| **3.** d | **3.** F |
| **4.** e | **4.** T |
| **5.** a | **5.** T |
| **6.** b | **6.** F |
| **7.** b | **7.** F |
| **8.** c | **8.** T |
| **9.** c | **9.** F |
| **10.** e | **10.** F |

# Functions in BASIC

10

## 10–1

## INTRODUCTION

In this chapter, we examine BASIC's built-in and user-defined functions.

## 10–2

## BUILT-IN FUNCTIONS

BASIC has many **built-in functions**. To calculate the natural logarithm of a number, for example, you don't need to do any extra coding. You can use the formula

$$X = LOG(W)$$

to store the natural logarithm of W in address X. The most commonly used built-in functions are summarized in table 10–1.

## 10–3

## TRIGONOMETRIC FUNCTIONS

Figure 10–1 shows a program that prints the SIN, COS, TAN, COT, and ATN of a 45 and a 60 degree angle. To do this, you must first convert degrees to radians as follows (Pi = 3.14159):

$$45 \text{ degrees} = \frac{Pi}{180} * 45 = \frac{Pi}{4}$$
$$60 \text{ degrees} = \frac{Pi}{180} * 60 = \frac{Pi}{3}$$

## 10–4

## ALGEBRAIC FUNCTIONS

Figure 10–2 shows a program that prints the exponentiation, the natural logarithm, and the square root of numbers 9, 16, and 25. Figure 10–3 shows the flowchart for this program.

**Table 10–1**
BASIC'S Built-In Functions

| Function | Result |
|---|---|
| SIN(x) | Sine of x, angle measured in radians |
| COS(x) | Cosine of x, angle measured in radians |
| TAN(x) | Tangent of x, angle measured in radians |
| COT(x) | Cotangent of x, angle measured in radians |
| ATN(x) | Arctangent of x, angle measured in radians |
| EXP(x) | E (2.718. . .) raised to the power x |
| LOG(x) | Natural logarithm of x (x must be positive) |
| ABS(x) | Absolute value of x |
| SQR(x) | Square root of x (x must be positive) |
| INT(x) | The greatest integer less than or equal to x |
| RND(x) | A random number between 0 and 1 |
| SGN(x) | −1 if x is negative, 0 if x=0, or 1 if x is positive |

```
100     REM THIS PROGRAM ILLUSTRATES BUILT-IN TRIGONOMETRIC FUNCTIONS.
110     REM
120     REM ****** VARIABLE TABLE
130     REM           PI = VALUE OF PI (3.14159)
140     REM
150     REM ****** INITIALIZATION SECTION
160     LET PI = 3.14159
170     REM
180     REM ****** OUTPUT SECTION
190     PRINT SIN(PI/4), COS(PI/4), TAN(PI/4), COT(PI/4), ATN(PI/4)
200     PRINT SIN(PI/3), COS(PI/3), TAN(PI/3), COT(PI/3), ATN(PI/3)
210     END
Ok
RUN
 .7071064       .7071073       .9999986       0            .6657733
 .866025        .5000007       1.732048       0            .8084485
Ok
```

**Figure 10–1**

An Example of a Trigonometric Function

```
100     REM THIS PROGRAM ILLUSTRATES ALGEBRAIC BUILT-IN FUNCTIONS.
110     REM
120     REM ****** VARIABLE TABLE
130     REM           NUM1, NUM2, NUM3 = INPUT VARIABLES
140     REM
150     REM ****** INITIALIZATION SECTION
160     READ NUM1, NUM2, NUM3
170     REM
180     REM ****** OUTPUT SECTION
190     PRINT "NUMBER","EXPONENT","LOG","SQUARE ROOT"
200     PRINT NUM1; TAB(13);
210     PRINT USING "##.##^^^^"; EXP(NUM1);
220     PRINT TAB(26); LOG(NUM1);TAB(42);SQR(NUM1)
230     PRINT NUM2; TAB(13);
240     PRINT USING "##.##^^^^"; EXP(NUM2);
250     PRINT TAB(26);LOG(NUM2);TAB(42);SQR(NUM2)
260     PRINT NUM3; TAB(13);
270     PRINT USING "##.##^^^^"; EXP(NUM3);
280     PRINT TAB(26);LOG(NUM3);TAB(42);SQR(NUM3)
290     REM
300     REM ****** DATA SECTION
310     DATA 9, 16, 25
320     END
Ok
RUN
NUMBER          EXPONENT       LOG           SQUARE ROOT
  9             8.10E+03       2.197225       3
 16             8.89E+06       2.772589       4
 25             7.20E+10       3.218876       5
Ok
```

**Figure 10–2**

Examples of Algebraic Functions

**Figure 10–3**

The Flowchart for the Program
in Figure 10–2

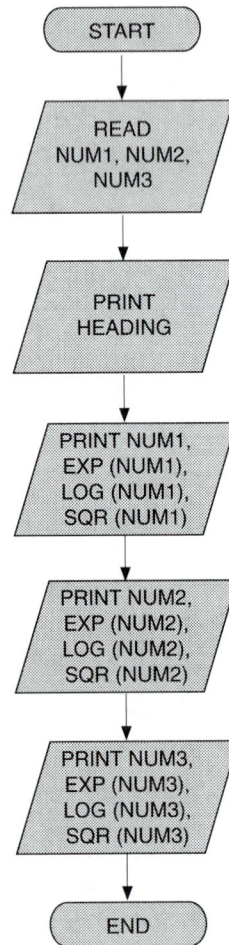

```
START

READ
NUM1, NUM2,
NUM3

PRINT
HEADING

PRINT NUM1,
EXP (NUM1),
LOG (NUM1),
SQR (NUM1)

PRINT NUM2,
EXP (NUM2),
LOG (NUM2),
SQR (NUM2)

PRINT NUM3,
EXP (NUM3),
LOG (NUM3),
SQR (NUM3)

END
```

```
100    REM THIS PROGRAM ILLUSTRATES THE ABSOLUTE VALUE FUNCTION
110    REM
120    REM ******* VARIABLE TABLE
130    REM          NUM1, NUM2, NUM3, NUM4, NUM5 = INPUT VARIABLES
140    REM
150    REM ******* INITIALIZATION SECTION
160    READ NUM1, NUM2, NUM3, NUM4, NUM5
170    REM
180    REM ******* OUTPUT SECTION
190    PRINT ABS(NUM1), ABS(NUM2), ABS(NUM3), ABS(NUM4), ABS(NUM5)
200    REM
210    REM ******* DATA SECTION
220    DATA -2, -1, 0, 1, 2
230    END
Ok
RUN
 2           1              0              1              2
Ok
```

**Figure 10–4**

The ABS Function

The ABS (absolute value) function returns the numeric value of the argument (with no sign). Figure 10–4 shows a program that prints the absolute values of the numbers −2, −1, 0, 1, and 2.

**THE ABS(X) FUNCTION**

The INT (integer) function truncates the argument. The INT function returns the greatest integer that is less than or equal to its argument.

Figure 10–5 shows a program that prints the integer values of −4.45, −7.60, 3.9, and 5.99.

**THE INT(X) FUNCTION**

Using the INT function, you can round any number to its nearest whole number. You do this by adding .5 to the argument.

Figure 10–6 shows a program that rounds the following numbers using the INT function: −6.20, −9.70, −11.20, 12.70, and 21.49.

**ROUNDING NUMBERS USING INT**

The RND (random) function generates random numbers between zero and one. The argument can be any variable or constant. This function is commonly used in programs involving probability. To generate different series of random numbers in GW-BASIC, the RANDOMIZE statement is used at the beginning of the program.

Figures 10–7 and 10–8 show programs that generate three random numbers between 0 and 1. Figure 10–9 shows a program that generates random numbers between 10 and 20.

**THE RND(X) FUNCTION**

```
100    REM THIS PROGRAM ILLUSTRATES THE INTEGER FUNCTION.
110    REM
120    REM ****** VARIABLE TABLE
130    REM          THERE ARE NO VARIABLES IN THIS PROGRAM.
140    REM
150    REM ****** OUTPUT SECTION
160    PRINT INT(-4.45)
170    PRINT INT(-7.6)
180    PRINT INT(3.9)
190    PRINT INT(5.99)
200    END
Ok
RUN
-5
-8
 3
 5
Ok
```

**Figure 10–5**
An Example of the INT Function

**Figure 10–6**
Rounding Numbers Using the
INT Function

```
100     REM THIS PROGRAM USES THE INTEGER FUNCTION TO ROUND
110     REM DIFFERENT NUMBERS.
120     REM
130     REM ******* VARIABLE TABLE
140     REM           THERE ARE NO VARIABLES IN THIS PROGRAM.
150     REM
160     REM ******* OUTPUT SECTION
170     PRINT INT(-6.2+.5)
180     PRINT INT(-9.7+.5)
190     PRINT INT(-11.2+.5)
200     PRINT INT(12.7+.5)
210     PRINT INT(21.49+.5)
220     END
Ok
RUN
-6
-10
-11
 13
 21
Ok
```

```
100     REM THIS PROGRAM USES THE RND FUNCTION WITH POSITIVE ARGUMENT.
110     REM
120     REM ******* VARIABLE TABLE
130     REM           THERE ARE NO VARIABLES IN THIS PROGRAM.
140     REM
150     REM ******* OUTPUT SECTION
160     RANDOMIZE
170     PRINT RND(1), RND(1), RND(1)
180     END
Ok
RUN
Random number seed (-32768 to 32767)? 365
 .3348138      .6637525       .8138384
Ok
```

**Figure 10–7**
An Example of the RND Function with Positive Argument

```
100     REM THIS PROGRAM USES RND FUNCTION WITH NEGATIVE ARGUMENT.
110     REM
120     REM ******* VARIABLE TABLE
130     REM           THERE ARE NO VARIABLES IN THIS PROGRAM.
140     REM
150     REM ******* OUTPUT SECTION
160     RANDOMIZE
170     PRINT RND(-1), RND(-1), RND(-1)
180     END
Ok
RUN
Random number seed (-32768 to 32767)? 794
 .65086        .65086         .65086
Ok
```

**Figure 10–8**
An Example of the RND Function with Negative Argument

```
100     REM THIS PROGRAM WILL GENERATE 3 RANDOM NUMBERS BETWEEN
110     REM 10 AND 20.  THE FORMULA FOR GENERATING RANDOM NUMBERS
120     REM IS INT((DIFF+1)*RND+LOWERBOUND), WHERE DIFF IS THE
130     REM DIFFERENCE BETWEEN THE UPPER BOUND AND THE LOWER
140     REM BOUND, AND LOWERBOUND IS THE LOWER BOUND.
150     REM
160     REM ****** VARIABLE TABLE
170     REM         THERE ARE NO VARIABLES IN THIS PROGRAM.
180     REM
190     REM ****** OUTPUT SECTION
200     PRINT "THE FIRST NUMBER =";INT((11)*RND(1)+10)
210     PRINT "THE SECOND NUMBER =";INT((11)*RND(1)+10)
220     PRINT "THE THIRD NUMBER =";INT((11)*RND(1)+10)
230     END
Ok
RUN
THE FIRST NUMBER = 11
THE SECOND NUMBER = 17
THE THIRD NUMBER = 19
Ok
```

**Figure 10–9**
Generating Random Numbers Between 10 and 20

**10–9**

**THE SGN(X) FUNCTION**

The SGN (sign) function returns one of three different values based on its argument. If X equals 0, then function SGN(x) equals 0; if X is less than 0, then function SGN(x) equals −1; if X is greater than 0, then function SGN(x) equals +1.

The program shown in figure 10–10 determines the sign of the following numbers: −11, 0, 22, −17.20, .56, and −.79.

```
100     REM THIS PROGRAM ILLUSTRATES THE SGN FUNCTION
110     REM
120     REM ****** VARIABLE TABLE
130     REM         THERE ARE NO VARIABLES FOR THIS PROGRAM.
140     REM
150     REM ****** OUTPUT SECTION
160     PRINT "THE SIGN OF -11 = ";SGN(-11)
170     PRINT "THE SIGN OF 0 = ";SGN(0)
180     PRINT "THE SIGN OF 22 = ";SGN(22)
190     PRINT "THE SIGN OF -17.2 = ";SGN(-17.2)
200     PRINT "THE SIGN OF .56 = ";SGN(.56)
210     PRINT "THE SIGN OF -.79 = ";SGN(-.79)
220     END
Ok
RUN
THE SIGN OF -11 = -1
THE SIGN OF 0 =  0
THE SIGN OF 22 =  1
THE SIGN OF -17.2 = -1
THE SIGN OF .56 =  1
THE SIGN OF -.79 = -1
Ok
```

**Figure 10–10**
The SGN Function

## 10–10

### USER-DEFINED FUNCTIONS

In addition to built-in functions, you can define your own calculations, which are known as **user-defined functions**. To do this, you must use the DEF (define) statement. The DEF statement tells the computer that you are going to define a function. This statement is followed by the name of your function, FN followed by any valid characters. If you are using a particular calculation several times, you can save time by making the calculation into a function.

Figure 10–11 shows a program that defines the equation of a parabola and solves this equation at points 10, 20, and 30.

The DEF statement must appear before the function is used. The expression to the right of the equal sign can contain any formula, built-in function, or user-defined function as long as it all fits on one line. Figure 10–12 shows more examples of user-defined functions.

**Figure 10–11**

Example of a User-Defined Function

```
100     REM THIS PROGRAM DEFINES A FUNCTION.  THIS FUNCTION
110     REM IS THE EQUATION FOR A PARABOLA.  THROUGHOUT THIS
120     REM PROGRAM DIFFERENT VALUES OF THIS EQUATION CAN
130     REM BE COMPUTED AS MANY TIMES AS NECESSARY JUST BY
140     REM SUBSTITUTING VALUES INTO THE FUNCTION.
150     REM ****** VARIABLE TABLE
160     REM          NUM1, NUM2, NUM3 = GLOBAL INPUT VARIABLES
170     REM          NUMBER = LOCAL FUNCTION VARIABLE
180     REM
190     REM ****** USER DEFINED FUNCTIONS
200     REM          FNA(NUMBER) = 5*NUMBER^2+10*NUMBER+25
210     REM
220     REM ****** INITIALIZATION SECTION
230     DEF FNA(NUMBER) = 5*NUMBER^2+10*NUMBER+25
240     LET NUM1 = FNA(10)
250     LET NUM2 = FNA(20)
260     LET NUM3 = FNA(30)
270     REM
280     REM ****** OUTPUT SECTION
290     PRINT "   DIFFERENT VALUES OF A PARABOLA"
300     PRINT "====================================="
310     PRINT "1 =";NUM1,"2 =";NUM2,"3 =";NUM3
320     END
Ok
RUN
    DIFFERENT VALUES OF A PARABOLA
=====================================
1 = 625        2 = 2225        3 = 4825
Ok
```

```
100    REM THIS PROGRAM ILLUSTRATES SOME EXAMPLES OF USER
110    REM DEFINED FUNCTIONS.
120    REM
130    REM ****** VARIABLE TABLE
140    REM          NUM1, NUM2 = GLOBAL INPUT VARIABLES
150    REM          NUMBER1 = LOCAL FUNCTION VARIABLE
160    REM          NUMBER2 = LOCAL FUNCTION VARIABLE
170    REM          NUMBER3 = LOCAL FUNCTION VARIABLE
180    REM          NUMBER4 = LOCAL FUNCTION VARIABLE
190    REM
200    REM ****** USER DEFINED FUNCTIONS
210    REM          FNA(NUMBER1) = EXP(NUMBER1^2)+NUM1^3
220    REM          FNB(NUMBER2) = INT(NUM2)+SQR(NUMBER2)+NUM2*5
230    REM          FNC(NUMBER3) = NUMBER3*NUM1*NUM2*25+NUM1^2
240    REM          FND(NUMBER4) = SQR(NUMBER4)+NUMBER4^3+EXP(NUMBER4)
250    REM
260    REM ****** INITIALIZATION SECTION
270    READ NUM1, NUM2
280    DEF FNA(NUMBER1) = EXP(NUMBER1^2)+NUM1^3
290    DEF FNB(NUMBER2) = INT(NUM2)+SQR(NUMBER2)+NUM2*5
300    DEF FNC(NUMBER3) = NUMBER3*NUM1*NUM2*25+NUM1^2
310    DEF FND(NUMBER4) = SQR(NUMBER4)+NUMBER4^3+EXP(NUMBER4)
320    REM
330    REM ****** OUTPUT SECTION
340    PRINT "FUNCTION 1","FUNCTION 2","FUNCTION 3","FUNCTION 4"
350    PRINT "==============================================="
360    PRINT FNA(2), FNB(3), FNC(4), FND(5)
370    REM
380    REM ****** DATA SECTION
390    DATA 5, 7.2
400    END
Ok
RUN
FUNCTION 1      FUNCTION 2      FUNCTION 3      FUNCTION 4
===============================================
 179.5982       44.73205        3625           275.6492
Ok
```

**Figure 10–12**
More User-Defined Functions

In this chapter, we discussed built-in and user-defined functions. Functions and arithmetic operations constitute a major part of the data processing cycle.  **SUMMARY**

*These questions are answered in Appendix D.  **REVIEW QUESTIONS**

*1. What symbol is used for exponentiation?

2. What is the equivalent of a 90 degree angle in radians?

3. What are the numeric answers to the following statements?

   a. 8*9^2*(25*6)

   b. 12/3+18^2−62*(32−8)

   c. 2*3^2+6*8^4/2

4. Write a program to compute the SIN, COS, TAN, and COT of a 90 degree angle.

*5. What is INT(−6.2)?

*6. What is SQR(9+16+75)?

7. What is ABS(−11.75)?

8. What is EXP(2.5)?

*9. What is SGN(−7.7)?

10. Define the area of a triangle as a function.

11. Define the area of a rectangle as a function.

*12. Define the volume of a sphere as a function. (The formula to calculate the volume of a sphere is 4/3*3.1416*R^3, where R is the radius.)

## HANDS-ON EXPERIENCE

1. Write a BASIC program to compute the following statements:

   a. T=62*18*2+16*3

   b. Y=18^2+16/2^3

2. Translate the following algebraic statements into BASIC:

   a. X=A−B*C

   b. D=(M)*(64Y2−12Y−16)

   c. $\dfrac{-B \pm \sqrt{B^2 - 4AC}}{2A}$

   d. Y=(16*3−18)^(1/2)

3. Define the following equation as a function, and then evaluate its value for X=1, X=2, and X=3.

$$X^4 + 2X^3 + 6X + 10$$

## KEY TERMS

Built-in function          User-defined function

## ARE YOU READY TO MOVE ON?

### Multiple Choice

1. Which of the following are true about the statement SIN(x)?

   a. It generates address X with a value of X

   b. X is the argument of the function

   c. X must be expressed in radians

   d. none of the above

   e. both c and b

What is the output of the following programs?

2.
```
10 PRINT INT(-2.06)
20 PRINT INT(-1.75+.50)
30 PRINT INT(7.65)
40 END
```

   a. −2
      −1
       8

   b. −3
      −3
      +8

   **c.**  −3
         −2
          7

   **d.**  −3
         −2
          8

**3.** 
```
10  A=5
20  C=12
30  D=A/SQR(-C)+5*A-16
40  PRINT D
50  END
```

   **a.** 26

   **b.** 28

   **c.** −16

   **d.** an error message

   **e.** none of the above

**4.** 
```
10  DEF FNA(X)=SQR(4)+2*X/2
20  PRINT FNA(3)
30  END
```

   **a.** 5

   **b.** 3

   **c.** 8

   **d.** A STATEMENT ERROR IN LINE 10

   **e.** none of the above

**5.** 
```
10  READ F,E
20  PRINT ABS(E), ABS(F)
30  DATA -4,3
40  END
```

   **a.** 4   3

   **b.** −1   1

   **c.** 3   4

   **d.** 3   −4

   **e.** 1   −1

**6.** 
```
10  PRINT INT(-4.37),
20  READ C
30  PRINT INT(C)
40  DATA 7.98
50  END
```

   **a.** −5   7

   **b.** −4   8

   **c.** 8   −5

   **d.** −4   7

   **e.** none of the above

**7.** 
```
10  PRINT SGN(-11.3)
20  END
```

   **a.** −12

   **b.** −1

   **c.** 11.3

   **d.** 1

   **e.** −11

8. ```
   10 DEF FNB(X)=2*X^2+35
   20 PRINT FNB(5)
   30 END
   ```
   a. 85
   b. 135
   c. 75
   d. 43
   e. none of the above

9. ```
   10 A=((3+3)/2+12)/5
   20 PRINT A
   30 END
   ```
   a. 5.4
   b. 3
   c. 6.9
   d. 4
   e. none of the above

10. Which function generates random numbers between 0 and 1?
    a. RAND
    b. INT
    c. ATN
    d. SGN
    e. RND

## True/False

1. The ABS function returns the numeric value of the argument without any sign.
2. The INT function returns the largest integer that is greater than or equal to its argument.
3. When using a user-defined function, the DEF statement may appear anywhere in the program.
4. The argument of the SQR function must be negative.
5. The argument of the SGN function can be zero, positive, or negative.
6. When evaluating an algebraic statement, the computer performs all exponentiations first before performing parentheses.
7. When using any built-in trigonometric function, the angle must be measured in radians.
8. LOG(x) is an example of a built-in function.
9. You can define your own functions by using the ABC statement.
10. The RND function generates random numbers between −1 and 1.

---

**ANSWERS**

**Multiple Choice**

1. e
2. c
3. d
4. a

**True/False**

1. T
2. F
3. F
4. F

5. c
6. a
7. b
8. a
9. b
10. e

5. T
6. F
7. T
8. T
9. F
10. F

# Using BASIC for Business and Economic Problem Solving

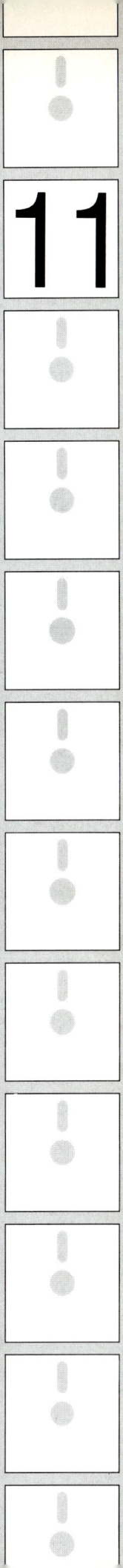

11

## 11–1

### INTRODUCTION

In this chapter, we present a series of programs that can be used in a variety of disciplines, including business and economics. These programs make complicated calculations easy and ensure accuracy. To see the dynamics of the example programs, you should load them from the disk provided and run them with your own data. The output you see on the screen for some programs may be slightly different from what is presented here. This is due to the printer. However, the outputs are correct.

## 11–2

### COMPOUND INTEREST: INVESTMENT INCREASING

An interesting question facing many investors is: How long does it take to double or triple an original investment using compounded interest? To answer this question, we use the following general formula:

$$A = P\left(1 + \frac{R}{Q}\right)^{QN}$$

where: A = amount at the end of the period
P = amount of initial investment
R = annual interest rate in percent format
Q = number of compounding periods per year
N = length of investment in years

In this problem, we need to solve for N using variable amounts for the initial investment, P, and the ending amount, A. To do this, we use the ratio A/P. Because the interest rate is in percent format, it must be multiplied by .01 to obtain a decimal. Let X = A/P, the ratio of increase. Substituting and solving for N, the process is as follows:

$$X = \left(1 + \frac{.01R}{Q}\right)^{QN}$$

$$QN = \frac{LOG(X)}{LOG\left(1 + \dfrac{.01R}{Q}\right)}$$

Therefore:

$$N = \frac{\left[\dfrac{LOG(X)}{LOG\left(1 + \dfrac{.01R}{Q}\right)}\right]}{Q}$$

This is the formula we will use to solve this problem. The values of Q, the number of compounding periods, are as follows:

| Period | Value |
|---|---|
| Annual | 1 |
| Semi-annual | 2 |
| Quarterly | 4 |
| Monthly | 12 |
| Daily | 360 |

There are some limits on the values of A, P, and X:

A < 10,000,000
P < 10,000,000
X < 10,000

These values will be checked before N is calculated and, if any value falls outside the limits, the program asks for other data. Because N is a decimal number after the calculation and the output is to be stated in years, months, and days, we must make the following calculations:

$$Y = INT(N)$$
$$M1 = (N - Y)12$$
$$M = INT(M1)$$
$$D = (INT(M1 - M))30$$

where: Y = the number of years
   M1 = the number of months in decimal form
   M = the number of months
   D = the number of days

   Suppose that a student studying finance wants to know how long it takes for an investment to double, triple, and so forth. He knows that the length of time depends on the interest rate and the number of compounding periods. Figure 11–1 shows a program that calculates the required length of time.

**Figure 11–1**

A Program for Increasing Investment

```
1000    REM PROGRAM TITLE:   INVESTMENT INCREASING
1010    REM
1020    REM THIS IS A COMPOUND INTEREST PROGRAM THAT DETERMINES THE
1030    REM LENGTH OF TIME IT TAKES TO INCREASE AN INVESTMENT
1040    REM A GIVEN MULTIPLE, AT A GIVEN INTEREST RATE.   FOR
1050    REM SIMPLICITY, THE OUTPUT WILL BE BASED ON A 360 DAY YEAR,
1060    REM AND THE TIME EXPRESSED IN YEARS, MONTHS AND DAYS.
1070    REM FIVE DIFFERENT COMPOUNDING PERIODS WILL BE USED AND SHOWN
1080    REM IN THE OUTPUT FOR COMPARISON.
1090    REM CONSTRAINTS WILL BE PLACED ON THE MULTIPLE SO THE
1100    REM LIMITS OF THE PROGRAM WILL NOT BE EXCEEDED.
1110    REM
1120    REM THE BASIC FORMULA USED IN THIS PROGRAM IS:
1130    REM MONEY = LOG(MULT)/LOG(1+RATE/COMP)/COMP, WHERE:
1140    REM
1150    REM MULT = AMOUNT/PRIN, THE NUMBER OF MULTIPLES THE INVESTMENT WILL
1160    REM INCREASE.   IT IS THE RATIO OF THE DESIRED AMOUNT (AMOUNT) TO
1170    REM THE ORIGINAL AMOUNT (PRIN). E. G. $2000/$1000 = 2 TIMES,
1180    REM OR A DOUBLING OF THE ORIGINAL INVESTMENT.
1190    REM
1200    REM ******* VARIABLE TABLE
1210    REM          RATE = ANNUAL INTEREST RATE
1220    REM          PRIN = PRINCIPAL AMOUNT OF INVESTMENT
1230    REM          AMOUNT = AMOUNT THE USER WISHES TO RECEIVE
1240    REM          YEARS = LENGTH OF TIME IN YEARS
1250    REM          MULT = AMOUNT/PRIN (NUMBER OF INCREASE MULTIPLES)
1260    REM          COUNT = LOOP CONTROL VARIABLE
1270    REM
1280    REM ******* ARRAY TABLE
1290    REM          COMP(5) = NUMBER OF COMPOUNDING PERIODS IN A YEAR
```

```
1300   REM           PER$(5) = OUTPUT FORMATTING ARRAY
1310   REM           NUMBER(5) = NUMBER OF YEARS EXPRESSED AS A DECIMAL
1320   REM           MONTHS(5) = NUMBER OF MONTHS EXPRESSED AS A DECIMAL
1330   REM           MONTH(5) = NUMBER OF MONTHS EXPRESSED AS AN INTEGER
1340   REM           DAYS(5) = NUMBER OF DAYS EXPRESSED AS A DECIMAL
1350   REM
1360   REM ******* INITIALIZATION SECTION
1370   REM THE FOLLOWING QUESTIONS ASK FOR THE INPUT DATA.
1380   PRINT "THIS IS THE COMPOUND INTEREST PROGRAM TO TELL YOU THE"
1390   PRINT "LENGTH OF TIME IT TAKES FOR AN INVESTMENT TO ";
1400   PRINT "INCREASE TO A NEW AMOUNT."
1410   PRINT
1420   PRINT "THE DOLLAR AMOUNTS MUST BE LESS THAN 10 MILLION, AND THE"
1430   PRINT "AMOUNT OF YOUR INVESTMENT MUST BE LESS THAN THE AMOUNT"
1440   PRINT "THAT YOU WISH TO RECEIVE AT THE END OF THE INVESTMENT TERM."
1450   PRINT
1460   PRINT
1470   PRINT "WHAT IS THE ANNUAL INTEREST RATE, IN PERCENT?"
1480   INPUT "(DO NOT USE THE % SIGN IN YOUR INPUT.) ";RATE
1490   PRINT
1500   PRINT "WHAT IS THE AMOUNT OF THE INVESTMENT? "
1510   PRINT "YOUR NUMBER MUST BE LESS THAN 10,000,000."
1520   INPUT "(DO NOT USE THE , OR $ SIGN IN YOUR INPUT.) ",PRIN
1530   PRINT
1540   PRINT "WHAT AMOUNT DO YOU WISH TO RECEIVE?"
1550   PRINT "YOUR NUMBER MUST BE GREATER THAN THE AMOUNT OF"
1560   PRINT "YOUR INVESTMENT, AND LESS THAN 10,000,000."
1570   INPUT "(DO NOT USE THE , OR $ SIGN IN YOUR INPUT.) ",AMOUNT
1580   REM
1590   REM THE MULTIPLE OF THE INVESTMENT IS DETERMINED AS FOLLOWS:
1600   LET MULT = AMOUNT/PRIN
1610   IF PRIN > 10000000# OR AMOUNT > 10000000# THEN 1630
1620   IF MULT > 1 AND MULT < 10000 THEN 1720
1630   PRINT
1640   PRINT "THE AMOUNTS YOU HAVE ENTERED ARE OUTSIDE THE LIMITS OF THE ";
1650   PRINT "PROGRAM."
1660   PRINT "CHANGE THE AMOUNT OF INVESTMENT AND/OR THE AMOUNT ";
1670   PRINT "OF RETURN."
1680   PRINT
1690   PRINT
1700   GOTO 1500
1710   REM THE FOLLOWING DATA ARE THE COMPOUNDING PERIODS PER YEAR.
1720   LET COMP(1) = 1
1730   LET COMP(2) = 2
1740   LET COMP(3) = 4
1750   LET COMP(4) = 12
1760   LET COMP(5) = 360
1770   REM THE FOLLOWING LOOP CALCULATES THE DIFFERENT LENGTHS OF
1780   REM TIME.
1790   REM YEARS = THE NUMBER OF YEARS, MONTHS = THE NUMBER OF MONTHS,
1800   REM AND DAYS = THE NUMBER OF DAYS.
1810   FOR COUNT = 1 TO 5
1820     REM NUMBER(COUNT) = THE NUMBER OF YEARS EXPRESSED AS A DECIMAL.
1830     LET NUMBER(COUNT)=LOG(MULT)/LOG(1+.01*RATE/COMP(COUNT))/COMP(COUNT)
1840     LET YEARS(COUNT)=INT(NUMBER(COUNT))
1850     REM MONTHS(COUNT)=THE NUMBER OF MONTHS, EXPRESSED AS A DECIMAL.
1860     LET MONTHS(COUNT)=(NUMBER(COUNT)-YEARS(COUNT))*12
1870     LET MONTH(COUNT)=INT(MONTHS(COUNT))
1880     REM DAYS(COUNT) IS THE NO OF DAYS EXPRESSED AS DECIMAL.
1890     LET DAYS(COUNT)=INT((MONTHS(COUNT)-MONTH(COUNT))*30)
1900   NEXT COUNT
1910   REM THE FOLLOWING STEPS FORMAT THE OUTPUT.
1920   LET PER$(1) = "ANNUAL"
1930   LET PER$(2) = "SEMI-ANNUAL"
```

**Figure 11–1**  *(Continued)*

204

```
1940     LET PER$(3) = "QUARTERLY"
1950     LET PER$(4) = "MONTHLY"
1960     LET PER$(5) = "DAILY"
1970     PRINT
1980     PRINT
1990     PRINT
2000     FOR COUNT = 1 TO 72
2010        PRINT "-";
2020     NEXT COUNT
2030     PRINT
2040     PRINT
2050     PRINT TAB(16); "TIME REQUIRED TO INCREASE AN INVESTMENT"
2060     PRINT "ANNUAL INTEREST RATE:";TAB(24);
2070     PRINT USING "##.###";RATE
2080     PRINT "THE AMOUNT OF THE ORIGINAL INVESTMENT:";TAB(39);
2090     PRINT USING "$$#######.##";PRIN
2100     PRINT "THE AMOUNT OF THE DESIRED RETURN:";TAB(34);
2110     PRINT USING "$$#######.##";AMOUNT
2120     PRINT "THE RATIO OF THE INCREASE IS:";TAB(30);
2130     PRINT USING "####.###";MULT
2140     PRINT
2150     PRINT
2160     PRINT "COMPOUNDING        COMPOUNDING        TIME TO INCREASE"
2170     PRINT TAB(4);"TIMES        PERIODS PER YEAR    YEARS   MONTHS   DAYS"
2180     PRINT
2190     FOR C = 1 TO 5
2200        PRINT PER$(C);TAB(21);
2210        PRINT USING "###";COMP(C);
2220        PRINT USING "         ###       ##      ##";YEARS(C),MONTH(C),DAYS(C)
2230     NEXT C
2240     PRINT
2250     PRINT
2260     PRINT
2270     FOR COUNT = 1 TO 72
2280        PRINT "-";
2290     NEXT COUNT
2300     PRINT
2310     PRINT
2320     REM
2330     REM ****** TERMINATION SECTION
2340     INPUT "DO YOU WISH TO CALCULATE ANOTHER (Y OR N): ";ANSWER$
2350     IF ANSWER$ = "Y" OR ANSWER$ = "y" THEN GOTO 1470
2360     IF ANSWER$ <> "N" AND ANSWER$ <> "n" THEN GOTO 2340
2370     PRINT
2380     PRINT
2390     PRINT
2410     PRINT
2420     PRINT "IT'S BEEN FUN!  TRY THE INVESTMENT INCREASING";
2430     PRINT " PROGRAM AGAIN SOON."
2440     END
Ok
RUN


THIS IS THE COMPOUND INTEREST PROGRAM TO TELL YOU THE
LENGTH OF TIME IT TAKES FOR AN INVESTMENT TO INCREASE TO A NEW AMOUNT.

THE DOLLAR AMOUNTS MUST BE LESS THAN 10 MILLION, AND THE
AMOUNT OF YOUR INVESTMENT MUST BE LESS THAN THE AMOUNT
THAT YOU WISH TO RECEIVE AT THE END OF THE INVESTMENT TERM.


WHAT IS THE ANNUAL INTEREST RATE, IN PERCENT?
(DO NOT USE THE , OR $ SIGN IN YOUR INPUT.) 18.000

WHAT IS THE AMOUNT OF THE INVESTMENT?
YOUR NUMBER MUST BE LESS THAN 10,000,000.
(DO NOT USE THE , OR $ SIGN IN YOUR INPUT.)                $3500.00
```

**Figure 11–1**   *(Continued)*

```
WHAT AMOUNT DO YOU WISH TO RECEIVE?
YOUR NUMBER MUST BE GREATER THAN THE AMOUNT OF
YOUR INVESTMENT, AND LESS THAN 10,000,000.
(DO NOT USE THE , OR $ SIGN IN YOUR INPUT.)                    $7000.00



--------------------------------------------------------------------

                TIME REQUIRED TO INCREASE AN INVESTMENT
ANNUAL INTEREST RATE:  18.000
THE AMOUNT OF THE ORIGINAL INVESTMENT:     $3500.00
THE AMOUNT OF THE DESIRED RETURN:     $7000.00
THE RATIO OF THE INCREASE IS:    2.000


COMPOUNDING       COMPOUNDING          TIME TO INCREASE
   TIMES       PERIODS PER YEAR    YEARS  MONTHS  DAYS

ANNUAL                1              4      2      7
SEMI-ANNUAL           2              4      0      7
QUARTERLY             4              3     11      7
MONTHLY              12              3     10     16
DAILY               360              3     10      6



--------------------------------------------------------------------

DO YOU WISH TO CALCULATE ANOTHER (Y OR N): ? N



IT'S BEEN FUN!   TRY THE INVESTMENT INCREASING PROGRAM AGAIN SOON.
```

**Figure 11–1**   *(Continued)*

The program prints the answer using the stated interest rate and shows the various lengths of time based on the common compounding periods of annual, semi-annual, quarterly, monthly, and daily. The input of the program includes the annual interest rate, the amount of initial investment, and the amount desired.The output of the program includes the input data, the ratio of increase, and the time to increase in years, months, and days for the five different compounding periods.

## 11–3

## COMPOUND INTEREST: PRESENT VALUE

Because different investments have different future cash inflows, comparing these investment alternatives becomes a difficult task. **Present value analysis** is one technique that can be very helpful in comparing different investment alternatives.

To calculate the present value of a future income or cash flow, we use the following general formula:

$$P = \frac{A}{\left(1 + \dfrac{R}{Q}\right)^{QN}}$$

where: P = amount of money to invest today
    A = amount of desired return
    R = annual interest rate in percent format
    Q = number of compounding periods per year
    N = number of years for the investment

To simplify this problem, we will assume quarterly compounding periods (Q = 4). Because R is expressed as a percent, it must be multiplied by .01 to obtain a decimal. Substitute these numbers into the general formula as follows:

$$P = \frac{A}{\left(1 + \frac{.01R}{4}\right)^{4N}}$$

If N is a part year, or years, we must express it as a decimal, and not in years, months, or days.

As another example, suppose that Northwest Successful Investment Company has various funds available for its clients' investments. The different funds have different annual interest rates, and interest is compounded quarterly. The investment counselor has to be able to tell a client the amount of money to invest today to receive the desired amount at the end of a specific period.

Figure 11–2 shows a program to calculate the present value of a future amount, based on a specified annual interest rate. The program allows interactive entry of the amount of desired return, the length of investment in years, and the annual interest rate. The program's output includes the input data and the amount required to invest today.

**Figure 11–2**
Present Value

```
100    REM PROGRAM TITLE: PRESENT VALUE
110    REM
120    REM THIS PROGRAM CALCULATES THE PRESENT VALUE OF A
130    REM FUTURE AMOUNT OF MONEY.  THE ANNUAL INTEREST
140    REM RATE IS REQUESTED AND THE COMPOUNDING IS QUARTERLY.
150    REM
160    REM THE MAIN FORMULA USED IS:
170    REM PRIN=AMOUNT/(1+.01*RATE/4)^(4YEARS) (SEE VARIABLE TABLE)
180    REM
190    REM ****** VARIABLE TABLE
200    REM        PRIN = THE PRESENT VALUE OF INVESTMENT REQUIRED TODAY
210    REM        AMOUNT = AMOUNT OF DESIRED RETURN
220    REM        RATE = THE ANNUAL INTEREST RATE
230    REM        YEARS = THE NUMBER OF YEARS FOR THE INVESTMENT
240    REM        COUNT = FOR-NEXT LOOP CONTROL VARIABLE
250    REM        ANSWER$ = REPEAT PROGRAM TEST VARIABLE
260    REM
270    REM ****** INITIALIZATION SECTION
280    REM
290    REM THESE STEPS ASK THE USER FOR THE REQUIRED DATA.
300    PRINT TAB(22);"CALCULATION OF PRESENT VALUE"
310    PRINT
320    PRINT "PLEASE ENTER THE AMOUNT OF DESIRED RETURN."
330    PRINT "DO NOT USE A COMMA (,) OR A DOLLAR ($) SIGN."
340    INPUT "THE NUMBER YOU ENTER MUST BE GREATER THAN ZERO. ",AMOUNT
350    REM
```

```
360     REM TEST FOR VALID INPUT
370     IF AMOUNT <= 0 THEN GOTO 340
380     REM
390     PRINT : PRINT "WHAT IS THE LENGTH OF INVESTMENT IN YEARS?"
400     PRINT "IF A PART YEAR, INPUT AS A DECIMAL, E.G. 4.5)."
410     INPUT "AGAIN, THE NUMBER YOU ENTER MUST BE GREATER THAN ZERO. ";YEARS
420     REM
430     REM TEST FOR VALID INPUT
440     IF YEARS <= 0 THEN GOTO 410
450     REM
460     PRINT : PRINT "PLEASE ENTER THE ANNUAL INTEREST RATE?"
470     PRINT "DO NOT USE A PERCENTAGE (%) SIGN."
480     INPUT "YOUR ENTRY MUST BE POSITIVE. ",RATE
490     REM
500     REM TEST FOR VALID INPUT
510     IF RATE <= 0 THEN GOTO 480
520     REM
530     REM ****** PROCESS SECTION
540     REM THE VALUE OF PRIN IS CALCULATED NEXT.
550     LET PRIN=AMOUNT/((1+.01*RATE/4)^(4*YEARS))
560     REM
570     REM ****** OUTPUT SECTION
580     REM THE OUTPUT IS NOW FORMATTED AND PRINTED.
590     PRINT
600     PRINT
610     PRINT
620     FOR COUNT = 1 TO 72
630     PRINT "-";
640     NEXT COUNT
650     PRINT
660     PRINT
670     PRINT TAB(24); "PRESENT VALUE CALCULATION"
680     PRINT
690     PRINT "THE AMOUNT OF DESIRED RETURN: ";TAB(31);
700     PRINT USING "$$#####,.##";AMOUNT
710     PRINT "THE INVESTMENT PERIOD, IN YEARS, IS:   ";TAB(39);
720     PRINT USING "###.##";YEARS
730     PRINT "THE ANNUAL INTEREST RATE IS:";TAB(30);
740     PRINT USING "###.##%";RATE
750     PRINT "THE AMOUNT TO BE INVESTED TODAY IS: ";TAB(38);
760     PRINT USING "$$#####,.##";PRIN
770     PRINT
780     PRINT
790     PRINT
800     FOR COUNT = 1 TO 72
810     PRINT "-";
820     NEXT COUNT
830     PRINT
840     PRINT
850     REM
860     REM ****** TERMINATION SECTION
870     INPUT "WOULD YOU LIKE TO CALCULATE ANOTHER (Y OR N)? ",ANSWER$
880     REM
890     REM TEST FOR VALID INPUT
900     IF ANSWER$ = "Y" OR ANSWER$ = "y" THEN GOTO 300
910     IF ANSWER$ <> "N" AND ANSWER$ <> "n" THEN GOTO 870
920     PRINT
930     PRINT "END OF PROGRAM"
940     END
```

**Figure 11–2**  *(Continued)*

```
Ok
LLIST
Ok
RUN


                    CALCULATION OF PRESENT VALUE

PLEASE ENTER THE AMOUNT OF DESIRED RETURN.
DO NOT USE A COMMA (,) OR A DOLLAR ($) SIGN.
THE NUMBER YOU ENTER MUST BE GREATER THAN ZERO.          15000

WHAT IS THE LENGTH OF INVESTMENT IN YEARS?
IF A PART YEAR, INPUT AS A DECIMAL, E.G. 4.5).
AGAIN, THE NUMBER YOU ENTER MUST BE GREATER THEN ZERO.   7.89

PLEASE ENTER THE ANNUAL INTEREST RATE?
DO NOT USE A PERCENTAGE (%) SIGN.
YOUR ENTRY MUST BE POSITIVE.                 35



-----------------------------------------------------------------

                     PRESENT VALUE CALCULATION

THE AMOUNT OF DESIRED RETURN:    $15,000.00
THE INVESTMENT PERIOD, IN YEARS, IS:     7.89
THE ANNUAL INTEREST RATE IS:   35.00%
THE AMOUNT TO BE INVESTED TODAY IS:      $1,062.64



-----------------------------------------------------------------

WOULD YOU LIKE TO CALCULATE ANOTHER (Y OR N)?          N

END OF PROGRAM
```

**Figure 11-2**   *(Continued)*

## 11-4

## COMPOUND INTEREST: FINANCING A NEW CAR

One of the most interesting applications of the compounded interest rate is its use in the calculation of the amount of an installment payment for a new car or house. We have applied this model to financing a new car with the following general formula:

$$A = \frac{P(R/Q)}{1 - \left[ \dfrac{1}{(1 + (R/Q)^{QY}} \right]}$$

where: A = amount of payment
       P = principal amount financed

R = annual interest rate in percent format
Q = number of payments per year
Y = number of years in the contract

We need to expand this formula to fit this particular problem. The variables needed are the contract period, the amount of principal, and the annual interest rate. The principal amount has three factors:

- The price of the car
- The amount of down payment
- The amount of trade-in

In our formula, the variables are as follows:

P1 = Cost of new car
P2 = Trade-in amount
P3 = Down payment

Therefore, P = P1 − P2 − P3, the total amount financed. We must specify R, the annual interest rate expressed as a percent. It must, however, be multiplied by 0.01 to obtain a decimal. The number of payments in a year, Q, is 12. We assume a 25 percent down payment and a monthly interest rate. Substitute these variables into the general formula as follows:

$$A = \frac{(P1 - P2 - P3)(.01R/12)}{1 - \left[\dfrac{1}{(1 + |.01R/12|)^{12Y}}\right]}$$

For the purpose of this problem, some of the calculations will be performed prior to the calculation of A. Assume that P = (P1 − P2 − P3) is the total principle financed, N = 12Y is the total number of payments, and R1 = .01R/12 is the monthly interest rate expressed as a decimal. This reduces to:

$$A = \frac{P(R1)}{1 - \left[\dfrac{1}{(1 + |R1|)^{N}}\right]}$$

This is the formula used in this problem. Other required calculations are as follows:

| Function | Purpose |
|---|---|
| P4 = .25(P1) | Determines the minimum down payment amount |
| $FNA(X) = INT(X) + \dfrac{INT(100(X - INT(X)) + .50)}{100}$ | Rounds a number to two decimal places, needed to maintain the accuracy of the output |
| P5 = FNA(P4) | Value of P4, rounded to two decimal places |
| P6 = P2 + P3 | Total amount of down payment |

| | | |
|---|---|---|
| $P7 = P5 - P6$ | Amount the down payment is lacking | |
| $A1 = FNA(A)$ | Monthly payment amount, rounded to two decimal places | |
| $T = (A1)N$ | Total amount of all payments | |
| $F = T - P$ | Total finance charge | |

BM-RM, a European automobile dealer, has been experiencing a loss of business because of erroneous loan information provided to customers by the salespeople. The dealer wants to provide his salespeople with understandable and accurate financial information so they can help potential customers make decisions based on the facts.

Figure 11–3 shows a program that verifies the input data for the minimum (25 percent) down payment and calculates the monthly payments for various payback periods, at a stated interest rate. In this program, the following data are entered in an interactive mode:

- Date
- Customer's name
- Salesperson
- New car price
- Trade-in amount
- Cash down payment amount
- Interest rate

The program outputs the following information:

- Input data
- Total down payment amount
- Amount financed
- Finance charge
- Total payments
- Number of payments
- Monthly payment amounts for 1-, 2-, 3-, 4-, and 5-year contracts

**Figure 11–3**

Financing a New Car

```
1000    REM PROGRAM TITLE: FINANCING A NEW CAR
1010    REM
1020    REM THIS PROGRAM IS AN APPLICATION OF THE INTEREST FORMULA
1030    REM TO FIND THE PAYMENT AMOUNT ON THE BASIS OF
1040    REM MONTHLY PAYMENTS.  IT IS DESIRED TO DETERMINE THE
1050    REM AMOUNT OF MONTHLY PAYMENT REQUIRED TO PURCHASE A
1060    REM NEW CAR.
1070    REM TWO VALUES MUST BE ROUNDED TO TWO DECIMAL PLACES TO
1080    REM MAINTAIN ACCURACY IN THE OUTPUT.  A USER DEFINED
1090    REM FUNCTION IS USED FOR THIS.
1100    REM THE FORMULA USED IN THIS PROGRAM IS:
1110    REM AMT=(NCAR-T.IN-DOWN)*(.01*RATE/12)/(1-(1/(1+(.01*RATE/12))^PAYS))
1120    REM (SEE VARIABLE TABLE BELOW)
1130    REM
```

```
1140    REM THE OUTPUT WILL BE BASED ON 1, 2, 3, 4, AND 5 YEAR
1150    REM PAYBACK TIMES, AT A SPECIFIED ANNUAL INTEREST RATE.
1160    REM
1170    REM ****** VARIABLE TABLE
1180    REM         AMT = AMOUNT OF MONTHLY PAYMENT
1190    REM         NCAR = NEW CAR PRICE
1200    REM         T.IN = TRADE IN AMOUNT
1210    REM         DOWN = DOWN PAYMENT
1220    REM         RATE = ANNUAL INTEREST RATE, EXPRESSED IN PERCENT
1230    REM         PAYS = NUMBER OF MONTHLY PAYMENTS
1240    REM         NAM$ = THE CUSTOMERS NAME
1250    REM         SALNAM$ = THE SALESMAN'S NAME
1260    REM         MINDOWN = THE MINIMUM DOWN PAYMENT AMOUNT
1270    REM         TOTDOWN = TOTAL AMOUNT OF DOWN PAYMENT TENDERED
1280    REM         DOWNSHORT = THE AMOUNT THE DOWN PAYMENT IS SHORT
1290    REM         DOWNREQ = THE AMOUNT OF DOWN PAYMENT REQUIRED
1300    REM         ANSWER$ = USER INPUT TEST VARIABLE
1310    REM         FINANCED = THE AMOUNT TO BE FINANCED
1320    REM         RATE1 = MONTHLY INTEREST RATE EXPRESSED AS A DECIMAL
1330    REM         COUNT = FOR-NEXT LOOP CONTROL VARIABLE
1340    REM         P.OUT = OUTPUT FORMAT STRING
1350    REM
1360    REM ****** ARRAY TABLE
1370    REM         NUMPAYS(5) = NUMBER OF PAYMENTS ARRAY
1380    REM         AMOUNT1(5) = MONTHLY AMOUNT ROUNDED TO 2 PLACES
1390    REM         TOTAL(5) = TOTAL OF THE PAYMENTS
1400    REM         FIN(5) = THE FINANCE CHARGE
1410    REM
1420    REM ****** INITIALIZATION SECTION
1430    REM THE FOLLOWING QUESTIONS ASK FOR THE DATA TO BE USED
1440    REM IN THE PROGRAM.
1450    PRINT TAB(17); "REQUEST FOR AMOUNT OF MONTHLY PAYMENT"
1460    PRINT : INPUT "PLEASE ENTER THE CUSTOMER'S NAME: ",NAM$
1470    PRINT : INPUT "PLEASE ENTER THE SALESMAN'S NAME: ",SALNAM$
1480    PRINT : PRINT "WHAT IS THE PRICE OF THE NEW CAR?"
1490    INPUT "DO NOT USE A COMMA (,) OR A DOLLAR ($) SIGN: ",NCAR
1500    PRINT : PRINT "WHAT IS THE TRADE IN AMOUNT?"
1510    INPUT "DO NOT USE A COMMA (,) OR A DOLLAR ($) SIGN: ",T.IN
1520    PRINT : PRINT "WHAT IS THE CASH DOWN PAYMENT AMOUNT?"
1530    INPUT "DO NOT USE A COMMA (,) OR A DOLLAR ($) SIGN: ",DOWN
1540    PRINT : PRINT "WHAT IS THE ANNUAL INTEREST RATE?"
1550    INPUT "DO NOT USE A PERCENTAGE (%) SIGN: ",RATE
1560    REM
1570    REM THE FOLLOWING FUNCTION ROUNDS A NUMBER TO 2 DECIMAL PLACES.
1580    DEF FNA(X)=INT(X)+INT(100*(X-INT(X))+.5)/100
1590    REM
1600    REM ****** PROCESS SECTION
1610    REM THE FOLLOWING IS A TEST TO DETERMINE IF THE DOWN PAYMENT
1620    REM AMOUNT IS ADEQUATE.  MINDOWN=THE MINIMUM DOWN PAYMENT.
1630    LET MINDOWN = FNA(.25*NCAR)
1640    REM
1650    REM TOTDOWN IS THE TOTAL AMOUNT OF DOWN PAYMENT TENDERED.
1660    LET TOTDOWN = T.IN+DOWN
1670    IF MINDOWN <= TOTDOWN THEN GOTO 1990
1680    REM
1690    REM THIS DETERMINES THE AMOUNT THE TOTAL DOWN PAYMENT IS SHORT
1700    LET DOWNSHORT = MINDOWN-(T.IN+DOWN)
1710    REM
1720    REM THIS DETERMINES THE TOTAL AMOUNT OF CASH DOWN PAYMENT REQUIRED
1730    LET DOWNREQ = MINDOWN-T.IN
1740    REM
1750    PRINT : PRINT : PRINT
1760    PRINT "SORRY, THE CASH DOWN PAYMENT IS NOT ADEQUATE!"
1770    PRINT "THE TOTAL DOWN PAYMENT REQUIRED IS ";
1780    PRINT USING "$$####.##";MINDOWN
1790    PRINT "THE TRADE-IN VALUE YOU HAVE IS WORTH ";
1800    PRINT USING "$$####.##";T.IN
1810    PRINT "YOUR CURRENT DOWN PAYMENT AMOUNT IS ";
```

**Figure 11–3** *(Continued)*

212

```
1820      PRINT USING "$$####.##";DOWN
1830      PRINT "THE ADDITIONAL CASH AMOUNT NEEDED IS ";
1840      PRINT USING "$$####.##";DOWNSHORT;
1850      PRINT ", FOR A TOTAL OF ";
1860      PRINT USING "$$#####.##";DOWNREQ
1870      REM
1880      PRINT : PRINT "CAN THE CUSTOMER PAY THE ADDITIONAL CASH DOWN";
1890      INPUT "PAYMENT (Y OR N): ";ANSWER$
1900      REM TEST USER INPUT
1910      IF ANSWER$ = "N" OR ANSWER$ = "n" THEN GOTO 2610
1920      IF ANSWER$ <> "Y" AND ANSWER$ <> "y" THEN GOTO 1880
1930      REM
1940      PRINT : PRINT "WHAT IS THE NEW AMOUNT OF CASH DOWN PAYMENT?"
1950      INPUT "DO NOT USE A COMMA (,) OR A DOLLAR ($) SIGN): ";DOWN
1960      GOTO 1630
1970      REM
1980      REM THE FOLLOWING DATA ARE THE NUMBER OF MONTHLY PAYMENTS.
1990      LET NUMPAYS(1) = 12
2000      LET NUMPAYS(2) = 24
2010      LET NUMPAYS(3) = 36
2020      LET NUMPAYS(4) = 48
2030      LET NUMPAYS(5) = 60
2040      REM
2050      REM FINANCED = THE AMOUNT TO BE FINANCED.
2060      LET FINANCED = NCAR-T.IN-DOWN
2070      REM
2080      REM RATE1 = THE MONTHLY INTEREST RATE EXPRESSED AS A DECIMAL.
2090      LET RATE1 = .01*RATE/12
2100      REM
2110      REM THE FOLLOWING LOOP IS USED TO CALCULATE THE DIFFERENT
2120      REM MONTHLY PAYMENT AMOUNTS.
2130      FOR COUNT = 1 TO 5
2140        LET AMT = FINANCED*RATE1/(1-(1/(1+RATE1)^NUMPAYS(COUNT)))
2150        REM AMT1 = THE MONTHLY AMOUNT ROUNDED TO 2 PLACES.
2160        LET AMT1(COUNT) = FNA(AMT)
2170        REM TOTAL(COUNT) = THE TOTAL OF THE PAYMENTS.
2180        LET TOTAL(COUNT) = AMT1(COUNT)*NUMPAYS(COUNT)
2190        REM FIN(COUNT) = THE FINANCE CHARGE.
2200        LET FIN(COUNT) = TOTAL(COUNT)-FINANCED
2210      NEXT COUNT
2220      REM
2230      REM ****** OUTPUT SECTION
2240      REM THE FOLLOWING STEPS FORMAT THE OUTPUT.
2250      PRINT : PRINT : PRINT
2260      FOR J=1 TO 72
2270        PRINT "-";
2280      NEXT J
2290      PRINT : PRINT : PRINT
2300      PRINT TAB(23); "AMOUNTS OF MONTHLY PAYMENT"
2310      PRINT : PRINT
2320      PRINT "DATE:",,DATE$
2330      PRINT "CUSTOMER'S NAME:"," ";NAM$
2340      PRINT "SALESMAN:",," ";SALNAM$
2350      PRINT "NEW CAR PURCHASE PRICE:";
2360      PRINT , USING "$$####,.##";NCAR
2370      PRINT "TRADE IN AMOUNT:";
2380      PRINT , USING "$$###,.##";T.IN
2390      PRINT "CASH DOWN PAYMENT AMOUNT:";
2400      PRINT , USING "$$###,.##";DOWN
2410      PRINT "TOTAL DOWN PAYMENT AMOUNT:";
2420      PRINT USING " $$###,.##";TOTDOWN
2430      PRINT "ANNUAL INTEREST RATE:";
2440      PRINT , USING "    ##.##%";RATE
2450      PRINT
2460      PRINT "YEARS TO    AMOUNT     FINANCE     TOTAL    NUMBER OF    AMOUNT OF"
2470      PRINT "FINANCE    FINANCED     CHARGE     PAYMENTS  PAYMENTS  MO. PAYMENT"
2480      PRINT
2490      FOR COUNT = 1 TO 5
```

**Figure 11–3** *(Continued)*

```
2500        PRINT USING "  #        $$####,.## $$####,.##";COUNT,FINANCED,FIN(COUNT);
2510        LET P.OUT$ = "   $$####,.##       ##        $$###,.##"
2520        PRINT USING P.OUT$;TOTAL(COUNT);NUMPAYS(COUNT),AMT1(COUNT)
2530   NEXT COUNT
2540   PRINT
2550   FOR COUNT = 1 TO 72
2560     PRINT "-";
2570   NEXT COUNT
2580   PRINT
2590   REM
2600   REM ****** TERMINATION SECTION
2610   INPUT "DO YOU HAVE ANOTHER REQUEST FOR INFORMATION (Y OR N): ";ANSWER$
2620   REM TEST FOR VALID INPUT
2630   IF ANSWER$ = "Y" OR ANSWER$ = "y" THEN GOTO 1450
2640   IF ANSWER$ <> "N" AND ANSWER$ <> "n" THEN GOTO 2610
2650   PRINT : PRINT : PRINT : PRINT
2660   PRINT "THANK YOU FOR USING OUR NEW CAR FINANCING PROGRAM."
2670   END
Ok
RUN
              REQUEST FOR AMOUNT OF MONTHLY PAYMENT

PLEASE ENTER THE CUSTOMER'S NAME: JOAN HARDIN

PLEASE ENTER THE SALESMAN'S NAME: JOE SMITH

WHAT IS THE PRICE OF THE NEW CAR?
DO NOT USE A COMMA (,) OR A DOLLAR ($) SIGN: 10500

WHAT IS THE TRADE IN AMOUNT?
DO NOT USE A COMMA (,) OR A DOLLAR ($) SIGN: 2000

WHAT IS THE CASH DOWN PAYMENT AMOUNT?
DO NOT USE A COMMA (,) OR A DOLLAR ($) SIGN: 1000

WHAT IS THE ANNUAL INTEREST RATE?
DO NOT USE A PERCENTAGE (%) SIGN: 10.8


                  AMOUNTS OF MONTHLY PAYMENT


DATE:                        01-11-1991
CUSTOMER'S NAME:              JOAN HARDIN
SALESMAN:                     JOE SMITH
NEW CAR PURCHASE PRICE:      $10,500.00
TRADE IN AMOUNT:             $2,000.00
CASH DOWN PAYMENT AMOUNT:    $1,000.00
TOTAL DOWN PAYMENT AMOUNT:   $3,000.00
ANNUAL INTEREST RATE:            10.80%

YEARS TO    AMOUNT     FINANCE    TOTAL     NUMBER OF   AMOUNT OF
FINANCE     FINANCED   CHARGE     PAYMENTS  PAYMENTS    MO. PAYMENT

   1      $7,500.00     $446.04  $7,946.04     12        $662.17
   2      $7,500.00     $872.88  $8,372.88     24        $348.87
   3      $7,500.00   $1,313.88  $8,813.88     36        $244.83
   4      $7,500.00   $1,769.76  $9,269.76     48        $193.12
   5      $7,500.00   $2,239.20  $9,739.20     60        $162.32

------------------------------------------------------------------------
DO YOU HAVE ANOTHER REQUEST FOR INFORMATION (Y OR N): ? N


THANK YOU FOR USING OUR NEW CAR FINANCING PROGRAM.
```

**Figure 11–3** *(Continued)*

## 11-5
## ECONOMIC ORDER QUANTITY

Many firms must contend with large inventory ordering, handling, and carrying costs. They develop inventory policies to keep the total costs of ordering and carrying inventory at a minimum. One inventory model is the **economic order quantity** (EOQ), which, when applied correctly, minimizes total inventory costs. This model determines the number of units that minimizes total inventory costs. The formula used for this model is as follows:

$$EOQ = \sqrt{\frac{2*A*O}{C*P}}$$

where: A = annual inventory requirements
O = cost of placing an order
C = single unit cost
P = percentage of inventory value allotted for carrying costs
EOQ = number of units to order to minimize the firm's total inventory costs
T = minimum total cost for carrying and ordering EOQ

With this formula, you can compute the EOQ for many different products with different selling prices and different annual sales. It is also possible to calculate the minimum total costs for carrying and ordering the EOQ.

Suppose that Beauty Green Shoe Company is planning to minimize total inventory costs. The sales manager has heard about the EOQ model. Figure 11-4 shows an interactive program that determines the Economic Order Quantity for this company. The program also determines the total costs of this order.

## 11-6
## BREAK-EVEN ANALYSIS

Many firms use a method known as **break-even analysis** to help determine at what production level sales revenue will equal production costs, assuming a certain selling price. This analysis helps a company decide on its output level. It also serves as a valuable pricing tool if the company's pricing objective is to maximize profits.

To determine the break-even point, you must enter the total fixed costs of production (overhead), the costs that vary with the number of units produced (variable cost), and the proposed selling price per unit. The difference between the unit price and the variable costs is the amount contributed to overhead. The break-even point is the number of units the company needs to sell at this price. The units' combined contributions to overhead equals the total overhead (see table 11-1).

Electro-Kamoko is a manufacturer of electronic devices. The production manager is faced with the question of how many units to produce in order to stay at the break-even point. Figure 11-5 shows an interactive program that computes the break-even point for different unit prices, variable costs, and fixed overhead costs. The program also determines the total cost of this quantity.

## 11-7
## PRODUCTION ANALYSIS

Suppliers of perishable products face a serious question: How much should they buy to satisfy demand while minimizing spoilage from overstocking? One method for determining this amount is known as **expected opportunity loss**.

```
100   REM PROGRAM TO ANALYZE VARIOUS COSTS OF ORDERING AND MAINTAINING
110   REM INVENTORY TO DETERMINE THE OPTIMUM ORDER QUANTITY OR THE
120   REM ECONOMIC ORDER QUANTITY (EOQ).
130   REM
140   REM ****** VARIABLE TABLE
150   REM         COST = THE SINGLE UNIT COST
160   REM         ANNUAL = THE ANNUAL INVENTORY REQUIREMENT
170   REM         ORDER = THE COST OF PLACING AND HANDLING AN ORDER
180   REM         PER = THE PERCENTAGE OF INVENTORY ALLOTTED FOR CARRYING COSTS
190   REM         EOQ = THE ECONOMIC ORDER QUANTITY
200   REM         TOTAL = THE TOTAL COST OF ORDERING AND CARRYING THE EOQ
210   REM         ANSWER$ = REPEAT PROGRAM TEST VARIABLE
220   REM
230   REM ****** INITIALIZATION SECTION
240   CLS
250   PRINT "THIS PROGRAM ANALYZES YOUR FIRM'S VARIOUS COSTS OF"
260   PRINT "INVENTORY AND DETERMINES THE ECONOMIC ORDER QUANTITY TO"
270   PRINT "MINIMIZE TOTAL INVENTORY COSTS."
280   PRINT
290   PRINT
300   PRINT "PLEASE INPUT THE FOLLOWING:"
310   PRINT : INPUT "     SINGLE UNIT COST: ",COST
320   INPUT "     NUMBER OF UNITS SOLD ANNUALLY: ",ANNUAL
330   INPUT "     THE COST OF PLACING AND HANDLING EACH ORDER: ",ORDER
340   PRINT "     THE PERCENTAGE OF THE INVENTORY VALUE ALLOTTED ";
350   INPUT "TO CARRYING COSTS: ",PER
360   REM
370   REM ****** PROCESS SECTION
380   LET PER = PER/100
390   LET EOQ = SQR(2*ANNUAL*ORDER/(PER*COST))
400   LET TOTAL = SQR(2*ANNUAL*PER*ORDER*COST)
410   PRINT
420   REM
430   REM ****** OUTPUT SECTION
440   PRINT "THE ECONOMIC ORDER QUANTITY IS ";
450   PRINT USING "#####";EOQ;
460   PRINT " UNITS PER ORDER"
470   PRINT
480   PRINT "THE COST OF PLACING AND HANDLING THIS ORDER WOULD BE ";
490   PRINT USING "####.##";TOTAL
500   PRINT
510   PRINT
520   REM
530   REM ****** TERMINATION SECTION
540   INPUT "WOULD YOU LIKE TO RECOMPUTE YOUR EOQ (Y OR N): ",ANSWER$
550   REM TEST FOR VALID USER INPUT
560   IF ANSWER$ = "Y" OR ANSWER$ = "y" THEN GOTO 240
570   IF ANSWER$ <> "N" AND ANSWER$ <> "n" THEN GOTO 540
580   END


THIS PROGRAM ANALYZES YOUR FIRM'S VARIOUS COSTS OF
INVENTORY AND DETERMINES THE ECONOMIC ORDER QUANTITY TO
MINIMIZE TOTAL INVENTORY COSTS.


PLEASE INPUT THE FOLLOWING:

     SINGLE UNIT COST: 2
     NUMBER OF UNITS SOLD ANNUALLY: 4000
     THE COST OF PLACING AND HANDLING EACH ORDER: 15
     THE PERCENTAGE OF THE INVENTORY VALUE ALLOTTED TO CARRYING COSTS: 10

THE ECONOMIC ORDER QUANTITY IS    775 UNITS PER ORDER

THE COST OF PLACING AND HANDLING THIS ORDER WOULD BE   154.92


WOULD YOU LIKE TO RECOMPUTE YOUR EOQ (Y OR N): N
Ok
```

**Figure 11–4**
Economic Order Quantity

| Unit<br>Price | Variable<br>Costs | Contribution<br>to Overhead | Overhead<br>(Total) | Break-Even<br>Point |
|---|---|---|---|---|
| $60 | $30 | $30 | $250 | 8.3 units |
| 80 | 30 | 50 | 250 | 5.0 units |
| 100 | 30 | 70 | 250 | 3.6 units |
| 150 | 30 | 120 | 250 | 2.1 units |
| 200 | 150 | 50 | 250 | 5.0 units |

**Table 11–1**
An Example Break-Even
Analysis

The manager of Happy Rental Car Company wants to know how many rental cars he should make available for his customers. Over-supply and under-supply is a problem. Past experience shows that the number of rental cars demanded ranges from 15 to 21 with the following probabilities:

| Cars | Probabilities |
|---|---|
| 15 | .12 |
| 16 | .12 |
| 17 | .10 |
| 18 | .08 |
| 19 | .20 |
| 20 | .25 |
| 21 | .13 |

The cost to Happy Rental Car Company for renting a car is $20; a customer pays $28 to rent a car.

Table 11–2 shows an opportunity loss table. Whenever the supply is equal to the demand, there is no opportunity loss. Each unit of over-supply costs the company $20. Each unit of under-supply means an $8 opportunity cost (the company would have made an $8 profit if the car had been available).

The expected opportunity loss of supplying 15 cars is $27.12. This amount is calculated as follows:

$$0(.12) + 8(.12) + 16(.10) + 24(.08) + 32(.20) + 40(.25) + 48(.13) = 27.12$$

The expected opportunity losses for the other units of supply are as follows:

| Cars | Loss |
|---|---|
| 15 | 27.12 |
| 16 | 22.48 |
| 17 | 21.20 |
| 18 | 22.72 |
| 19 | 26.48 |
| 20 | 35.84 |
| 21 | 52.20 |

As you can see, supplying 17 cars results in the minimum opportunity loss.

The manager of Delicious Super Star Restaurant is deciding how many dishes to prepare for tomorrow. He is dealing with perishable products, so he must produce enough to satisfy the demand without creating an over-supply so that spoilage is a problem. Draw a flowchart and write and run an interactive

```
100   REM PROGRAM TO DETERMINE BREAK-EVEN POINT.
110   REM
120   REM ****** VARIABLE TABLE
130   REM           FIXED = TOTAL FIXED COSTS OR OVERHEAD
140   REM           VARIABLE = VARIABLE COSTS PER UNIT
150   REM           UNIT =  IS THE UNIT SELLING PRICE
160   REM           CONTRIB = UNIT CONTRIBUTION TO OVERHEAD
170   REM           BEP = BREAK-EVEN POINT UNITS
180   REM           ANSWER$ = REPEAT PROGRAM TEST VARIABLE
190   REM
200   REM ****** INITIALIZATION SECTION
210   CLS
220   PRINT "THIS PROGRAM WILL DETERMINE THE BREAK-EVEN POINT FOR"
230   PRINT "A PRODUCT WITH A GIVEN UNIT SELLING PRICE AND KNOWN"
240   PRINT "PRODUCTION COSTS."
250   PRINT : PRINT
260   PRINT "PLEASE INPUT THE FOLLOWING:"
270   PRINT
280   INPUT "       (1)  YOUR TOTAL FIXED PRODUCTION COSTS (OVERHEAD): ",FIXED
290   INPUT "       (2)  YOUR VARIABLE COSTS PER UNIT: ",VARIABLE
300   INPUT "       (3)  YOUR UNIT SELLING PRICE: ",UNIT
310   PRINT : PRINT
320   REM
330   REM ****** PROCESS SECTION
340   LET CONTRIB = UNIT-VARIABLE
350   LET BEP = FIXED/CONTRIB
360   REM
370   REM ****** OUTPUT SECTION
380   PRINT "UNIT PRICE    VARIABLE COSTS    OVERHEAD    BREAK-EVEN POINT"
390   PRINT "-----------------------------------------------------------"
400   PRINT USING "#####.##        ####.##";UNIT,VARIABLE;
410   PRINT USING "         #####.##     ######.# UNITS";FIXED,BEP
420   PRINT : PRINT
430   REM
440   REM ****** TERMINATION SECTION
450   INPUT "DO YOU WANT TO COMPUTE ANOTHER BREAK-EVEN POINT (Y OR N): ",ANSWER$
460   REM TEST FOR VALID USER INPUT
470   IF ANSWER$ = "Y" OR ANSWER$ = "y" THEN GOTO 210
480   IF ANSWER$ <> "N" AND ANSWER$ <> "n" THEN GOTO 450
490   END


THIS PROGRAM WILL DETERMINE THE BREAK-EVEN POINT FOR
A PRODUCT WITH A GIVEN UNIT SELLING PRICE AND KNOWN
PRODUCTION COSTS.


PLEASE INPUT THE FOLLOWING:

      (1)  YOUR TOTAL FIXED PRODUCTION COSTS (OVERHEAD): 250
      (2)  YOUR VARIABLE COSTS PER UNIT: 30
      (3)  YOUR UNIT SELLING PRICE: 60


UNIT PRICE     VARIABLE COSTS     OVERHEAD    BREAK-EVEN POINT
-----------------------------------------------------------
   60.00          30.00            250.00       8.3 UNITS


DO YOU WANT TO COMPUTE ANOTHER BREAK-EVEN POINT (Y OR N): N
Ok
```

**Figure 11–5**
Break-Even Analysis

| Number of Rental Cars Demanded | Probability of Past Demand | Number of Rental Cars Supplied | | | | | | |
|---|---|---|---|---|---|---|---|---|
| | | **15** | **16** | **17** | **18** | **19** | **20** | **21** |
| 15 | .12 | 0 | 20 | 40 | 60 | 80 | 100 | 120 |
| 16 | .12 | 8 | 0 | 20 | 40 | 60 | 80 | 100 |
| 17 | .10 | 16 | 8 | 0 | 20 | 40 | 60 | 80 |
| 18 | .08 | 24 | 16 | 8 | 0 | 20 | 40 | 60 |
| 19 | .20 | 32 | 24 | 16 | 8 | 0 | 20 | 40 |
| 20 | .25 | 40 | 32 | 24 | 16 | 8 | 0 | 20 |
| 21 | .13 | 48 | 40 | 32 | 24 | 16 | 8 | 0 |

**Table 11–2**
Opportunity Loss Table for Happy Rental Car Company

program to accept up to 20 different supplies and demands with different probabilities and to generate the number of dishes that has the minimum expected opportunity loss (see figs. 11–6 and 11–7). We have used the LOCATE command in some of our programs in the next two chapters. This command positions the cursor on the screen. See Figure A–12 in Appendix A for more explanation.

## 11–8
## MARKET AND SALES FORCE ANALYSIS

**Market analysis** and **sales force analysis** are two methods that can be used for monitoring the overall sales performance of a company. With market analysis, you can spot high and low sales performances in different regions, and you can see the performances of different salespeople in different regions. You can use this information to make decisions regarding promotions, media selection, advertising campaigns, distribution channels, and so forth.

Suppose that, as the sales manager of a large Northwest manufacturing firm, you are asked to give a presentation on sales performance at the next meeting of the board of directors. You want to have a computer printout showing overall sales, total sales in each region, and the total sales generated by each salesperson. Using READ and DATA statements, write and run a program to generate bar graphs showing the sales of individual salespeople and the sales of each region. The graphs should express sales as a percent of total sales, and they should show the actual dollar amounts. Because you also want performance information, the individual graphs should be ranked in order, from highest to lowest sales (see fig. 11–8).

The input data are as follows:

| Salesperson | Washington | Oregon | Idaho | California |
|---|---|---|---|---|
| J. Allen | 1000 | 2990 | 4185 | 7240 |
| L. Carter | 6000 | 7205 | 8165 | 28810 |
| A. Darsfan | 6750 | 7880 | 8215 | 15760 |
| P. Flemming | 5870 | 6210 | 6440 | 8500 |
| M. Heinlein | 2330 | 5970 | 5320 | 9525 |
| H. Hogle | 6150 | 17165 | 5600 | 1535 |
| J. Newall | 23650 | 13140 | 9195 | 19710 |
| A. Rush | 16050 | 11555 | 8220 | 25935 |
| J. Taylor | 12420 | 9035 | 6325 | 14680 |
| F. Williams | 3340 | 6375 | 2595 | 3115 |
| A. Wood | 6790 | 7350 | 3860 | 1300 |

**Figure 11–6**

The Flowchart for the Program in Figure 11–7

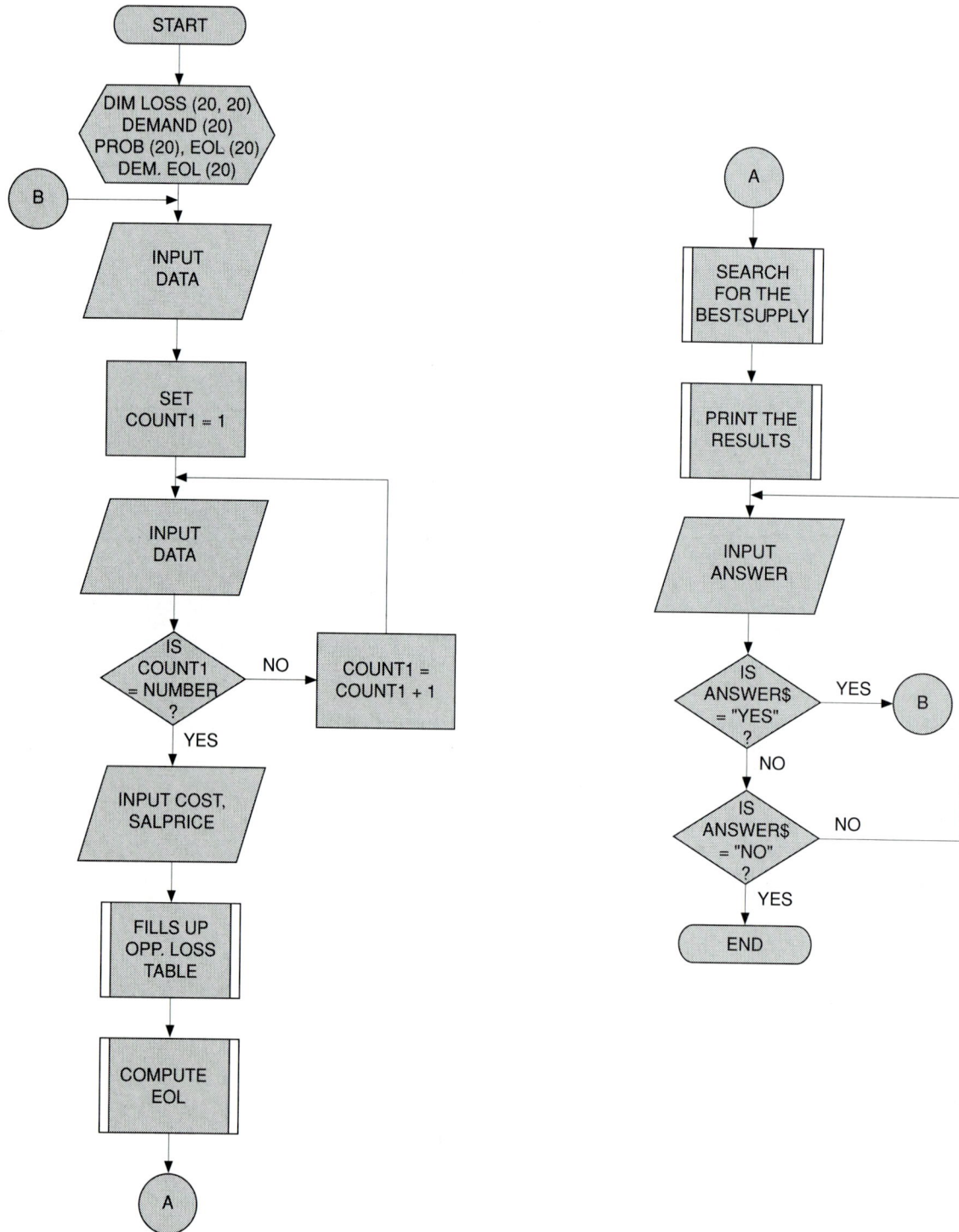

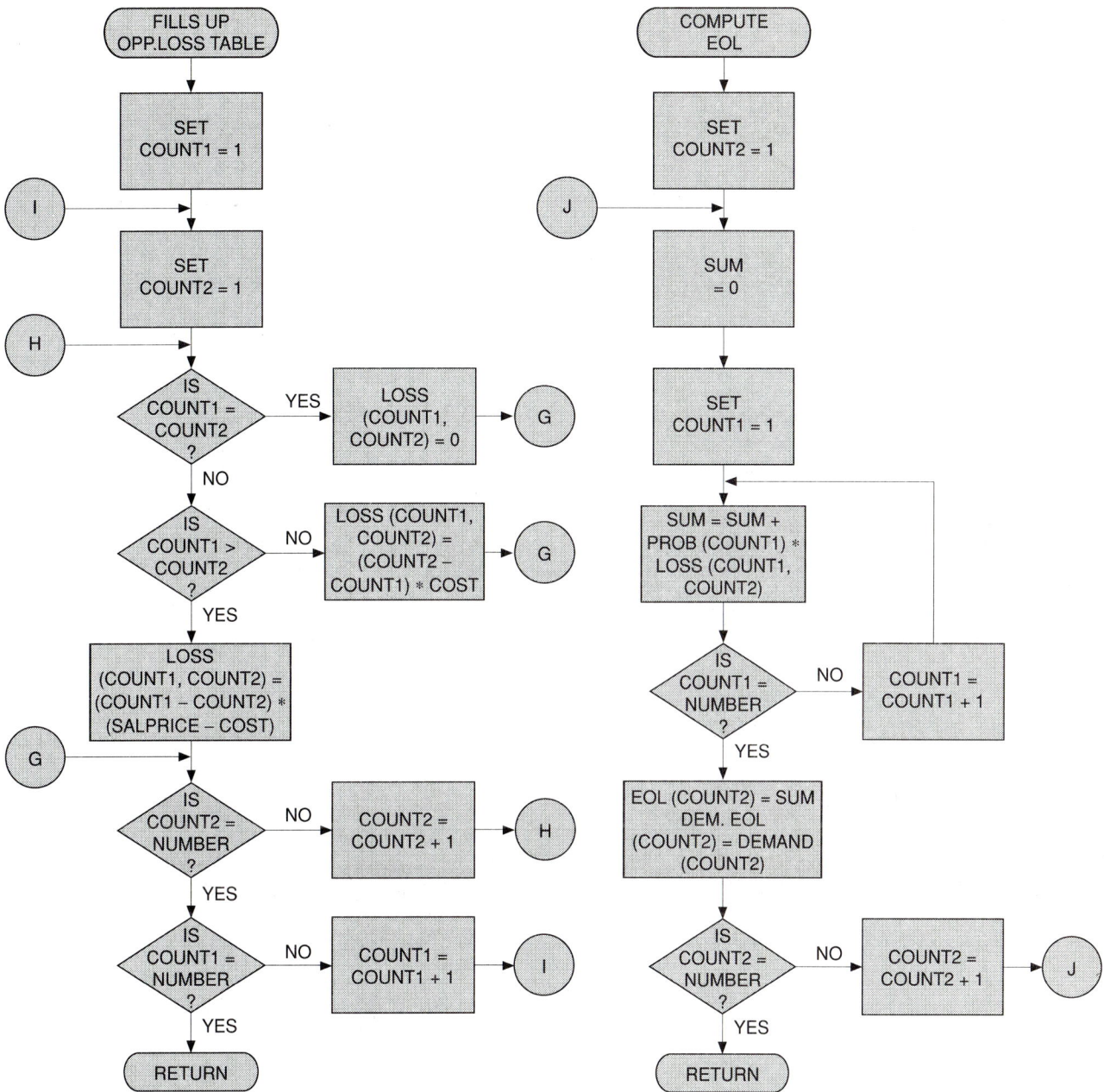

**Figure 11–6** *(Continued)*

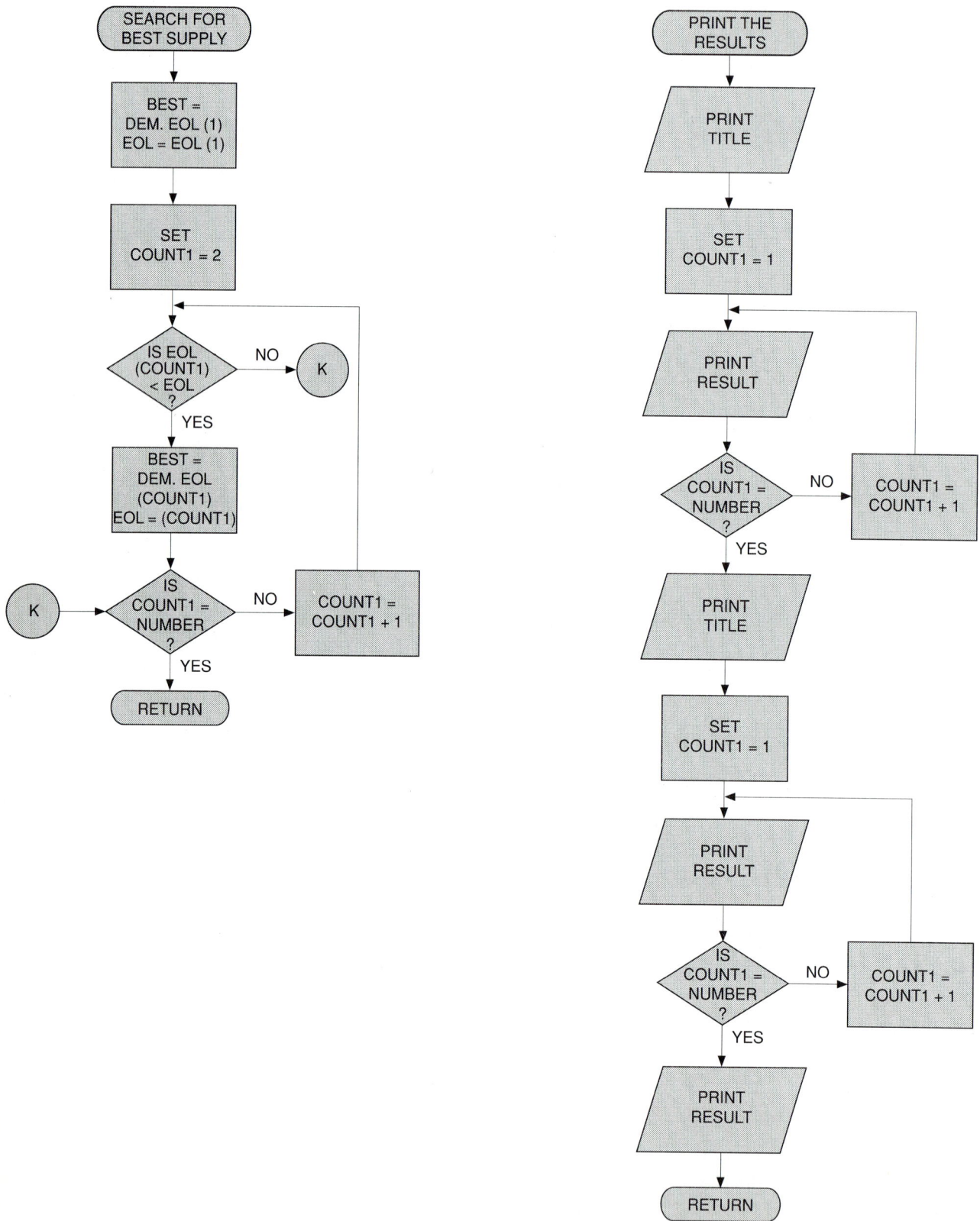

**Figure 11-6** *(Continued)*

**Figure 11–7**
Production Analysis

```
1000 REM THIS PROGRAM ACCEPTS UP TO 20 PAIRS OF DATA
1010 REM (DEMAND AND ASSOCIATED PROBABILITIES) AND COMPUTES
1020 REM THE MINIMUM EOL (EXPECTED OPPORTUNITY LOSS).
1030 REM IF THE NUMBER OF THESE PAIRS EXCEEDS 20, THE DIM STATEMENT
1040 REM MUST BE MODIFIED.
1050 REM
1060 REM ****** VARIABLE TABLE
1070 REM           COUNT1, COUNT2 = FOR-NEXT LOOP CONTROL VARIABLES
1080 REM           NUMBER = THE NUMBER OF DATA PAIRS TO CONSIDER
1090 REM           SALPRICE = THE SALES PRICE
1100 REM           COST = THE PRODUCTION COST
1110 REM           SUM = FOR-NEXT LOOP ACCUMULATOR VARIABLE
1120 REM           EOL = THE LOWEST EXPECTED OPPORTUNITY LOSS
1130 REM           BEST = THE BEST SUPPLY
1140 REM
1150 REM ****** MATRIX AND ARRAY TABLE
1160 REM           LOSS(20,20) = THE MATRIX FOR THE OPPORTUNITY LOSS
1170 REM           DEMAND(20) = THE ARRAY FOR THE DEMAND
1180 REM           PROB(20) = THE ARRAY FOR THE PROBABILITIES
1190 REM           EOL(20) = THE ARRAY FOR THE EXPECTED OPPORTUNITY LOSS
1200 REM           DEM.EOL(20) = THE ARRAY FOR ASSOCIATED DEMAND WITH EOL
1210 REM
1220 REM ****** INITIALIZATION SECTION
1230 DIM LOSS(20,20), DEMAND(20), PROB(20), EOL(20), DEM.EOL(20)
1240 CLS
1250 INPUT "PLEASE ENTER THE NUMBER OF DATA PAIRS YOU WANT TO CONSIDER: ",NUMBER
1260 PRINT "PLEASE ENTER THE DIFFERENT VALUES OF DEMAND AND THEIR ";
1270 PRINT "ASSOCIATED PROBABILITIES."
1280 REM
1290 FOR COUNT1 = 1 TO NUMBER
1300 LOCATE 6,1
1310    PRINT "PLEASE ENTER DEMAND #";COUNT1;":";
1320    INPUT " ",DEMAND(COUNT1)
1330    PRINT "PLEASE ENTER PROBABILITY #";COUNT1;":";
1340    INPUT " ",PROB(COUNT1)
1350 NEXT COUNT1
1360 REM
1370 INPUT "PLEASE ENTER THE PRODUCTION COST: ",COST
1380 INPUT "PLEASE ENTER THE SALES PRICE: ",SALPRICE
1390 REM
1400 REM ****** PROCESS SECTION
1410 GOSUB 1540
1420 GOSUB 1700
1430 GOSUB 1850
1440 GOSUB 1980
1450 REM
1460 REM ****** TERMINATION SECTION
1470 PRINT "++++++++++++++++++++++++++++++++++++++++++++++++++++++++"
1480 INPUT "DO YOU WANT TO ENTER ANOTHER SERIES OF DATA (Y OR N): ",ANSWER$
1490 REM TEST FOR VALID USER INPUT
1500 IF ANSWER$ = "Y" OR ANSWER$ = "y" THEN GOTO 1240
1510 IF ANSWER$ <> "N" AND ANSWER$ <> "n" THEN GOTO 1480
1520 GOTO 2180
1530 REM
1540 REM THIS SUBROUTINE FILLS UP THE OPPORTUNITY LOSS TABLE.
1550 FOR COUNT1 = 1 TO NUMBER
1560    FOR COUNT2 = 1 TO NUMBER
1570       IF COUNT1 = COUNT2 THEN 1600
1580       IF COUNT1 > COUNT2 THEN 1640
1590       GOTO 1620
1600       LET LOSS(COUNT1,COUNT2) = 0
```

```
1610      GOTO 1650
1620      LET LOSS(COUNT1,COUNT2) = (COUNT2-COUNT1)*COST
1630      GOTO 1650
1640      LET LOSS(COUNT1,COUNT2) = (COUNT1-COUNT2)*(SALPRICE-COST)
1650    NEXT COUNT2
1660 NEXT COUNT1
1670 REM
1680 RETURN
1690 REM
1700 REM THIS SUBROUTINE COMPUTES THE EXPECTED OPPORTUNITY LOSS
1710 REM AND STORES THE RESULT INTO ARRAY EOL.
1720 REM DEM_EOL KEEPS TRACK OF EXPECTED OPPORTUNITY LOSS FOR
1730 REM EACH SPECIFIC DEMAND AND/OR SUPPLY.
1740 REM
1750 FOR COUNT2 = 1 TO NUMBER
1760    LET SUM = 0
1770    FOR COUNT1 = 1 TO NUMBER
1780      LET SUM = SUM+PROB(COUNT1)*LOSS(COUNT1,COUNT2)
1790    NEXT COUNT1
1800    LET EOL(COUNT2) = SUM
1810    LET DEM.EOL(COUNT2) = DEMAND(COUNT2)
1820 NEXT COUNT2
1830 REM
1840 RETURN
1850 REM THIS SUBROUTINE SEARCHES FOR THE BEST SUPPLY.
1860 LET BEST = DEM.EOL(1)
1870 LET EOL = EOL(1)
1880 FOR COUNT1 = 2 TO NUMBER
1890    IF EOL(COUNT1) < EOL THEN 1910
1900    GOTO 1930
1910    LET BEST = DEM.EOL(COUNT1)
1920    LET EOL = EOL(COUNT1)
1930 NEXT COUNT1
1940 REM
1950 RETURN
1960 REM
1970 REM ******  OUTPUT SECTION
1980 REM THIS SUBROUTINE PRINTS THE RESULT.
1990 PRINT "*********************************************************"
2000 PRINT TAB(15); "PRODUCTION ANALYSIS"
2010 PRINT "THE FOLLOWING ARE THE ORIGINAL DATA"
2020 REM
2030 FOR COUNT1 = 1 TO NUMBER
2040    PRINT USING "##.##                ##.##";DEMAND(COUNT1),PROB(COUNT1)
2050 NEXT COUNT1
2060 REM
2070 PRINT "THE FOLLOWING ARE DIFFERENT SUPPLIES AND THEIR EOL"
2080 REM
2090 FOR COUNT1 = 1 TO NUMBER
2100    PRINT USING "##.##        ###.##";DEMAND(COUNT1),EOL(COUNT1)
2110 NEXT COUNT1
2120 REM
2130 PRINT "SUPPLY OF ";
2140 PRINT USING "##    ";BEST;
2150 PRINT "UNITS WILL HAVE THE MINIMUM EOL OF ";
2160 PRINT USING "$$##.##";EOL
2170 RETURN
2180 END
PLEASE ENTER THE NUMBER OF DATA PAIRS YOU WANT TO CONSIDER:
 10
PLEASE ENTER THE DIFFERENT VALUES OF DEMAND AND THEIR ASSOCIATED PROBABILITIES.
PLEASE ENTER DEMAND # 1 :     20
PLEASE ENTER PROBABILITY # 1 :               .1
PLEASE ENTER DEMAND # 2 :     21
```

**Figure 11–7** (Continued)

224

```
PLEASE ENTER PROBABILITY # 2 :               .05
PLEASE ENTER DEMAND # 3 :      22
PLEASE ENTER PROBABILITY # 3 :               .02
PLEASE ENTER DEMAND # 4 :      23
PLEASE ENTER PROBABILITY # 4 :               .2
PLEASE ENTER DEMAND # 5 :      24
PLEASE ENTER PROBABILITY # 5 :               .15
PLEASE ENTER DEMAND # 6 :      25
PLEASE ENTER PROBABILITY # 6 :               .18
PLEASE ENTER DEMAND # 7 :      26
PLEASE ENTER PROBABILITY # 7 :               .1
PLEASE ENTER DEMAND # 8 :      27
PLEASE ENTER PROBABILITY # 8 :               .12
PLEASE ENTER DEMAND # 9 :      28
PLEASE ENTER PROBABILITY # 9 :               .03
PLEASE ENTER DEMAND # 10 :      29
PLEASE ENTER PROBABILITY # 10 :              .05
PLEASE ENTER THE PRODUCTION COST:           25
PLEASE ENTER THE SALES PRICE:               35
*******************************************************
               PRODUCTION ANALYSIS
THE FOLLOWING ARE THE ORIGINAL DATA
20.00                    0.10
21.00                    0.05
22.00                    0.02
23.00                    0.20
24.00                    0.15
25.00                    0.18
26.00                    0.10
27.00                    0.12
28.00                    0.03
29.00                    0.05
THE FOLLOWING ARE DIFFERENT SUPPLIES AND THEIR EOL
20.00          43.20
21.00          36.70
22.00          31.95
23.00          27.90
24.00          30.85
25.00          39.05
26.00          53.55
27.00          71.55
28.00          93.75
29.00         117.00
SUPPLY OF 23    UNITS WILL HAVE THE MINIMUM EOL OF  $27.90
+++++++++++++++++++++++++++++++++++++++++++++++++++++++
DO YOU WANT TO ENTER ANOTHER SERIES OF DATA (Y OR N):    N
```

**Figure 11–7**  (Continued)


**Figure 11–8**

Market and Sales Force Analysis

```
1000    REM PROGRAM TITLE:  MARKET/SALES FORCE ANALYSIS
1010    REM
1020    REM THIS PROGRAM READS DATA ON THE AMOUNT OF SALES GENERATED
1030    REM IN 4 REGIONS BY 11 SALESPEOPLE AND TOTALS THE INFORMATION
1040    REM FOR EACH CATEGORY.   THE INFORMATION IS PRINTED IN
1050    REM BAR GRAPH FORM.   ONE GRAPH FOR REGIONAL SALES AND
1060    REM ONE FOR SALESPEOPLE.   THEY ARE SHOWN IN PERCENT OF OVERALL
1070    REM TOTAL SALES.   THE GRAPHS ARE RANKED FROM TOP TO BOTTOM,
1080    REM HIGHEST TO LOWEST SALES.
1090    REM
1100    REM ****** DATA SECTION
```

```
1110    REM THE FOLLOWING ARE THE SALES DATA.
1120    DATA 1000,2990,4185,7240,6000,7205,8165,28810
1130    DATA 6750,7880,8215,15760,5870,6210,6440,8500
1140    DATA 2330,5970,5320,9525,6150,17165,5600,1535
1150    DATA 23650,13140,9195,19710,16050,11555,8220,25935
1160    DATA 12420,9035,6325,14680,3340,6375,2595,3115
1170    DATA 6790,7350,3860,1300
1180    REM THE FOLLOWING DATA ARE THE NAMES OF THE SALESPEOPLE.
1190    DATA J. ALLEN,L. CARTER,A. DARSFAN,P. FLEMING,M. HEINLEIN
1200    DATA H. HOGLE,J. NEWALL,A. RUSH,J. TAYLOR,F. WILLIAMS
1210    DATA A. WOOD
1220    REM THE FOLLOWING DATA ARE THE NAMES OF THE REGIONS.
1230    DATA WASHINGTON,OREGON,IDAHO,CALIFORNIA
1240    REM
1250    REM ****** VARIABLE TABLE
1260    REM          COUNT1, COUNT2 = FOR-NEXT LOOP CONTROL VARIABLES
1270    REM          TOTAL = TEMPORARY ADDRESS FOR THE TOTALS
1280    REM          TEMP = TEMPORARY SORT SWITCHING VARIABLE
1290    REM          TEMP$ = TEMPORARY SORT SWITCHING VARIABLE
1300    REM          TOT.OVER.SAL = TOTAL OVERALL SALES
1310    REM          NUM1 = SCALE FACTOR, EITHER 1 OR 2
1320    REM          NUM2 = COUNTER, EITHER 4 OR 11
1330    REM          OUT.P$ = PRINT USING OUTPUT IMAGE
1340    REM
1350    REM ****** MATRIX AND ARRAY TABLE
1360    REM          SALES(11,4) = MATRIX FOR THE SALES DATA
1370    REM          NAM$(11) = NAMES OF THE SALESPEOPLE
1380    REM          REGION$(4) = NAMES OF THE REGIONS
1390    REM          SALTOT(11) = TOTAL OF SALES BY SALESPERSON
1400    REM          REGTOT(4) = TOTAL OF SALES BY REGION
1410    REM          DO(11) = VARIABLE HOLDER FOR SALTOT(11) OR REGTOT(4)
1420    REM          DO$(11) = VARIABLE HOLDER FOR NAM$(11) OR REGION$(4)
1430    REM          FILL(50) = THE NUMBER OF "*" TO PRINT
1440    REM          NUM(11) = A COUNTER, EITHER 4 OR 11
1450    REM
1460    REM ****** INITIALIZATION SECTION
1470    REM THE FOLLOWING ARE THE DIMENSIONS OF THE MATRIX AND ARRAYS.
1480    DIM SALES(11,4), NAM$(11), REGION$(4), SALTOT(11), REGTOT(4)
1490    DIM DO(11), DO$(11), FILL(50), NUM(11)
1500    REM
1510    REM ****** PROCESS SECTION
1520    REM THE SALES MATRIX IS FILLED IN THIS SECTION.
1530    FOR COUNT1 = 1 TO 11
1540      FOR COUNT2 = 1 TO 4
1550        READ SALES(COUNT1,COUNT2)
1560      NEXT COUNT2
1570    NEXT COUNT1
1580    REM
1590    REM THE TOTAL SALES FOR EACH SALESPERSON IS DETERMINED, AND
1600    REM THE SALESPERSON NAME ARRAY IS FILLED.
1610    REM TOTAL IS A TEMPORARY ADDRESS FOR THE TOTALS.
1620    REM
1630    LET TOTAL = 0
1640    FOR COUNT1 = 1 TO 11
1650      READ NAM$(COUNT1)
1660      FOR COUNT2 = 1 TO 4
1670        LET TOTAL = TOTAL+SALES(COUNT1,COUNT2)
1680      NEXT COUNT2
1690      LET SALTOT(COUNT1) = TOTAL
1700      LET TOTAL = 0
1710    NEXT COUNT1
1720    REM
1730    REM THE TOTAL SALES FOR EACH REGION IS DETERMINED AND THE
1740    REM REGION NAME ARRAY FILLED.
1750    LET TOTAL = 0
1760    FOR COUNT1 = 1 TO 4
1770      READ REGION$(COUNT1)
1780      FOR COUNT2 = 1 TO 11
```

**Figure 11–8** *(Continued)*

226

```
1790        LET TOTAL = TOTAL+SALES(COUNT2,COUNT1)
1800      NEXT COUNT2
1810      LET REGTOT(COUNT1) = TOTAL
1820      LET TOTAL = 0
1830    NEXT COUNT1
1840    REM
1850    REM THE FOLLOWING "BUBBLE SORT" ROUTINE SORTS THE SALES FROM
1860    REM HIGH TO LOW, STARTING WITH SALESPEOPLE AND THEN BY REGION.
1870    REM COUNT1 AND COUNT2 ARE COUNTERS AND TEMP AND TEMP$ ARE
1880    REM TEMPORARY ADDRESSES.
1890    REM
1900    FOR COUNT1 = 1 TO 10
1910      FOR COUNT2 = COUNT1+1 TO 11
1920        IF SALTOT(COUNT1) >= SALTOT(COUNT2) THEN GOTO 1990
1930        LET TEMP = SALTOT(COUNT1)
1940        LET SALTOT(COUNT1) = SALTOT(COUNT2)
1950        LET SALTOT(COUNT2) = TEMP
1960        LET TEMP$ = NAM$(COUNT1)
1970        LET NAM$(COUNT1) = NAM$(COUNT2)
1980        LET NAM$(COUNT2) = TEMP$
1990      NEXT COUNT2
2000    NEXT COUNT1
2010    REM
2020    FOR COUNT1 = 1 TO 3
2030      FOR COUNT2 = COUNT1+1 TO 4
2040        IF REGTOT(COUNT1) >= REGTOT(COUNT2) THEN GOTO 2110
2050        LET TEMP = REGTOT(COUNT1)
2060        LET REGTOT(COUNT1) = REGTOT(COUNT2)
2070        LET REGTOT(COUNT2) = TEMP
2080        LET TEMP$ = REGION$(COUNT1)
2090        LET REGION$(COUNT1) = REGION$(COUNT2)
2100        LET REGION$(COUNT2) = TEMP$
2110      NEXT COUNT2
2120    NEXT COUNT1
2130    REM
2140    REM THE FOLLOWING DETERMINES OVERALL TOTAL SALES.
2150    REM TOT.OVER.SAL  = TOTAL OVERALL SALES.
2160    LET TOT.OVER.SAL = 0
2170    FOR COUNT1 = 1 TO 4
2180      LET TOT.OVER.SAL = TOT.OVER.SAL+REGTOT(COUNT1)
2190    NEXT COUNT1
2200    REM
2210    REM THE FOLLOWING TRANSFERS THE SALESPERSON INFORMATION
2220    REM INTO THE BAR GRAPH SUBROUTINE ARRAYS.
2230    LET NUM1 = 2
2240    LET NUM2 = 11
2250    LET OUT.P$ = "SALES BY PERSON AS A PERCENT OF TOTAL SALES"
2260    FOR COUNT1 = 1 TO 11
2270      LET DO(COUNT1) = SALTOT(COUNT1)
2280      LET DO$(COUNT1) = NAM$(COUNT1)
2290    NEXT COUNT1
2300    REM
2310    GOSUB 2510
2320    REM
2330    REM THE FOLLOWING TRANSFERS THE REGION INFORMATION
2340    REM INTO THE BAR GRAPH SUBROUTINE ARRAYS.
2350    REM
2360    REM THE FOLLOWING FILLS THE SUBROUTINE ARRAYS.
2370    LET NUM1 = 1
2380    LET NUM2 = 4
2390    REM
2400    LET OUT.P$ = "SALES BY REGION AS A PERCENT OF TOTAL SALES"
2410    FOR COUNT1 = 1 TO 4
2420      LET DO(COUNT1) = REGTOT(COUNT1)
2430      LET DO$(COUNT1) = REGION$(COUNT1)
2440    NEXT COUNT1
2450    REM
2460    GOSUB 2510
```

**Figure 11–8**  *(Continued)*

```
2470     REM THIS COMPLETES THE PROGRAM.
2480     GOTO 2960
2490     REM
2500     REM ****** OUTPUT SECTION
2510     REM THE FOLLOWING SUBROUTINE CALCULATES THE INFORMATION AND
2520     REM PRINTS THE BAR GRAPH FOR DIFFERENT REGIONS OR SALESPERSONS.
2530     PRINT : PRINT : PRINT : PRINT
2540     FOR COUNT1 = 1 TO 72
2550       PRINT "-";
2560     NEXT COUNT1
2570     REM
2580     PRINT : PRINT
2590     PRINT TAB(15);OUT.P$
2600     PRINT
2610     PRINT "TOTAL SALES TO DATE IS ";
2620     PRINT USING "$$######,.##";TOT.OVER.SAL
2630     PRINT : PRINT : PRINT
2640     REM
2650     REM THE FULL GRAPH REPRESENTS EITHER 25% OR 50% OF TOTAL
2660     REM SALES, AND THE INFORMATION IS SCALED TO FIT THE GRAPH.
2670     FOR COUNT1 = 1 TO NUM2
2680       LET FILL(COUNT1) = INT(100*DO(COUNT1)/TOT.OVER.SAL+.5)*NUM1
2690       PRINT DO$(COUNT1);
2700       FOR COUNT2 = 1 TO FILL(COUNT1)
2710         PRINT TAB(15+COUNT2);"*";
2720       NEXT COUNT2
2730       PRINT
2740       PRINT "SALES"
2750       PRINT USING "$$######,";DO(COUNT1)
2760       PRINT
2770     NEXT COUNT1
2780     REM
2790     PRINT : PRINT
2800     REM THE FOLLOWING PRINTS THE SCALE FOR THE GRAPH.
2810     PRINT TAB(15);
2820     FOR COUNT1 = 1 TO 5
2830       PRINT "#########+";TAB(15+10*COUNT1);
2840     NEXT COUNT1
2850     REM
2860     IF NUM1 = 2 THEN 2890
2870     PRINT TAB(15);"0         10%       20%       30%       40%       50%"
2880     GOTO 2900
2890     PRINT TAB(15);"0          5%       10%       15%       20%       25%"
2900     PRINT : PRINT : PRINT
2910     FOR COUNT1 = 1 TO 72
2920       PRINT TAB(COUNT1);"-";
2930     NEXT COUNT1
2940     PRINT : PRINT
2950     RETURN
2960     END
```

--------------------------------------------------------------------------

```
            SALES BY PERSON AS A PERCENT OF TOTAL SALES

TOTAL SALES TO DATE IS   $389,455.00



J. NEWALL      *******************************
SALES
  $65,695

A. RUSH        *****************************
SALES
  $61,760
```

**Figure 11–8**  *(Continued)*

```
L. CARTER        **************************
SALES
  $50,180

J. TAYLOR        *********************
SALES
  $42,460

A. DARSFAN       *******************
SALES
  $38,605

H. HOGLE         ***************
SALES
  $30,450

P. FLEMING       *************
SALES
  $27,020

M. HEINLEIN      ************
SALES
  $23,145

A. WOOD          **********
SALES
  $19,300

F. WILLIAMS      ********
SALES
  $15,425

J. ALLEN         ********
SALES
  $15,415




          #########+#########+#########+#########+#########+
          0        5%       10%       15%       20%       25%




------------------------------------------------------------------




------------------------------------------------------------------

          SALES BY REGION AS A PERCENT OF TOTAL SALES

TOTAL SALES TO DATE IS  $389,455.00



CALIFORNIA       ***********************************
SALES
  $136,110

OREGON           ***********************
SALES
  $94,875

WASHINGTON       **********************
SALES
  $90,350
```

**Figure 11–8**  *(Continued)*

```
IDAHO                ****************
SALES
  $68,120



           ########+########+########+########+########+
           0       10%      20%      30%      40%      50%



---------------------------------------------------------------
```

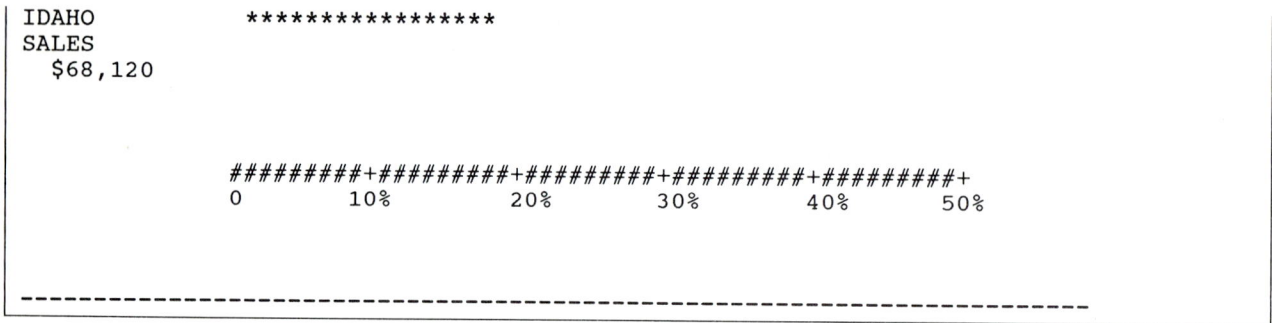

**Figure 11–8**   *(Continued)*

## 11–9
## FINANCIAL ANALYSIS

To measure the financial status of a company, many analysts use **financial statement analysis**. To perform this task, a series of ratios are computed and are compared with the same ratios from other companies in the same industry or from the company in past years. Some of the most commonly used ratios are as follows:

| Ratio | Formula | Key |
|---|---|---|
| Return on investment | $R = I/E$ | $R$ = return on investment<br>$I$ = net income<br>$E$ = owner equity |
| Earnings per share | $G = I/S$ | $G$ = earnings per share<br>$I$ = net income<br>$S$ = shares outstanding |
| Price to earnings ratio | $C = P/G$ | $C$ = price to earnings ratio<br>$P$ = market price per share<br>$G$ = earnings per share |
| Quick ratio | $Q = A/L1$ | $Q$ = quick ratio<br>$A$ = quick assets<br>$L1$ = current liabilities |
| Debt to equity ratio | $D = L2/E$ | $D$ = debt to equity ratio<br>$L2$ = total liabilities<br>$E$ = owners' equity |

You are interested in buying the stock of a corporation, hopefully as a hedge against inflation. However, each analyst you talk with tells you something different about the company. Confused and unhappy, you decide to gather selected financial data from several companies and, using some common financial ratios, make the investment analysis yourself.

Using the following data in READ/DATA statements, write a program to calculate the ratios and print them for comparison:

| Company Name | Net Inc. | Owner Equity | Shares Out. | Market Price | Quick Assets | Current Liab. | Total Liab. |
|---|---|---|---|---|---|---|---|
| Heinlein | 22380 | 18750 | 75000 | 2.50 | 43600 | 100200 | 219300 |
| How Chem. | 260456 | 200978 | 125000 | 16.00 | 78600 | 300870 | 807680 |
| Edsel Co. | 56890 | 124000 | 350000 | 3.50 | 62000 | 14680 | 35966 |
| Sounds | 26800 | 18000 | 15000 | 5.50 | 23090 | 10005 | 37416 |
| De Beer | 1330000 | 12135000 | 600000 | 45.00 | 6570000 | 5000000 | 13000000 |

Your program's output should include a listing of the input data and the following information listed by company name:

- Return on investment
- Earnings per share
- Price/earnings ratio
- Quick ratio
- Debt/equity ratio

Figure 11–9 shows this program.

**Figure 11–9**
Financial Statement Analysis

```
1000   REM PROGRAM NAME: FINANCIAL STATEMENT ANALYSIS
1010   REM
1020   REM THIS PROGRAM PRODUCES INFORMATION FROM DIFFERENT COMPANY'S
1030   REM FINANCIAL STATEMENTS IN TERMS OF FIVE COMMON RATIOS.  THESE
1040   REM RATIOS, WHEN EVALUATED AND COMPARED, GIVE A RELATIVE IDEA OF
1050   REM HOW EACH COMPANY IS DOING FINANCIALLY.
1060   REM
1070   REM *****CAUTION*****  INFORMATION FROM THIS PROGRAM IS NOT AN
1080   REM END IN ITSELF BUT ONLY PRODUCES INFORMATION THAT MUST BE
1090   REM CAREFULLY ANALYZED.  RATIOS ARE A STARTING POINT AS INDICATORS
1100   REM OF WHAT TO LOOK FOR IN GREATER DEPTH.
1110   REM
1120   REM THE RATIOS DETERMINED AND FORMULAS USED ARE;
1130   REM RETURN ON INVESTMENT = NET INCOME/OWNERS EQUITY
1140   REM RET = NET.INC/EQUITY
1150   REM EARNINGS PER SHARE = NET INCOME/NUMBER OF SHARES
1160   REM OUTSTANDING
1170   REM EPS = NET.INC/NUMSHARES
1180   REM PRICE TO EARNINGS RATIO = MARKET PRICE PER SHARE/
1190   REM EARNINGS PER SHARE
1200   REM PTE = PRICE.P.S/EPS
1210   REM QUICK RATIO = QUICK ASSETS/CURRENT LIABILITIES
1220   REM QUICK.R = QUICK.A/CURR.L
1230   REM DEBT TO EQUITY RATIO = TOTAL LIABILITIES/OWNERS EQUITY
1240   REM D.TO.E = TOT.L/EQUITY
1250   REM
1260   REM ****** VARIABLE TABLE
1270   REM        COUNT = FOR-NEXT LOOP CONTROL VARIABLE
1280   REM
1290   REM ****** ARRAY TABLE
1300   REM        NET.INC(5) = NET INCOME ARRAY
1310   REM        EQUITY(5) = OWNER'S EQUITY ARRAY
1320   REM        NUMSHARES(5) = NUMBER OF SHARES OUTSTANDING ARRAY
1330   REM        PRICE.P.S(5) = PRICE PER SHARE ARRAY
1340   REM        QUICK.A(5) = QUICK ASSETS ARRAY
```

```
1350   REM           CURR.L(5) = CURRENT LIABILITIES ARRAY
1360   REM           TOT.L(5) = TOTAL LIABILITIES ARRAY
1370   REM           NAM$ = COMPANY NAME ARRAY
1380   REM           RET$ = RETURN ON INVESTMET ARRAY
1390   REM           EPS = EARNINGS PER SHARE ARRAY
1400   REM           P.TO.E = PRICE TO EARNINGS RATIO ARRAY
1410   REM           QUICK.R = QUICK RATIO ARRAY
1420   REM           D.TO.E = DEBT TO EQUITY ARRAY
1430   REM
1440   REM ******* INITIALIZATION SECTION
1450   REM
1460   FOR COUNT = 1 TO 5
1470     READ NAM$(COUNT)
1480   NEXT COUNT
1490   REM
1500   REM ******* DATA SECTION
1510   DATA HEINLEIN INC., NOW CHEMICAL, EDSEL CO., SOUND DESIGN
1520   DATA DE BEER CO.
1530   DATA 22380, 18750,75000,2.5,43600,100200,219300
1540   DATA 260456, 200978, 125000,16.00, 78600,300870,807680
1550   DATA 56890, 124000,350000, 3.50,62000,14680,35966
1560   DATA 26800,18000,15000,5.50,23090,10005,37416
1570   DATA 1330000,1213500,600000,45.00, 6570000,5000000, 13000000
1580   REM
1590   REM ******* PROCESS SECTION
1600   REM THIS LOOP READS THE DATA AND CALCULATES THE RATIOS
1610   REM
1620   FOR COUNT = 1 TO 5
1630     READ NET.INC(COUNT), EQUITY(COUNT), NUMSHARES(COUNT), PRICE.P.S(COUNT)
1640     READ QUICK.A(COUNT), CURR.L(COUNT), TOT.L(COUNT)
1650     LET RET(COUNT) = NET.INC(COUNT)/EQUITY(COUNT)
1660     LET EPS(COUNT) = NET.INC(COUNT)/NUMSHARES(COUNT)
1670     LET P.TO.E(COUNT) = PRICE.P.S(COUNT)/EPS(COUNT)
1680     LET QUICK.R(COUNT) = QUICK.A(COUNT)/CURR.L(COUNT)
1690     LET D.TO.E(COUNT) = TOT.L(COUNT)/EQUITY(COUNT)
1700   NEXT COUNT
1710   REM
1720   REM ******* OUTPUT SECTION
1730   REM THIS LOOP PRINTS THE DATA AND INFORMATION.
1740   PRINT : PRINT : PRINT
1750   REM
1760   FOR COUNT = 1 TO 72
1770     PRINT "-";
1780   NEXT COUNT
1790   PRINT
1800   PRINT
1810   PRINT "  COMPANY         NET    OWNERS   SHARES   MARKET   QUICK";
1820   PRINT "    CURRENT   TOTAL"
1830   PRINT "    NAME         INCOME  EQUITY   OUT.     PRICE    ASSETS";
1840   PRINT "  LIAB.     LIAB."
1850   PRINT
1860   REM
1870   FOR COUNT = 1 TO 5
1880     PRINT NAM$(COUNT);TAB(15);
1890     PRINT USING "#######";NET.INC(COUNT),EQUITY(COUNT),NUMSHARES(COUNT);
1900     PRINT USING "    ##.##";PRICE.P.S(COUNT);
1910     PRINT USING "########";QUICK.A(COUNT),CURR.L(COUNT),TOT.L(COUNT)
1920     PRINT
1930   NEXT COUNT
1940   REM
1950   PRINT : PRINT
```

**Figure 11-9**  *(Continued)*

```
1960   PRINT "  COMPANY     RETURN    EARNINGS    PRICE     QUICK     DEBT/"
1970   PRINT "   NAME         ON        PER      EARNINGS   RATIO    EQUITY"
1980   PRINT "              INVEST.    SHARE      RATIO                RATIO"
1990   PRINT
2000   FOR COUNT = 1 TO 5
2010     PRINT NAM$(COUNT);TAB(14)
2020     PRINT USING "##.###%   ";RET(COUNT);
2030     PRINT USING "##.###    ";EPS(COUNT);
2040     PRINT USING "##.###    ";P.TO.E(COUNT);
2050     PRINT USING "##.###    ";QUICK.R(COUNT);
2060     PRINT USING "##.###    ";D.TO.E(COUNT)
2070     PRINT
2080   NEXT COUNT
2090   REM
2100   REM ****** TERMINATION SECTION
2110   PRINT : PRINT
2120   FOR COUNT = 1 TO 72
2130     PRINT "-";
2140   NEXT COUNT
2150   PRINT : PRINT : PRINT
2160   PRINT TAB(20);"PROCESSING COMPLETED."
2170   END
```

----------------------------------------------------------------

| COMPANY NAME | NET INCOME | OWNERS EQUITY | SHARES OUT. | MARKET PRICE | QUICK ASSETS | CURRENT LIAB. | TOTAL LIAB. |
|---|---|---|---|---|---|---|---|
| HEINLEIN INC. | 22380 | 18750 | 75000 | 2.50 | 43600 | 100200 | 219300 |
| NOW CHEMICAL | 260456 | 200978 | 125000 | 16.00 | 78600 | 300870 | 807680 |
| EDSEL CO. | 56890 | 124000 | 350000 | 3.50 | 62000 | 14680 | 35966 |
| SOUND DESIGN | 26800 | 18000 | 15000 | 5.50 | 23090 | 10005 | 37416 |
| DE BEER CO. | 13300001 | 213500 | 600000 | 45.00 | 6570000 | 5000000 | 13000000 |

| COMPANY NAME | RETURN ON INVEST. | EARNINGS PER SHARE | PRICE EARNINGS RATIO | QUICK RATIO | DEBT/ EQUITY RATIO |
|---|---|---|---|---|---|
| HEINLEIN INC. | 1.194% | 0.298 | 8.378 | 0.435 | 11.696 |
| NOW CHEMICAL | 1.296% | 2.084 | 7.679 | 0.261 | 4.019 |
| EDSEL CO. | 0.459% | 0.163 | 21.533 | 4.223 | 0.290 |
| SOUND DESIGN | 1.489% | 1.787 | 3.078 | 2.308 | 2.079 |
| DE BEER CO. | 1.096% | 2.217 | 20.301 | 1.314 | 10.713 |

----------------------------------------------------------------

PROCESSING COMPLETED.

**Figure 11-9** *(Continued)*

## 11–10

## DEPRECIATION ASSESSMENT

There are many different ways in which you can compute the depreciation of equipment. Straight-line, sum-of-the-years, and double-declining balance methods are probably the most commonly used techniques for **depreciation assessment**. These techniques are as follows:

| Method | Formula | Key |
|---|---|---|
| Straight-line | $A1 = (C - S)/L$ | $A1$ = annual depreciation amount<br>$C$ = original equipment cost<br>$S$ = salvage value<br>$L$ = years of equipment life |
| Sum-of-the-years | $A2 = (Y/L(L + 1)/2)(C - S)$ | $A2$ = annual depreciation amount<br>$Y$ = year number in declining order (for example, $Y = 4$ for a four-year life the first year, $Y = 3$ the second year, and so on)<br>$L$ = years of equipment life<br>$C$ = original equipment cost<br>$S$ = salvage value |
| Double-declining | $A3 = 2(C - D)/L$ | $A3$ = annual depreciation amount<br>$C$ = original equipment cost<br>$D$ = accumulated depreciation amount (for example, if the first year amount is $500, the second year accumulated amount is $500; if the second year amount is $300, the third year accumulated amount is $800)<br>$L$ = useful equipment life in years |

When calculating the double-declining balance amount, the salvage value is not part of the calculation. However, the cost is not depreciated below the salvage value.

A CPA firm, as a service, calculates depreciation for its clients. The firm has a microcomputer and wants to develop a program to calculate depreciation using these three methods. Write a program to interactively accept the following input data:

- Original equipment cost
- Salvage value
- Useful equipment life, in years

Your program should list the amounts calculated side by side so that you can compare them easily (see fig. 11–10).

**Figure 11–10**
Depreciation Analysis

```
1000    REM PROGRAM NAME:  DEPRECIATION
1010    REM
1020    REM THIS IS A PROGRAM THAT CALCULATES DEPRECIATION AMOUNTS
1030    REM USING THREE DIFFERENT DEPRECIATION RATES: STRAIGHT LINE,
1040    REM SUM-OF-THE-YEARS DIGITS, AND DOUBLE-DECLINING BALANCE.
1050    REM THE INPUT DATA REQUIRED IS:  USEFUL LIFE OF THE EQUIPMENT IN
1060    REM YEARS, EQUIPMENT COST, AND ESTIMATED SALVAGE VALUE.
1070    REM
1080    REM ****** VARIABLE TABLE
1090    REM         COST = EQUIPMENT COST IN DOLLARS
1100    REM         SALVAGE = ESTIMATED SALVAGE VALUE IN DOLLARS
1110    REM         LIFE = ESTIMATED EQUIPMENT LIFE IN YEARS
1120    REM         STRAIGHT = STRAIGHT LINE CALCULATION RESULT
1130    REM         COUNTER = COUNTER TO ESTABLISH THE YEAR NUMBER
1140    REM         COUNT = FOR-NEXT LOOP CONTROL VARIABLE
1150    REM         YEAR = YEAR NUMBER IN DECLINING ORDER
1160    REM         ACCUM.DEP = ACCUMULATED DEPRECIATION AMOUNT
1170    REM         ANSWER$ = REPEAT PROGRAM TEST VARIABLE
1180    REM
1190    REM ****** ARRAY TABLE
1200    REM         SUM(99) = SUM-OF-THE-YEARS DIGITS CALCULATION RESULTS
1210    REM         D.D.B.(99) = DOUBLE-DECLINING BALANCE CALCULATION RESULTS
1220    REM
1230    REM ****** INITIALIZATION SECTION
1240    REM THE FOLLOWING QUESTIONS ASK FOR THE INPUT DATA.
1250    PRINT : PRINT
1260    PRINT TAB(10);"THIS IS THE DEPRECIATION AMOUNT PROGRAM."
1270    PRINT TAB(15);"PLEASE ENTER THE REQUIRED DATA."
1280    PRINT
1290    PRINT "WHAT IS THE EQUIPMENT COST IN DOLLARS?"
1300    INPUT "(DO NOT USE THE DOLLAR ($) SIGN OR INSERT COMMAS): ",COST
1310    PRINT
1320    PRINT "WHAT IS THE ESTIMATED SALVAGE VALUE IN DOLLARS?"
1330    INPUT "(DO NOT USE THE DOLLAR ($) SIGN OR INSERT COMMAS): ",SALVAGE
1340    PRINT
1350    INPUT "WHAT IS THE ESTIMATED EQUIPMENT LIFE IN YEARS? ",LIFE
1360    REM
1370    REM THE FOLLOWING ARE THE DIMENSIONS OF THE ARRAYS
1380    REM THE DIMENSION OF 99 ALLOWS VALUES OF LIFE UP TO 99 YEARS
1390    DIM SUM(99), D.D.B.(99)
1400    REM
1410    REM ****** PROCESS SECTION
1420    REM THE FOLLOWING STEPS CALCULATE THE AMOUNTS
1430    REM
1440    REM STRAIGHT_LINE CALCULATION
1450    LET STRAIGHT = (COST-SALVAGE)/LIFE
1460    REM
1470    REM SUM-OF-THE-YEARS DIGITS CALCULATION
1480    REM COUNTER IS A COUNTER TO ESTABLISH THE YEAR NUMBER
1490    LET COUNTER = 0
```

```
1500    FOR COUNT = 1 TO LIFE
1510       LET YEAR = LIFE-COUNTER
1520       LET SUM(COUNT) = (YEAR/(LIFE*(LIFE+1)/2))*(COST-SALVAGE)
1530       LET COUNTER = COUNTER+1
1540    NEXT COUNT
1550    REM
1560    REM DOUBLE DECLINING BALANCE CALCULATION
1570    REM USING THIS METHOD, THE COST SHOULD NOT BE DEPRECIATED
1580    REM BELOW THE SALVAGE VALUE.  A TEST IS USED FOR THIS AND IF IT
1590    REM HAS, THE FINAL VALUE IS THE REMAINING DEPRECIATION AMOUNT.
1600    LET ACCUM.DEP = 0
1610    FOR COUNT = 1 TO LIFE
1620       LET D.D.B.(COUNT) = 2*(COST-ACCUM.DEP)/LIFE
1630       LET ACCUM.DEP = ACCUM.DEP+D.D.B.(COUNT)
1640       IF ACCUM.DEP < (COST-SALVAGE) THEN GOTO 1670
1650       LET ACCUM.DEP = ACCUM.DEP-D.D.B.(COUNT)
1660       LET D.D.B.(COUNT) = (COST-SALVAGE)-ACCUM.DEP
1670    NEXT COUNT
1680    REM
1690    REM ****** OUTPUT SECTION
1700    REM THE FOLLOWING STEPS PRINT THE INPUT DATA AND OUTPUT INFORMATION.
1710    PRINT : PRINT : PRINT
1720    REM
1730    FOR COUNT = 1 TO 72
1740       PRINT "*";
1750    NEXT COUNT
1760    REM
1770    PRINT : PRINT
1780    PRINT "THE EQUIPMENT COST IS: ";
1790    PRINT USING "$$#######,.##";COST
1800    PRINT "THE SALVAGE VALUE IS: ";
1810    PRINT USING "$$#######,.## ";SALVAGE
1820    PRINT "THE ESTIMATED USEFUL LIFE IS: ";
1830    PRINT USING "### ";LIFE
1840    PRINT
1850    PRINT TAB(16);"DEPRECIATION AMOUNTS FOR YEAR"
1860    PRINT TAB(13);"STRAIGHT      SUM-OF-YRS       DOUB-DECL"
1870    PRINT " YEAR          LINE          DIGITS         BALANCE"
1880    PRINT
1890    REM
1900    FOR COUNT = 1 TO LIFE
1910       PRINT USING "  ##     ";COUNT;
1920       PRINT USING "$$#######,.##";STRAIGHT;
1930       PRINT USING "   $$#######,.##";SUM(COUNT);
1940       PRINT USING "   $$#######,.##";D.D.B.(COUNT)
1950    NEXT COUNT
1960    REM
1970    PRINT : PRINT
1980    REM
1990    FOR COUNT = 1 TO 72
2000    PRINT TAB(COUNT);"*";
2010    NEXT COUNT
2020    REM
2030    REM ****** TERMINATION SECTION
2040    PRINT : PRINT : PRINT : PRINT : PRINT
2050    PRINT "DO YOU HAVE ANOTHER DEPRECIATION AMOUNT TO CALCULATE (Y OR N)";
2060    INPUT ANSWER$
2070    IF ANSWER$ = "Y" OR ANSWER$ = "y" THEN GOTO 1280
2080    IF ANSWER$ <> "N" AND ANSWER$ <> "n" THEN GOTO 2050
2090    CLS : PRINT TAB(20);"HAVE A GOOD DAY!"
2100    END


        THIS IS THE DEPRECIATION AMOUNT PROGRAM.
             PLEASE ENTER THE REQUIRED DATA.
```

**Figure 11-10**  (Continued)

```
WHAT IS THE EQUIPMENT COST IN DOLLARS?
(DO NOT USE THE DOLLAR ($) SIGN OR INSERT COMMAS):        10000

WHAT IS THE ESTIMATED SALVAGE VALUE IN DOLLARS?
(DO NOT USE THE DOLLAR ($) SIGN OR INSERT COMMAS):        500

WHAT IS THE ESTIMATED EQUIPMENT LIFE IN YEARS?            10



*********************************************************************

THE EQUIPMENT COST IS:        $10,000.00
THE SALVAGE VALUE IS:            $500.00
THE ESTIMATED USEFUL LIFE IS:  10

                 DEPRECIATION AMOUNTS FOR YEAR
              STRAIGHT     SUM-OF-YRS     DOUB-DECL
   YEAR         LINE        DIGITS        BALANCE

    1          $950.00     $1,727.27     $2,000.00
    2          $950.00     $1,554.55     $1,600.00
    3          $950.00     $1,381.82     $1,280.00
    4          $950.00     $1,209.09     $1,024.00
    5          $950.00     $1,036.36       $819.20
    6          $950.00       $863.64       $655.36
    7          $950.00       $690.91       $524.29
    8          $950.00       $518.18       $419.43
    9          $950.00       $345.45       $335.54
   10          $950.00       $172.73       $268.44


*********************************************************************



DO YOU HAVE ANOTHER DEPRECIATION AMOUNT TO CALCULATE (Y OR N)N
            HAVE A GOOD DAY!
```

**Figure 11–10** *(Continued)*

## SUMMARY

In this chapter, we developed a series of programs that can solve many different problems in business and economics. We presented a brief description of the different techniques used in these programs. Most of the programs were written in an interactive mode to allow them to be used in many different situations.

In the next chapter, we present a series of statistics and statistical forecasting programs.

## HANDS-ON EXPERIENCE

1. Using the compound interest rate formula, how much money should you invest today in order to receive a total of $18,000 at the end of the year 2000. The interest rate can be either 18, 15, or 21 percent.

2. Jacky, a student in our BASIC class, has invested $1,000 in Neighborhood First Bank. The bank uses daily compounding periods with a 12 percent yearly interest rate. Using the compound interest rate, how long will it take Jacky to accumulate $2,500 in her savings account?

3. Azam and Akram, friendly sisters, have saved $60,000 for a down payment on a new house. The price of the house is $300,000. They are planning to pay the rest in a 30-year contract with an interest rate of 11.50 percent. Write and run a program to calculate the monthly mortgage payment for Azam and Akram.

4. The Blue-Green Shoe Company is a supplier of different kinds of shoes in the Northwest. To minimize the cost of placing an order and carrying costs, the sales manager has decided to use the EOQ model. If the annual inventory requirement is 25,000 pairs of shoes, the cost of placing an order is $1.75, the cost of each pair of shoes is $88, and the percentage of inventory value allotted for carrying costs is 7 percent, how much is the EOQ?

5. You have been hired as the analyst programmer for Tely-Tac-Tic, a manufacturer of electronic devices. The marketing manager of this company is performing different kinds of analyses to estimate the sales price of a new product. The question is how many units to produce and how much to sell each unit for to reach the break-even point. You have been asked to write a program to compute the break-even points using the following situations assuming the fixed costs are $5000:

   **a.** The unit price is $30, the variable cost is $15.

   **b.** Decrease the unit price by 10 percent, the rest is the same.

   **c.** Decrease the unit price by 15 percent, decrease the variable cost by 5 percent, the rest is the same.

6. The Down-Town Donut Shop is preparing a number of cheese cakes for tomorrow. The cost of production is $8 and the sales price is $12. Past experience shows the numbers of units demanded and the associated probabilities to be as follows:

   | Units | Probability |
   | --- | --- |
   | 41 | .10 |
   | 42 | .03 |
   | 43 | .06 |
   | 44 | .20 |
   | 45 | .15 |
   | 46 | .18 |
   | 47 | .12 |
   | 48 | .06 |
   | 49 | .10 |

   How many cheese cakes should be produced to minimize the expected opportunity loss?

7. The total sales for the past 10 years of Alpha-T, a manufacturer of fancy sailboats, is as follows:

   **Total Sales**

   | Year | Dollars (thousands) |
   | --- | --- |
   | 1990 | 25000 |
   | 1989 | 24000 |
   | 1988 | 18750 |
   | 1987 | 27000 |
   | 1986 | 26000 |
   | 1985 | 14000 |
   | 1984 | 19600 |
   | 1983 | 27000 |
   | 1982 | 26000 |
   | 1981 | 19250 |

   Write and run a program to generate a bar graph to show the company's sales performances in ascending order.

8. The cost of a new car is $28,000, the salvage value is $8,000, and the estimated life is 6 years. Write and run a program to calculate the depreciation of this car for the next 15 years using the straight-line, sum-of-the-years, and double-declining balance methods.

---

| | | | |
|---|---|---|---|
| Break-even analysis | Expected opportunity loss | Market analysis | **KEY TERMS** |
| Depreciation assessment | Financial statement analysis | Present value analysis | |
| Economic order quantity | | Sales force analysis | |

# Using BASIC for Statistical Problem Solving and Forecasting

**12**

## 12-1

## INTRODUCTION

In this chapter, we introduce statistics and some statistical forecasting problems. First we give a short description of a problem, and then we present a BASIC program to solve that problem. We have written these programs in a very general way to increase their adaptability to many different uses. Most of these programs have been written in an interactive mode; therefore, the reader does not need to know the details of each particular formula. To see the dynamics of these programs, load them from the disk provided and run them with your own data.

## 12-2

## ARITHMETIC MEAN, STANDARD DEVIATION, AND VARIANCE

Often, it is useful to know the average of a series of numbers. You might, for example, want to know the average score on your computer class midterm exam. You find the average score by adding all the scores and dividing the sum by the number of scores.

To compute the arithmetic mean, use the following formula:

$$A = \frac{\sum_{i=1}^{n} Y_i}{n}$$

where: A = the average or the mean

Y$_i$ = an individual score

n = the number of individuals

To find out how scattered the individual scores are around their mean, you calculate either their variance or their standard deviation. These measures are usually called measures of variability.

If two classes have the same mean, for example, the class with the smaller standard deviation will be considered the more harmonic class. This means that the students' performances are more similar.

To compute the variance, you use the following formula:

$$V^2 = \frac{\sum_{i=1}^{n} (Y_i - A)^2}{n}$$

The standard deviation is the positive square root of the variance, as follows:

$$S = \sqrt{V^2} = \frac{\sqrt{\sum_{i=1}^{n} (Y_i - A)^2}}{n}$$

Write and run a BASIC program to compute the mean, variance, and standard deviation of the following five scores: 6, 7, 8, 9, and 10 (see fig. 12-1). Then, write and run a program to accept up to 100 scores from the keyboard and to compute their mean, variance, and standard deviation (see fig. 12-2).

```
100    REM THIS PROGRAM COMPUTES THE MEAN, VARIANCE AND
110    REM STANDARD DEVIATION OF FIVE SCORES.
120    REM THIS PART OF THE PROGRAM COMPUTES THE MEAN.
130    REM
140    REM ******* VARIABLE TABLE
150    REM          NUM1, NUM2, NUM3, NUM4, NUM5 = INPUT VARIABLES
160    REM          MEAN = MEAN OF NUM1, NUM2, NUM3, NUM4, NUM5
170    REM          DEV1, DEV2, DEV3, DEV4, DEV5 = DEVIATIONS FROM THE MEAN
180    REM          SQ1, SQ2, SQ3, SQ4, SQ5 = SQUARES OF THE DEVIATIONS
190    REM          VARIANCE = VARIANCE OF SQ1, SQ2, SQ3, SQ4, AND SQ5
200    REM          STANDARD = STANDARD DEVIATION OF THE VARIANCE
210    REM
220    REM ******* INITIALIZATION SECTION
230    READ NUM1, NUM2, NUM3, NUM4, NUM5
240    REM
250    REM ******* PROCESS SECTION
260    LET MEAN = (NUM1+NUM2+NUM3+NUM4+NUM5)/5
270    PRINT "THE MEAN OF 6, 7, 8, 9, AND 10 =";MEAN
280    REM
290    REM THIS PART OF THE PROGRAM COMPUTES THE
300    REM VARIANCE OF THE ABOVE SCORES.
310    REM
320    LET DEV1 = (NUM1-MEAN)
330    LET DEV2 = (NUM2-MEAN)
340    LET DEV3 = (NUM3-MEAN)
350    LET DEV4 = (NUM4-MEAN)
360    LET DEV5 = (NUM5-MEAN)
370    REM
380    LET SQ1 = DEV1^2
390    LET SQ2 = DEV2^2
400    LET SQ3 = DEV3^2
410    LET SQ4 = DEV4^2
420    LET SQ5 = DEV5^2
430    REM
440    LET VARIANCE = (SQ1+SQ2+SQ3+SQ4+SQ5)/5
450    REM
460    PRINT "THE VARIANCE OF 6, 7, 8, 9, AND 10 =";VARIANCE
470    REM THIS PART OF THE PROGRAM COMPUTES THE STANDARD DEVIATION.
480    REM STANDARD IS THE STANDARD DEVIATION.
490    LET STANDARD = SQR(VARIANCE)
500    PRINT "THE STANDARD DEVIATION OF 6, 7, 8, 9, AND 10 =";STANDARD
510    REM
520    REM ******* DATA SECTION
530    DATA 6,7,8,9,10
540    END
Ok
RUN
THE MEAN OF 6, 7, 8, 9, AND 10 = 8
THE VARIANCE OF 6, 7, 8, 9, AND 10 = 2
THE STANDARD DEVIATION OF 6, 7, 8, 9, AND 10 = 1.414214
Ok
```

**Figure 12–1**
Mean, Variance, and Standard Deviation

## 12–3
## GEOMETRIC MEAN

Besides the arithmetic mean, another type of mean, and one that is more appropriate for index numbers, percentages, and ratios, is the geometric mean. You calculate the geometric mean of a series of scores by adding the logarithms

**Figure 12–2**

Interactive Version of the Program Shown in Figure 12–1

```
100    REM THIS PROGRAM ACCEPTS UP TO 100 SCORES FROM THE KEYBOARD
110    REM AND COMPUTES THEIR MEAN, VARIANCE AND STANDARD
120    REM DEVIATION.  IF THE NUMBER OF SCORES EXCEEDS 100, THE
130    REM DIM STATEMENT IN LINE 300 MUST BE REDEFINED.
140    REM
150    REM ****** VARIABLE TABLE
160    REM          NUMBER = THE NUMBER OF SCORES TO BE CONSIDERED
170    REM          COUNT = FOR-NEXT LOOP CONTROL VARIABLE
180    REM          ACCUMULATOR = ACCUMULATOR FOR THE SCORES
190    REM          MEAN = MEAN OF THE SCORES
200    REM          VARIANCE = VARIANCE OF THE SCORES
210    REM          STANDARD = STANDARD DEVIATION OF THE SCORES
220    REM
230    REM ****** ARRAY TABLE
240    REM          SCORES(100) = THE ARRAY FOR SCORES
250    REM          DEVIATE(100) = ARRAY FOR THE DEVIATIONS FROM THE MEAN
260    REM          SQUARES(100) = ARRAY FOR THE SQUARES OF THE DEVIATIONS
270    REM
280    REM ****** INITIALIZATION SECTION
290    CLS : PRINT : PRINT : PRINT
300    DIM SCORES(100), DEVIATE(100), SQUARES(100)
310    REM
320    INPUT "HOW MANY SCORES WOULD YOU LIKE TO CONSIDER? ",NUMBER
330    REM
340    REM ****** PROCESS SECTION
350    FOR COUNT = 1 TO NUMBER
360       LOCATE 8,1
370       PRINT "PLEASE ENTER SCORE NUMBER";COUNT;": ";
380       INPUT "",SCORES(COUNT)
390    NEXT COUNT
400    REM
410    PRINT "THE FOLLOWING ARE YOUR ORIGINAL SCORES"
420    REM
430    FOR COUNT = 1 TO NUMBER
440       PRINT SCORES(COUNT);
450    NEXT COUNT
460    REM
470    PRINT
480    REM THIS PART OF THE PROGRAM COMPUTES THE MEAN.
490    LET ACCUMULATOR = 0
500    REM
510    FOR COUNT = 1 TO NUMBER
520       LET ACCUMULATOR = ACCUMULATOR+SCORES(COUNT)
530    NEXT COUNT
540    REM
550    LET MEAN = ACCUMULATOR/NUMBER
560    PRINT "THE MEAN OF THE ABOVE SCORES IS =";MEAN
570    REM
580    REM THIS PART OF THE PROGRAM COMPUTES THE VARIANCE OF
590    REM THE ABOVE SCORES.
600    REM LET US FIRST COMPUTE THE DEVIATIONS OF THE SCORES
610    REM FROM THEIR MEAN.
620    REM
630    FOR COUNT = 1 TO NUMBER
640       LET DEVIATE(COUNT) = SCORES(COUNT)-MEAN
650    NEXT COUNT
660    REM
670    REM LET US NOW COMPUTE THE SQUARES OF THE DEVIATIONS.
680    REM
690    FOR COUNT = 1 TO NUMBER
700       LET SCORES(COUNT) = DEVIATE(COUNT)^2
710    NEXT COUNT
720    REM
730    REM VARIANCE IS THE VARIANCE.
740    LET ACCUMULATOR = 0
```

```
750    REM
760    FOR COUNT = 1 TO NUMBER
770      LET ACCUMULATOR = ACCUMULATOR+SCORES(COUNT)
780    NEXT COUNT
790    REM
800    LET VARIANCE = ACCUMULATOR/NUMBER
810    PRINT "THE VARIANCE OF THE ABOVE SCORES IS";VARIANCE
820    REM
830    REM THIS PART OF THE PROGRAM COMPUTES THE STANDARD DEVIATION.
840    REM S IS THE STANDARD DEVIATION.
850    LET STANDARD = SQR(VARIANCE)
860    PRINT "THE STANDARD DEVIATION OF THE ABOVE SCORE IS";STANDARD
870    END



HOW MANY SCORES WOULD YOU LIKE TO CONSIDER?                     10
PLEASE ENTER SCORE NUMBER 1 :            1
PLEASE ENTER SCORE NUMBER 2 :            2
PLEASE ENTER SCORE NUMBER 3 :            3
PLEASE ENTER SCORE NUMBER 4 :            4
PLEASE ENTER SCORE NUMBER 5 :            5
PLEASE ENTER SCORE NUMBER 6 :            6
PLEASE ENTER SCORE NUMBER 7 :            7
PLEASE ENTER SCORE NUMBER 8 :            8
PLEASE ENTER SCORE NUMBER 9 :            9
PLEASE ENTER SCORE NUMBER 10 :           15
THE FOLLOWING ARE YOUR ORIGINAL SCORES
 1   2   3   4   5   6   7   8   9   15
THE MEAN OF THE ABOVE SCORES IS = 6
THE VARIANCE OF THE ABOVE SCORES IS 15
THE STANDARD DEVIATION OF THE ABOVE SCORE IS 3.872984
```

**Figure 12–2**    *(Continued)*

of the scores and dividing the sum by the number of scores. The formula for the geometric mean is as follows:

$$LOG(G) = \frac{\sum_{i=1}^{n} LOG\ Y_i}{n}$$

where: G = the geometric mean

Y$_i$ = an individual score

n = the number of scores

The scores used in this formula must be greater than zero (negative numbers don't have logarithms).

Write and run a program to accept up to 100 scores from the keyboard and to compute their geometric mean (see fig. 12–3).

## 12–4
## MEDIAN

The median of a series of scores is the value of the middle score if the number of scores is odd. If the number of scores is even, the median is the average of the two middle values. Half of the scores are lower than the median and half of the

```
100     REM THIS PROGRAM ACCEPTS UP TO 100 SCORES FROM THE KEYBOARD
110     REM AND COMPUTES THEIR GEOMETRIC MEAN.   THESE SCORES
120     REM MUST BE POSITIVE.   IF THE NUMBER OF SCORES EXCEEDS
130     REM 100, THE DIM STATEMENT MUST BE REDEFINED.
140     REM
150     REM ****** VARIABLE TABLE
160     REM          NUMBER = THE NUMBER OF SCORES TO CONSIDER
170     REM          COUNT = FOR-NEXT LOOP CONTROL VARIABLE
180     REM          ACCUMULATOR = ACCUMULATOR FOR THE LOGARITHMS
190     REM          AVERAGE = AVERAGE OF THE LOGARITHMS
200     REM          GEOMEAN = THE GEOMETRIC MEAN
210     REM
220     REM ****** ARRAY TABLE
230     REM          SCORES(100) = THE ARRAY OF SCORES
240     REM          LOGARITHMS(100) = THE ARRAY OF LOGARITHMS OF SCORES
250     REM
260     REM ****** INITIALIZATION SECTION
270     DIM SCORES(100), LOGS(100)
280     INPUT "PLEASE ENTER THE NUMBER OF SCORES TO CONSIDER: ",NUMBER
290     REM
300     REM ****** PROCESS SECTION
310     FOR COUNT = 1 TO NUMBER
320     PRINT "PLEASE ENTER SCORE NUMBER";COUNT;": ";
330       INPUT "",SCORES(COUNT)
340     NEXT COUNT
350     REM
360     PRINT "THE FOLLOWING ARE YOUR ORIGINAL SCORES"
370     REM
380     FOR COUNT = 1 TO NUMBER
390       PRINT SCORES(COUNT);
400     NEXT COUNT
410     REM
420     PRINT
430     REM LET US FIRST CALCULATE THE LOGARITHMS OF THE SCORES
440     LET ACCUMULATOR = 0
450     REM ACCUMULATOR WILL KEEP TRACK OF THE SUM OF THE LOGARITHMS
460     REM
470     FOR COUNT = 1 TO NUMBER
480       LET LOGARITHMS(COUNT) = LOG(SCORES(COUNT))
490       LET ACCUMULATOR = ACCUMULATOR+LOGARITHMS(COUNT)
500     NEXT COUNT
510     REM
520     LET AVERAGE = ACCUMULATOR/NUMBER
530     REM NOW LOG(GEOMEAN) = AVERAGE, IN ORDER TO COMPUTE GEOMEAN,
540     REM WE MUST TAKE THE ANTILOGARITHM I. E. GEOMEAN = EXP(AVERAGE).
550     LET GEOMEAN = EXP(AVERAGE)
560     PRINT "THE GEOMETRIC MEAN OF THE ABOVE SCORES IS =";GEOMEAN
570     END
Ok
RUN
PLEASE ENTER THE NUMBER OF SCORES TO CONSIDER: 10
PLEASE ENTER SCORE NUMBER 1 : 10
PLEASE ENTER SCORE NUMBER 2 : 20
PLEASE ENTER SCORE NUMBER 3 : 30
PLEASE ENTER SCORE NUMBER 4 : 40
PLEASE ENTER SCORE NUMBER 5 : 50
PLEASE ENTER SCORE NUMBER 6 : 60
PLEASE ENTER SCORE NUMBER 7 : 70
PLEASE ENTER SCORE NUMBER 8 : 80
PLEASE ENTER SCORE NUMBER 9 : 90
PLEASE ENTER SCORE NUMBER 10 : 100
THE FOLLOWING ARE YOUR ORIGINAL SCORES
 10  20  30  40  50  60  70  80  90  100
THE GEOMETRIC MEAN OF THE ABOVE SCORES IS = 45.28729
Ok
```

**Figure 12-3**
Geometric Mean

scores are higher than the median. For example, the median of 1, 5, 3, 2, and 4 is 3. The median of 18, 4, 12, 28, 22, and 14 is 16.

Write and run an interactive program that accepts up to 100 values and calculates their median (see fig. 12–4).

**Figure 12–4**
Median

```
100    REM THIS PROGRAM ACCEPTS UP TO 100 VALUES FROM THE KEYBOARD
110    REM AND COMPUTES THEIR MEDIAN.  THE NUMBER OF THESE VALUES
120    REM CAN BE EITHER ODD OR EVEN.  IF THE NUMBER OF SCORES
130    REM EXCEEDS 100 THE DIM STATEMENT MUST BE REDEFINED.
140    REM
150    REM ******* VARIABLE TABLE
160    REM         NUMBER = NUMBER OF SCORES TO BE CONSIDERED
170    REM         MEDIAN = MEDIAN OF THE SCORES
180    REM         COUNT1, COUNT2 = FOR-NEXT LOOP CONTROL VARIABLES
190    REM         TEMP = TEMPORARY DATA SWITCHING VARIABLE
200    REM         ODD.EVEN = ODD OR EVEN NUMBER OF SCORES DETERMINATION VARIABLE
210    REM         ANSWER$ = REPEAT PROGRAM TEST VARIABLE
220    REM
230    REM ******* ARRAY TABLE
240    REM         SCORES(100) = THE ARRAY OF SCORES
250    REM
260    REM ******* INITIALIZATION SECTION
270    DIM SCORES(100)
280    CLS
290    INPUT "HOW MANY SCORES DO YOU WANT TO CONSIDER";NUMBER
300    REM
310    REM ******* PROCESS SECTION
320    REM FILL THE SCORES ARRAY
330    FOR COUNT1 = 1 TO NUMBER
340      LOCATE 8,1 : PRINT "ENTER SCORE NUMBER";COUNT1;": ";
350      INPUT "",SCORES(COUNT1)
360    NEXT COUNT1
370    REM
380    PRINT "THE SCORES YOU ENTERED ARE AS FOLLOWS:"
390    REM DISPLAY THE CONTENTS OF THE SCORES ARRAY
400    FOR COUNT1 = 1 TO NUMBER
410      PRINT SCORES(COUNT1);
420    NEXT COUNT1
430    REM
440    REM IN ORDER TO COMPUTE THE MEDIAN OF A SERIES OF SCORES,
450    REM THESE SCORES MUST BE SORTED.
460    GOSUB 540
470    GOSUB 640
480    PRINT "BELOW IS A SORTED LISTING OF THE SCORES (IN ASCENDING ORDER):"
490    FOR COUNT1 = 1 TO NUMBER
500      PRINT SCORES(COUNT1)
510    NEXT COUNT1
520    PRINT "THE MEDIAN OF THE ABOVE SCORES IS";MEDIAN
530    GOTO 800
540    REM THIS SUBROUTINE SORTS THE SCORES.
550    FOR COUNT1 = 1 TO NUMBER-1
560      FOR COUNT2 = COUNT1+1 TO NUMBER
570        IF SCORES(COUNT1) <= SCORES(COUNT2) THEN GOTO 610
580        LET TEMP = SCORES(COUNT1)
590        LET SCORES(COUNT1) = SCORES(COUNT2)
600        LET SCORES(COUNT2) = TEMP
610      NEXT COUNT2
620    NEXT COUNT1
630    RETURN
640    REM THIS SUBROUTINE CALCULATES THE MEDIAN.
```

```
650    REM FIRST WE CHECK TO SEE IF THE NUMBER OF SCORES IS
660    REM EVEN OR ODD.
670    LET ODD.EVEN = NUMBER
680    REM
690    FOR COUNT1 = 1 TO NUMBER/2
700      LET ODD.EVEN = ODD.EVEN-2
710    NEXT COUNT1
720    REM
730    IF ODD.EVEN = 0 THEN 760
740    LET MEDIAN = SCORES(INT(NUMBER/2)+1)
750    GOTO 770
760    LET MEDIAN = (SCORES(NUMBER/2)+SCORES(NUMBER/2+1))/2
770    RETURN
780    REM
790    REM ****** TERMINATION SECTION
800    INPUT "WOULD YOU LIKE TO TRY ANOTHER (Y OR N): ",ANSWER$
810    IF ANSWER$ = "Y" OR ANSWER$ = "y" THEN GOTO 280
820    IF ANSWER$ <> "N" AND ANSWER$ <> "n" THEN GOTO 800
830    PRINT TAB(35);"THANK YOU!"
840    END
HOW MANY SCORES DO YOU WANT TO CONSIDER 9
ENTER SCORE NUMBER 1 :        25
ENTER SCORE NUMBER 2 :        19
ENTER SCORE NUMBER 3 :        62
ENTER SCORE NUMBER 4 :        100
ENTER SCORE NUMBER 5 :        200
ENTER SCORE NUMBER 6 :        41
ENTER SCORE NUMBER 7 :        15
ENTER SCORE NUMBER 8 :        1
ENTER SCORE NUMBER 9 :        500
THE SCORES YOU ENTERED ARE AS FOLLOWS:
 25  19  62  100  200  41  15  1  500
BELOW IS A SORTED LISTING OF THE SCORES (IN ASCENDING ORDER):
 1
 15
 19
 25
 41
 62
 100
 200
 500
THE MEDIAN OF THE ABOVE SCORES IS 41
WOULD YOU LIKE TO TRY ANOTHER (Y OR N):    N
                              THANK YOU!
```

**Figure 12–4**  *(Continued)*

## 12–5

## EXPECTED VALUE

The expected value of variable Y is defined as follows:

$$E(Y) = \sum_{i=1}^{n} Y_i P(Y_i)$$

where: E(Y) = the expected value of Y

P($Y_i$) = the probability of $Y_i$

Expected value is a very useful technique for choosing a particular alternative from several possibilities. The alternative with the highest expected value is considered the best.

Suppose, for example, that Northwest Gama Oil Company is considering several alternatives for one of its oil fields. Different alternatives and

Table 12–1
Profit Table
(in millions of dollars)

| Alternative | State of Nature | | | |
| | S1 | S2 | S3 | S4 |
|---|---|---|---|---|
| Probability | .20 | .22 | .18 | .40 |
| Drill for Oil | 1310 | 410 | −55 | −144 |
| Unconditionally Lease | 88 | 88 | 88 | 88 |
| Conditionally Lease | 480 | 202 | 10 | 20 |

different states of nature with their relevant probabilities of occurrence have been summarized in table 12–1.

Write and run a program to choose the best alternative based on the computed expected value (see fig. 12–5).

## 12–6
## FORECASTING ACCURACY

Whenever the value of a particular item has been forecasted, the next question concerns the accuracy of this forecast. One way to measure this accuracy is to add all the errors and divide the sum by the number of errors. However, in this case, the negative errors may be canceled out by the positive ones. To avoid this, there are other ways to measure the accuracy of a forecast.

One method of measuring the accuracy of the forecast is to compute the mean absolute deviation (MAD). To compute the MAD, you add the absolute values of the errors and divide their sum by the number of errors.

Another method of measuring the accuracy of the forecast is to compute the mean absolute percentage error (MAPE). You find the percentage of absolute errors by dividing the absolute error by the actual value of the item. Then you add the absolute percentage errors and divide the sum by the number of errors.

The third method of measuring the accuracy of the forecast is to compute the mean squared error (MSE). You square the errors and divide their sum by the number of errors.

Finally, you can compute the mean percentage error (MPE) by adding the percentage errors and dividing the result by the number of errors.

Write and run a program that accepts up to 100 pairs of data items (a pair consists of the actual value and the predicted value) from the keyboard and that computes the ME, MAD, MAPE, MSE, and MPE (see fig. 12–6).

## 12–7
## SINGLE EXPONENTIAL SMOOTHING

Single exponential smoothing is a mathematical forecasting model appropriate for immediate (less than one month) or short-range (one to three months) forecasting. Forecasting with this model is based on the following formula:

$$F(t + 1) = X(t) + (1 − \alpha)F(t)$$

where: F = the forecast
X = actual value
t = present time
Alpha ($\alpha$) = a constant whose value is between 0 and 1

```
100    REM THIS PROGRAM CALCULATES THE EXPECTED VALUE OF
110    REM SEVERAL ALTERNATIVES.  IT ALSO CHOOSES THE
120    REM BEST ALTERNATIVE BASED UPON ITS EXPECTED VALUE.
130    REM EXPECT IS THE ARRAY FOR THE EXPECTED VALUES.
140    REM
150    REM ****** VARIABLE TABLE
160    REM         PER1, PER2, PER3, PER4 = PERCENTAGE OF LIKLIHOOD
170    REM         ALT1, ALT2, ALT3, ALT4 = ALTERNATIVES
180    REM         COUNT = FOR-NEXT LOOP CONTROL VARIABLE
190    REM         BEST = THE BEST ALTERNATIVE
200    REM         ALTNUM = THE NUMBER OF THE BEST ALTERNATIVE
210    REM
220    REM ****** ARRAY TABLE
230    REM         EXPECT(3) = EXPECTED RESULTS
240    REM
250    REM ****** INITIALIZATION SECTION
260    READ PER1, PER2, PER3, PER4
270    REM
280    REM ****** PROCESS SECTION
290    REM THIS PART READS THE ALTERNATIVES AND CALCULATES THE EXPECTED RESULTS
300    FOR COUNT = 1 TO 3
310       READ ALT1, ALT2, ALT3, ALT4
320       LET EXPECT(COUNT) = ALT1*PER1+ALT2*PER2+ALT3*PER3+ALT4*PER4
330    NEXT COUNT
340    REM
350    REM THIS PART OF THE PROGRAM SELECTS THE BEST ALTERNATIVE.
360    LET ALTNUM = 1
370    LET BEST = EXPECT(1)
380    REM
390    FOR COUNT = 2 TO 3
400       IF EXPECT(COUNT) > BEST THEN GOTO 420
410       GOTO 440
420       LET ALTNUM = COUNT
430       LET BEST = EXPECT(COUNT)
440    NEXT COUNT
450    REM
460    PRINT TAB(15); "EXPECTED VALUE"
470    REM
480    FOR COUNT = 1 TO 3
490       PRINT "THE EXPECTED VALUE FOR ALTERNATIVE ";COUNT;"=";
500       PRINT USING " ###.##";EXPECT(COUNT)
510    NEXT COUNT
520    REM
530    REM ****** OUTPUT SECTION
540    PRINT "ALTERNATIVE NUMBER ";
550    PRINT USING "#";ALTNUM;
560    PRINT " IS THE BEST WITH THE EXPECTED VALUE ";
570    PRINT USING "###.##";BEST
580    DATA .20,.22,.18,.40
590    DATA 1310,410,-55,-144
600    DATA 88,88,88,88
610    DATA 480,202,10,20
620    END
Ok
RUN
                EXPECTED VALUE
THE EXPECTED VALUE FOR ALTERNATIVE   1 = 284.70
THE EXPECTED VALUE FOR ALTERNATIVE   2 =  88.00
THE EXPECTED VALUE FOR ALTERNATIVE   3 = 150.24
ALTERNATIVE NUMBER 1 IS THE BEST WITH THE EXPECTED VALUE 284.70
```

**Figure 12–5**
Expected Value Analysis

**Figure 12–6**

Forecasting Accuracy

```
1000    REM THIS PROGRAM COMPUTES THE ACCURACY OF A FORECAST BY
1010    REM CALCULATION OF ME, MAD, MAPE, MSE, AND MPE.
1020    REM THIS PROGRAM CAN HANDLE UP TO 100 PAIRS OF DATA.
1030    REM IF THE NUMBER OF DATA ITEMS EXCEEDS 100, THE DIM
1040    REM STATEMENT MUST BE MODIFIED.
1050    REM
1060    REM ****** VARIABLE TABLE
1070    REM         NUMBER = NUMBER OF PAIRS OF DATA TO CONSIDER
1080    REM         COUNT = FOR-NEXT LOOP CONTROL VARIABLE
1090    REM         ANSWER$ = REPEAT PROGRAM TEST VARIABLE
1100    REM         SUM.ERR = SUM OF THE ERRORS
1110    REM         SUM.ABS = SUM OF THE ABSOLUTE ERRORS
1120    REM         SUM.PER.ABS = SUM OF THE PERCENT OF THE ABSOLUTE ERRORS
1130    REM         SUM.SQU.ERR = SUM OF THE SQUARED ERRORS
1140    REM         SUM.PER.ERR = SUM OF THE PERCENT OF ERRORS
1150    REM         ME.NUM = MEAN OF THE ERRORS
1160    REM         MAD.NUM = MEAN OF THE ABSOLUTE DEVIATIONS
1170    REM         MAPE.NUM = MEAN OF THE ABSOLUTE PERCENT ERRORS
1180    REM         MSE.NUM = MEAN OF THE SQUARED ERRORS
1190    REM         MPE.NUM = MEAN OF THE PERCENTAGE ERRORS
1200    REM
1210    REM ****** ARRAY TABLE
1220    REM         REAL(100) = THE ARRAY OF REAL VALUES
1230    REM         PRED(100) = THE ARRAY OF PREDICTED VALUES
1240    REM         ME(100) = THE ARRAY FOR ERRORS
1250    REM         MAD(100) = THE ARRAY FOR ABSOLUTE ERRORS
1260    REM         MAPE(100) = THE ARRAY FOR PERCENT OF ABSOLUTE ERRORS
1270    REM         MSE(100) = THE ARRAY FOR SQUARED ERRORS
1280    REM         MPE(100) = THE ARRAY FOR THE PERCENT OF ERRORS
1290    REM
1300    REM ****** INITIALIZATION SECTION
1310    DIM REAL(100), PRED(100), ME(100)
1320    DIM MAD(100), MAPE(100), MSE(100), MPE(100)
1330    LET SUM.ERR = 0
1340    LET SUM.ABS = 0
1350    LET SUM.PER.ABS = 0
1360    LET SUM.SQU = 0
1370    LET SUM.PER.ERR = 0
1380    CLS
1390    INPUT "ENTER THE NUMBER OF DATA PAIRS YOU WANT TO CONSIDER: ",NUMBER
1400    PRINT : PRINT "TELL ME THE REAL VALUES AND THEIR FORECASTED VALUES."
1410    PRINT
1420    REM
1430    FOR COUNT = 1 TO NUMBER
1440      LOCATE 5,1
1450      PRINT "PLEASE ENTER REAL VALUE NUMBER";COUNT;":";
1460      INPUT " ",REAL(COUNT)
1470      PRINT "PLEASE ENTER PREDICTED FORECAST FOR NUMBER";COUNT;":";
1480      INPUT " ",PRED(COUNT)
1490    NEXT COUNT
1500    REM
1510    REM ****** PROCESS SECTION
1520    PRINT : PRINT TAB(17); "FORECAST ACCURACY MEASUREMENT"
1530    PRINT "  THE FOLLOWING ARE THE REAL VALUES AND THEIR FORECASTED VALUES"
1540    PRINT "                          ----------        ------------------
1550    REM
1560    FOR COUNT = 1 TO NUMBER
1570      PRINT , ,REAL(COUNT);,"                ";PRED(COUNT)
1580    NEXT COUNT
1590    REM
1600    GOSUB 1700
```

```
1610    PRINT "********************************************************"
1620    REM
1630    REM ****** TERMINATION SECTION
1640    INPUT "DO YOU WANT TO TRY ANY OTHER PAIRS OF DATA (Y OR N): ";ANSWER$
1650    IF ANSWER$ = "Y" OR ANSWER$ = "y" THEN GOTO 1380
1660    IF ANSWER$ <> "N" AND ANSWER$ <> "n" THEN GOTO 1640
1670    PRINT : PRINT TAB(35);"THANK YOU!"
1680    GOTO 2030
1690    REM
1700    REM THE NEXT SECTION OF THE PROGRAM CALCULATES THE OUTPUT
1710    REM
1720    FOR COUNT = 1 TO NUMBER
1730       LET ME(COUNT) = REAL(COUNT)-PRED(COUNT)
1740       LET MAD(COUNT) = ABS(ME(COUNT))
1750       LET MAPE(COUNT) = MAD(COUNT)/REAL(COUNT)
1760       LET MSE(COUNT) = ME(COUNT)^2
1770       LET MPE(COUNT) = ME(COUNT)/REAL(COUNT)
1780       LET SUM.ERR = SUM.ERR+ME(COUNT)
1790       LET SUM.ABS = SUM.ABS+MAD(COUNT)
1800       LET SUM.PER.ABS = SUM.PER.ABS+MAPE(COUNT)
1810       LET SUM.SQU.ERR = SUM.SQU.ERR+MSE(COUNT)
1820       LET SUM.PER.ERR = SUM.PER.ERR+MPE(COUNT)
1830    NEXT COUNT
1840    REM
1850    LET ME.NUM = SUM.ERR/NUMBER
1860    LET MAD.NUM = SUM.ABS/NUMBER
1870    LET MAPE.NUM = SUM.PER.ABS/NUMBER
1880    LET MSE.NUM = SUM.SQU.ERR/NUMBER
1890    LET MPE.NUM = SUM.PER.ERR/NUMBER
1900    REM
1910    REM ****** OUTPUT SECTION
1920    PRINT "THE MEAN OF THE ERRORS = ";
1930    PRINT USING "######.## ";ME.NUM
1940    PRINT "THE MEAN OF THE ABSOLUTE DEVIATIONS = ";
1950    PRINT USING "######.## ";MAD.NUM
1960    PRINT "THE MEAN OF THE ABSOLUTE PERCENT ERRORS = ";
1970    PRINT USING "######.## ";MAPE.NUM
1980    PRINT "THE MEAN OF THE SQUARED ERRORS = ";
1990    PRINT USING "######.## ";MSE.NUM
2000    PRINT "THE MEAN OF THE PERCENTAGE ERRORS = ";
2010    PRINT USING "######.## ";MPE.NUM
2020    RETURN
2030    END
ENTER THE NUMBER OF DATA PAIRS YOU WANT TO CONSIDER:       10

TELL ME THE REAL VALUES AND THEIR FORECASTED VALUES.

PLEASE ENTER REAL VALUE NUMBER 1 :            100
PLEASE ENTER PREDICTED FORECAST FOR NUMBER 1 :              105
PLEASE ENTER REAL VALUE NUMBER 2 :            100
PLEASE ENTER PREDICTED FORECAST FOR NUMBER 2 :              90
PLEASE ENTER REAL VALUE NUMBER 3 :            98
PLEASE ENTER PREDICTED FORECAST FOR NUMBER 3 :              118
PLEASE ENTER REAL VALUE NUMBER 4 :            150
PLEASE ENTER PREDICTED FORECAST FOR NUMBER 4 :              172
PLEASE ENTER REAL VALUE NUMBER 5 :            160
PLEASE ENTER PREDICTED FORECAST FOR NUMBER 5 :              160
PLEASE ENTER REAL VALUE NUMBER 6 :            211
PLEASE ENTER PREDICTED FORECAST FOR NUMBER 6 :              290
PLEASE ENTER REAL VALUE NUMBER 7 :            240
PLEASE ENTER PREDICTED FORECAST FOR NUMBER 7 :              230
PLEASE ENTER REAL VALUE NUMBER 8 :            250
PLEASE ENTER PREDICTED FORECAST FOR NUMBER 8 :              295
PLEASE ENTER REAL VALUE NUMBER 9 :            700
PLEASE ENTER PREDICTED FORECAST FOR NUMBER 9 :              762
PLEASE ENTER REAL VALUE NUMBER 10 :            550
PLEASE ENTER PREDICTED FORECAST FOR NUMBER 10 :              620
```

**Figure 12–6**    (Continued)

```
                    FORECAST ACCURACY MEASUREMENT
        THE FOLLOWING ARE THE REAL VALUES AND THEIR FORECASTED VALUES
                         ------------                  ------------------
                              100                             105
                              100                              90
                               98                             118
                              150                             172
                              160                             160
                              211                             290
                              240                             230
                              250                             295
                              700                             762
                              550                             620
THE MEAN OF THE ERRORS =          -28.30
THE MEAN OF THE ABSOLUTE DEVIATIONS =          32.30
THE MEAN OF THE ABSOLUTE PERCENT ERRORS =          0.13
THE MEAN OF THE SQUARED ERRORS =      1811.90
THE MEAN OF THE PERCENTAGE ERRORS =        -0.10
*****************************************************************
DO YOU WANT TO TRY ANY OTHER PAIRS OF DATA (Y OR N): N

                              THANK YOU!
```

**Figure 12-6**  *(Continued)*

Based on this formula, the forecasts for periods 11, 10, . . . , and 2 are as follows:

$$F(11) = X(10) + (1 - \alpha)F(10)$$
$$F(10) = X(9) + (1 - \alpha)F(9)$$
.
.
.
$$F(2) = X(1) + (1 - \alpha)F(1)$$

To use this formula, you must assume that the forecast for period 1 is equal to the actual value of period 1 or any other constant. The $\alpha$ value must be chosen to minimize the MSE.

Northwest Textile Company is making a sales forecast for the next period based on the total sales of the previous periods. The sales manager wants to use single exponential smoothing as his forecasting tool. Write and run a program to accept up to 100 pairs of sales data items from the keyboard and to predict the total sales for the next period. Your program should perform this forecast by choosing an alpha value that generates the smallest MSE (see fig. 12-7).

**Figure 12-7**
Single Exponential Smoothing

```
1000    REM THIS PROGRAM ACCEPTS UP TO 100 ITEMS FROM THE KEYBOARD
1010    REM AND GENERATES THE BEST POSSIBLE FORECAST FOR THE NEXT
1020    REM PERIOD BY CHOOSING THE ALPHA VALUE WHICH MINIMIZES THE
1030    REM VALUE OF MSE.  IF THE NUMBER OF DATA POINTS EXCEEDS 100
1040    REM THE DIM STATEMENT MUST BE MODIFIED.
1050    REM
1060    REM ****** VARIABLE TABLE
1070    REM         NUMBER = THE NUMBER OF PERIODS OF DATA TO CONSIDER
```

```
1080   REM          COUNT1 = FOR-NEXT LOOP CONTROL VARIABLE
1090   REM          BEG.ALP = BEGINNING VALUE OF ALPHA
1100   REM          END.ALP = ENDING VALUE OF ALPHA
1110   REM          STEPSIZE = FOR-NEXT LOOP STEP INCREMENT VARIABLE
1120   REM          ANSWER$ = REPEAT PROGRAM TEST VARIABLE
1130   REM          SUM.SQ = SUM OF THE SQUARED ERRORS
1140   REM          COUNTER = COUNTER VARIABLE
1150   REM          ALPHA = ALPHA VARIABLE
1160   REM          MSE = SQUARED ERROR VARIABLE
1170   REM          MIN.MSE = THE SMALLEST MSE
1180   REM          ALP.MSE = THE ALPHA OF THE SMALLEST MSE
1190   REM          BEST = THE BEST FORECAST
1200   REM
1210   REM ****** ARRAY TABLE
1220   REM          TIME(100) = THE ARRAY FOR THE TIME PERIOD
1230   REM          ACTUAL(100) = THE ARRAY FOR THE ACTUAL VALUES
1240   REM          FORECAST(100) = THE ARRAY FOR THE FORECAST
1250   REM          ERRORS(100) = THE ARRAY FOR THE ERRORS
1260   REM          SQ.ERRORS(100) = THE ARRAY FOR THE SQUARED ERRORS
1270   REM          ALPHA(1000) = THE ARRAY FOR THE DIFFERENT VALUES OF ALPHA
1280   REM          MSE(1000) = THE ARRAY FOR THE DIFFERENT VALUES OF MSE'S
1290   REM
1300   REM ****** INITIALIZATION SECTION
1310   DIM TIME(100), ACTUAL(100), FORECAST(100), ERRORS(100)
1320   DIM SQ.ERRORS(100), ALPHA(1001), MSE(1001)
1330   REM
1340   CLS
1350   INPUT "HOW MANY PERIODS OF DATA WOULD YOU LIKE TO CONSIDER? ",NUMBER
1360   PRINT : PRINT "PLEASE ENTER YOUR PERIODS AND YOUR DATA ITEMS."
1370   REM
1380   FOR COUNT1 = 1 TO NUMBER
1390      LOCATE 5,1
1400      PRINT "ENTER TIME PERIOD NUMBER";COUNT1;": ";
1410      INPUT "",TIME(COUNT1)
1420      PRINT "ENTER DATA ITEM NUMBER";COUNT1;": ";
1430      INPUT "",ACTUAL(COUNT1)
1440   NEXT COUNT1
1450   REM
1460   INPUT "PLEASE ENTER THE BEGINNING VALUE OF ALPHA: ",BEG.ALP
1470   INPUT "PLEASE ENTER THE ENDING VALUE OF ALPHA: ",END.ALP
1480   INPUT "PLEASE ENTER THE STEP SIZE: ",STEPSIZE
1490   REM
1500   REM ****** PROCESS SECTION
1510   GOSUB 1620
1520   GOSUB 1960
1530   GOSUB 2110
1540   REM
1550   REM ****** TERMINATION SECTION
1560   PRINT "**************************************************"
1570   INPUT "WOULD YOU LIKE TO RUN ANOTHER SET OF DATA (Y OR N)? ",ANSWER$
1580   IF ANSWER$ = "Y" OR ANSWER$ = "y" THEN GOTO 1340
1590   IF ANSWER$ <> "N" AND ANSWER$ <> "n" THEN GOTO 1570
1600   GOTO 2390
1610   REM
1620   REM THIS SUBROUTINE TRIES DIFFERENT VALUES FOR ALPHA
1630   REM AND COMPUTES THE MSE'S FOR THESE VALUES.
1640   REM FIRST WE MUST ASSUME THAT THE FORECAST FOR THE SECOND
1650   REM PERIOD IS EQUAL TO THE ACTUAL VALUE OF THE FIRST PERIOD.
1660   LET SUM.SQ = 0
1670   REM SUM.SQ KEEPS TRACK OF THE SUM OF SQUARED ERRORS
1680   LET FORECAST(1) = 0
1690   LET ERRORS(1) = 0
1700   LET SQ.ERRORS(1) = 0
1710   LET FORECAST(2) = ACTUAL(1)
1720   LET ERRORS(2) = ACTUAL(2)-FORECAST(2)
```

**Figure 12–7** *(Continued)*

254

```
1730     LET SQ.ERRORS(2) = ERRORS(2)^2
1740     LET COUNTER = 0
1750     PRINT "BEGINNING        ENDING" : PRINT " ALPHA        ALPHA"
1760     PRINT "---------       ------"
1770     PRINT USING "   #.##              #.##";BEG.ALP,END.ALP
1780     REM
1790     FOR ALPHA1= BEG.ALP TO END.ALP STEP STEPSIZE
1800       LET SUM.SQ = SUM.SQ+SQ.ERRORS(2)
1810       FOR COUNT1 = 3 TO NUMBER
1820        FORECAST(COUNT1)=ALPHA1*ACTUAL(COUNT1-1)+(1-ALPHA1)*FORECAST(COUNT1-1)
1830         LET ERRORS(COUNT1) = ACTUAL(COUNT1)-FORECAST(COUNT1)
1840         LET SQ.ERRORS(COUNT1) = ERRORS(COUNT1)^2
1850         LET SUM.SQ = SUM.SQ+SQ.ERRORS(COUNT1)
1860       NEXT COUNT1
1870       LET MSE1= SUM.SQ/(NUMBER-1)
1880       LET COUNTER = COUNTER+1
1890       LET MSE(COUNTER) = MSE1
1900       LET ALPHA(COUNTER) = ALPHA1
1910       LET SUM.SQ = 0
1920     NEXT ALPHA1
1930     REM
1940     RETURN
1950     REM
1960     REM THIS SUBROUTINE SEARCHES FOR THE SMALLEST MSE.
1970     LET MIN.MSE = MSE(1)
1980     ALP.MSE = ALPHA(1)
1990     REM WE ARE ASSUMING THAT THE FIRST MSE IS THE
2000     REM SMALLEST ONE WHICH HAS BEEN GENERATED BY THE
2010     REM FIRST ALPHA.
2020     FOR COUNT1 = 2 TO COUNTER
2030       IF MSE(COUNT1) < MIN.MSE THEN GOTO 2050
2040       GOTO 2070
2050       LET MIN.MSE = MSE(COUNT1)
2060       LET ALP.MSE = ALPHA(COUNT1)
2070     NEXT COUNT1
2080     REM
2090     RETURN
2100     REM
2110     REM THIS SUBROUTINE PRINTS THE BEST FORECAST.
2120     PRINT "SINGLE EXPONENTIAL SMOOTHING"
2130     PRINT "THE FOLLOWING ARE THE ORIGINAL DATA"
2140     REM
2150     FOR COUNT1 = 1 TO NUMBER
2160       PRINT TIME(COUNT1), ACTUAL(COUNT1)
2170     NEXT COUNT1
2180     REM
2190     REM FINDING THE BEST FORECAST.
2200     LET FORECAST(1) = 0
2210     LET FORECAST(2) = ACTUAL(1)
2220     REM
2230     FOR COUNT1 = 3 TO NUMBER
2240       FORECAST(COUNT1)=ALP.MSE*ACTUAL(COUNT1-1)+(1-ALP.MSE)*FORECAST(COUNT1-1)
2250     NEXT COUNT1
2260     REM
2270     LET BEST = ALP.MSE*ACTUAL(NUMBER)+(1-ALP.MSE)*FORECAST(NUMBER)
2280     REM
2290     REM ****** OUTPUT SECTION
2300     PRINT "THE BEST FORECAST FOR PERIOD";
2310     PRINT USING " ## ";NUMBER+1;
2320     PRINT "IS ";
2330     PRINT USING "######.## ";BEST
2340     PRINT "THE ALPHA = ";
2350     PRINT USING "#.### ";ALP.MSE
2360     PRINT "THE MSE = ";
```

**Figure 12-7** *(Continued)*

```
2370    PRINT USING "#######.## ";MIN.MSE
2380    RETURN
2390    END
```
HOW MANY PERIODS OF DATA WOULD YOU LIKE TO CONSIDER?      10

PLEASE ENTER YOUR PERIODS AND YOUR DATA ITEMS.
ENTER TIME PERIOD NUMBER 1 :                1
ENTER DATA ITEM NUMBER 1 :    480
ENTER TIME PERIOD NUMBER 2 :                2
ENTER DATA ITEM NUMBER 2 :    450
ENTER TIME PERIOD NUMBER 3 :                3
ENTER DATA ITEM NUMBER 3 :    420
ENTER TIME PERIOD NUMBER 4 :                4
ENTER DATA ITEM NUMBER 4 :    451
ENTER TIME PERIOD NUMBER 5 :                5
ENTER DATA ITEM NUMBER 5 :    459
ENTER TIME PERIOD NUMBER 6 :                6
ENTER DATA ITEM NUMBER 6 :    419
ENTER TIME PERIOD NUMBER 7 :                7
ENTER DATA ITEM NUMBER 7 :    448
ENTER TIME PERIOD NUMBER 8 :                8
ENTER DATA ITEM NUMBER 8 :    395
ENTER TIME PERIOD NUMBER 9 :                9
ENTER DATA ITEM NUMBER 9 :    370
ENTER TIME PERIOD NUMBER 10 :               10
ENTER DATA ITEM NUMBER 10 :                 400
PLEASE ENTER THE BEGINNING VALUE OF ALPHA:              .001
PLEASE ENTER THE ENDING VALUE OF ALPHA:     .999
PLEASE ENTER THE STEP SIZE:                 .001
BEGINNING       ENDING
  ALPHA         ALPHA
---------       ------
  0.00          1.00
SINGLE EXPONENTIAL SMOOTHING
THE FOLLOWING ARE THE ORIGINAL DATA
  1             480
  2             450
  3             420
  4             451
  5             459
  6             419
  7             448
  8             395
  9             370
 10             400
THE BEST FORECAST FOR PERIOD 11 IS      394.56
THE ALPHA = 0.655
THE MSE =      968.35
*****************************************************
WOULD YOU LIKE TO RUN ANOTHER SET OF DATA (Y OR N)?      N
```

**Figure 12–7**    *(Continued)*

## 12–8

## SIMPLE LINEAR REGRESSION

Simple linear regression is a forecasting tool usually used for either medium range (less than two years) or long-range (two years or more) forecasting. The formula for a simple linear regression is as follows:

$$Y = A + BX$$

where: Y = dependent variable
       X = independent variable
```

A = intercept
B = slope of the line

To apply this model to forecasting problems, the values for A and B must be estimated. One way of estimating these values is by using the least squares method.

The least squares method estimates the values of A and B in such a way that the mean squared deviation between actual and predicted values is as small as possible. The following two formulas satisfy the requirements of the least squares method:

$$B = \frac{N\Sigma(XY) - \Sigma X \Sigma Y}{N\Sigma X^2 - (\Sigma X)^2}$$

$$A = \frac{\Sigma Y}{N} - \frac{B\Sigma X}{N}$$

## 12–9
## CORRELATION COEFFICIENT

To measure the strength of relative association between two variables, you use the correlation coefficient. The correlation coefficient, r, can vary from −1 to +1, where:

r = 0 indicates no correlation
r = −1 indicates perfect negative correlation
r = +1 indicates perfect positive correlation

The formula to use for calculating the correlation coefficient is as follows:

$$r = \frac{N\Sigma(XY) - \Sigma X \Sigma Y}{\sqrt{(N\Sigma X^2 - (\Sigma X^2))(N\Sigma Y^2 - (\Sigma Y)^2)}}$$

## 12–10
## COEFFICIENT OF DETERMINATION

The square of the correlation coefficient is called the coefficient of determination. The coefficient of determination is the ratio of the sum of explained variation over the sum of total variation. The formula is as follows:

$$r^2 = \frac{(N\Sigma(XY) - \Sigma X \Sigma Y)^2}{(N\Sigma X^2 - (\Sigma X)^2)(N\Sigma Y^2 - (\Sigma Y)^2)}$$

This ratio shows how well a regression line can define the total variation in a series of data points. This ratio varies from 0 to 1, where 0 means that the regression line does not explain any variation in the data points and 1 means that total variation is perfectly explained by the regression line.

Suppose that TR-North Pacific Glass Company is conducting a long-range production cost forecast. Write and run a program that accepts up to 100 pairs of data items from the keyboard and computes the regression line for these pairs, the correlation coefficient, and the coefficient of determination. Your program should also be able to accept any value for the independent variable and calculate the estimated value of the dependent variable based on the computed regression line (see fig. 12–8).

**Figure 12-8**

Regression Analysis

```
1000 REM THIS PROGRAM ACCEPTS UP TO 100 PAIRS OF DATA FROM THE
1010 REM KEYBOARD AND COMPUTES THE REGRESSION LINE FOR THESE PAIRS.
1020 REM IF THE NUMBER OF THESE PAIRS EXCEEDS 100, THE DIM STATEMENT
1030 REM MUST BE MODIFIED.
1040 REM
1050 REM ******* VARIABLE TABLE
1060 REM           NUMBER = THE NUMBER OF DATA PAIRS TO CONSIDER
1070 REM           COUNT = FOR-NEXT LOOP CONTROL VARIABLE
1080 REM           ANSWER1$= PERFORM PREDICTION TEST VARIABLE
1090 REM           ANSWER2$ = COMPUTE REGRESSION OF OTHER PAIRS TEST VARIABLE
1100 REM           DEP.VAR = ESTIMATED VALUE OF THE DEPENDENT VARIABLE
1110 REM           INT.REG = THE INTERCEPT FOR THE REGRESSION LINE
1120 REM           SLO.REG = THE SLOPE OF THE REGRESSION LINE
1130 REM           SUM.IND = THE SUM OF THE VALUES FOR INDEPENDENT VARIABLES
1140 REM           SUM.DEP =THE SUM OF THE VALUES FOR DEPENDENT VARIABLES
1150 REM           SUM.SQ.IND = THE SUM OF THE SQUARES OF INDEPENDENT VALUES
1160 REM           SUM.SQ.DEP = THE SUM OF THE SQUARES OF DEPENDENT VALUES
1170 REM           SUM.PROD = THE SUM OF THE PRODUCTS OF IND. BY DEP. VALUES
1180 REM           CORR = THE CORRELATION COEFFICIENT
1190 REM           CORR.2 = THE COEFFICIENT OF DETERMINATION
1200 REM           INTER1 = INTERMEDIATE CORRELATION CALCULATION VARIABLE
1210 REM           INTER2 = INTERMEDIATE CORRELATION CALCULATION VARIABLE
1220 REM
1230 REM
1240 REM ******* ARRAY TABLE
1250 REM           IND(100) = ARRAY FOR THE INDEPENDENT VARIABLES
1260 REM           DEP(100) = ARRAY FOR THE DEPENDENT VARIABLES
1270 REM
1280 REM ******* INITIALIZATION SECTION
1290 DIM IND(100), DEP(100)
1300 CLS : INPUT "HOW MANY PAIRS OF DATA DO YOU WANT TO CONSIDER? ",NUMBER
1310 PRINT : PRINT "TELL ME THE VALUE OF ALL YOUR INDEPENDENT AND DEPENDENT";
1320 PRINT " VARIABLES."
1330 REM
1340 FOR COUNT = 1 TO NUMBER
1350     LOCATE 5,1
1360     PRINT "ENTER THE VALUE OF INDEPENDENT VARIABLE NUMBER";COUNT;": ";
1370     INPUT "",IND(COUNT)
1380     PRINT "ENTER THE VALUE OF DEPENDENT VARIABLE NUMBER";COUNT;": ";
1390     INPUT "",DEP(COUNT)
1400 NEXT COUNT
1410 REM
1420 REM ******* PROCESS SECTION
1430 PRINT TAB(15); "SIMPLE REGRESSION"
1440 PRINT "THE FOLLOWING ARE THE VALUES FOR INDEPENDENT AND ";
1450 PRINT "DEPENDENT VARIABLES"
1460 REM
1470 FOR COUNT = 1 TO NUMBER
1480     PRINT IND(COUNT), DEP(COUNT)
1490 NEXT COUNT
1500 REM
1510 GOSUB 1740
1520 GOSUB 2010
1530 GOSUB 2100
1540 REM
1550 PRINT "********************************************************"
1560 INPUT "DO YOU WANT TO DO ANY PREDICTION (Y OR N)? ",ANSWER1$
1570 IF ANSWER1$ = "Y" OR ANSWER1$ = "y" THEN GOTO 1690
1580 IF ANSWER1$ <> "N" AND ANSWER1$ <> "n" THEN GOTO 1560
1590 REM
1600 REM ******* TERMINATION SECTION
1610 PRINT "++++++++++++++++++++++++++++++++++++++++++++++++++++++++"
```

```
1620 PRINT "+++++++++++++++++++++++++++++++++++++++++++++++++++++++++++++"
1630 PRINT "DO YOU WANT TO COMPUTE THE REGRESSION FOR ANY OTHER PAIRS ";
1640 INPUT "(Y OR N)? ",ANSWER2$
1650 IF ANSWER2$ = "Y" OR ANSWER2$ = "y" THEN GOTO 1300
1660 IF ANSWER2$ <> "N" AND ANSWER2$ <> "n" THEN GOTO 1630
1670 GOTO 2150
1680 REM
1690 INPUT "PLEASE ENTER THE VALUE OF THE INDEPENDENT VARIABLE: ",IND.VAR
1700 LET DEP.VAR = INT.REG+(SLO.REG)*IND.VAR
1710 PRINT "THE ESTIMATED VALUE OF THE DEPENDENT VARIABLE = ";
1720 PRINT USING "###.##";DEP.VAR
1730 GOTO 1610
1740 REM THIS SUBROUTINE COMPUTES THE REGRESSION EQUATION.
1750 LET SUM.IND = 0
1760 LET SUM.DEP = 0
1770 LET SUM.SQ.IND = 0
1780 LET SUM.SQ.DEP = 0
1790 LET SUM.PROD = 0
1800 REM
1810 FOR COUNT = 1 TO NUMBER
1820    LET SUM.IND = SUM.IND+IND(COUNT)
1830    LET SUM.DEP = SUM.DEP+DEP(COUNT)
1840    LET SUM.SQ.IND = SUM.SQ.IND+IND(COUNT)^2
1850    LET SUM.SQ.DEP = SUM.SQ.DEP+DEP(COUNT)^2
1860    LET SUM.PROD = SUM.PROD+IND(COUNT)*DEP(COUNT)
1870 NEXT COUNT
1880 REM
1890 REM INT.REG IS THE INTERCEPT
1900 REM SLO.REG IS THE SLOPE OF THE REGRESSION LINE
1910 LET SLO.REG=(NUMBER*SUM.PROD-SUM.IND*SUM.DEP)/(NUMBER*SUM.SQ.IND-SUM.IND^2)
1920 LET INT.REG = (SUM.DEP/NUMBER)-SLO.REG*(SUM.IND/NUMBER)
1930 REM
1940 REM ****** OUTPUT SECTION
1950 PRINT "THE INTERCEPT FOR THE REGRESSION LINE = ";
1960 PRINT USING "#######.## ";INT.REG
1970 PRINT "THE SLOPE FOR THE REGRESSION LINE   = ";
1980 PRINT USING "#######.## ";SLO.REG
1990 RETURN
2000 REM
2010 REM THIS SUBROUTINE COMPUTES THE CORRELATION COEFFICIENT.
2020 LET INTER1 = (NUMBER*SUM.PROD-SUM.IND*SUM.DEP)
2030 LET INTER2=SQR((NUMBER*SUM.SQ.IND-SUM.IND^2)*(NUMBER*SUM.SQ.DEP-SUM.DEP^2))
2040 LET CORR=INTER1/INTER2
2050 REM
2060 PRINT "THE CORRELATION COEFFICIENT = ";
2070 PRINT USING "#######.##";CORR
2080 RETURN
2090 REM
2100 REM THIS SUBROUTINE COMPUTES THE COEFFICIENT OF DETERMINATION.
2110 LET CORR.2 = CORR^2
2120 PRINT "THE COEFFICIENT OF DETERMINATION = ";
2130 PRINT USING "#######.## ";CORR.2
2140 RETURN
2150 END
HOW MANY PAIRS OF DATA DO YOU WANT TO CONSIDER?               10

TELL ME THE VALUE OF ALL YOUR INDEPENDENT AND DEPENDENT VARIABLES.
ENTER THE VALUE OF INDEPENDENT VARIABLE NUMBER 1 :            15
ENTER THE VALUE OF DEPENDENT VARIABLE NUMBER 1 :              27
ENTER THE VALUE OF INDEPENDENT VARIABLE NUMBER 2 :            18
ENTER THE VALUE OF DEPENDENT VARIABLE NUMBER 2 :              32
ENTER THE VALUE OF INDEPENDENT VARIABLE NUMBER 3 :            22
ENTER THE VALUE OF DEPENDENT VARIABLE NUMBER 3 :              36
ENTER THE VALUE OF INDEPENDENT VARIABLE NUMBER 4 :            25
ENTER THE VALUE OF DEPENDENT VARIABLE NUMBER 4 :              41
```

**Figure 12–8**   *(Continued)*

```
ENTER THE VALUE OF INDEPENDENT VARIABLE NUMBER 5 :        27
ENTER THE VALUE OF DEPENDENT VARIABLE NUMBER 5 :          42
ENTER THE VALUE OF INDEPENDENT VARIABLE NUMBER 6 :        32
ENTER THE VALUE OF DEPENDENT VARIABLE NUMBER 6 :          44
ENTER THE VALUE OF INDEPENDENT VARIABLE NUMBER 7 :        39
ENTER THE VALUE OF DEPENDENT VARIABLE NUMBER 7 :          50
ENTER THE VALUE OF INDEPENDENT VARIABLE NUMBER 8 :        42
ENTER THE VALUE OF DEPENDENT VARIABLE NUMBER 8 :          60
ENTER THE VALUE OF INDEPENDENT VARIABLE NUMBER 9 :        40
ENTER THE VALUE OF DEPENDENT VARIABLE NUMBER 9 :          49
ENTER THE VALUE OF INDEPENDENT VARIABLE NUMBER 10 :       32
ENTER THE VALUE OF DEPENDENT VARIABLE NUMBER 10 :         40
                  SIMPLE REGRESSION
THE FOLLOWING ARE THE VALUES FOR INDEPENDENT AND DEPENDENT VARIABLES
  15              27
  18              32
  22              36
  25              41
  27              42
  32              44
  39              50
  42              60
  40              49
  32              40
THE INTERCEPT FOR THE REGRESSION LINE =        14.25
THE SLOPE FOR THE REGRESSION LINE    =        0.95
THE CORRELATION COEFFICIENT =        0.95
THE COEFFICIENT OF DETERMINATION =        0.89
*********************************************************
DO YOU WANT TO DO ANY PREDICTION (Y OR N)?            N
++++++++++++++++++++++++++++++++++++++++++++++++++++++++++
++++++++++++++++++++++++++++++++++++++++++++++++++++++++++
DO YOU WANT TO COMPUTE THE REGRESSION FOR ANY OTHER PAIRS        N
```

**Figure 12–8**   *(Continued)*

## 12–11

## PARABOLIC REGRESSION

Parabolic regression is a forecasting tool for medium- or long-range forecasting. In the previous section, we discussed a method for fitting a line among a series of data points. Linear regression is helpful only if the relationship between the two variables is linear. Often, however, the relationship is not linear but curved. In such cases, a parabolic fit may produce a better result. The formula for a parabolic regression is as follows:

$$Y = A + BX + CX^2$$

where: Y = the dependent variable

X = the independent variable

A, B, and C = the parameters

Again, the least squares method can be used to estimate the values of these parameters. To satisfy the requirements of the least squares method, the following three equations must be solved:

$$\Sigma Y = NA + B\Sigma X + C\Sigma X^2$$
$$\Sigma XY = A\Sigma X + B\Sigma X^2 + C\Sigma X^3$$
$$\Sigma X^2Y = A\Sigma X^2 + B\Sigma X^3 + C\Sigma X^4$$

Suppose that North Atlantic Copper Company is conducting a long-range manpower plan. Write and run a program to accept up to 100 pairs of data items from the keyboard and to compute the parameters of the parabolic regression for these pairs. Your program should be able to accept any value for the independent variable and compute the value of the dependent variable based on the computed parabolic regression (see fig. 12–9).

**Figure 12–9**
Parabolic Regression

```
1000 REM THIS PROGRAM ACCEPTS UP TO 100 PAIRS OF DATA FROM THE
1010 REM KEYBOARD AND COMPUTES THE PARABOLIC REGRESSION FOR THESE PAIRS.
1020 REM IF THE NUMBER OF THESE PAIRS EXCEEDS 100, THE DIM STATEMENT
1030 REM MUST BE MODIFIED.
1040 REM
1050 REM ****** VARIABLE TABLE
1060 REM          NUMBER = THE NUMBER OF DATA PAIRS TO CONSIDER
1070 REM          COUNT = FOR-NEXT LOOP CONTROL VARIABLE
1080 REM          ANSWER1$, ANSWER$ = USER INPUT TEST VARIABLES
1090 REM          IND = VALUE OF INDEPENDENT VARIABLE
1100 REM          DEP = VALUE OF DEPENDENT VARIABLE
1110 REM          A, B, C = FORMULA PLUG-IN VARIABLES
1120 REM          S1 = SUM OF INDEPENDENT VARIABLE VALUES
1130 REM          S2 = SUM OF SQUARES OF INDEPENDENT VARIABLE VALUES
1140 REM          S3 = SUM OF CUBES OF INDEPENDENT VARIABLE VALUES
1150 REM          S4 = SUM OF INDEPENDENT VARIABLE VALUES TO POWER OF FOUR
1160 REM          S5 = SUM OF DEPENDENT VARIABLE VALUES
1170 REM          S6 = SUM OF PRODUCTS OF IND. BY DEPENDENT VARIABLE VALUES
1180 REM          S7 = SUM OF PRODUCTS OF SQUARES OF IND. BY DEP. VARIABLE VALS
1190 REM
1200 REM ****** ARRAY AND MATRIX TABLE
1210 REM          IND(100) = THE ARRAY FOR THE INDEPENDENT VARIABLES
1220 REM          DEP(100) = THE ARRAY FOR THE DEPENDENT VARIABLES
1230 REM          COEF(3,3) = MATRIX OF THE COEFFICIENTS
1240 REM          INV(3,3) = INVERSE OF THE MATRIX OF THE COEFFICIENTS
1250 REM          RHS(3) = RIGHT-HAND-SIDE ARRAY
1260 REM          SOL(3) = MATRIX OF THE SOLUTION
1270 REM
1280 REM ****** INITIALIZATION SECTION
1290 DIM IND(100), DEP(100)
1300 DIM COEF(3,3), INV(3,3), RHS(3), SOL(3)
1310 CLS : INPUT "HOW MANY PAIRS OF DATA DO YOU WANT TO CONSIDER? ",NUMBER
1320 REM
1330 REM ****** PROCESS SECTION
1340 PRINT : PRINT "TELL ME THE VALUE OF ALL YOUR INDEPENDENT AND DEPENDENT ";
1350 PRINT " VARIABLES"
1360 REM
1370 FOR COUNT = 1 TO NUMBER
1380    LOCATE 6,1
1390    PRINT "PLEASE ENTER INDEPENDENT VARIABLE NUMBER";COUNT;": ";
1400    INPUT "",IND(COUNT)
1410    PRINT "PLEASE ENTER DEPENDENT VARIABLE NUMBER";COUNT;": ";
1420    INPUT "",DEP(COUNT)
1430 NEXT COUNT
1440 REM
1450 PRINT TAB(15); "PARABOLIC REGRESSION"
1460 PRINT "THE FOLLOWING ARE THE VALUES FOR INDEPENDENT AND ";
1470 PRINT "DEPENDENT VARIABLES"
1480 REM
1490 FOR COUNT = 1 TO NUMBER
1500    PRINT IND(COUNT), DEP(COUNT)
1510 NEXT COUNT
1520 REM
1530 GOSUB 1730
```

```
1540 REM
1550 REM ****** TERMINATION SECTION
1560 PRINT "*********************************************"
1570 INPUT "WOULD YOU LIKE TO DO ANY PREDICTIONS (Y OR N): ",ANSWER1$
1580 IF ANSWER1$ = "Y" OR ANSWER1$ = "y" THEN GOTO 1680
1590 IF ANSWER1$ <> "N" AND ANSWER1$ <> "n" THEN GOTO 1570
1600 PRINT "++++++++++++++++++++++++++++++++++++++++++++++++++++"
1610 PRINT "++++++++++++++++++++++++++++++++++++++++++++++++++++"
1620 PRINT "DO YOU WANT TO COMPUTE THE REGRESSION FOR ANY OTHER PAIRS";
1630 INPUT " (Y OR N): ",ANSWER2$
1640 IF ANSWER2$ = "Y" OR ANSWER2$ = "y" THEN GOTO 1310
1650 IF ANSWER2$ <> "N" AND ANSWER2$ <> "n" THEN GOTO 1620
1660 GOTO 2250
1670 REM
1680 INPUT "PLEASE ENTER THE VALUE OF THE INDEPENDENT VARIABLE: ",IND
1690 LET DEP = A+(B)*IND+(C)*IND^2
1700 PRINT "THE ESTIMATED VALUE OF THE DEPENDENT VARIABLE = ";
1710 PRINT USING "###.##";DEP
1720 GOTO 1600
1730 REM PARABOLIC SUBROUTINE.
1740 REM THIS SUBROUTINE COMPUTES THE PARABOLIC REGRESSION.
1750 REM IN ORDER TO COMPUTE THE PARABOLIC REGRESSION THE
1760 REM THREE EQUATIONS DESCRIBED IN THE TEXT MUST BE SOLVED.
1770 REM DEP IS THE DEPENDENT VARIABLE AND IND IS THE INDEPENDENT VARIABLE.
1780 LET S1 = 0
1790 REM
1800 LET S2 = 0
1810 LET S3 = 0
1820 LET S4 = 0
1830 LET S5 = 0
1840 LET S6 = 0
1850 LET S7 = 0
1860 REM
1870 FOR COUNT = 1 TO NUMBER
1880    LET S1 = S1+IND(COUNT)
1890    LET S2 = S2+IND(COUNT)^2
1900    LET S3 = S3+IND(COUNT)^3
1910    LET S4 = S4+IND(COUNT)^4
1920    LET S5 = S5+DEP(COUNT)
1930    LET S6 = S6+IND(COUNT)*DEP(COUNT)
1940    LET S7 = S7+(IND(COUNT)^2*DEP(COUNT))
1950 NEXT COUNT
1960 REM
1970 REM THIS PART OF THE PROGRAM FILLS THE MATRIX OF THE COEFFICIENTS.
1980 LET COEF(2,2) = S2
1990 REM THIS PART OF THE PROGRAM FILLS THE RIGHT HAND SIDE ARRAY.
2000 REM THIS PART OF THE PROGRAM SOLVES THE THREE SIMULTANEOUS
2010 REM EQUATIONS IN ORDER TO FIND THE VALUES OF A, B, AND C.
2020 LET ACCUM1 = 0
2030 REM
2040 LET ACCUM1 = NUMBER*S2*S4-NUMBER*(S3^2)-S4*(S1^2)
2050 LET ACCUM2 = 2*S1*S2*S3-(S2^3)
2060 LET ACCUM1 = ACCUM1+ACCUM2
2070 REM
2080 LET A = S5*(S2*S4-(S3^2))+S6*(S2*S3-S1*S4)+S7*(-S2^2+S1*S3)
2090 LET A = A/ACCUM1
2100 LET B = S4*(NUMBER*S6-S1*S5)+S7*(S1*S2-NUMBER*S3)+S2*(S5*S3-S2*S6)
2110 LET B = B/ACCUM1
2120 LET C = S7*(-S1^2+NUMBER*S2)+S3*(S1*S5-NUMBER*S6)+S2*(S1*S6-S2*S5)
2130 LET C = C/ACCUM1
2140 REM
2150 REM ****** OUTPUT SECTION
2160 PRINT "THE SOLUTIONS OF THE PARAMETERS OF THE PARABOLIC REGRESSION"
2170 PRINT "ARE AS FOLLOWS:"
2180 PRINT "A = ";
```

**Figure 12-9** *(Continued)*

```
2190 PRINT USING "#######.##";A
2200 PRINT "B = ";
2210 PRINT USING "#######.##";B
2220 PRINT "C = ";
2230 PRINT USING "#######.## ";C
2240 RETURN
2250 END
```
HOW MANY PAIRS OF DATA DO YOU WANT TO CONSIDER?            14

TELL ME THE VALUE OF ALL YOUR INDEPENDENT AND DEPENDENT  VARIABLES
PLEASE ENTER INDEPENDENT VARIABLE NUMBER 1 :   5
PLEASE ENTER DEPENDENT VARIABLE NUMBER 1 :   15
PLEASE ENTER INDEPENDENT VARIABLE NUMBER 2 :   24
PLEASE ENTER DEPENDENT VARIABLE NUMBER 2 :   128
PLEASE ENTER INDEPENDENT VARIABLE NUMBER 3 :   39
PLEASE ENTER DEPENDENT VARIABLE NUMBER 3 :   250
PLEASE ENTER INDEPENDENT VARIABLE NUMBER 4 :   44
PLEASE ENTER DEPENDENT VARIABLE NUMBER 4 :   174
PLEASE ENTER INDEPENDENT VARIABLE NUMBER 5 :   48
PLEASE ENTER DEPENDENT VARIABLE NUMBER 5 :   139
PLEASE ENTER INDEPENDENT VARIABLE NUMBER 6 :   58
PLEASE ENTER DEPENDENT VARIABLE NUMBER 6 :   348
PLEASE ENTER INDEPENDENT VARIABLE NUMBER 7 :   66
PLEASE ENTER DEPENDENT VARIABLE NUMBER 7 :   313
PLEASE ENTER INDEPENDENT VARIABLE NUMBER 8 :   71
PLEASE ENTER DEPENDENT VARIABLE NUMBER 8 :   245
PLEASE ENTER INDEPENDENT VARIABLE NUMBER 9 :   79
PLEASE ENTER DEPENDENT VARIABLE NUMBER 9 :   303
PLEASE ENTER INDEPENDENT VARIABLE NUMBER 10 :   86
PLEASE ENTER DEPENDENT VARIABLE NUMBER 10 :   441
PLEASE ENTER INDEPENDENT VARIABLE NUMBER 11 :   93
PLEASE ENTER DEPENDENT VARIABLE NUMBER 11 :   511
PLEASE ENTER INDEPENDENT VARIABLE NUMBER 12 :   99
PLEASE ENTER DEPENDENT VARIABLE NUMBER 12 :   448
PLEASE ENTER INDEPENDENT VARIABLE NUMBER 13 :   106
PLEASE ENTER DEPENDENT VARIABLE NUMBER 13 :   525
PLEASE ENTER INDEPENDENT VARIABLE NUMBER 14 :   111
PLEASE ENTER DEPENDENT VARIABLE NUMBER 14 :   666
                    PARABOLIC REGRESSION
THE FOLLOWING ARE THE VALUES FOR INDEPENDENT AND DEPENDENT VARIABLES
   5              15
   24             128
   39             250
   44             174
   48             139
   58             348
   66             313
   71             245
   79             303
   86             441
   93             511
   99             448
   106            525
   111            666
THE SOLUTIONS OF THE PARAMETERS OF THE PARABOLIC REGRESSION
ARE AS FOLLOWS:
A =     38.14
B =      2.29
C =      0.02
*************************************************
WOULD YOU LIKE TO DO ANY PREDICTIONS (Y OR N):           N
+++++++++++++++++++++++++++++++++++++++++++++++++
+++++++++++++++++++++++++++++++++++++++++++++++++
DO YOU WANT TO COMPUTE THE REGRESSION FOR ANY OTHER PAIRS         N

**Figure 12–9**   *(Continued)*

## 12–12

## S-CURVE

The S-curve model is a long-range forecasting model (two years or more). An S-curve model has a slow start, a steep growth, and a saturation point that comes after some period of time. There are several mathematical presentations of the S-curve model. The following formula is one way of showing this model:

$$Y_t = e^{A + B/t}$$

where: $Y_t$ = S-curve estimate
$\quad$ e = a constant equal to 2.718
$\quad$ A = the equivalent of the intercept in the linear regression model
$\quad$ B = the equivalent of the slope in the linear regression model
$\quad$ t = time

Because the relationship between the independent variable (t) and the dependent variable (Y) is not linear, the classical least squares method does not apply to this model. However, by taking the logarithm of both sides, you can convert this form to a linear one, as follows:

$$\text{Log } Y_t = \left( A + \frac{B}{t} \right) \log e^e$$

If you replace 1/t with T′ and replace Log e $Y_t$ with $Y'_t$, you have the following (remember, log $e^e$ = 1):

$$Y'_t = A + BT'$$

As you see, this equation has a linear form, and we can apply the classical least squares method to estimate the values of A and B.

Suppose that Southern International Merchant is conducting a long-range sales forecast for its new product. Write and run a program to accept up to 100 pairs of data items from the keyboard and to compute the parameters of an S-curve model (intercept and slope). Your program should be able to accept any value for the independent variable and compute the value of the dependent variable based on the computed S-curve model. (In this case, the independent variable is time and the dependent variable is any item to be predicted. See fig. 12–10.)

**Figure 12–10**
S-Curve Model

```
1000   REM THIS PROGRAM ACCEPTS UP TO 100 PAIRS OF DATA FROM THE
1010   REM KEYBOARD AND COMPUTES THE S-CURVE MODEL FOR THESE PAIRS.
1020   REM IF THE NUMBER OF THESE PAIRS EXCEEDS 100, THE DIM STATEMENT
1030   REM MUST BE MODIFIED.
1040   REM
1050   REM ******* VARIABLE TABLE
1060   REM          NUMBER = THE NUMBER OF DATA PAIRS THE USER WISHES TO CONSIDER
1070   REM          COUNT = FOR-NEXT LOOP CONTROL VARIABLE
1080   REM          ANSWER1$, ANSWER2$ = USER INPUT TEST VARIABLES
1090   REM          IND = THE VALUE OF THE INDEPENDENT VARIABLE
1100   REM          DEP = THE VALUE OF THE DEPENDENT VARIABLE
1110   REM          INTCPT = THE INTERCEPT OF THE LINE
1120   REM          SLOPE = THE SLOPE OF THE LINE
```

```
1130   REM          S1 = SUM OF THE REVERSE OF THE INDEPENDENT VARIABLE VALUES
1140   REM          S2 = SUM OF THE LOGARITHM OF ALL THE DEPENDENT VARIABLE VALUES
1150   REM          S3 = SUM OF PRODUCTS OF THE REVERSE OF THE INDEPENDENT VAR.
1160   REM          S4 = SUM OF THE SQUARES OF THE REVERSE OF THE INDEPENDENT VAR.
1170   REM
1180   REM ****** ARRAY TABLE
1190   REM          IND(100) = ARRAY FOR THE INDEPENDENT VARIABLE
1200   REM          DEP(100) = ARRAY FOR THE DEPENDENT VARIABLE
1210   REM          IND.REV(100) = ARRAY FOR THE REVERSE OF THE INDEPENDENT VAR.
1220   REM          LOG.DEP(100) = ARRAY FOR THE LOGARITHM OF THE DEPENDENT VAR.
1230   REM
1240   REM ****** INITIALIZATION SECTION
1250   DIM IND(100), DEP(100), IND.REV(100), LOG.DEP(100)
1260   CLS : INPUT "HOW MANY PAIRS OF DATA DO YOU WANT TO CONSIDER? ",NUMBER
1270   PRINT : PRINT "TELL ME THE VALUE OF ALL YOUR INDEPENDENT AND ";
1280   PRINT "DEPENDENT VARIABLES."
1290   REM
1300   FOR COUNT = 1 TO NUMBER
1310      LOCATE 5,1
1320      PRINT "PLEASE ENTER INDEPENDENT VARIABLE NUMBER";COUNT;": ";
1330      INPUT "",IND(COUNT)
1340      PRINT "PLEASE ENTER DEPENDENT VARIABLE NUMBER";COUNT;": ";
1350      INPUT "",DEP(COUNT)
1360   NEXT COUNT
1370   REM
1380   REM ****** PROCESS SECTION
1390   PRINT TAB(15); "S-CURVE MODEL"
1400   PRINT "THE FOLLOWING ARE THE VALUES FOR INDEPENDENT AND DEPENDENT";
1410   PRINT " VARIABLES"
1420   REM
1430   FOR COUNT = 1 TO NUMBER
1440      PRINT IND(COUNT),DEP(COUNT)
1450   NEXT COUNT
1460   REM
1470   GOSUB 1680
1480   REM
1490   REM ****** TERMINATION SECTION
1500   PRINT "*****************************************************"
1510   INPUT "DO YOU WANT TO DO ANY PREDICTION (Y OR N)? ",ANSWER1$
1520   IF ANSWER1$ = "Y" OR ANSWER1$ = "y" THEN GOTO 1620
1530   IF ANSWER1$ <> "N" AND ANSWER1$ <> "n" THEN GOTO 1510
1540   PRINT "+++++++++++++++++++++++++++++++++++++++++++++++++++++"
1550   PRINT "+++++++++++++++++++++++++++++++++++++++++++++++++++++"
1560   PRINT "DO YOU WANT TO COMPUTE THE S-CURVE MODEL FOR ANY OTHER PAIRS ";
1570   INPUT "(Y OR N): ",ANSWER2$
1580   IF ANSWER2$ = "Y" OR ANSWER2$ = "y" THEN GOTO 1260
1590   IF ANSWER2$ <> "N" AND ANSWER2$ <> "n" THEN GOTO 1560
1600   GOTO 1910
1610   REM
1620   INPUT "PLEASE ENTER THE VALUE OF THE INDEPENDENT VARIABLE: ",IND
1630   LET DEP = EXP(INTCPT+SLOPE/IND)
1640   PRINT "THE ESTIMATED VALUE OF THE DEPENDENT VARIABLE = ";
1650   PRINT USING "###.## ";DEP
1660   GOTO 1540
1670   REM
1680   REM THIS SUBROUTINE COMPUTES THE PARAMETERS FOR THE S-CURVE MODEL.
1690   LET S1 = 0
1700   LET S2 = 0
1710   LET S3 = 0
1720   LET S4 = 0
1730   REM
1740   FOR COUNT = 1 TO NUMBER
1750      LET IND.REV(COUNT) = (1/IND(COUNT))
1760      LET LOG.DEP(COUNT) = LOG(DEP(COUNT))
```

**Figure 12–10**  *(Continued)*

```
1770      LET S1 = S1+IND.REV(COUNT)
1780      LET S2 = S2+LOG.DEP(COUNT)
1790      LET S3 = (S3+IND.REV(COUNT)*LOG.DEP(COUNT))
1800      LET S4 = S4+IND.REV(COUNT)^2
1810   NEXT COUNT
1820   REM
1830   REM ****** OUTPUT SECTION
1840   LET SLOPE = (NUMBER*S3-S1*S2)/(NUMBER*S4-S1^2)
1850   LET INTCPT = (S2/NUMBER)-SLOPE*(S1/NUMBER)
1860   PRINT "THE INTERCEPT FOR THE S-CURVE MODEL = ";
1870   PRINT USING "#######.## ";INTCPT
1880   PRINT "THE SLOPE FOR THE S-CURVE MODEL = ";
1890   PRINT USING "#######.## ";SLOPE
1900   RETURN
1910   END
HOW MANY PAIRS OF DATA DO YOU WANT TO CONSIDER?            10

TELL ME THE VALUE OF ALL YOUR INDEPENDENT AND DEPENDENT VARIABLES.
PLEASE ENTER INDEPENDENT VARIABLE NUMBER 1 :  1
PLEASE ENTER DEPENDENT VARIABLE NUMBER 1 :   75
PLEASE ENTER INDEPENDENT VARIABLE NUMBER 2 :   2
PLEASE ENTER DEPENDENT VARIABLE NUMBER 2 :   98
PLEASE ENTER INDEPENDENT VARIABLE NUMBER 3 :   3
PLEASE ENTER DEPENDENT VARIABLE NUMBER 3 :   160
PLEASE ENTER INDEPENDENT VARIABLE NUMBER 4 :   4
PLEASE ENTER DEPENDENT VARIABLE NUMBER 4 :   238
PLEASE ENTER INDEPENDENT VARIABLE NUMBER 5 :   5
PLEASE ENTER DEPENDENT VARIABLE NUMBER 5 :   300
PLEASE ENTER INDEPENDENT VARIABLE NUMBER 6 :   6
PLEASE ENTER DEPENDENT VARIABLE NUMBER 6 :   341
PLEASE ENTER INDEPENDENT VARIABLE NUMBER 7 :   7
PLEASE ENTER DEPENDENT VARIABLE NUMBER 7 :   399
PLEASE ENTER INDEPENDENT VARIABLE NUMBER 8 :   8
PLEASE ENTER DEPENDENT VARIABLE NUMBER 8 :   480
PLEASE ENTER INDEPENDENT VARIABLE NUMBER 9 :   9
PLEASE ENTER DEPENDENT VARIABLE NUMBER 9 :   590
PLEASE ENTER INDEPENDENT VARIABLE NUMBER 10 :   10
PLEASE ENTER DEPENDENT VARIABLE NUMBER 10 :   720
                 S-CURVE MODEL
THE FOLLOWING ARE THE VALUES FOR INDEPENDENT AND DEPENDENT VARIABLES
   1            75
   2            98
   3            160
   4            238
   5            300
   6            341
   7            399
   8            480
   9            590
  10            720
THE INTERCEPT FOR THE S-CURVE MODEL =        6.31
THE SLOPE FOR THE S-CURVE MODEL =       -2.40
*****************************************************
DO YOU WANT TO DO ANY PREDICTION (Y OR N)?               Y
PLEASE ENTER THE VALUE OF THE INDEPENDENT VARIABLE:       12
THE ESTIMATED VALUE OF THE DEPENDENT VARIABLE = 451.56
+++++++++++++++++++++++++++++++++++++++++++++++++++++++
+++++++++++++++++++++++++++++++++++++++++++++++++++++++
DO YOU WANT TO COMPUTE THE S-CURVE MODEL FOR ANY OTHER PAIRS (Y OR N): N
```

**Figure 12–10** *(Continued)*

In this chapter, we presented a selection of statistics and statistical forecasting problems along with a brief explanation of each technique. These problems have a variety of applications. Many small-scale computerized models can be designed based on these techniques.

**SUMMARY**

**HANDS-ON EXPERIENCE**

1. Write and run a BASIC program to calculate the arithmetic mean, standard deviation, and variance of the following numbers: 5, 9, 16, 22, 3, 8, and 7.

2. Write and run a program to calculate the geometric mean of the following numbers: 16, 22, 80, 40, and 11.

3. Write and run a program to calculate the median of the following two data sets:

   5, 11, 22, 6, 14, 3, and 19
   15, 21, 32, 16, 24, 13, 29, and 11

4. The following table shows four different alternatives and five different states of nature and their associated probabilities of occurrence. Write and run a program to calculate the expected value of each alternative, and then choose the best alternative based on its expected value.

| | State of Nature | | | | |
| --- | --- | --- | --- | --- | --- |
| | S1 | S2 | S3 | S4 | S5 |
| Probability | .20 | .15 | .25 | .30 | .10 |
| Alternative 1 | 1,200 | 1,800 | 2,500 | 3,000 | 4,200 |
| Alternative 2 | 1,600 | 2,700 | 2,600 | 3,100 | 1,200 |
| Alternative 3 | 1,600 | 3,100 | 2,200 | 1,550 | 1,000 |
| Alternative 4 | 1,110 | 4,100 | 1,500 | 1,620 | 5,000 |

5. The following data show the sales for product X for the past 10 months. Using single exponential smoothing, what is the best forecast for the next month?

   | | |
   | --- | --- |
   | January | 220 |
   | February | 210 |
   | March | 285 |
   | April | 240 |
   | May | 265 |
   | June | 310 |
   | July | 340 |
   | August | 295 |
   | September | 300 |
   | October | 305 |

6. Most people believe there is a high correlation between income and level of education. The following data have been collected from ten different regions and show the number of years of education and present salary. Write and run a program to calculate the correlation coefficient between level of education and salary. Based on this answer, what is your reaction to this general belief?

   | Years of Education | Salary |
   | --- | --- |
   | 16 | $23,000 |
   | 23 | 46,000 |
   | 12 | 22,000 |
   | 16 | 32,000 |
   | 18 | 29,000 |

| | |
|---|---|
| 19 | 21,000 |
| 21 | 43,500 |
| 12 | 23,000 |
| 24 | 57,000 |
| 12 | 16,000 |

7. The following data show the consumption of natural gas for the past 11 years for six different states. Using three different forecasting models (simple regression, parabolic regression, and S-curve), what is the forecast for the year 1992?

| Year | Consumption (Million Metric Tons) |
|---|---|
| 1981 | 52 |
| 1982 | 59 |
| 1983 | 53 |
| 1984 | 49 |
| 1985 | 71 |
| 1986 | 79 |
| 1987 | 86 |
| 1988 | 91 |
| 1989 | 97 |
| 1990 | 105 |
| 1991 | 119 |

# APPENDICES

# Appendix A
# GW-BASIC's Advanced Features

This appendix lists some of the most important advanced features of GW-BASIC. We present these features through a series of fully documented programs. We provide a listing and an execution of each feature. The programs perform some interesting tasks.

To see the dynamics of these programs, either type them into your computer or load them from the disk provided.

```
100    REM CHR$(X) CONVERTS THE ASCII CODE X TO ITS CHARACTER EQUIVALENT.
110    REM THE FOLLOWING LOOP PRINTS THE CHARACTERS CORRESPONDING TO
120    REM ASCII CODES 64 TO 91.
130    REM
140    REM ****** VARIABLE TABLE
150    REM          COUNT = FOR-NEXT LOOP CONTROL VARIABLE
160    REM          OUTPUT$ = CHR$(COUNT)
170    REM
180    REM ****** PROCESS SECTION
190    FOR COUNT = 64 TO 91
200      LET OUTPUT$ = CHR$(COUNT)
210      PRINT " ";OUTPUT$;
220    NEXT COUNT
230    END
Ok
RUN
 @ A B C D E F G H I J K L M N O P Q R S T U V W X Y Z [
Ok
```

**Figure A–1**

The CHR$(X) Function

```
100    REM THIS PROGRAM GIVES AN EXAMPLE OF THE USE OF CINT(x).
110    REM CINT(x) CONVERTS x TO AN INTEGER.
120    REM x IS CONVERTED TO AN INTEGER BY ROUNDING THE
130    REM FRACTIONAL PORTION.
140    REM x, A NUMERIC EXPRESSION, WILL GIVE "OVERFLOW" ERROR
150    REM IF IT IS NOT IN THE RANGE -32768 TO 32767.
160    REM
170    REM ****** VARIABLE TABLE
180    REM          NUM1, NUM2, NUM3, NUM4 = INPUT VARIABLES
190    REM
200    REM ****** PROCESS SECTION
210    LET NUM1 = 123.556
220    LET NUM2 = CINT(NUM1)
230    PRINT NUM2
240    NUM3 = 123.456
250    NUM4 = CINT(NUM3)
260    PRINT NUM4
270    END
Ok
RUN
 124
 123
Ok
```

**Figure A–2**

The CINT(X) Function

**Figure A–3**

The CONT Command

```
100    REM THIS PROGRAM DEMONSTRATES THE USE OF CONT.
110    REM THE INSTRUCTION CONT CAUSES THE PROGRAM TO
120    REM RESUME EXECUTION AFTER A BREAK.
130    REM THE CONT COMMAND CAN BE USED TO RESUME PROGRAM
140    REM EXECUTION AFTER CTRL-BREAK HAS BEEN PRESSED; A
150    REM STOP OR END STATEMENT HAS BEEN EXECUTED; OR AN
160    REM ERROR HAS OCCURRED.
170    REM
180    REM ****** VARIABLE TABLE
190    REM          COUNT = FOR-NEXT LOOP CONTROL VARIABLE
200    REM          NUM = FOR-NEXT LOOP OUTPUT VARIABLE
210    REM
220    REM ****** INITIALIZATION SECTION
```

272

```
230    PRINT "INTERRUPT THE LOOP BY PRESSING CTRL-BREAK"
240    PRINT "THEN USE CONT TO CONTINUE"
250    REM
260    REM ****** PROCESS SECTION
270    FOR COUNT = 1 TO 50
280       LET NUM = 2*COUNT+3
290       PRINT NUM
300    NEXT COUNT
310    REM
320    REM ****** TERMINATION SECTION
330    PRINT "END"
340    END
 23
 25
 27
 29
 31
 33
 35
 37
 39
 41
 43
 45
 47
 49
 51
 53
 55
 57
 59
 61
^C
Break in 290
Ok


 63
 65
 67
 69
 71
 73
 75
 77
 79
 81
 83
 85
^C
Break in 290
Ok

CONT
 87
 89
 91
 93
 95
 97
 99
 101
 103
END
Ok
```

**Figure A–3**  *(Continued)*

273

```
100    REM THIS PROGRAM DEMONSTRATES THE USE OF CVI, CVD, CVS.
110    REM THESE COMMANDS CONVERT STRING VARIABLE TYPES TO
120    REM NUMERIC VARIABLE TYPES. NUMERIC VALUES READ FROM
130    REM A RANDOM FILE MUST BE CONVERTED FROM STRINGS INTO
140    REM NUMBERS.
150    REM CVI CONVERTS A 2-BYTE STRING TO AN INTEGER.
160    REM CVS CONVERTS A 4-BYTE STRING TO A SINGLE-PRECISION
170    REM NUMBER.
180    REM CVD CONVERTS AN 8-BYTE STRING TO A DOUBLE-PRECISION
190    REM NUMBER.
200    REM BE SURE THAT THE FILE JOHN HAS THE APPROPRIATE VALUES
210    REM IN JFLD$ AND EDFLD$.
220    REM THE STATEMENT "SCREEN" SETS THE ATTRIBUTES TO BE USED
230    REM BY SUBSEQUENT STATEMENTS.  THE FORMAT IS: SCREEN mode,
240    REM WHERE mode MAY BE 0, 1, OR 2.  mode 0 MEANS THAT THE
250    REM TEXT MODE IS AT THE CURRENT WIDTH (40 OR 80).
260    REM THE STATEMENT "OPEN" ALLOWS INPUT OR OUTPUT TO OR FROM
270    REM A FILE OR DEVICE.  THE FORMAT IS: OPEN mode2,
280    REM filenum, filespec, recl, where mode2=R SPECIFIES
290    REM RANDOM INPUT/OUTPUT, filenum IS THE NUMBER THAT
300    REM IS ASSOCIATED WITH THE FILE OR DEVICE FOR AS
310    REM LONG AS IT IS OPEN, filespec IS A STRING EXPRESSION
320    REM FOR THE FILE SPECIFICATION AND recl IS AN INTEGER
330    REM EXPRESSION WHICH SETS THE RECORD LENGTH FOR RANDOM
340    REM FILES.
350    REM
360    REM ******* VARIABLE TABLE
370    REM          WORD1$, WORD2$, WORD3$ = INPUT STRING VARIABLES
380    REM          NUM1, NUM2, NUM3 = CONVERTED NUMERIC VARIABLES
390    REM
400    REM ******* INITIALIZATION SECTION
410    OPEN "R",2,"A:JOHN", 14
420    FIELD 2, 2 AS WORD1$, 8 AS WORD2$, 4 AS WORD3$
430    GET #2
440    NUM1 = CVI(WORD1$)
450    NUM2 = CVD(WORD2$)
460    NUM3 = CVS(WORD3$)
470    REM
480    REM ******* OUTPUT SECTION
490    PRINT NUM1, NUM2, NUM3
500    PRINT "END"
510    END
Ok
RUN
 23            9898.123      3456789
END
Ok
```

**Figure A-4**
The CVI, CVD, and CVS Commands

274

```
100     REM THIS PROGRAM DEMONSTRATES THE USE OF DEF.
110     REM DEF DECLARES VARIABLE TYPE AS INTEGER, SINGLE-
120     REM PRECISION, DOUBLE-PRECISION, OR STRING.
130     REM A DEF STATEMENT DECLARES THAT THE VARIABLE NAMES
140     REM BEGINNING WITH THE LETTER OR LETTERS SPECIFIED
150     REM WILL BE THAT TYPE OF VARIABLE.
160     REM TYPE IS INT(INTEGER), SNG(SINGLE-PRECISION),
170     REM DBL(DOUBLE-PRECISION) OR STR(STRING).
180     REM VARIABLE W IS SINGLE-PRECISION.
190     REM
200     REM ****** VARIABLE TABLE
210     REM          NUM.ORIGINAL = ORIGINAL INPUT NUMBER
220     REM          W = SINGLE PRECISION VERSION OF NUM.ORIGINAL
230     REM          X = DOUBLE PRECISION VERSION OF NUM.ORIGINAL
240     REM          NUM.OUT1, NUM.OUT2 = NUMERIC VARIABLES
250     REM          Y = INTEGER VERSION OF NUM.OUT1
260     REM          Z = INTEGER VERSION OF NUM.OUT2
270     REM
280     REM ****** INITIALIZATION SECTION
290     DEFSNG W
300     LET NUM.ORIGINAL = 1.98765432#
310     LET W = NUM.ORIGINAL
320     REM VARIABLE X IS DOUBLE-PRECISION.
330     DEFDBL X
340     LET X = NUM.ORIGINAL
350     REM
360     REM VARIABLES NUM.OUT1 TO NUM.OUT4 ARE INTEGERS.
370     DEFINT Y-Z
380     LET NUM.OUT1 = 1.756
390     LET NUM.OUT2 = 1.459
400     LET Y = NUM.OUT1
410     LET Z = NUM.OUT2
420     REM
430     REM ****** OUTPUT SECTION
440     PRINT "THE ORIGINAL NUMBER = ";NUM.ORIGINAL
450     PRINT "EXPRESSED AS SINGLE-PRECISION, THE ORIGINAL NUMBER IS ";W
460     PRINT "EXPRESSED AS DOUBLE-PRECISION, THE ORIGINAL NUMBER IS ";X
470     PRINT "THE FIRST NON-INTEGER OUTPUT NUMBER IS ";NUM.OUT1
480     PRINT "THE SECOND NON-INTEGER OUTPUT NUMBER IS ";NUM.OUT2
490     PRINT "EXPRESSED AS AN INTEGER, THE FIRST NON-INTEGER NUMBER IS ";Y
500     PRINT "EXPRESSED AS AN INTEGER, THE SECOND NON-INTEGER NUMBER IS ";Z
510     END
Ok
RUN
THE ORIGINAL NUMBER =  1.987654
EXPRESSED AS SINGLE-PRECISION, THE ORIGINAL NUMBER IS  1.987654
EXPRESSED AS DOUBLE-PRECISION, THE ORIGINAL NUMBER IS  1.987654328346252
THE FIRST NON-INTEGER OUTPUT NUMBER IS  1.756
THE SECOND NON-INTEGER OUTPUT NUMBER IS  1.459
EXPRESSED AS AN INTEGER, THE FIRST NON-INTEGER NUMBER IS  2
EXPRESSED AS AN INTEGER, THE SECOND NON-INTEGER NUMBER IS  1
Ok
```

**Figure A–5**
The DEF Function

275

```
100    REM THIS PROGRAM DEMONSTRATES THE USE OF "LSET",
110    REM "PUT" AND "FIELD"
120    REM THE FIELD STATEMENT ALLOCATES SPACE FOR VARIABLES
130    REM IN A RANDOM FILE BUFFER.  IN THIS EXAMPLE HOSSRAN1
140    REM IS A RANDOM FILE WHICH WAS OPENED.  THE FORMAT OF
150    REM FIELD STATEMENT CALLS FOR THE NUMBER UNDER WHICH
160    REM THE FILE WAS OPENED FOLLOWED BY THE WIDTH OF THE
170    REM STRING VARIABLE.  THIS IN TURN IS FOLLOWED BY THE
180    REM WORD "AS" WHICH IS FOLLOWED BY THE NAME OF THE
190    REM STRING VARIABLE. IN THIS CASE 2 IS THE NUMBER UNDER
200    REM WHICH HOSSRAN1 WAS OPENED, 10 IS THE WIDTH OF EACH OF
210    REM THE TWO STRING VARIABLES FLD1$ AND FLD2$.
220    REM THE STATEMENT "LSET" MOVES DATA INTO A RANDOM BUFFER
230    REM IN PREPARATION FOR A "PUT" STATEMENT. IN OUR EXAMPLE
240    REM "LSET" LEFT JUSTIFIES THE STRING IN THE FIELD.
250    REM THE STATEMENT "PUT" WRITES A RECORD FROM A RANDOM
260    REM BUFFER TO A RANDOM FILE.  THE FORMAT IS "PUT" filenumber,
270    REM number. filenumber IS THE NUMBER UNDER WHICH THE FILE
280    REM WAS OPENED, IN OUR EXAMPLE #2, AND number IS THE RECORD
290    REM TO BE WRITTEN, IN OUR EXAMPLE 2.
300    REM
310    REM ****** VARIABLE TABLE
320    REM          FLD1$, FLD2$ = RANDOM ACCESS FILE VARIABLES
330    REM          COUNT = FOR-NEXT LOOP CONTROL VARIABLE
340    REM          ACCUMULATOR = ACCUMULATOR VARIABLE
350    REM
360    REM ****** ARRAY TABLE
370    REM          SPANISH(3) = A 3-ELEMENT RANDOM FILE VARIABLE ARRAY
380    REM          ENGLISH(3) = A 3-ELEMENT RANDOM FILE VARIABLE ARRAY
390    REM
400    REM ****** INITIALIZATION SECTION
410    DIM SPANISH$(3), ENGLISH$(3)
420    OPEN "R", 2, "A:HOSSRAN1",20
430    PRINT "HOSSRAN1 IS OPEN FOR RANDOM ACCESS FILE PROCESSING."
440    FIELD 2, 10 AS FLD1$, 10 AS FLD2$
450    REM
460    REM ****** PROCESS SECTION
470    FOR COUNT = 1 TO 3
480      READ SPANISH$(COUNT), ENGLISH$(COUNT)
490    NEXT COUNT
500    REM
510    LET ACCUMULATOR = 0
520    REM
530    FOR COUNT = 1 TO 3
540      LSET FLD1$ = SPANISH$(COUNT)
550      LSET FLD2$ = ENGLISH$(COUNT)
560      LET ACCUMULATOR = ACCUMULATOR+1
570      PUT #2,ACCUMULATOR
580    NEXT COUNT
590    REM
600    REM ****** TERMINATION SECTION
610    CLOSE #2
620    PRINT "FILE CLOSED"
630    REM TO SEE THE CONTENTS OF HOSSRAN1 GO TO DOS, AT
640    REM THE DOS PROMPT ENTER "TYPE HOSSRAN1" AND PRESS
650    REM ENTER. THE CONTENTS OF HOSSRAN1 WILL APPEAR
660    REM ON THE SCREEN.
670    REM
680    REM ****** DATA SECTION
690    DATA MARY,DAVID,RUTH,PAT,COCO,ERNIE
700    END
Ok
RUN
HOSSRAN1 IS OPEN FOR RANDOM ACCESS FILE PROCESSING.
FILE CLOSED
Ok
```

**Figure A–6**
The LSET, PUT, and FIELD Commands

```
100     REM THIS PROGRAM DEMONSTRATES THE USE OF "FIX".
110     REM THE FUNCTION "FIX(X)" TRUNCATES X TO AN
120     REM INTEGER.   "FIX" STRIPS ALL DIGITS TO THE RIGHT
130     REM OF THE DECIMAL POINT AND RETURNS THE VALUE OF
140     REM THE DIGITS TO THE LEFT OF THE DECIMAL POINT.
150     REM "FIX" DOES NOT RETURN THE NEXT LOWER NUMBER WHEN
160     REM X IS NEGATIVE.
170     REM
180     REM ****** VARIABLE TABLE
190     REM          NUM1, NUM3 = INPUT VARIABLES
200     REM          NUM2, NUM4 = "FIXED" INPUT VARIABLES (NUM1 AND NUM3)
210     REM
220     REM ****** PROCESS SECTION
230     LET NUM1 = 123.567
240     LET NUM2 = FIX(NUM1)
250     PRINT NUM1,NUM2
260     LET NUM3 = -765.68
270     LET NUM4 = FIX(NUM3)
280     PRINT NUM3,NUM4
290     END
Ok
RUN
 123.567         123
-765.68          -765
Ok
```

**Figure A–7**

The FIX(X) Function

```
100     REM THIS PROGRAM DEMONSTRATES THE USE OF GET.
110     REM THE STATEMENT "GET" READS A RECORD FROM A RANDOM
120     REM FILE INTO A RANDOM BUFFER.   THE FORMAT IS;
130     REM GET filenum, number WHERE filenum IS THE NUMBER
140     REM UNDER WHICH THE FILE WAS OPENED AND number IS THE
150     REM NUMBER OF THE RECORD TO BE READ IN.   IF number IS
160     REM OMITTED, THE NEXT RECORD IS READ INTO THE BUFFER.
170     REM
180     REM ****** VARIABLE TABLE
190     REM          FLD1$, FLD2$ = RANDOM FILE INPUT VARIABLES
200     REM
210     REM ****** INITIALIZATION SECTION
220     OPEN "R",2,"A:HOSSRAN1",20
230     FIELD 2, 10 AS FLD1$, 10 AS FLD2$
240     GET #2,3
250     REM
260     REM ****** OUTPUT SECTION
270     PRINT FLD1$, FLD2$
280     PRINT "END"
290     END
Ok
RUN
     COCO         ERNIE

END
Ok
```

**Figure A–8**

The GET Command

```
100     REM THIS PROGRAM DEMONSTRATES THE USE OF INPUT #
110     REM THIS STATEMENT READS DATA ITEMS FROM A SEQUENTIAL
120     REM DEVICE OR FILE AND ASSIGNS THEM TO PROGRAM VARIABLES.
130     REM THE FORMAT IS INPUT #,filenum,variable.  filenum IS
140     REM THE NUMBER USED WHEN THE FILE WAS OPENED FOR INPUT.
150     REM variable IS THE NAME OF A VARIABLE THAT WILL HAVE AN
160     REM ITEM IN THE FILE ASSIGNED TO IT.  IT CAN BE A STRING
170     REM OR NUMERIC VARIABLE, OR AN ARRAY ELEMENT. IN OUR EXAMPLE
180     REM filenum IS 1 AND variable IS SPANISH$ OR ENGLISH$.
190     REM
200     REM ****** VARIABLE TABLE
210     REM           SPANISH$ = RANDOM FILE INPUT VARIABLE
220     REM           ENGLISH$ = RANDOM FILE INPUT VARIABLE
230     REM
240     REM ****** INITIALIZATION SECTION
250     OPEN "A:TRANSL.TXT" FOR INPUT AS #1
260     REM
270     REM ****** PROCESS SECTION
280     INPUT #1,SPANISH$
290     PRINT SPANISH$
300     INPUT #1,ENGLISH$
310     PRINT ENGLISH$
320     REM
330     REM ****** TERMINATION SECTION
340     PRINT "END"
350     END
Ok
RUN
JOSE
JOSEPH
END
Ok
```

**Figure A–9**

The INPUT# Command

```
100     REM THIS PROGRAM DEMONSTRATES THE USE OF INPUT$(x).
110     REM THE FUNCTION INPUT$(n,filenum) RETURNS A STRING
120     REM OF n CHARACTERS, READ FROM FILE NUMBER filenum.
130     REM IF filenum IS OMITTED, THE KEYBOARD IS READ.
140     REM IF THE KEYBOARD IS USED FOR INPUT, NO CHARACTERS
150     REM ARE DISPLAYED ON THE SCREEN.
160     REM
170     REM ****** VARIABLE TABLE
180     REM           CHARACTER$ = THE CHARACTER TO BE INPUT BY THE USER
190     REM
200     REM ****** INITIALIZATION SECTION
210     PRINT "PRESS ANY KEY, AND I WILL TELL YOU WHICH KEY YOU PRESSED."
220     REM
230     REM ****** PROCESS SECTION
240     LET CHARACTER$ = INPUT$(1)
250     REM
260     REM ****** OUTPUT SECTION
270     PRINT "YOU PRESSED --------------> ";
280     PRINT CHARACTER$;" <------------- YOU PRESSED."
290     END
Ok
RUN
PRESS ANY KEY, AND I WILL TELL YOU WHICH KEY YOU PRESSED.
YOU PRESSED --------------> a <------------- YOU PRESSED.
Ok
```

**Figure A–10**

The INPUT$(X) Command

278

```
100    REM THIS PROGRAM DEMONSTRATES THE USE OF KEY.
110    REM THE STATEMENT "KEY" SETS OR DISPLAYS THE SOFT KEYS.
120    REM "KEY ON" CAUSES THE SOFT KEY VALUES TO BE DISPLAYED
130    REM ON THE 25TH LINE ON THE SCREEN.  ONLY THE FIRST 6
140    REM CHARACTERS OF EACH VALUE ARE DISPLAYED.  "KEY OFF"
150    REM ERASES THE SOFT DISPLAY FROM THE 25TH LINE.  THE KEY
160    REM COMMAND DOES NOT DISABLE THE FUNCTION KEYS.
170    REM
180    REM ****** VARIABLE TABLE
190    REM          ANYKEY$ = ANY KEY THE USER PRESSES
200    REM
210    REM ****** INITIALIZATION SECTION
220    PRINT "PRESS ANY KEY TO SUPPRESS THE DISPLAY OF"
230    PRINT "THE SOFT KEYS AT THE BOTTOM OF THE SCREEN."
240    LET ANYKEY$ = INPUT$(1)
250    REM
260    REM ****** PROCESS SECTION
270    KEY OFF
280    PRINT : PRINT "THE SOFT KEY DISPLAY HAS BEEN SUPPRESSED."
290    PRINT "PRESS ANY KEY TO REDISPLAY THE SOFT KEYS."
300    REM
310    LET ANYKEY$ = INPUT$(1)
320    REM
330    REM ****** TERMINATION SECTION
340    KEY ON
350    PRINT : PRINT "YOU PRESSED '";ANYKEY$;
360    PRINT "', AND THE SOFT KEYS WERE  AUTOMATICALLY RESTORED."
370    END
Ok
RUN
PRESS ANY KEY TO SUPPRESS THE DISPLAY OF
THE SOFT KEYS AT THE BOTTOM OF THE SCREEN.

THE SOFT KEY DISPLAY HAS BEEN SUPPRESSED.
PRESS ANY KEY TO REDISPLAY THE SOFT KEYS.

YOU PRESSED 'J', AND THE SOFT KEYS WERE  AUTOMATICALLY RESTORED.
Ok




1LIST   2RUN   3LOAD"  4SAVE"  5CONT  6,"LPT1 7TRON  8TROFF 9KEY    0SCREEN
```

**Figure A-11**
The KEY Command

```
100     REM THIS PROGRAM DEMONSTRATES THE USE OF LEFT$(n).
110     REM THE FUNCTION LEFT$ RETURNS THE LEFTMOST n CHARACTERS
120     REM OF x$.   x$ IS ANY STRING EXPRESSION AND n IS A
130     REM NUMERIC EXPRESSION WHICH MUST BE IN THE RANGE 0 TO 255.
140     REM n SPECIFIES THE NUMBER OF CHARACTERS THAT ARE TO BE IN
150     REM THE RESULT.   IN OUR EXAMPLE THE FIRST 7 CHARACTERS OF
160     REM THE STRING "JOHN HOLLOWAY" ARE EXTRACTED.
170     REM
180     REM ****** VARIABLE TABLE
190     REM         NAM$ = STRING VARIABLE
200     REM         NAM.LEFT7$ = THE FIRST 7 CHARACTERS OF NAM$
210     REM
220     REM ****** INITIALIZATION SECTION
230     LET NAM$ = "JOHN HOLLOWAY"
240     LET NAM.LEFT7$ = LEFT$(NAM$,7)
250     REM
260     REM ****** OUTPUT SECTION
270     PRINT "THE FIRST 7 CHARACTERS OF 'JOHN HOLLOWAY' ARE: ";NAM.LEFT7$
280     END
Ok
RUN
THE FIRST 7 CHARACTERS OF 'JOHN HOLLOWAY' ARE: JOHN HO
Ok
```

**Figure A–12**

The LEFT$(N) Function

```
100     REM THIS PROGRAM DEMONSTRATES THE USE OF THE STATEMENT
110     REM "LOCATE", WHICH POSITIONS THE CURSOR ON THE ACTIVE
120     REM SCREEN.   OPTIONAL PARAMETERS (WHICH ARE NOT DEMONSTRATED
130     REM HERE) TURN THE BLINKING CURSOR ON AND OFF AND DEFINE
140     REM THE SIZE OF THE BLINKING CURSOR.   THE FORMAT USED IN
150     REM THIS EXAMPLE IS LOCATE row,col.   row IS A NUMERIC
160     REM EXPRESSION (FROM 1 TO 25) WHICH INDICATES THE SCREEN LINE
170     REM NUMBER WHERE YOU WANT TO PLACE THE CURSOR.   col IS A
180     REM NUMERIC EXPRESSION WHICH INDICATES THE SCREEN COLUMN
190     REM NUMBER WHERE YOU WANT TO PLACE THE CURSOR.
200     REM
210     REM ****** VARIABLE TABLE
220     REM         THERE ARE NO VARIABLES IN THIS PROGRAM
230     REM
240     REM ****** OUTPUT SECTION
250     CLS
260     LOCATE 15,50 : PRINT " *"
270     LOCATE 18,65 : PRINT "******"
280     END




                                                    *

                                                          ******
Ok
```

**Figure A–13**

The LOCATE Command

```
100     REM THIS PROGRAM DEMONSTRATES SEVERAL COMMANDS.
110     REM AMONG THESE ARE RSET, PUT AND FIELD.
120     REM THE STATEMENT "FIELD" ALLOCATES SPACE FOR VARIABLES
130     REM IN A RANDOM FILE BUFFER. THE FORMAT FOR THIS
140     REM STATEMENT IS FIELD filenum, width AS stringvar.
150     REM IN THIS STATEMENT filenum :
160     REM IS THE NUMBER UNDER WHICH THE FILE WAS OPENED,
170     REM width IS A NUMERIC EXPRESSION SPECIFYING THE NUMBER
180     REM OF CHARACTER POSITIONS TO BE ALLOCATED TO stringvar,
190     REM AND stringvar IS A STRING VARIABLE THAT IS USED FOR
200     REM RANDOM FILE ACCESS. A "FIELD" STATEMENT DEFINES
210     REM VARIABLES USED TO GET DATA OUT OF A RANDOM BUFFER
220     REM AFTER A "GET" OR TO ENTER DATA INTO THE BUFFER FOR
230     REM A "PUT" STATEMENT.
240     REM THE "PUT" STATEMENT WRITES A RECORD FROM A RANDOM
250     REM BUFFER TO A RANDOM FILE.  THE FORMAT IS: PUT filenum,
260     REM number WHERE filenum IS THE NUMBER UNDER WHICH THE
270     REM FILE WAS OPENED AND number IS THE RECORD NUMBER FOR
280     REM THE RECORD TO BE WRITTEN.
290     REM "RSET" MOVES DATA INTO A RANDOM FILE BUFFER IN
300     REM PREPARATION FOR A "PUT" STATEMENT.  THE FORMAT
310     REM IS: RSET  stringvar = x$, WHERE stringvar  IS THE
320     REM NAME OF THE VARIABLE DEFINED IN THE "FIELD" STATE-
330     REM MENT, AND x$ IS A STRING EXPRESSION TO PLACE THE
340     REM INFORMATION INTO THE FIELD IDENTIFIED BY stringvar.
350     REM
360     REM ******* VARIABLE TABLE
370     REM          FLD1$, FLD2$ = RANDOM FILE INPUT VARIABLES
380     REM          COUNT = FOR-NEXT LOOP CONTROL VARIABLE
390     REM          ACCUMULATOR = FOR-NEXT LOOP ACCUMULATOR VARIABLE
400     REM
410     REM ******* ARRAY TABLE
420     REM          SPANISH$(3), ENGLISH(3) = 3-ELEMENT RANDOM FILE DATA ARRAYS
430     REM
440     REM ******* INITIALIZATION SECTION
450     DIM SPANISH$(3), ENGLISH$(3)
460     OPEN "R", 2, "A:HOSSRAN1", 20
470     PRINT "THE FILE 'HOSSRAN1' IS OPEN FOR PROCESSING."
480     FIELD 2, 10 AS FLD1$, 10 AS FLD2$
490     REM
500     REM ******* PROCESS SECTION
510     FOR COUNT = 1 TO 3
520       READ SPANISH$(COUNT), ENGLISH$(COUNT)
530     NEXT COUNT
540     REM
550     LET ACCUMULATOR = 0
560     REM
570     FOR COUNT = 1 TO 3
580       RSET FLD1$ = SPANISH$(COUNT)
590       RSET FLD2$ = ENGLISH$(COUNT)
600       LET ACCUMULATOR = ACCUMULATOR+1
610       PUT #2, ACCUMULATOR
620     NEXT COUNT
630     REM
640     REM ******* TERMINATION SECTION
650     CLOSE #2
660     PRINT "PROCESSING COMPLETED.  FILE CLOSED"
670     REM
680     REM ******* DATA SECTION
690     DATA "MARY","DAVID","RUTH","PAT","COCO","ERNIE"
700     END
Ok
RUN
THE FILE 'HOSSRAN1' IS OPEN FOR PROCESSING.
PROCESSING COMPLETED.  FILE CLOSED
Ok
```

**Figure A–14**

The PSET, PUT, and FIELD Commands

```
100    REM THIS PROGRAM GIVES AN EXAMPLE OF THE USE OF
110    REM THE FUNCTION "MID$".   THIS FUNCTION RETURNS
120    REM THE REQUESTED PART OF A GIVEN STRING. THE FORMAT IS
130    REM v$ = MID$(x$,n,m), WHERE THE FUNCTION RETURNS A
140    REM STRING OF LENGTH m CHARACTERS FROM x$ BEGINNING
150    REM WITH THE nTH CHARACTER.   IF m IS OMITTED OR IF
160    REM FEWER THAN m CHARACTERS ARE TO THE RIGHT OF THE
170    REM nTH CHARACTER, ALL RIGHTMOST CHARACTERS BEGINNING
180    REM WITH THE nTH CHARACTER ARE RETURNED.
190    REM
200    REM ****** VARIABLE TABLE
210    REM          WORD1$, WORD2$ = STRING VARIABLES
220    REM          MARY$, JOHN$ = STRING VARIABLES
230    REM
240    REM ****** PROCESS SECTION
250    LET WORD1$= "ABCDEFGHIJ"
260    LET WORD2$ = MID$(WORD1$,4,5)
270    PRINT WORD2$
280    REM
290    REM FOLLOWING IS AN EXAMPLE OF THE "MID$" STATEMENT.
300    REM WHEN USED AS A STATEMENT, MID$ REPLACES A PORTION
310    REM OF ONE STRING WITH ANOTHER STRING.   THE FORMAT IS:
320    REM MID$(v$,n,m) = y$, WHERE v$ IS A STRING VARIABLE
330    REM OR ARRAY ELEMENT THAT WILL HAVE ITS CHARACTERS
340    REM REPLACED, n IS AN INTEGER EXPRESSION IN THE RANGE
350    REM 1 TO 255, m IS AN INTEGER EXPRESSION IN THE RANGE
360    REM 0 TO 255, AND y$ IS A STRING EXPRESSION.   THE
370    REM CHARACTERS IN v$, BEGINNING AT POSITION n, ARE
380    REM REPLACED BY THE CHARACTERS IN y$.   THE OPTIONAL
390    REM m REFERS TO THE NUMBER OF CHARACTERS FROM y$
400    REM USED IN THE REPLACEMENT.  IF m IS OMITTED, ALL
410    REM OF y$ IS USED.
420    REM
430    LET MARY$ = "APPLE FARM"
440    LET JOHN$ = "ABC"
450    PRINT "ORIGINAL STRING -----------> ";MARY$
460    MID$(MARY$,3,2) = JOHN$
470    PRINT "STRING TO BE BLENDED ------>    ";LEFT$(JOHN$,2)
480    PRINT "RESULT --------------------> ";MARY$
490    END
Ok
RUN
DEFGH
ORIGINAL STRING -----------> APPLE FARM
STRING TO BE BLENDED ------>    AB
RESULT --------------------> APABE FARM
Ok
```

**Figure A–15**
The MID$ Function

```
100    REM THIS PROGRAM DEMONSTRATES THE USE OF MKI$, MKS$,
110    REM AND MKD$.   THESE FUNCTIONS CONVERT NUMERIC TYPE
120    REM VALUES TO STRING TYPE VALUES.   ANY NUMERIC VALUE
130    REM THAT IS PLACED IN A RANDOM FILE BUFFER WITH AN
140    REM "LSET" OR "RSET" STATEMENT MUST BE CONVERTED TO A
150    REM STRING.   "MKI$" CONVERTS AN INTEGER TO A 2-BYTE
160    REM STRING.   "MKS$" CONVERTS A SINGLE PRECISION NUMBER
170    REM TO A 4-BYTE STRING.   "MKD$" CONVERTS A DOUBLE PRECI-
180    REM SION NUMBER TO AN 8-BYTE STRING.   THE FORMATS ARE AS
190    REM FOLLOWS: v$ = MKI$(integer expression),
200    REM v$ = MKS$(single-precision expression),
210    REM v$ = MKD$(double-precision expression).
220    REM
230    REM ****** VARIABLE TABLE
240    REM        WORD1$, WORD2$, WORD3$ = RANDOM FILE VARIABLES
250    REM        NEW.WORD1$, NEW.WORD2$, NEW.WORD3$ = CONVERTED VARIABLES
260    REM        NUM1, NUM2, NUM3 = NUMERIC CONVERSION VARIABLES
270    REM
280    REM ****** INITIALIZATION SECTION
290    OPEN "R",1,"A:JOHN",14
300    FIELD 1, 2 AS WORD1$, 8 AS WORD2$, 4 AS WORD3$
310    LET NUM1 = 23
320    LET NUM2 = 3456789#
330    LET NUM3 = 9898.123
340    REM
350    REM ****** PROCESS SECTION
360    LET NEW.WORD1$ = MKI$(NUM1)
370    LET NEW.WORD2$ = MKD$(NUM3)
380    LET NEW.WORD3$ = MKS$(NUM2)
390    LSET WORD1$ = NEW.WORD1$
400    LSET WORD2$ = NEW.WORD2$
410    LSET WORD3$ = NEW.WORD3$
420    PUT #1, 1
430    REM
440    REM ****** TERMINATION SECTION
450    CLOSE #1
460    PRINT "OPERATION COMPLETE.   PROGRAM STATUS: END."
470    END
Ok
RUN
OPERATION COMPLETE.   PROGRAM STATUS: END.
Ok
```

**Figure A–16**
The MKI$, MKS$, and MKD$ Functions

```
100     REM THIS PROGRAM DEMONSTRATES THE COMMAND ON-GOTO.
110     REM THE "ON - GOTO" STATEMENT ENABLES A PROGRAM
120     REM TO BRANCH TO ONE OF SEVERAL SPECIFIED LINE
130     REM NUMBERS, DEPENDING ON THE VALUE OF AN EXPRESSION.
140     REM THE FORMAT IS "ON n GOTO line1, line2, line3,....
150     REM WHERE n IS A NUMERIC EXPRESSION, ROUNDED TO AN
160     REM INTEGER, IF NECESSARY.  n MUST BE IN THE RANGE
170     REM 0 TO 255.  line1, line2,..., IS THE LINE NUMBER
180     REM TO WHICH THE PROGRAM BRANCHES.  THE VALUE OF
190     REM n DETERMINES WHICH LINE NUMBER IN THE LIST THE
200     REM PROGRAM USES FOR BRANCHING.  FOR EXAMPLE, IF n HAS
210     REM THE VALUE 2 THE PROGRAM BRANCHES TO THE SECOND LINE
220     REM NUMBER  IN THE LIST.
230     REM ****** VARIABLE TABLE
240     REM         NUM1 = NUMBER TO BE INPUT BY THE USER
250     REM         NUM2 = NUM1, CONVERTED TO -1, 0, OR 1
260     REM
270     REM ****** INITIALIZATION SECTION
280     PRINT "PRESS ANY NUMBER ON THE KEYBOARD, AND I WILL TELL YOU"
290     PRINT "THE NUMBER YOU PRESSED WAS NEGATIVE, ZERO, OR POSITIVE. "
300     INPUT "PLEASE PRESS RETURN AFTER YOU TYPE YOUR NUMBER.   NUMBER: ",NUM1
310     REM
320     REM ****** PROCESS SECTION
330     LET NUM2 = SGN(NUM1)+2
340     ON NUM2 GOTO 370,390,410
350     REM
360     REM ****** OUTPUT SECTION
370     PRINT "YOUR NUMBER WAS ";NUM1;"----> STATUS: ----> NEGATIVE."
380     GOTO 440
390     PRINT "YOUR NUMBER WAS ";NUM1;"----> STATUS: ----> ZERO."
400     GOTO 440
410     PRINT "YOUR NUMBER WAS ";NUM1;"----> STATUS: ----> POSITIVE."
420     REM
430     REM ****** TERMINATION SECTION
440     PRINT "END"
450     END
Ok
RUN
PRESS ANY NUMBER ON THE KEYBOARD, AND I WILL TELL YOU
THE NUMBER YOU PRESSED WAS NEGATIVE, ZERO, OR POSITIVE.
PLEASE PRESS RETURN AFTER YOU TYPE YOUR NUMBER.   NUMBER: -5
YOUR NUMBER WAS -5 ----> STATUS: ----> NEGATIVE.
END
Ok
RUN
PRESS ANY NUMBER ON THE KEYBOARD, AND I WILL TELL YOU
THE NUMBER YOU PRESSED WAS NEGATIVE, ZERO, OR POSITIVE.
PLEASE PRESS RETURN AFTER YOU TYPE YOUR NUMBER.   NUMBER: 9
YOUR NUMBER WAS  9 ----> STATUS: ----> POSITIVE.
END
Ok
RUN
PRESS ANY NUMBER ON THE KEYBOARD, AND I WILL TELL YOU
THE NUMBER YOU PRESSED WAS NEGATIVE, ZERO, OR POSITIVE.
PLEASE PRESS RETURN AFTER YOU TYPE YOUR NUMBER.   NUMBER: 0
YOUR NUMBER WAS  0 ----> STATUS: ----> ZERO.
END
Ok
```

**Figure A–17**
The ON-GOTO Command

```
100    REM THIS PROGRAM GIVES AN EXAMPLE OF THE STATEMENT "PLAY".
110    REM THIS STATEMENT PLAYS MUSIC AS SPECIFIED BY string.
120    REM THE FORMAT IS PLAY string, WHERE string IS A STRING
130    REM EXPRESSION CONSISTING OF SINGLE- OR DOUBLE-CHARACTER
140    REM MUSIC COMMANDS.
150    REM
160    REM ****** VARIABLE TABLE
170    REM          MARY$ = MUSICAL NOTE STRING
180    REM
190    REM ****** INITIALIZATION SECTION
200    LET MARY$ = "GFE-FGGG"
210    REM
220    REM ****** PROCESS SECTION
230    PLAY "MB T100 O3 L8;XMARY$;P8 FFF4"
240    PLAY "GB-B-4; XMARY$; GFFGFE-...."
250    REM
260    REM ****** TERMINATION SECTION
270    PRINT "THIS COMPLETES OUR RENDITION OF 'MARY HAD A LITTLE LAMB'."
280    END
Ok
RUN
THIS COMPLETES OUR RENDITION OF 'MARY HAD A LITTLE LAMB'.
Ok
```

**Figure A–18**
The PLAY Command

```
100    REM THIS PROGRAM DEMONSTRATES THE USE OF THE FUNCTION
110    REM "RIGHT$".  THIS FUNCTION RETURNS THE RIGHTMOST n
120    REM CHARACTERS OF STRING x$.  THE FORMAT IS v$ = RIGHT$(x$,n).
130    REM WHERE x$ IS ANY STRING EXPRESSION AND n IS AN INTEGER
140    REM EXPRESSION THAT SPECIFIES THE NUMBER OF CHARACTERS
150    REM TO BE IN THE RESULT.
160    REM
170    REM ****** VARIABLE TABLE
180    REM          FIRST.WORD$ = INPUT STRING VARIABLE
190    REM          SECOND.WORD$ = LAST 5 CHARACTERS OF FIRST.WORD$
200    REM
210    REM ****** INITIALIZATION SECTION
220    LET FIRST.WORD$ = "HOSSEIN BIDGOLI"
230    LET SECOND.WORD$ = RIGHT$(FIRST.WORD$,5)
240    REM
250    REM ****** OUTPUT SECTION
260    PRINT "THE LAST 5 CHARACTERS OF 'HOSSEIN BIDGOLI' ARE: ";SECOND.WORD$
270    END
Ok
RUN
THE LAST 5 CHARACTERS OF 'HOSSEIN BIDGOLI' ARE: DGOLI
Ok
```

**Figure A–19**
The RIGHT$ Command

```
100     REM THIS PROGRAM DEMONSTRATES THE USE OF THE STATEMENT
110     REM "SOUND".  THIS STATEMENT GENERATES SOUND THROUGH THE
120     REM SPEAKER.  THE FORMAT IS: SOUND freq, duration, WHERE
130     REM freq IS THE DESIRED FREQUENCY IN HERTZ.  IT MUST BE
140     REM A NUMERIC EXPRESSION IN THE RANGE 37 TO 32767.  duration
150     REM IS THE DESIRED DURATION IN CLOCK TICKS.  duration MUST
160     REM BE A NUMERIC EXPRESSION.
170     REM THIS PROGRAM DEMONSTRATES THE USE OF SOUND, WITH THE
180     REM SOUND GOING UP THE SCALE.
190     REM
200     REM ****** VARIABLE TABLE
210     REM           COUNT = FOR-NEXT LOOP CONTROL VARIABLE
220     REM
230     REM ****** PROCESS SECTION
240     FOR COUNT = 40 TO 1000 STEP 10
250        SOUND COUNT,.5
260     NEXT COUNT
270     REM
280     PRINT "PROGRAM COMPLETE."
290     END
Ok
RUN
PROGRAM COMPLETE.
Ok
```

**Figure A–20**
The SOUND Command

```
100     REM THIS PROGRAM DEMONSTRATES THE USE OF THE COMMAND SWAP
110     REM WHICH EXCHANGES THE VALUES OF TWO VARIABLES.  THE FORMAT IS:
120     REM SWAP variable1, variable2.  variable1 AND variable2 ARE THE
130     REM NAMES OF THE TWO VARIABLES OR ARRAY ELEMENTS.  ANY TYPE OF
140     REM VARIABLE CAN BE EXCHANGED BUT THE TWO VARIABLES MUST BE OF
150     REM THE SAME TYPE OR A TYPE MISMATCH ERROR OCCURS.
160     REM
170     REM ****** VARIABLE TABLE
180     REM           NUM1, NUM2 = INPUT VARIABLES
190     REM
200     REM ****** INITIALIZATION SECTION
210     LET NUM1 = 1234
220     LET NUM2 = 6789
230     REM
240     REM ****** PROCESS SECTION
250     PRINT "THE FIRST NUMBER IS =";NUM1;"--- THE SECOND NUMBER IS =";NUM2
260     SWAP NUM1, NUM2
270     PRINT
280     PRINT TAB(23);"SWAP COMPLETE."
290     PRINT
300     PRINT "THE FIRST NUMBER IS =";NUM1;"--- THE SECOND NUMBER IS =";NUM2
310     END
Ok
RUN
THE FIRST NUMBER IS = 1234 --- THE SECOND NUMBER IS = 6789

                      SWAP COMPLETE.

THE FIRST NUMBER IS = 6789 --- THE SECOND NUMBER IS = 1234
Ok
```

**Figure A–21**
The SWAP Command

```
100    REM THIS PROGRAM DEMONSTRATES THE USE OF THE FUNCTION
110    REM "SPC".  THIS FUNCTION SKIPS n SPACES IN A PRINT
120    REM STATEMENT.  THE FORMAT IS: PRINT SPC(N).  n MUST
130    REM BE IN THE RANGE 0 TO 255.  IF n IS GREATER THAN
140    REM THE DEFINED WIDTH OF THE DEVICE THE VALUE USED IS
150    REM n MOD width.  "SPC" CAN BE USED ONLY WITH PRINT,
160    REM LPRINT AND PRINT#.
170    REM THIS PROGRAM DEMONSTRATES THE USE OF SPC(n).
180    REM
190    REM ****** VARIABLE TABLE
200    REM          NUM1, NUM2 = INPUT VARIABLES
210    REM
220    REM ****** INITIALIZATION SECTION
230    LET NUM1 = 1234
240    LET NUM2 = 78901!
250    REM
260    REM ****** OUTPUT SECTION
270    PRINT NUM1;
280    PRINT NUM2
290    PRINT NUM2;SPC(5);NUM1
300    END
Ok
RUN
 1234   78901
 78901          1234
Ok
```

**Figure A–22**
The SPC Function

```
100    REM THIS PROGRAM DEMONSTRATES THE USE OF THE FUNCTION VAL.
110    REM THIS FUNCTION RETURNS THE NUMERICAL VALUE OF THE STRING
120    REM x$.  THE FORMAT IS v = VAL(x$), WHERE x$ IS A STRING
130    REM EXPRESSION.  THE VAL FUNCTION STRIPS BLANKS, TABS,
140    REM AND LINE FEEDS FROM THE ARGUMENT TO DETERMINE THE RESULT.
150    REM IF THE FIRST CHARACTERS OF x$ ARE NOT NUMERIC VAL(x$)
160    REM RETURNS 0.
170    REM
180    REM ****** VARIABLE TABLE
190    REM          WORD$ = INPUT STRING VARIABLE
200    REM          NUM = INPUT NUMERIC VARIABLE
210    REM
220    REM ****** INITIALIZATION SECTION
230    LET WORD$ = "1234"
240    LET NUM = VAL(WORD$)
250    REM
260    REM ****** OUTPUT SECTION
270    PRINT "THE NUMERIC VALUE OF THE STRING VARIABLE WORD$ =";NUM
280    PRINT "PROGRAM COMPLETE."
290    END
Ok
RUN
THE NUMERIC VALUE OF THE STRING VARIABLE WORD$ = 1234
PROGRAM COMPLETE.
Ok
```

**Figure A–23**
The VAL(X$) Function

287

```
100    REM THIS PROGRAM DEMONSTRATES THE USE OF THE
110    REM STATEMENT "LINE". THE "LINE" STATEMENT DRAWS
120    REM A LINE OR A BOX ON THE SCREEN. THE FORMAT IS
130    REM LINE((x1,y1)-(x2,y2)).  THIS IS THE SIMPLEST
140    REM FORM OF THE "LINE" STATEMENT. IT DRAWS A LINE
150    REM BETWEEN THE TWO POINTS (x1,y1) AND (x2,y2).
160    REM THERE ARE NUMEROUS REFINEMENTS TO THIS STATEMENT,
170    REM INVOLVING COLOR, STYLE, BOX, ETC.  THESE OPTIONS PERMIT
180    REM THE DRAWING OF RECTANGLES, WITH OR WITHOUT THE INTERIORS
190    REM FILLED IN WITH COLOR.  DOTTED LINES MAY ALSO BE DRAWN.
200    REM IT SHOULD BE NOTED THAT THIS STATEMENT CAN BE USED ONLY
210    REM IN THE GRAPHICS MODE.
220    REM THE STATEMENT "SCREEN" SETS THE ATTRIBUTES TO BE
230    REM USED BY SUBSEQUENT STATEMENTS.  THE STATEMENT SCREEN 2
240    REM SETS THE MODE TO HIGH RESOLUTION GRAPHICS, AND THE
250    REM STATEMENT SCREEN 0 SETS THE MODE TO TEXT AT CURRENT WIDTH.
260    REM IT SHOULD BE NOTED THAT THE STATEMENT "SCREEN" IS MEANINGFUL
270    REM ONLY WITH THE COLOR GRAPHICS MONITOR ADAPTERS.
280    REM
290    REM ****** VARIABLE TABLE
300    REM          KEYSTROKE$ = ANY KEY THE USER PRESSES
310    REM
320    REM ****** INITIALIZATION SECTION
330    SCREEN 2 : CLS : KEY OFF
340    LINE (0,0) - (60,70)
350    REM
360    REM ****** PROCESS SECTION
370    PRINT "PRESS ANY LETTER TO CLEAR SCREEN"
380    KEYSTROKE$ = INPUT$(1)
390    REM
400    REM ****** TERMINATION SECTION
410    CLS : SCREEN 0 : KEY ON
420    PRINT "PROGRAM COMPLETE."
430    END



PRESS ANY LETTER TO CLEAR SCREEN
```

**Figure A-24**
The LINE Function

```
100    REM THIS PROGRAM DEMONSTRATES THE USE OF THE
110    REM STATEMENT "CIRCLE".  THE PURPOSE OF THIS
120    REM STATEMENT IS TO DRAW AN ELLIPSE ON THE SCREEN
130    REM WITH CENTER (x,y) AND RADIUS r.  THE FORMAT IS:
140    REM CIRCLE (x,y),r.  THIS FORMAT IS THE SIMPLEST
150    REM FORM OF THE STATEMENT.  IT IS POSSIBLE TO ADD
160    REM OTHER FEATURES SUCH AS color,start,end, AND aspect.
170    REM color IS AN INTEGER EXPRESSION THAT CHOOSES A
180    REM COLOR ATTRIBUTE RANGE FROM THE CURRENT SCREEN
190    REM MODE.  start AND end SPECIFY WHERE THE DRAWING
200    REM OF THE ELLIPSE WILL BEGIN AND END.  IT IS POSSIBLE
210    REM TO DRAW A PORTION OF THE ELLIPSE, USING CERTAIN
220    REM COMBINATIONS OF start AND end.  aspect CAN BE USED
230    REM TO DETERMINE THE SHAPE OF THE ELLIPSE.  IF aspect
240    REM IS LESS THAN 1, THEN r IS THE X-AXIS.  (x,y) ARE THE
250    REM COORDINATES OF THE CENTER OF THE ELLIPSE, r IS
260    REM THE RADIUS.  AGAIN IT SHOULD BE NOTED THAT THIS
270    REM STATEMENT CAN BE USED IN GRAPHICS MODE ONLY.
280    REM
290    REM ****** VARIABLE TABLE
300    REM           KEYSTROKE$ = ANY KEY THE USER PRESSES
310    REM
320    REM ****** INITIALIZATION SECTION
330    SCREEN 2 : CLS : KEY OFF
340    REM
350    REM ****** PROCESS SECTION
360    CIRCLE (200,100),80
370    PRINT "PRESS ANY LETTER TO CLEAR SCREEN "
380    KEYSTROKE$ = INPUT$(1)
390    REM
400    REM ****** TERMINATION SECTION
410    CLS : SCREEN 0 : KEY ON
420    PRINT "PROGRAM COMPLETE."
430    END
```

PRESS ANY LETTER TO CLEAR SCREEN

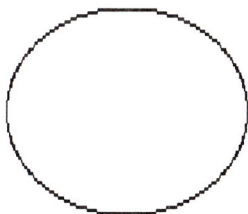

**Figure A–25**
The CIRCLE Function

```
100    REM THIS PROGRAM DEMONSTRATES THE USE OF THE
110    REM STATEMENTS "COLOR" AND "PAINT".  THE STATEMENT
120    REM "COLOR" DETERMINES WHICH COLORS WILL BE USED
130    REM WITH THE "PAINT" STATEMENT. SINCE THE STATEMENT
140    REM "COLOR" APPEARS FIRST WE WILL GIVE THE FORMAT
150    REM FOR THAT FIRST.  THE STATEMENT "COLOR" SETS THE
160    REM COLORS FOR FOREGROUND, BACKGROUND AND BORDER
170    REM SCREENS. THE FORMAT IS: COLOR foreground, back-
180    REM ground, border.  EACH OF THE VARIABLES foreground,
190    REM background AND border ARE NUMERIC VALUES
200    REM REPRESENTING SOME COLOR.  THE FORMAT FOR
210    REM THE STATEMENT "PAINT" IS: PAINT(x,y),paint,
220    REM boundary,background.  THE COORDINATES (x,y)
230    REM ARE FOR A POINT WITHIN THE AREA TO BE FILLED IN,
240    REM paint,boundary AND background ARE PARAMETERS
250    REM USED TO SPECIFY THE FIGURE TO BE PRODUCED.
260    REM
270    REM ****** VARIABLE TABLE
280    REM          COUNT = FOR-NEXT LOOP CONTROL VARIABLE
290    REM          KEYSTROKE$ = CONTINUATION VARIABLE - USER SELECTED
300    REM
310    REM ****** INITIALIZATION SECTION
320    SCREEN 1 : COLOR 0,1 : KEY OFF : CLS
330    REM
340    REM ****** PROCESS SECTION
350    REM THE LINE STATEMENTS IN LINES 420 AND 430 INDICATE THAT
360    REM THE FIGURES TO BE DRAWN ARE BOXES.  THE "B" IN THE STATE-
370    REM MENTS TELLS BASIC TO DRAW TWO SQUARES, ONE WITH THE POINTS
380    REM (20,20) AND (50,50) AS OPPOSITE CORNERS.  THE OTHER SQUARE
390    REM HAS THE POINTS (30,30) AND (90,90) AS OPPOSITE CORNERS.
400    REM THE NUMBER 2 SPECIFIES AN ATTRIBUTE.
410    FOR COUNT = 1 TO 3
420       LINE (20,20)-(50,50),2,B
430       LINE (30,30)-(90,90),2,B
440       LOCATE 1,1
450       PRINT "PRESS ANY LETTER TO PAINT SQUARE";COUNT
460       KEYSTROKE$ = INPUT$(1)
470       IF COUNT = 1 THEN PAINT (25,25),COUNT,2 : GOTO 500
480       IF COUNT = 2 THEN PAINT (35,35),COUNT,2 : GOTO 500
490       PAINT (55,55),COUNT,2
500    NEXT COUNT
510    REM
520    REM ****** TERMINATION SECTION
530    PRINT "PRESS ANY LETTER TO CLEAR SCREEN"
540    KEYSTROKE$ = INPUT$(1)
550    CLS : SCREEN 0 : KEY ON : WIDTH 80
560    PRINT "PROCESSING COMPLETED."
570    END


PRESS ANY LETTER TO PAINT SQUARE 1
```

**Figure A–26**
The Color Function

```
100    REM THIS PROGRAM DEMONSTRATES THE USE OF THE STATEMENT
110    REM "PSET", THE PURPOSE OF WHICH IS TO DRAW A POINT
120    REM AT THE SPECIFIED POSITION ON THE SCREEN.  THE
130    REM FORMAT IS: PSET(x,y),color, WHERE (x,y) ARE THE
140    REM COORDINATES OF THE POINT TO BE SET.  color DETERMINES
150    REM CERTAIN ATTRIBUTES. IN OUR EXAMPLE WE HAVE DRAWN
160    REM A SINE CURVE.
170    REM THE STATEMENT COLOR 0,1 SETS THE COLORS FOR THE
180    REM BACKGROUND AS WELL AS FOR THE FIGURE DRAWN BY PSET.
190    REM COLOR ATTRIBUTE 0 IS THE CURRENT BACKGROUND, THE
200    REM NUMBER 1 DETERMINES THE COLOR OF THE FIGURE.
210    REM
220    REM ****** VARIABLE TABLE
230    REM          COLUMN = FOR-NEXT LOOP CONTROL VARIABLE
240    REM          HEIGHT = FOR-NEXT LOOP VARIABLE
250    REM          KEYSTROKE$ = CONTINUATION VARIABLE, USER SELECTED
260    REM
270    REM ****** INITIALIZATION SECTION
280    SCREEN 1: COLOR 0,1: CLS : KEY OFF
290    REM
300    REM ****** PROCESS SECTION
310    FOR COLUMN = 0 TO 80   STEP .05
320      LET HEIGHT = 50*SIN(COLUMN)
330      PSET(COLUMN,HEIGHT),3
340    NEXT COLUMN
350    REM
360    REM ****** TERMINATION SECTION
370    PRINT "PRESS ANY LETTER TO CLEAR SCREEN "
380    KEYSTROKE$ = INPUT$(1)
390    CLS : SCREEN 0 : KEY ON : WIDTH 80
400    PRINT "PROCESSING COMPLETED."
410    END


PRESS ANY LETTER TO CLEAR SCREEN
```

**Figure A–27**
The PSET Command

```
100    REM THIS PROGRAM DEMONSTRATES THE USE OF THE
110    REM STATEMENT "WIDTH", WHICH SETS THE OUTPUT LINE
120    REM IN NUMBER OF CHARACTERS.  AFTER OUTPUTTING THE
130    REM INDICATED NUMBER OF CHARACTERS BASIC ADDS A
140    REM CARRIAGE RETURN. WE HAVE USED THE SIMPLEST
150    REM FORMAT, WHICH IS: WIDTH size, WHERE size IS
160    REM A NUMERIC EXPRESSION IN THE RANGE 0 TO 255.
170    REM size GIVES THE NEW WIDTH.  IN OUR CASE WE HAVE
180    REM USED THE WIDTH OF 40 WHICH MEANS THAT ONLY 40
190    REM CHARACTERS OCCUPY THE ENTIRE WIDTH OF THE SCREEN.
200    REM THERE ARE OTHER OPTIONS WHICH DESIGNATE THE DEVICE
210    REM BEING USED AND THE NUMBER OF A FILE OPENED TO AN
220    REM OUTPUT DEVICE.
230    REM
240    REM ****** VARIABLE TABLE
250    REM          COUNT = FOR-NEXT LOOP CONTROL VARIABLE
260    REM          KEYSTROKE$ = CONTINUATION VARIABLE, USER SELECTED
270    REM
280    REM ****** INITIALIZATION SECTION
290    SCREEN 1 : KEY OFF : CLS : WIDTH 40
300    REM
310    REM ****** PROCESS SECTION
320    FOR COUNT = 1 TO 60
330      PRINT "ABCDEFGHIJ";
340    NEXT COUNT
350    PRINT
360    REM
370    REM ****** TERMINATION SECTION
380    PRINT "PRESS ANY LETTER TO CLEAR SCREEN"
390    KEYSTROKE$ = INPUT$(1)
400    CLS : SCREEN 0 : KEY ON : WIDTH 80
410    PRINT "PROCESSING COMPLETED."
420    END
```

```
ABCDEFGHIJABCDEFGHIJABCDEFGHIJABCDEFGHIJ
ABCDEFGHIJABCDEFGHIJABCDEFGHIJABCDEFGHIJ
ABCDEFGHIJABCDEFGHIJABCDEFGHIJABCDEFGHIJ
ABCDEFGHIJABCDEFGHIJABCDEFGHIJABCDEFGHIJ
ABCDEFGHIJABCDEFGHIJABCDEFGHIJABCDEFGHIJ
ABCDEFGHIJABCDEFGHIJABCDEFGHIJABCDEFGHIJ
ABCDEFGHIJABCDEFGHIJABCDEFGHIJABCDEFGHIJ
ABCDEFGHIJABCDEFGHIJABCDEFGHIJABCDEFGHIJ
ABCDEFGHIJABCDEFGHIJABCDEFGHIJABCDEFGHIJ
ABCDEFGHIJABCDEFGHIJABCDEFGHIJABCDEFGHIJ
ABCDEFGHIJABCDEFGHIJABCDEFGHIJABCDEFGHIJ
ABCDEFGHIJABCDEFGHIJABCDEFGHIJABCDEFGHIJ
ABCDEFGHIJABCDEFGHIJABCDEFGHIJABCDEFGHIJ
ABCDEFGHIJABCDEFGHIJABCDEFGHIJABCDEFGHIJ
ABCDEFGHIJABCDEFGHIJABCDEFGHIJABCDEFGHIJ
PRESS ANY LETTER TO CLEAR SCREEN
```

**Figure A–28**
The WIDTH Command

```
100   REM THIS PROGRAM DEMONSTRATES THE USE OF THE
110   REM "DRAW" STATEMENT.  THE PURPOSE OF THIS STATEMENT IS
120   REM TO DRAW AN OBJECT AS SPECIFIED BY string.
130   REM THE FORMAT IS: DRAW string, WHERE string
140   REM CONTAINS A graphics definition language.
150   REM THE STRING DEFINES AN OBJECT, WHICH IS DRAWN
160   REM WHEN BASIC EXECUTES THE DRAW STATEMENT.
170   REM DURING EXECUTION, BASIC EXAMINES THE VALUE
180   REM OF string AND INTERPRETS SINGLE-LETTER
190   REM COMMANDS FROM THE CONTENTS OF THE STRING.
200   REM IN OUR EXAMPLE "U60" INDICATES THAT A LINE IS
210   REM DRAWN UPWARD FOR 60 POINTS, "L50" PRODUCES A LINE
220   REM DRAWN LEFT FOR 50 POINTS, ETC. THE ENTIRE SETS OF
230   REM INSTRUCTIONS IN THIS LINE PRODUCE A LARGE SQUARE.
240   REM
250   REM ****** VARIABLE TABLE
260   REM           KEYSTROKE$ = USER SELECTED CONTINUATION VARIABLE
270   REM
280   REM ****** INITIALIZATION SECTION
290   SCREEN 1,0 : CLS : KEY OFF
300   REM
310   REM ****** PROCESS SECTION
320   DRAW "U60 L50 D60 R50"
330   DRAW "U10 L10 D10 R10"
340   REM
350   REM ****** TERMINATION SECTION
360   PRINT "PRESS ANY LETTER TO CLEAR SCREEN"
370   KEYSTROKE$ = INPUT$(1)
380   CLS : SCREEN 0 : WIDTH 80 : KEY ON
390   END


PRESS ANY LETTER TO CLEAR SCREEN
```

**Figure A–29**
The DRAW Command

```
100     REM THIS PROGRAM DEMONSTRATES THE USE OF THE "PRESET"
110     REM AND "PSET" STATEMENTS.   EACH OF THESE STATEMENTS
120     REM DRAWS A POINT AT THE SPECIFIED POSITION ON THE
130     REM SCREEN.   THE FORMAT IS: PSET (x,y),color AND
140     REM PRESET (x,y),color.   (x,y) ARE THE COORDINATES
150     REM OF THE POINT TO BE SET, color IS AN INTEGER
160     REM EXPRESSION THAT CHOOSES AN ATTRIBUTE FROM THE
170     REM ATTRIBUTE RANGE FOR THE CURRENT SCREEN MODE.
180     REM 0 IS ALWAYS THE ATTRIBUTE FOR THE BACKGROUND.
190     REM PRESET IS ALMOST IDENTICAL TO PSET. THE ONLY
200     REM DIFFERENCE IS THAT IF NO color PARAMETER IS GIVEN
210     REM TO PRESET, THE BACKGROUND ATTRIBUTE (0) IS SELECTED.
220     REM IF color IS INCLUDED, PRESET IS IDENTICAL TO PSET.
230     REM IN OUR EXAMPLE WE USE PSET TO DRAW A SINE CURVE
240     REM USING A VALUE OF 3 FOR color IN PSET.   THEN WE USE
250     REM PRESET WITH NO color DESIGNATION.   PRESET NOW SETS
260     REM EACH POINT OF THE FIRST PORTION OF THIS CURVE TO A
270     REM color OF 0, THAT IS, PRESET ERASES A PORTION OF THE
280     REM SINE CURVE DRAWN BY PSET.
290     REM
300     REM ****** VARIABLE TABLE
310     REM          COLUMN = FOR-NEXT LOOP CONTROL VARIABLE
320     REM          HEIGHT = FOR-NEXT LOOP VARIABLE
330     REM          KEYSTROKE$ = USER SELECTED CONTINUATION VARIABLE
340     REM
350     REM ****** INITIALIZATION SECTION
360     SCREEN 1 : COLOR 0,1 : CLS : KEY OFF
370     REM
380     REM ****** PROCESS SECTION
390     REM START DRAWING SINE CURVE
400     FOR COLUMN = 0 TO 80 STEP .05
410        LET HEIGHT = 50*SIN(COLUMN)
420        PSET(COLUMN,HEIGHT),3
430     NEXT COLUMN
440     REM
450     FOR COLUMN = 0 TO 80 STEP .05
460        HEIGHT = 25*SIN(COLUMN)+100
470        PSET(COLUMN,HEIGHT),3
480     NEXT COLUMN
490     REM
500     PRINT "PRESS ANY KEY TO START ERASING."
510     KEYSTROKE$ = INPUT$(1)
520     REM
530     FOR COLUMN = 0 TO 30 STEP .05
540        LET HEIGHT = 50*SIN(COLUMN)
550        PRESET(COLUMN,HEIGHT)
560     NEXT COLUMN
570     REM
580     REM ****** TERMINATION SECTION
590     PRINT "PRESS ANY KEY TO CLEAR THE SCREEN."
600     KEYSTROKE$ = INPUT$(1)
610     CLS : SCREEN 0 : WIDTH 80 : KEY ON
620     PRINT "PROCESSING COMPLETED."
630     END
```

**Figure A–30**
The PSET and PRESET Commands

294

```
100    REM THIS PROGRAM WILL CREATE A STRUCTURED SEQUENTIAL FILE.
110    REM
120    REM ****** VARIABLE TABLE
130    REM          SPANISH$ = VARIABLE TO HOLD A USER INPUT SPANISH NAME
140    REM          ENGLISH$ = VARIABLE TO HOLD A USER INPUT ENGLISH NAME
150    REM          SPAN$ = THE FIRST 38 CHARACTERS OF SPANISH$
160    REM          ENGL$ = THE FIRST 38 CHARACTERS OF ENGLISH$
170    REM
180    REM ****** INITIALIZATION SECTION
190    OPEN "A:TRANSL.TXT" FOR OUTPUT AS #1
200    REM
210    GOSUB 340
220    REM
230    REM ****** TERMINATION SECTION
240    PRINT
250    REM "LOF" RETURNS THE NUMBER OF BYTES ALLOCATED TO THE FILE.
260    PRINT "THE FILE CREATED, TRANSL.TXT, REQUIRES";
270    PRINT LOF(1);"BYTES OF DISK STORAGE SPACE."
280    CLOSE #1
290    END
300    REM
310    REM ****** PROCESS SECTION
320    REM SUBROUTINE:  ENTER RECORDS & WRITE TO FILE.
330    REM EACH RECORD HAS 2 FIELDS.
340    PRINT "WHEN PROMPTED, PLEASE ENTER A SPANISH OR ENGLISH NAME."
350    REM
360    REM TO RETURN FROM THE SUBROUTINE AND END THE FILE TYPE A
370    REM Z WHEN THE PROMPT FOR A SPANISH NAME IS GIVEN.
380    PRINT "TO END FILE, PRESS Z WHEN A SPANISH NAME IS REQUESTED."
390    REM
400    LINE INPUT "ENTER A SPANISH NAME: ";SPANISH$
410    REM
420    REM TEST USER INPUT
430    IF SPANISH$ = "Z" OR SPANISH$ = "z" THEN RETURN
440    REM
450    LINE INPUT "ENTER AN ENGLISH NAME: ";ENGLISH$
460    REM
470    SPAN$ = LEFT$(SPANISH$,38)
480    ENGL$ = LEFT$(ENGLISH$,38)
490    WRITE #1, SPAN$, ENGL$
500    GOTO 400
Ok
RUN
WHEN PROMPTED, PLEASE ENTER A SPANISH OR ENGLISH NAME.
TO END FILE, PRESS Z WHEN A SPANISH NAME IS REQUESTED.
ENTER A SPANISH NAME: JOSE
ENTER AN ENGLISH NAME: JOSEPH
ENTER A SPANISH NAME: MARIA
ENTER AN ENGLISH NAME: MARY
ENTER A SPANISH NAME: JUAN
ENTER AN ENGLISH NAME: JOHN
ENTER A SPANISH NAME: Z

THE FILE CREATED, TRANSL.TXT, REQUIRES 48 BYTES OF DISK STORAGE SPACE.
Ok
```

**Figure A–31**
Creating a Sequential File and Determining its Storage Space Requirements

# Appendix B
# The World of Microcomputers

B

## B–1

## INTRODUCTION

In this appendix we discuss microcomputer fundamentals. Hardware and software for micros are explained, and different classes of application software are introduced. We present guidelines for successful selection and maintenance of microcomputers and we discuss the advantages of micros compared to mainframes. The appendix concludes with a hands-on session with a microcomputer.

## B–2

## DEFINING A MICROCOMPUTER

The terms personal computer, PC, micro, and **microcomputer** refer to the smallest type of computer when measured by such attributes as memory, cost, size, speed, and sophistication. Although small, the ever-increasing power and capability of personal computers sometimes blur the difference between PCs and larger computers.

Since the beginning of the microcomputer era in about 1975, the capability of these computers has improved beyond imagination. Still, some experts believe this is only the beginning and there is much more to be done by these computers.

A typical microcomputer consists of input, output, and memory devices. Figure B–1 illustrates a typical microcomputer system. The **input device** is usually a keyboard. A PC keyboard is similar to a typewriter keyboard, with some additional keys. Figure B–2 displays an IBM enhanced keyboard. Other input devices include the mouse, touch technology, light pens, graphics tablets, optical character readers (OCR), magnetic ink character recognition (MICR), cameras, sensors, and bar codes. In the future, there may be voice input devices as well.

The most common **output devices** for microcomputers are a monitor— sometimes called a CRT (cathode-ray tube) or VDT (video display terminal)—

**Figure B–1**
A Typical Microcomputer System. (Cobalt Productions/ Macmillan).

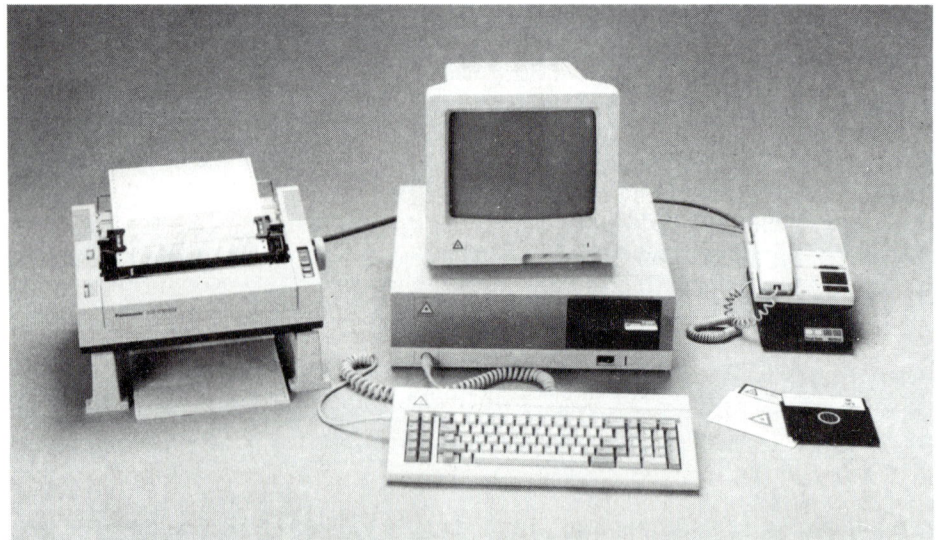

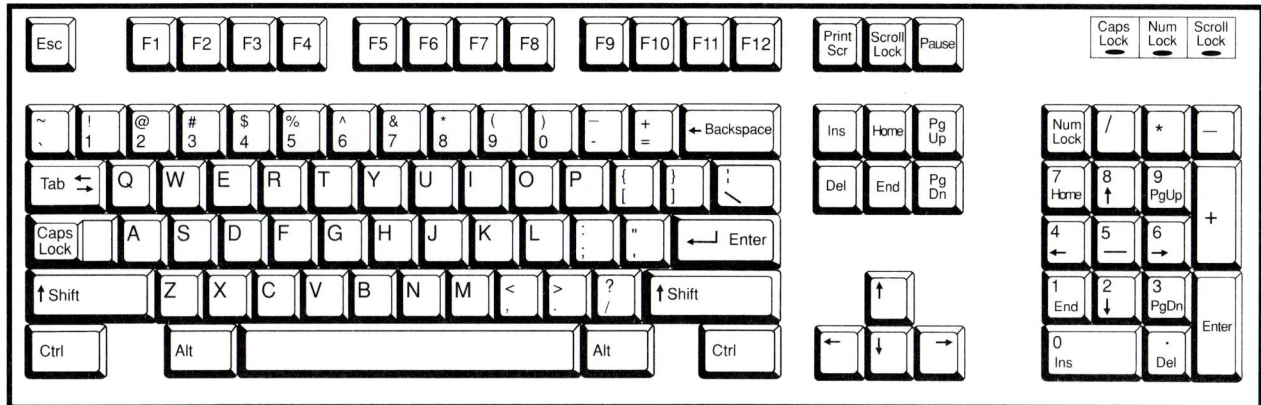

**Figure B–2**
An IBM Enhanced Keyboard

and a printer. The output generated on the monitor is called soft copy, and the printed output is referred to as hard copy. Other kinds of output devices include cameras and plotters.

There are two types of monitors. The majority of microcomputers use a monochrome screen. As the name indicates, this type of screen generates one color, such as green or amber. Monochrome monitors can generate graphics output if your computer is equipped with a graphics card or graphics adapter.

The other type of monitor is a color monitor—sometimes referred to as an RGB (red-green-blue) monitor. Color monitors come in several types: CGA, EGA, and VGA.

The sharpness of images on the display monitor is referred to as the resolution. The intersection of a row and a column is called a pixel; the greater the number of pixels, the higher the resolution. CGA, EGA, and VGA monitors present different resolutions. A CGA (Color Graphics Adapter) monitor displays 320 by 200 pixels in four colors.

An EGA (Enhanced Graphics Adapter) monitor displays 640 by 350 pixels in 16 colors. More advanced versions of EGA monitors can display 640 by 480 pixels in 16 colors and 320 by 200 pixels in 256 colors.

A VGA (Video Graphics Array) monitor can display 640 by 480 pixels in 16 colors and 320 by 200 pixels in 256 colors. The most recent graphics add-on board, this card was introduced in 1987 by the IBM PS/2 series computers.

Boards or cards are used to upgrade or expand the computer's capacities. These boards or cards perform many tasks. Some are used to expand memory, others are used as peripheral devices.

The processing part of a microcomputer is the CPU (central processing unit). Also called the microprocessor, the CPU includes three components. The main memory stores data, information, and instructions. The arithmetic logic unit (ALU) performs arithmetic and logical operations. Arithmetic operations include addition, subtraction, division, and multiplication. Logical operations include any types of comparisons, such as sorting (putting data into a particular order) or searching (choosing a particular data item). The control unit serves as the commander of the system. It tells the microcomputer what to do and how to do it. Figure B–3 shows two different microprocessor chips or microchips.

A.

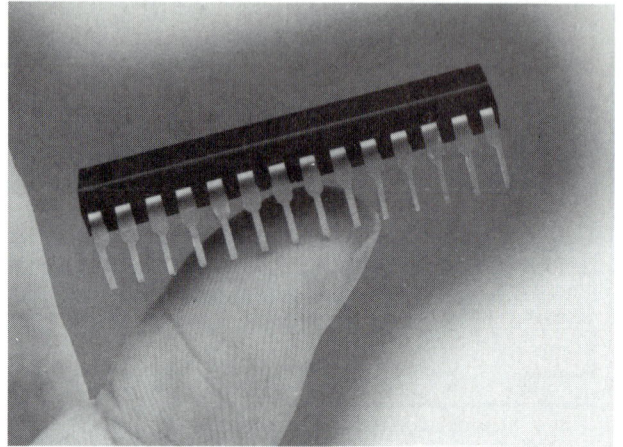

B.

**Figure B–3**
A. The Motorola MC 68020 Microprocessor in the Protective Ceramic Package (Courtesy of Motorola, Inc.). B. A Microprocessor. (Courtesy of Radio Shack, A Division of Tandy Corporation).

## B–3

# MORE ON THE KEYBOARD

As you can see in figure B–2, an enhanced keyboard is divided into three sections. Across the top are 12 function keys. Some keyboards have the function keys on the left. With most application software, these keys perform special functions, or they can be programmed to perform a particular task. For example, Lotus 1-2-3, dBASE, and WordPerfect use function keys F1 through F10 for performing different tasks.

The middle part of the keyboard is similar to a typewriter keyboard. However, there are some special keys that a typewriter does not have—the Alt and Ctrl keys, for example.

On the right side of the keyboard is a numeric keypad similar to that of an adding machine, used for cursor movement or, when the Num Lock key is pressed, to facilitate numeric data entry.

The purpose of function keys and some of the special keys varies in different application programs. For example, in WordPerfect, the F1 key performs undelete operations. In 1-2-3 or dBASE, it accesses on-line help.

## B–4

# OTHER NECESSARY DEVICES

Besides typical input/output devices, some additional devices are required for effective use of a microcomputer. These devices include disk drives and adapter cards.

### B–4–1   Disk Drives

Disk drives are used to read and store data or information from and to a disk into the memory. Disk drives come in various capacities. You may have one or more floppy disk drives, and you also may have a **hard disk** drive. As you will

0 or 1 is equal to one bit

8 bits is equal to one byte

1,024 ($2^{10}$) bytes is equal to one kilobyte (K)

1,048,576 ($2^{20}$) bytes is equal to one megabyte (M)

1,073,741,824 ($2^{30}$) bytes is equal to one gigabyte

1,099,511,627,776 ($2^{40}$) bytes is equal to one terabyte

read later, hard disks are capable of storing large quantities of information. The capacity of a hard disk is many times greater than a **floppy disk**. A floppy disk can hold from 360K (kilobytes) to 1.44M (megabytes) of information. The capacity of a hard disk varies from 5M to 300M or more.

The capacity of a storage device is measured in terms of bits or bytes. A bit (BInary digiT) is the smallest piece of information understood by a computer. A bit is either a 1 or a 0, indicating either an on or an off condition. A byte is a string of eight bits acting as a single piece of information. A byte is roughly equivalent to one character. For example, if you type "Susan" on your computer, it will occupy approximately five bytes of memory. Table B–1 shows various memory equivalents.

## B–4–2   Adapter Cards

Adapter cards are used to attach a particular option to the system unit. They are installed in expansion slots (channels) inside the system unit. Typical adapter cards may include the following:

- Disk drive card for connecting disk drives to the system unit
- Display card for connecting CRT to the system unit
- Memory card for connecting additional RAM to the existing memory
- Clock card for connecting a clock to the system unit
- Modem card for connecting a modem to your PC
- Printer interface card for connecting a printer to your computer

The original IBM PC has five expansion slots, the IBM XT and AT have eight slots. The adapter cards usually have outlet ports that are accessed at the back of the system unit. It is important to remember that the newer PCs do not require as many adapter cards. Ports are either parallel or serial and are used to connect devices to the system. You must connect a serial device to a serial port and a parallel device to a parallel port. Serial devices transfer one bit of data at a time, parallel devices transfer groups of bits at a time.

# B–5

# TYPES OF PRIMARY MEMORIES

There are two kinds of memory: main, or **primary memory,** and auxiliary, or secondary memory. Main memory is the heart of the microcomputer, usually referred to as **RAM** (Random-Access Memory). This is volatile memory—data stored in RAM are lost when you turn off your computer. To avoid this type of loss, you should always save your work on a storage device, such as a disk.

Three other types of memory also are referred to as main memory, but the user does not have direct control over them. These include:

- **ROM** (Read-Only Memory): A prefabricated chip supplied by vendors. This memory stores some general-purpose instructions or programs—DOS commands, for example.
- **PROM** (Programmable Read-Only Memory): By using a special device, the user can program this memory. However, once programmed, the user cannot erase this type of memory.
- **EPROM** (Erasable Programmable Read-Only Memory): This type of read-only memory can be programmed by the user and, as the name indicates, erased and programmed again.

## B–6

# TYPES OF SECONDARY MEMORIES

Because the main memory of a microcomputer is limited, expensive, and volatile, secondary storage devices are used for mass data storage. **Secondary memory** is nonvolatile, and can be broadly classified into magnetic and optical.

### B–6–1   Magnetic Storage Devices

Magnetic storage devices include floppy disks, mini-floppy disks, hard disks, and the Bernoulli Box. The capacity of a floppy or hard disk depends on its technical features. There are three types of standard disks: 3-½ inches, 5-¼ inches, and 8 inches. The most recent floppy just entering into the market is a 2-inch floppy.

Disks can be single-density, double-density, or high-density. Density refers to the amount of information that can be stored on a disk. They can also be single-sided or double-sided. A 5-¼ inch, single-sided, single-density floppy can hold roughly 125K; a 5-¼ inch, single-sided, double-density floppy can hold about 250K; a 5-¼ inch, double-sided, double-density floppy can hold approximately 360K; and a high-density disk (sometimes called quad-density) can hold up to 1.2M. A 3-½ inch floppy disk can store 720K per side, or 1.44M on a double-sided disk.

A hard disk (sometimes called a Winchester disk) can be either 14, 8, 5-¼, or less than 4 inches in diameter. The capacity of these devices varies from 5 megabytes to 1 gigabyte.

A Bernoulli Box is a removable medium. This means after finishing your computer work you can pull this device out and store it in a safe location. This is not possible with a hard disk. A Bernoulli Box uses high-capacity floppy disks to store 10M or more of information. Generally speaking, it is less damage-prone than a hard disk, because the Bernoulli Box drive head, which records the data, does not move as a hard disk drive head does. In a Bernoulli Box the floppy disk moves toward the stationary read/write head. Figure B–4 shows a Bernoulli Box.

Currently, the most commonly used secondary storage device is the 3-½ inch floppy disk. However, at the beginning of the PC era 5-¼ inch floppy disks were the most commonly used secondary storage devices. A 5-¼ inch disk is enclosed in a permanent vinyl jacket to protect the disk. A floppy disk is made of plastic material coated with magnetic material. After using a floppy disk you should put it back in its paper cover to protect it against dirt and dust. Don't put

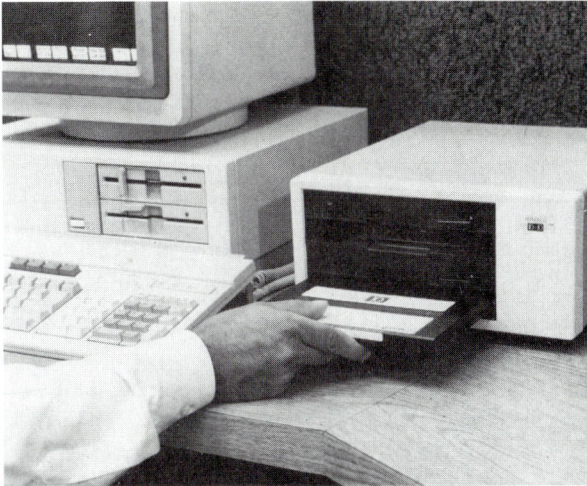

**Figure B–4**
A Bernoulli Box (Cobalt Productions/Macmillan)

your fingers on exposed portions of the disk or data loss may result. Figure B–5 highlights important areas of a 5-¼ inch disk.

## B–6–2    Optical Technologies

Three types of optical storage have attracted much attention in recent years: CD ROM, WORM, and erasable optical disk. The advantages of optical technology devices are their durability and storage capacity. The major drawback of optical

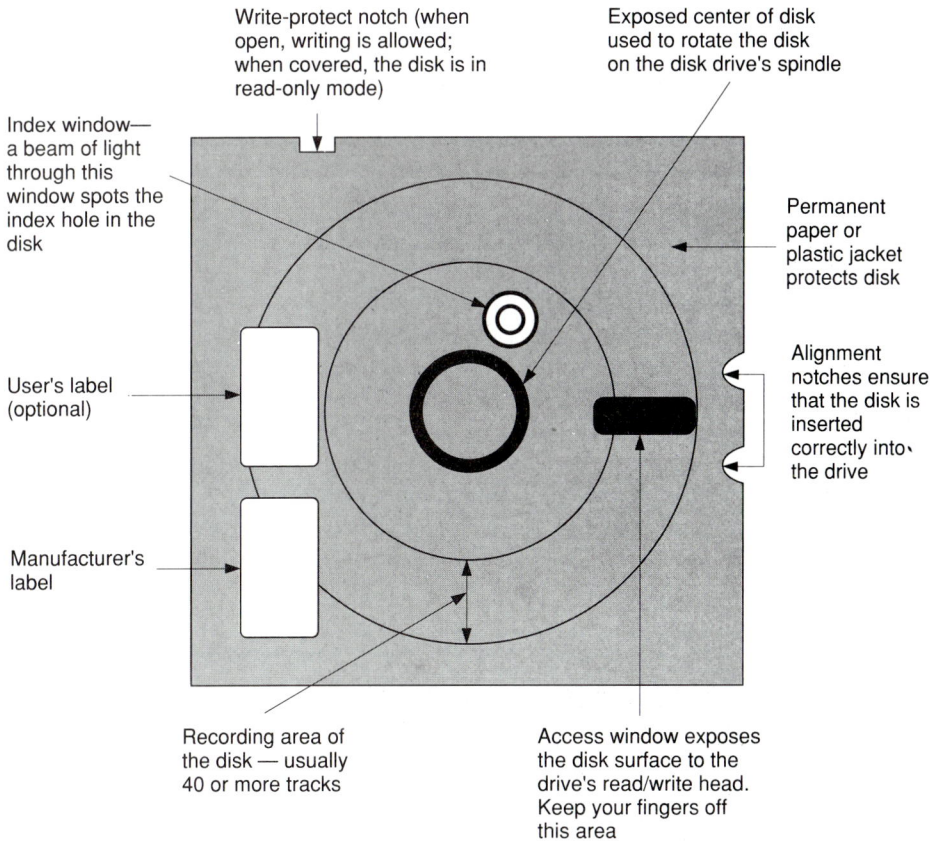

Write-protect notch (when open, writing is allowed; when covered, the disk is in read-only mode)

Exposed center of disk used to rotate the disk on the disk drive's spindle

Index window— a beam of light through this window spots the index hole in the disk

Permanent paper or plastic jacket protects disk

User's label (optional)

Alignment notches ensure that the disk is inserted correctly into the drive

Manufacturer's label

Recording area of the disk — usually 40 or more tracks

Access window exposes the disk surface to the drive's read/write head. Keep your fingers off this area

**Figure B–5**
A 5-¼ Inch Floppy Disk

**Figure B–6**
Optical Storage Devices for
Microcomputers

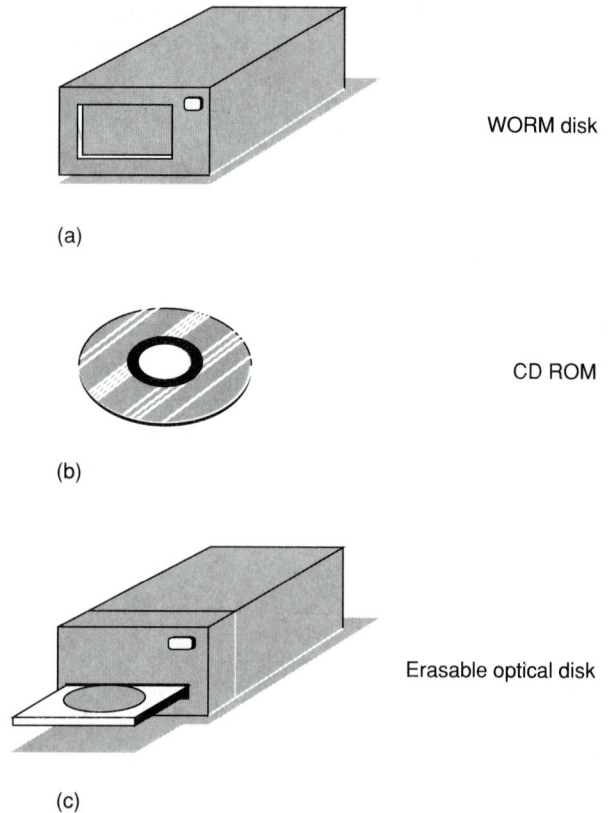

WORM disk

(a)

CD ROM

(b)

Erasable optical disk

(c)

technology is its slow speed. However, the speed problem is being resolved gradually.

As the name indicates, **CD ROM** (compact disk read-only memory) is a permanent device. Information is recorded by disk-mastering machines. A CD ROM is similar to an audio compact disk. It can be duplicated and distributed throughout the organization. Its major application is for large permanent databases; for example, public-domain databases such as libraries, real estate information, and corporate financial information.

**WORM** (Write Once, Read Many) also is a permanent device. Information can be recorded once and cannot be altered. Its major drawback compared to CD ROM is that you cannot duplicate the disk. You use a WORM for storing information that must be kept permanently; for example, information related to annual reports, nuclear power plants, airports, and railroads.

An **erasable optical disk** is used when high-volume storage and updating are essential. The information can be recorded and erased repeatedly. Figure B–6 shows these different technologies.

## B–7

# MEMORY CAPACITY AND PROCESSOR SPEED

Microcomputer RAM capacity usually starts at 256K, but most vendors now offer 512K or 640K PCs. PCs with capacities of 1 to 4 megabytes are becoming more common and, in the future, will approach minicomputer capacity.

When you purchase a computer, you should calculate the memory requirements for your computing needs. Although you may have a PC with 640K of RAM, all of it is not accessible to you. A large portion of this memory is used by the application software. As an example, Lotus 1-2-3 Release 2.01 uses almost 200K of RAM. So in a 640K PC, you are left with only 440K of user memory.

Another consideration regarding your computer is speed. The speed of the processor is measured in megahertz (MHz) and usually varies from 4 MHz to 33 MHz. Soon, speeds of 50 MHz or more may be available. The higher the processor speed, the faster the computer.

A factor that has direct effect on speed is the word size of the processor. Word size indicates the number of characters that can be processed simultaneously. Word size varies from 8 to 32 bits for microcomputers. The bigger the word size, the faster the computer. The speed of your microcomputer may have a direct effect on your business operation. With a faster computer you can process more information in a shorter period of time. However, you should consider the additional cost incurred by buying the more powerful PCs and the marginal benefit to be gained.

# B–8
# GENERAL CAPABILITIES OF MICROCOMPUTER SOFTWARE

A microcomputer can perform a variety of tasks by using either commercial software or software developed in-house. In-house developed software is usually more expensive than commercial software. However, this software is customized and should better fit your needs. Thousands of software programs are available for PCs. The following are typical commercial programs and applications available for microcomputers.

## B–8–1   Word Processing Software

A microcomputer used as a **word processor** is similar to a typewriter with a memory. With a word processor, you can generate documents, make deletions and insertions, and cut and paste. Word processing programs are becoming more sophisticated, and some of these programs provide limited graphics and data management features.

There are many word processing programs on the market. Some of the most popular ones are Multimate from Ashton-Tate, Officewriter from Office Solutions, WordPerfect from WordPerfect Corp., WordStar from WordStar International, PC-Write from Quicksoft, Word from Microsoft, and Volkswriter from Lifetree Software, Inc.

## B–8–2   Spreadsheet Software

A spreadsheet is simply a table of rows and columns. **Spreadsheet software** can be broadly classified into two types.

The first type is a dedicated spreadsheet. This means that the program performs only spreadsheet analysis. VisiCalc (by Visicorp) is a good example. The other type of spreadsheet package is integrated software, which means it can perform more than one type of analysis. You can use 1-2-3, for example, to perform spreadsheet analysis as well as maintaining a database and doing graphics. Some experts believe 1-2-3 is not a truly integrated package because it does not offer word processing and communication. However, although this is true, 1-2-3 can easily use these features from other software.

Other popular integrated packages include Electronic Desk from the Software Group, Inc., Framework from Ashton-Tate, Smart Software System from Innovative Software, Inc., Symphony from Lotus Development Corporation, UniCalc from Lattice, Inc., Excel from Microsoft, SuperCalc 5.0 from Computer Associates International, Inc., and Quattro from Borland International.

The number of jobs that can be performed by a spreadsheet program is unlimited. Generally speaking, any application suitable for a row and column analysis is a candidate for a typical spreadsheet. For example, you can use a spreadsheet to prepare a budget, and then, manipulating variables, the spreadsheet can perform some impressive "what-if" analysis. You could reduce your predicted income by 2 percent and ask the spreadsheet to calculate the effect of this change on other items in the spreadsheet.

## B-8-3   Database Software

**Database software** is designed to perform database operations such as file creation, deletion, modification, search, sort, merge, and join (combining two files based on a common key). A **file** is a collection of records, a record is a collection of fields, and a field is a collection of characters.

Popular database programs include Business Filevision from Telos Software Products, dBASE III PLUS and IV from Ashton-Tate, PC-File III from Buttonware, Inc., Q&A from Symantec, Paradox from Ansa Software, Omnis Quartz from Blyth Software, DataEase from DataEase International, FoxBase and FoxPro from Fox Software, and R-Base from Microrim Corporation.

A database also can be compared to a table of rows and columns. The rows correspond to a record, and the columns correspond to the fields within the record. Two common applications of a database are sorting and searching records. In sort operations, the operator enters a series of records in any order then asks the database management program to sort the records in ascending or descending order, based on the data in the fields. Search operations are even more interesting. You can search for data items that meet certain criteria. You can, for example, search for all the MIS students who have GPAs greater than 3.6 and who are under 20 years of age. Some databases (such as Q&A) allow you to search for key words within a text file.

## B-8-4   Graphics Software

**Graphics software** is designed to present data in graphic format. With this software, data can be converted into a line graph to show a trend, to a pie chart to highlight the components of a data item, and to other types of graphs for various analyses. Masses of data can be converted to a graph and, in a glance, you can discover the general pattern of the data. Graphs can highlight patterns and correlation of data items. They also make data presentation a more manageable job. Integrated packages such as 1-2-3 or Symphony have graphics capabilities, or you can use a dedicated graphics package.

Three popular graphics packages are Energraphics from Enertronics Research, Inc., Harvard Graphics from Software Publishing Corporation, and Freelance from Lotus Development Corporation.

## B−8−5   Communications Software

Using a modem and **communications software,** your microcomputer can connect you to a wealth of information available in public and private databases. Several executives can simultaneously work on the same report in several different states or countries by using communications software. The report is sent back and forth to each location until it is completed. With communications software and a modem, remote job entry becomes an easy task. A modem converts computer signals (digital signals) to signals that can be transferred on a telephone line (analog signals).

Some programs, such as Symphony, include a communications program within the package itself. However, there are many other communications software products on the market, among them Crosstalk from Microstuf, Inc., On-Line from Micro-Systems Software, Inc., PFS: Access from Software Publishing Corp., and Smartcom II from Hayes Microcomputer Products, Inc.

## B−8−6   Desktop Publishing Software

Desktop publishing software is used to produce professional-quality documents (with or without graphics) using relatively inexpensive hardware and software. All that is needed is a PC, a desktop publishing software package, and a letter-quality or laser printer. Desktop publishing has evolved as a result of three major factors: inexpensive PCs, inexpensive laser printers, and sophisticated and easy-to-use software.

Desktop publishing enables you to produce high quality screen output, and then transfer it to the printer in a "what you see is what you get" (WYSIWYG) environment. You can use desktop publishing for creating newsletters, brochures, training manuals, transparencies, posters, and books (see fig. B−7).

There are several desktop publishing software packages available. Pagemaker from Aldus and Ventura Publisher from Xerox Corporation are two of the most popular ones.

## B−8−7   Financial Planning Software

**Financial planning software** works with large amounts of data and performs diverse financial analyses. These analyses include present value, future value, rate of return, cash flow, depreciation, and budgeting.

Some popular programs for financial planning are DTFPS from Desk Top Financial Solutions, Inc., Excel from Microsoft Corp., Finar from Finar Research Systems, Ltd., Javelin from Javelin Software Corp., Micro-DSS/Finance from Addison-Wesley Publishing Co., 1-2-3 from Lotus Development Corporation, IFPS from Execucom Systems, and Micro Plan from Chase Laboratories, Inc.

With these programs, you can plan and analyze your financial situation. For example, you can calculate how much your $2,000 IRA will be at 10 percent interest in 30 years, or you can discount all future cash flows into today's dollar.

**Figure B–7**
A. Desktop Publishing Combines Text, Graphics, and Illustrations (Courtesy of Hewlett-Packard).
B. With Desktop Publishing, Business Professionals Can Prepare High Quality Documents (Courtesy of Hewlett-Packard)

A.

B.

You can figure out how much you have to deposit in the bank in order to save $60,000 in 10 years for your child's education.

## B–8–8  Accounting Software

Aside from spreadsheet software, which has widespread applications in the accounting field, there are many dedicated **accounting programs** that are able to perform accounting tasks. The tasks performed by these programs include general ledgers, accounts receivable, accounts payable, payrolls, balance sheets, and income statements. Depending on the price, these programs vary in sophistication.

Some of the more popular accounting programs are One Write Plus from Great American Software, Business Works PC from Manzanita Software

Systems, 4-in-1 Basic Accounting from Real World Corp., Peachtree from Peachtree Software, Inc., and DacEasy Accounting from Dac Software, Inc.

## B–8–9  Project-Management Software

A project consists of a series of related activities. Building a house, designing an order-entry system, or writing a thesis are examples of projects. The goal of **project-management software** is to help decision-makers keep the time and budget under control by resolving scheduling problems. Project-management software helps managers to plan and set achievable goals. It also highlights the bottlenecks and the relationships among different activities. These programs enable you to study the cost, time, and resource effect of any change in the schedule.

Popular project-management programs include Harvard Total Project Manager from Software Publishing Corp., Micro Planner 6 from Micro Planning International, Microsoft Project from Microsoft Corp., Superproject Expert from Computer Associates, and Time Line from Symantec.

## B–8–10  Computer-Aided Design (CAD) Software

**Computer-aided design** (CAD) software is used for drafting and design. CAD has replaced the traditional tools of drafting and design such as T-square, triangle, paper, and pencil, and it is being used extensively in the architectural and engineering industries. CAD software does not belong only to the large corporations any more. With the new 286-, 386-, and 486-based PCs and significant price reduction, small companies and individuals can afford this software. Because the new PCs have larger memory and are significantly faster than earlier PCs, they are able to take advantage of the majority of features offered by CAD programs.

There are several CAD programs on the market, including AutoCAD from Autodesk, Cadkey from Cadkey, and VersaCAD from VersaCAD (see fig. B–8).

# B–9

# GUIDELINES FOR SELECTING A MICROCOMPUTER

There are many kinds of microcomputers on the market, making the selection task a difficult one. In this section and the next, we provide you with some general guidelines regarding the purchase and maintenance of a microcomputer. These guidelines will help you choose a suitable computer and maintain it more easily.

Before you start looking, you should define your requirements. Sometimes this is called the "wish list" approach. When you are ready to buy, you should have a clear idea of the microcomputer you need and the specific applications you want it to handle. Remember, if you need a particular kind of software, you must have the hardware to run it.

After defining your software and hardware needs, you should look at technical support and vendor reputation. Important factors regarding selection and maintenance of a microcomputer follow.

A.

B.

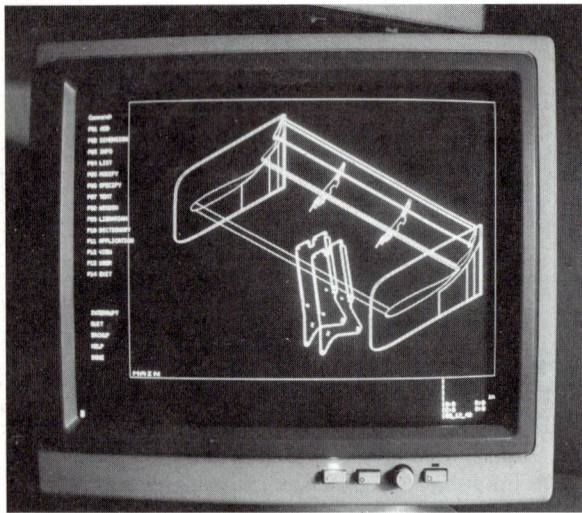
C.

**Figure B–8**
A. A CAD System for Detailed
Architectural Design (Larry
Hamill/Macmillan). B. A CAD
System for Design of a Multi-
component Product (Larry
Hamill/Macmillan). C. A CAD
System of an Indy Car Rear
Wing (Larry Hamill/Macmillan)

Good software should:

- be easy to use
- be able to handle your business volume
- have good documentation
- have training available
- have updates available (free of charge or for a minimum charge)
- have local support
- come from a reputable vendor
- have a low cost

Good hardware should:

- have a comfortable keyboard
- have function keys
- have a general operating system (OS/2, MS-DOS, PC-DOS, or UNIX)

- have 16-bit or bigger processor (word) size
- be expandable (memory and peripheral)
- have adequate channel capacity or expansion slots
- have a low cost

A good monitor should:

- be separated from the system unit (not be built-in)
- be easy to read
- have a standard number of characters per row and column (80 columns by 25 rows)

A good disk drive should:

- have a built-in, not separate, disk drive
- have adequate storage capacity
- have a hard disk option

A good printer should:

- have a standard printer interface (without additional devices)
- produce quality output
- have high speed
- have a reasonable amount of noise suppression
- let you change tape, ribbons, or toner cartridge easily
- have a low cost

A good vendor should:

- have a good reputation
- have a knowledgeable staff
- have training available for hardware and software
- have a hot line available
- support newsletters and user groups
- provide a "loaner" in case of breakdown
- provide updates (trade-in options)

A good contract should:

- have a warranty period
- state a flexible time for repair
- limit down time and inconvenience by providing flexible repair visits and timely repair of the computer
- have reasonable terms for contract renewal
- allow relocation or reassignment of the present contract
- observe confidentiality issues

## B-10

# TAKING CARE OF YOUR MICROCOMPUTER

To maintain the health of your microcomputer you should follow these guidelines:

- Protect your microcomputer against dirt, dust, and smoke.
- Make backups and keep your backups in different locations.
- Avoid any kind of liquid spills.
- Maintain steady power. Use surge protectors and lightning arresters.
- Protect the machine from static by using humidifiers or antistatic spray devices.
- Do not use a disk that you are not familiar with (to avoid computer viruses—the deadly programs that can corrupt data).
- Don't download information to your computer from unknown bulletin boards. (Downloading means importing information from other computers by using a telephone line.)
- Acquire insurance for your computer equipment.

## B-11

# ADVANTAGES OF MICROCOMPUTERS

Generally speaking, a microcomputer offers several advantages compared to a mainframe computer. With extended memory and increased speed, microcomputers can perform on a smaller scale many of the tasks performed by a mainframe. We can summarize the advantages of microcomputers compared with mainframes as follows:

- They are easier to use.
- They are less threatening to non-computer experts.
- The user has more control.
- They are relatively inexpensive.
- They can be portable.

## B-12

# YOU AND YOUR PC: A HANDS-ON SESSION

If the disk operating system (DOS) is in drive A (the top disk drive, or the left disk drive, in a two-drive system), when you turn the computer on, your microcomputer will ask for the date. Most IBM or IBM-compatible computers come with a DOS disk. Either type the date in the desired format or press Enter to skip this prompt. The computer then asks you for the time. Either type the time in the desired format or press Enter. Now you are at the A> prompt. Figure B-9 shows how your screen looks during the getting-started procedure.

If your computer has a hard disk this procedure is slightly different. You will start the system from the hard disk, and your prompt will be C> instead of A>. From the prompt, or disk operating system mode, you can go to any

```
Current date is Tue 1-01-80
Enter new date (mm-dd-yy): 1-1-91
Current time is 0:00:52.89
Enter new time: 15:25


Microsoft(R) MS-DOS(R)   Version 3.30
          (C)Copyright Microsoft Corp 1981-1987


A>
```

**Figure B–9**
Starting the System

application software. For example, pull the DOS disk out of the drive, insert the Lotus System disk, type 123, and press Enter to load 1-2-3 into RAM.

When you are at the A> prompt, you are in RAM. We call this area a working or temporary area. This means any work in this area will disappear if you turn the computer off. To make your work permanent, you must transfer it to a **permanent area**. Any application program provides you with some type of save or copy command for transferring your work from RAM to disk. The permanent area can be either floppy disk, hard disk, or cassette. Your work stays in the permanent area until you erase it.

Beginning computer users are always worried about making mistakes. What happens if you make a mistake? Don't panic. Your mistakes can easily be corrected. Some computers and application programs have an UNDO command. In the worst case, you can correct your mistake by typing over your previous material. Remember, any address or cell in the computer memory can hold only one value at a time. As soon as you type a new value, the old one disappears.

## B–13

## DEFINING A COMPUTER FILE

A computer file is basically an electronic document. One way to create a document is to enter it using the keyboard. As soon as you save the document, you have generated a computer file.

To differentiate one file from another, you must save each file under a unique name—a file name. A file name is any combination of up to eight valid characters (MYFILE, for example). Valid characters include letters of the alphabet (upper- or lowercase), digits 0 through 9, the underscore, and some special characters. If you provide a name longer than eight characters, some application programs give you an error message, others truncate the name and accept only the first eight characters. In addition to a file name, a file is usually saved with a file extension (MYFILE.TXT, for example). Some application programs automatically provide a file extension when you save the file. In other application programs, providing a file extension is the user's responsibility.

There are several characters that have special meanings in different application software. The asterisk (*) can represent up to eight characters. The question mark (?) can represent any single character. These two characters are called **wild card** characters. These wild cards can significantly improve your efficiency while working with application programs. For example, all your 1-2-3 graphics files are identified by *.PIC. The * represents any file name, and the PIC indicates that your file is a 1-2-3 graphics file.

As an illustration of the usefulness of these wild card characters, suppose that you want to copy all your 1-2-3 graphics files from the disk in drive A to the disk in drive B. You would simply type the DOS command COPY *.PIC B:. If the * wild card feature was not available, you would have to type the COPY command as many times as the number of graphics files.

## B–14

## TYPES OF DATA

Any application program or computer language accepts different types of data. The most commonly used data types are numeric and alphanumeric.

**Numeric data** include any combination of digits 0 through 9 and decimal points. Numeric data can be integer or real. Integer data include only whole numbers without any decimal points, for example, 656 or 986. Real data include digits and decimal points, 696.25 or 729.793, for example. Real data are sometimes called floating point data, which means the decimal point can move—222.2, 22.22, or 2.222, for example. Another type of real data is fixed point data, which means that the decimal point is always fixed.

**Nonnumeric,** or alphanumeric, **data** (sometimes called labels or strings) include any types of valid characters (for example, Jackson or 123 Broadway Street). Remember, you cannot perform any arithmetic operations with nonnumeric data or labels.

## B–15

## TYPES OF VALUES

Computers usually handle two types of values: variables and constants.

**Variables** are valid computer addresses (locations) that hold different values at different times. For example, when you specify A=65, A is the variable and 65 is the constant. When you specify B="Brown", B is the variable and Brown is the constant. As soon as you enter a new value into this variable, the old value disappears. The **constant** is always fixed. Figure B–10 illustrates this concept.

**Figure B–10**
An Example of a Variable and a Constant

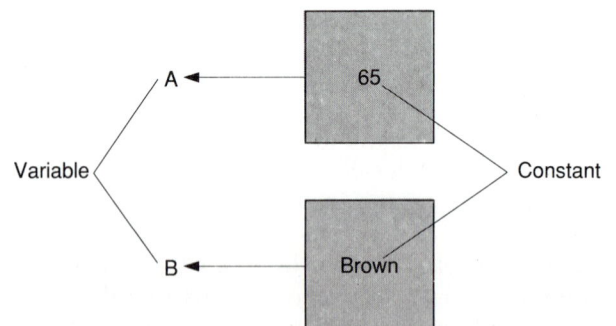

## B–16

## TYPES OF FORMULAS

There are two types of formulas or functions handled by computers: user-defined and built-in.

**User-defined formulas** or functions are a combination of computer addresses designed to perform a certain task. For example, the area of a triangle can be presented as A=B*H/2 meaning base multiplied by height divided by 2. In this case, A is a formula or a function. You can enter different values for B and H and a different value for A (the area of the triangle) will be calculated.

**Built-in formulas** or functions are already available within the application program or the computer language. As soon as the user provides values for a given variable or variables, the application program or the computer language calculates these formulas. For example, SQRT(X) is a function that calculates the square root of a variable, X. The X or any other information needed by these functions is called an argument. As soon as you provide a value for X, the square root is immediately calculated. For example, SQRT(25) is equal to 5. The function FV(payment,interest rate,term) calculates the future value of a series of equal payments with a given interest rate over a period of time (term).

## B–17

## PRIORITY (PRECEDENCE) OF OPERATIONS

When application programs perform arithmetic operations, they follow a series of rules. These **priority rules** are as follows:

1. Expressions inside parentheses have the highest priority.
2. Exponentiation (raising to power) is performed next.
3. Multiplication and division have the third highest priority.
4. Addition and subtraction have the lowest priority.
5. When there are two or more operations with the same priority, operations proceed from left to right.

The following examples should make this clear. A program uses * for multiplication, ˆ for exponentiation, and / for division. If A=5, B=10, and C=2, a computer will calculate the following answers:

```
A+B/C=10
(A+B)/C=7.5
A*B/C=25
(A*B)/C=25
AˆC/2=12.50
```

## SUMMARY

In this appendix we discussed microcomputers in general. Input and output, and primary and secondary memory devices were explained. General capabilities of microcomputers were introduced, and we presented a series of guidelines for successful selection and maintenance of a microcomputer. We discussed the advantages of microcomputers compared to mainframe computers. The appendix concluded with a hands-on session. We explained computer files, data, values, formulas, and the priority of operations.

## REVIEW QUESTIONS

*These questions are answered in Appendix D.

1. What is a microcomputer? What components does a typical minicomputer have?
*2. What are some typical input devices for a PC ?
3. What are some typical output devices for a PC?
4. What is the difference between a primary memory device and a secondary memory device?
5. What is RAM? ROM? PROM? EPROM?
*6. What is the most commonly used secondary memory device for a PC?
7. What are optical technologies? What are their advantages?
8. How do you measure the memory capacity of a PC?
9. Besides memory, what other attributes are important when you buy a computer?
10. What is the difference between a floppy and a hard disk?
11. What is the speed range for a typical microcomputer?
*12. What is the memory size of a typical personal computer?
13. What constitutes good software?
14. What constitutes good hardware?
15. What factors constitute a good contract?
*16. List important things to do when caring for your computer.
17. What are some application programs for a PC?
18. What are some of the advantages of a personal computer compared to a mainframe computer?
19. What is permanent memory in a PC? What is temporary memory?
20. How do you send information from RAM to a disk?
*21. How do you correct your mistakes?
22. What is a computer file?
23. What is a wild card character?
24. Name some different types of data.
25. What is a variable? A constant?
*26. What is priority of operations?
27. What symbols are used for arithmetic operations?
28. Turn on a PC. What do you see? Turn it off. Insert the DOS disk in drive A and turn the computer back on. What do you see this time?
29. Enter the correct date and time into your computer. What happens if you make a mistake?
30. Type DIR and press Enter. What is displayed?
31. How many generations of micros have we seen? What are the most powerful PCs on the market?
32. What types of PCs do you have on your campus? Describe different input/output devices used by the PCs in your school micro lab. Do you have a Bernoulli Box in the lab? What are some of the advantages of a Bernoulli Box over a hard disk?

33. What are the most commonly used disks on your campus? 3-½ or 5-¼? Compare and contrast these two types of storage devices.

34. Consult computer magazines to find out which computer at the present time is using optical disks.

35. Out of 10 application software packages introduced in this chapter, which ones are available on your campus? What are the applications of each?

36. If you want to buy a PC for your personal use, how do you start shopping? What attributes make a PC attractive?

## KEY TERMS

| | | |
|---|---|---|
| Accounting software | Graphics software | PROM |
| Built-in formulas | Hard disk | RAM |
| CD ROM | Input device | ROM |
| Communications software | Microcomputer | Secondary memory |
| Computer-aided design | Nonnumeric data | Spreadsheet software |
| Constants | Numeric data | User-defined formulas |
| Database software | Output device | Variables |
| EPROM | Permanent area | Wild card |
| Erasable optical disk | Primary memory | Word processor |
| File | Priority rules | WORM |
| Financial planning software | Project-management software | |
| Floppy disk | | |

## ARE YOU READY TO MOVE ON?

### Multiple Choice

1. Choose the correct ranking of monitor display resolutions from lowest to highest:
   a. VGA, CGA, EGA
   b. EGA, VGA, CGA
   c. EGA, CGA, VGA
   d. CGA, EGA, VGA
   e. none of the above

2. Which of the following is not a typical adapter card?
   a. printer interface card
   b. clock card
   c. disk drive card
   d. display card
   e. punch card

3. Of the various types of main memory, the user has direct control over
   a. ROM
   b. REM
   c. RAM
   d. PROM
   e. all of the above

4. At the present time, the most commonly used secondary storage device is the
   a. 5-¼ inch floppy disk
   b. 3-½ inch floppy disk
   c. Bernoulli Box
   d. hard disk
   e. none of the above

5. The major advantage(s) of optical storage technology is (are)
   a. storage capacity
   b. cost
   c. durability
   d. both a and c
   e. all of the above

6. When we refer to memory and storage capacity sizes, we use the term K (as in 360K). 1K equals approximately
   a. 1 byte
   b. 1,000 bytes
   c. 1,000,000 bytes
   d. 1,048,576 bytes
   e. none of the above

7. Word size directly affects
   a. the speed of the computer
   b. the ability of the user to understand what is being said
   c. the maximum amount of data that can be displayed on the CRT
   d. the choice of which type of disk drive to use
   e. the meaning of the function keys on the keyboard

8. Which of the following are disadvantages of mainframes when compared to microcomputers?
   a. they are more difficult to use
   b. they are more threatening to non-computer users
   c. the user has less control
   d. they are relatively more expensive
   e. all of the above

9. After "booting" the computer with the DOS disk (loading DOS and entering the date and time), you are at
   a. the Lotus Access Menu
   b. the DOS prompt (A>)
   c. the parallel/serial interface
   d. the BASIC prompt
   e. none of the above

10. An example of alphanumeric data would be
    a. 123
    b. 123.
    c. LOTUS-123
    d. A=(123−2)/4
    e. none of the above

## True/False

1. The terms personal computer, PC, and microcomputer refer to different types of computers.
2. A typical microcomputer consists of input, output, and memory devices.
3. Monochrome (or amber) CRTs cannot generate graphic output.
4. The purpose of function keys and special keys on a computer keyboard does not vary in different application programs.
5. The capacity of a hard disk is greater than the capacity of a floppy disk.
6. A WORM drive can be recorded and erased repeatedly when high volume storage and updating are essential.
7. Typical microcomputer software packages and applications include spreadsheet, database, graphics, communications, and word processing.
8. The first step in selecting a microcomputer is to define your needs, then think about software.
9. The commands DIR *.* and DIR ????????.??? produce the same results.
10. Expressions inside parentheses have the lowest priority when it comes to performing arithmetic operations.

## ANSWERS

### Multiple Choice
1. d
2. e
3. c
4. b
5. d
6. b
7. a
8. e
9. b
10. c

### True/False
1. F
2. T
3. F
4. F
5. T
6. F
7. T
8. T
9. T
10. F

# Appendix C
# A Quick Trip with MS- and PC-DOS

C

## C-1

## INTRODUCTION

In this appendix, we explain the basics of the disk operating system (DOS). We define the differences between internal and external DOS commands, and explain how you use system time and date. We review file specifications in the DOS environment and discuss how to use the DIR command. Important keys are highlighted, and you learn how to create a data disk using the FORMAT command. We also review the different versions of MS- and PC-DOS. The appendix concludes with a table summarizing most of the important DOS commands.[1]

## C-2

## TURNING ON YOUR PC

When you access a personal computer, it is either on or off. If the computer is off, put the DOS disk into drive A and turn on the computer (DOS comes with the computer). This procedure is called a **cold boot** (boot means starting the computer).

If the computer is already on, insert the DOS disk into drive A and press Ctrl-Alt-Del (press all three keys simultaneously). This procedure is called a **warm boot**. A warm boot is faster than a cold boot because the computer does not check its memory when you do a warm boot.

When the computer is booted, it prompts you for the current date. Enter the date in the format requested (mm-dd-yy) and press Enter. Next, the computer requests the current time. Enter the time in the correct format (hh:mm:ss) and press Enter. Remember that DOS operates on a 24-hour clock. This means that 2:30 p.m., for example, is entered as 14:30.

You should see the A> prompt, which indicates that the necessary portions of DOS have been loaded into random-access memory (RAM) and drive A is the default drive. Default means that this is the drive the computer will use unless you indicate otherwise. If DOS is installed on your hard disk (which is usually drive C), your default drive will be C.

You can avoid entering the date and time by pressing Enter at the prompts. Your PC will then use the default date and time when saving files. However, it is a good habit to enter the correct date and time each time you start your computer. That way you know your files will be saved with the current time and date stamps. The correct date and time help you determine the most or least recent versions of your files in a directory. (A directory is a listing of all your files.)

If you forget to enter the current date and time at boot-up, you can enter this information at any time with the DATE and TIME commands. At the A> prompt, type *DATE* and press Enter. The computer prompts you to enter the current date in the format mm-dd-yy. Type the date and press Enter. To enter the current time, type *TIME* at the A> prompt and press Enter. You are prompted to enter a new time in the format hh:mm:ss. Then press Enter. The computer holds this information in memory and updates it automatically until you turn off your computer. Some computers have a battery-operated clock on

---

[1]For a detailed discussion of DOS commands, see *Information Systems Literacy and Software Productivity Tools: DOS* by Hossein Bidgoli (Macmillan, 1991).

their motherboard, which keeps the time and date current even when the computer is turned off.

**Internal commands** (sometimes called memory-resident commands) are those commands that are loaded into the computer at boot-up. You can use internal commands without the DOS disk in a drive. CLS (clear screen) is an example of an internal DOS command. If you type *CLS* and press Enter, your screen is cleared.

**External commands** (sometimes called non-memory-resident commands) are those commands that you can execute only when the DOS disk is in a drive. These commands are sometimes called DOS utilities. They are separate programs stored on the DOS disk. DISKCOPY (disk copy), for example, is an external DOS command. You can find a listing of most of these commands at the end of this appendix.

## C–3
# DOS PROMPTS

Depending on how you start your computer, you will see different prompts. If you have a hard disk and you boot your system from it, your prompt will probably be C>. The prompt indicates the current default drive. The computer uses the default drive unless you specify a different one. Changing the default drive is an easy task. For example, if the default drive is A (indicated by the A> prompt) and you want to change it to drive B, at the A> prompt, type *B:* and press Enter. You prompt should now be B>. To change it back, type *A:* and press Enter. You can customize the DOS prompt with the PROMPT command.

## C–4
# DOS FILE SPECIFICATIONS

DOS files follow the same general naming conventions as other software. A DOS file name can be up to eight characters long and can contain the digits 0 through 9, as well as special characters, such as an underscore (_) and a pound sign (#). Usually, you should avoid using special symbols.

File extensions can be up to three characters long, and they follow the same conventions as file names. Important file extensions in the DOS environment include the following:

■ BAK—Backup files are generated by some word processing, spreadsheet, and database management programs. BAK files are backup copies of original files.
■ BAT—Batch files are text files that the user generates. Batch files contain DOS commands that are executed when you type the name of the file.
■ COM—Command files can be executed by typing the name of the file.
■ EXE—Like COM files, you run executable files by typing the file name.
■ SYS—System files can be used only by DOS.

## C–5
# THE DIR COMMAND

If you type *DIR* and press Enter, you will receive a listing of your current directory. It will resemble the listing shown in figure C–1. At the top of this

**Figure C–1**

A Directory Listing

```
DIR

Volume in drive A is MSDOS_330A
Directory of  A:\

ANSI     SYS      1647    3-01-88   8:00a
APPEND   EXE      5794    3-01-88   8:00a
ASSIGN   COM      1530    3-01-88   8:00a
ATTRIB   EXE     10656    3-01-88   8:00a
CHKDSK   COM      9819    3-01-88   8:00a
COMMAND  COM     25308    3-01-88   8:00a
COMP     COM      4183    3-01-88   8:00a
COUNTRY  SYS     11254    3-01-88   8:00a
DISKCOMP COM      5848    3-01-88   8:00a
DISKCOPY COM      6264    3-01-88   8:00a
DISPLAY  SYS     11259    3-01-88   8:00a
DRIVER   SYS      1165    3-01-88   8:00a
EDLIN    COM      7495    3-01-88   8:00a
EXE2BIN  EXE      3050    3-01-88   8:00a
FASTOPEN EXE      3888    3-01-88   8:00a
FDISK    COM     48983    3-01-88   8:00a
FIND     EXE      6403    3-01-88   8:00a
FORMAT   COM     11671    3-01-88   8:00a
GRAFTABL COM      6136    3-01-88   8:00a
GRAPHICS COM     13943    3-01-88   8:00a
JOIN     EXE      9612    3-01-88   8:00a
KEYB     COM      9041    3-01-88   8:00a
LABEL    COM      2346    3-01-88   8:00a
MODE     COM     15440    3-01-88   8:00a
MORE     COM       282    3-01-88   8:00a
NLSFUNC  EXE      3029    3-01-88   8:00a
PRINT    COM      9011    3-01-88   8:00a
RECOVER  COM      4268    3-01-88   8:00a
SELECT   COM      4132    3-01-88   8:00a
SORT     EXE      1946    3-01-88   8:00a
SUBST    EXE     10552    3-01-88   8:00a
SYS      COM      4725    3-01-88   8:00a
TREE     COM      3540    3-01-88   8:00a
       33 File(s)      19456 bytes free

A>
```

figure, you can see that the volume in drive A is MSDOS-3.30A, which is the internal name for this disk. You can use the LABEL command to change the volume names of your disks.

The DIR command displays the name of each file, the file extension, the size of the file in bytes, and the date and time at which the file was created. At the end of the listing, you see the number of files in the current directory and the number of bytes available on the disk.

You can use the DIR command with wild card characters. DOS accepts the asterisk (*) and the question mark (?) as wild cards. These characters substitute for other characters in the file name or extension. The ? substitutes for only one character; the * can substitute for one or more characters. For example, if you type

DIR PLAN?.MON

DOS lists all the files that begin with PLAN and end with .MON, such as PLAN1.MON, PLAN2.MON, or PLANA.MON. If you type

DIR *.MON

DOS lists all the .MON files, such as LETTER.MON, 123.MON, or CHART_1.MON.

# C–6

## USING DIR WITH SWITCHES

You can use the DIR command with different switches (parameters) to provide different types of listings. The /W switch lists your files in a wide format. Only the file names and extensions are listed. For example, we generated the wide listing of our drive A shown in figure C–2 by placing our DOS disk in drive A and typing *DIR/W*.

When you use the /P switch, DOS pauses when a directory listing fills your screen and waits for you to press a key before it continues listing files. In figure C–3, we used the DIR/P command to display the directory of drive A.

You can use the DIR command to list files on any drive, regardless of whether it is the current drive. For example, if your current drive is A and you want to see a listing of drive B, type

DIR B:

Remember to include at least one space between the DIR command and the drive name.

# C–7

## IMPORTANT KEYS IN THE DOS ENVIRONMENT

Figure C–4 shows a typical PC keyboard. Several keys perform special tasks in the DOS environment. Table C–1 lists these keys and their functions.

```
DIR/W

 Volume in drive A is MSDOS_330A
 Directory of  A:\

ANSI     SYS     APPEND   EXE     ASSIGN   COM     ATTRIB   EXE     CHKDSK   COM
COMMAND  COM     COMP     COM     COUNTRY  SYS     DISKCOMP COM     DISKCOPY COM
DISPLAY  SYS     DRIVER   SYS     EDLIN    COM     EXE2BIN  EXE     FASTOPEN EXE
FDISK    COM     FIND     EXE     FORMAT   COM     GRAFTABL COM     GRAPHICS COM
JOIN     EXE     KEYB     COM     LABEL    COM     MODE     COM     MORE     COM
NLSFUNC  EXE     PRINT    COM     RECOVER  COM     SELECT   COM     SORT     EXE
SUBST    EXE     SYS      COM     TREE     COM
       33 File(s)     19456 bytes free

A>
```

**Figure C–2**
A Wide Directory Listing

**Figure C–3**
Pausing a Directory Listing

```
DIR/P

 Volume in drive A is MSDOS_330A
 Directory of  A:\

ANSI     SYS    1647    3-01-88    8:00a
APPEND   EXE    5794    3-01-88    8:00a
ASSIGN   COM    1530    3-01-88    8:00a
ATTRIB   EXE   10656    3-01-88    8:00a
CHKDSK   COM    9819    3-01-88    8:00a
COMMAND  COM   25308    3-01-88    8:00a
COMP     COM    4183    3-01-88    8:00a
COUNTRY  SYS   11254    3-01-88    8:00a
DISKCOMP COM    5848    3-01-88    8:00a
DISKCOPY COM    6264    3-01-88    8:00a
DISPLAY  SYS   11259    3-01-88    8:00a
DRIVER   SYS    1165    3-01-88    8:00a
EDLIN    COM    7495    3-01-88    8:00a
EXE2BIN  EXE    3050    3-01-88    8:00a
FASTOPEN EXE    3888    3-01-88    8:00a
FDISK    COM   48983    3-01-88    8:00a
FIND     EXE    6403    3-01-88    8:00a
FORMAT   COM   11671    3-01-88    8:00a
GRAFTABL COM    6136    3-01-88    8:00a
GRAPHICS COM   13943    3-01-88    8:00a
JOIN     EXE    9612    3-01-88    8:00a
KEYB     COM    9041    3-01-88    8:00a
LABEL    COM    2346    3-01-88    8:00a
Strike a key when ready . . .
MODE     COM   15440    3-01-88    8:00a
MORE     COM     282    3-01-88    8:00a
NLSFUNC  EXE    3029    3-01-88    8:00a
PRINT    COM    9011    3-01-88    8:00a
RECOVER  COM    4268    3-01-88    8:00a
SELECT   COM    4132    3-01-88    8:00a
SORT     EXE    1946    3-01-88    8:00a
SUBST    EXE   10552    3-01-88    8:00a
SYS      COM    4725    3-01-88    8:00a
TREE     COM    3540    3-01-88    8:00a
      33 File(s)    19456 bytes free

A>
```

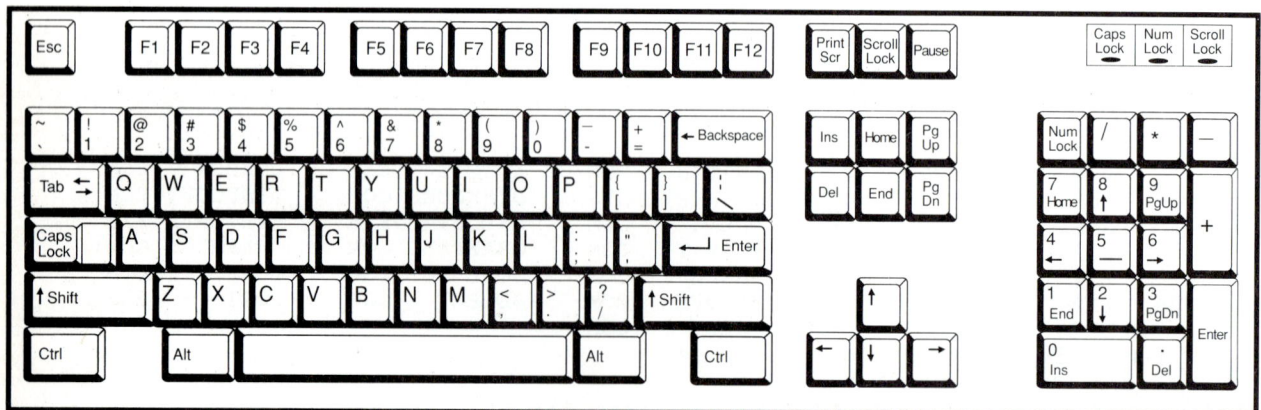

**Figure C–4**
A PC Keyboard

| Key | Description |
| --- | --- |
| Ctrl-Alt-Del | Warm boots your system. Equivalent to turning your computer off, and then on. |
| Ctrl-C or Ctrl-Break | Cancels a command while it is being executed. |
| Ctrl-PrtSc or Ctrl-P | Sends a copy of each line on-screen to the printer as it is displayed. This command is a toggle; it remains in effect until you press it again. |
| Shift-PrtSc (or PrtSc on enhanced keyboards) | Sends a copy of the entire screen to the printer. This command is not a toggle. |
| Ctrl-S or Ctrl-Num Lock | Pauses the directory listing for viewing. |
| F1 function key | Displays one character of the previous command with each press. Useful for editing a DOS command. |
| F3 function key | Displays the previous command. Useful for repetitive tasks. |
| Esc | Erases the current command or statement. |

**Table C–1**
Special Keyboard Keys

## C–8

# THE FORMAT COMMAND

Before you can use a new disk on your computer, it must be formatted. To format a disk, place the DOS disk into drive A, type

FORMAT A:

and press Enter. Remove the DOS disk, insert the disk to be formatted into drive A, and press Enter. When DOS is finished formatting the disk, you are asked if you want to format another. If you answer yes, you are prompted to insert another disk. If you answer no, the DOS prompt reappears.

When you format a disk, DOS checks it for defective spots and tells you whether the disk is usable. The FORMAT command also divides a disk into tracks and sectors, and creates a File Allocation Table (FAT). The FAT tells DOS where the data are stored on the disk.

When you format a disk, everything on it is erased. Make sure that the disk you are formatting is either brand new or contains files that you no longer need.

Figure C–5 shows what your screen looks like when you have completed formatting a disk in drive A. You also can format a disk in a different drive. For

```
A>FORMAT A:
Insert new diskette for drive A:
and strike ENTER when ready

Format complete

    362496 bytes total disk space
    362496 bytes available on disk

Format another (Y/N)?N
A>
```

**Figure C–5**
Formatting a Disk in Drive A

example, if you have your DOS disk in drive A, you can format a disk in drive B by typing

    FORMAT B:

## C–9

## DIFFERENT VERSIONS OF MS- AND PC-DOS

PC-DOS is used with the IBM computer, and MS-DOS is used with IBM-compatible computers. Both versions have evolved through several levels. Major versions are numbered 1.0, 2.0, 3.0, and so forth. Minor revisions are numbered 1.01, 2.2, 3.02, and so on. The current version is 5.0. Each new version has added new commands and corrected the bugs in previous versions. Versions 3.1 and later include commands for a LAN (Local Area Network).

Versions of MS- and PC-DOS are upwardly compatible, which means that all the commands in earlier versions are available in later versions. To a typical microcomputer user, PC-DOS and MS-DOS are almost identical. To find out which version of DOS you are using, type *VER* and press Enter. Figure C–6 illustrates this process. As you can see, our version of DOS is 3.3. All commands discussed in this book work with all versions of DOS unless otherwise specified.

## C–10

## BATCH AND AUTOEXEC FILES

Batch files contain a series of DOS commands that are executed as if you typed them individually. These files are helpful when you must perform repetitive operations. A batch file can have any standard name and the extension must always be BAT. Batch files can be any length, and you can include any valid command or statement. To generate a batch file, you can use EDLIN (the DOS line editor) or any word processing program.

For simple files, you can use a version of the copy command as follows:

    COPY CON MYFILE.BAT
    command or statement
    command or statement
    command or statement

You must press Enter after each command or statement in your batch file. To end a batch file, press Ctrl-Z or the F6 function key. To execute a batch file, insert the disk containing the file into your default drive and type the name of the file.

**Figure C–6**

Displaying the DOS Version Number

```
A>VER

MS-DOS Version 3.30

A>
```

Enter the following batch file at the A> prompt, pressing keys as indicated:

```
COPY CON HELLO.BAT (Enter)
DIR (Enter)
CLS (Enter)
BASICA (Enter)(Ctrl-Z)
```

If you type *HELLO* at the A> prompt, you will see a directory of that drive, the screen will clear, and BASICA will be loaded into RAM (assuming that the disk in drive A contains BASICA).

The only limitation with using the COPY CON command is that you cannot edit your batch file. You must recreate the entire file or import the file created by COPY CON into EDLIN or a word processing program to make changes.

To stop execution of your batch file, press Ctrl-Break.

You can have your batch file execute automatically when you start your computer system by naming it AUTOEXEC.BAT. DOS always looks for this file first. You can use this file to create custom menus for your system, to load a particular program that you use frequently, or anything else you want to have done automatically when you first turn on your computer.

Table C–2 lists some DOS commands and their functions. In this table, we assume that you are working from the A> prompt. A means drive A, B means drive B, ext stands for any valid file extension, and filename stands for any valid file name.

| Command | Function |
| --- | --- |
| ATTRIB +R filename.ext | Makes a file a read-only file (Release 3 and higher) |
| ATTRIB -R filename.ext | Removes the read-only status (Release 3 and higher) |
| CHDIR (CD) | Changes the current directory or displays the current path |
| CHKDSK | Displays amount of free disk space or the amount of free memory on your computer |
| CHKDSK B: | Displays amount of free disk space in drive B |
| CLS | Clears the screen |
| COMP A:filename.ext B:filename.ext | Compares two files |
| COPY filename.ext B: | Copies filename.ext to drive B |
| COPY B:filename.ext | Copies filename.ext to drive A |
| COPY *.ext B: | Copies all files with the ext extension from A to B |
| COPY B:*.ext | Copies all files with the ext extension from B to A |
| COPY *.* B: | Copies all files from A to B |

**Table C–2**
Important DOS Commands

**Table C–2** *(Continued)*

| Command | Function |
|---|---|
| COPY B:*.* | Copies all files from B to A |
| COPY filename1.ext filename2.ext | Copies a file from A to A with a different name |
| COPY filename1.ext B:filename2.ext | Copies a file from A to B with a different name |
| COPY B:filename1.ext filename2.ext | Copies a file from B to A with a different name |
| COPY CON B:filename.BAT | Creates a batch file in drive B |
| Ctrl-Alt-Del | Resets system (warm boot) |
| DATE | Sets system date |
| DEL filename.ext | Erases filename.ext from A |
| DEL B:filename.ext | Erases filename.ext from B |
| DEL B:filename.* | Erases filename with any extension from B |
| DEL B:*.ext | Erases files with the same extension from B |
| DIR | Displays directory of A |
| DIR B: | Displays directory of B |
| DIR/P | Pauses while displaying directory of A |
| DIR B:/P | Pauses while displaying directory of B |
| DIR/W | Displays directory of A in wide format |
| DIR B:/W | Displays directory of B in wide format |
| DIR \| SORT | Displays a sorted directory of A |
| DIR B: \| SORT | Displays a sorted directory of B |
| DISKCOPY A: B: | Copies disk in A to disk in B |
| DISKCOMP | Compares two disks, track by track and sector by sector to determine whether the contents are identical |
| ERASE filename.ext | Erases filename.ext on A |
| ERASE B:filename.ext | Erases filename.ext on B |
| ERASE *.ext | Erases all files with same extension on A |
| ERASE B:*.ext | Erases all files with same extension on B |
| FORMAT | Formats disk in A |
| FORMAT B: | Formats disk in B |
| FORMAT/V | Formats disk in A with volume label |
| FORMAT B:/V | Formats disk in B with volume label |
| LABEL | Creates, changes, or deletes a volume label |
| MKDIR (MD) | Creates a subdirectory |
| PATH | Searches a specified directory for a program that cannot be found in current directory |
| PROMPT | Customizes DOS system prompt |
| RENAME filename1.ext filename2.ext | Renames a file on A |

**Table C–2**   *(Continued)*

| Command | Function |
|---|---|
| RENAME B:filename1.ext filename2.ext | Renames a file on B |
| RMDIR (RD) | Removes a subdirectory |
| Shift-PrtSc (PrtSc on enhanced keyboards) | Prints the screen |
| SYS | Places operating system files (IBM.DOS and IBMBIO.COM) on the disk specified |
| TIME | Sets system time |
| TREE | Displays structure of current directory |
| TYPE filename.ext | Displays contents of filename.ext |
| TYPE B:filename.ext | Displays contents of filename.ext on B |
| VER | Displays DOS version |
| VERIFY | Checks data just written to disk to be sure the data has been recorded correctly |
| VERIFY ON/VERIFY OFF | Sets verify status |
| VOL | Displays volume label of disk (if label exists) |

# SUMMARY

This appendix reviewed simple DOS operations. We explained the difference between internal and external DOS commands, and we discussed the types of DOS prompts and file name specifications. You learned how to use the DIR command with various switches and how to format a disk using FORMAT.

# Appendix D
## Answers to Selected
## Review Questions

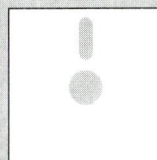

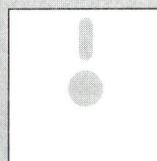

## Chapter 1

2. Problem definition is very important—it is the first step. If you don't define the problem clearly, you may end up solving the wrong problem. An algorithm is a series of steps or a "road map" for solving a problem.

8. Flowcharts and pseudocodes are used to simplify the logic of a problem. They are also used to split a large problem into a series of smaller modules.

16. Sequence, selection, iteration, and CASE.

## Chapter 2

2. The temporary memory area (RAM) is volatile. If your computer should lose power, all your work in RAM will be lost. The permanent memory area (hard or floppy disk) is non-volatile.

5. File name c (ABC 11) is not valid because it includes a space.

7. With DELETE you can delete the entire program or segments of the program. With NEW you can erase only the entire program.

10. Use FILES.

11. Use Ctrl-Break or Ctrl-C.

13. Only a copy of it is transferred to RAM. The original program stays on the disk.

## Chapter 3

2. In program a, line 10 must be READ X, Y. In program b, the data are missing. In program c, the line should read as follows:

X=B+C

6.
```
10 A$="JACKI"
20 B$="MARY"
30 C$="CATHY"
40 PRINT A$,B$,C$
50 END
```

11. Interactive programming means allowing data entry during program execution.

12. Names, addresses, product descriptions, colors, sex, and so on.

14. In program a, zero (0), because c has not been defined. In program b, 15 10 5.

## Chapter 4

**2.** Program a does not print anything. Program b prints 10. Program c generates an endless loop, printing COMPUTER over and over. Program d prints the following:

```
5
10
15
OUT OF DATA IN 10 error message
```

**5.** You need 24 data items.

**10.** Line 10 should be changed to the following:

```
10 FOR I=2 TO 6 STEP N
```

N must be a negative number.

## Chapter 5

**1.** On two different lines, enter two PRINT statements (followed by nothing).

**2.** The program prints a 5 in column 1, three spaces, another 5, one more space, and another 5.

## Chapter 6

**1.** A(1) and A1(25) are valid. A(WW), W1(2*A+11), and W5(2*A−10) are valid as long as the values in parentheses are greater than or equal to zero.

**3.** The program prints the following:

```
11 12 18 0 22 40
```

## Chapter 7

**1.** The statement

```
A(21,22)=64
```

is out of range because your DIM statement has defined a table of only 20 rows and 35 columns.

**2.** You need 600 numeric data items for A(20,30), 720 numeric data items for B(18,40), and 55 non-numeric data items for C$(55) (assuming that you are starting from address 1, not 0).

## Chapter 8

**3. a.** There are no data in this program.

   **b.** The subroutine does not have a RETURN statement.

   **c.** You must enter the subroutine by using the GOSUB command.

   **d.** The GOTO in line 520 is not needed.

## Chapter 9

**3.** A random file can be processed in any order. It is faster than a sequential file.

**5.** You use the following format:

OPEN filename FOR INPUT AS #1

**13.** Files are used to make a set of data available to several programs.

## Chapter 10

**1.** You use the ˆ (caret) symbol.

**5.** The answer is −7.

**6.** The answer is 10.

**9.** The answer is −1.

**12.** `DEF FN(R)=4/3*3.1416*R^3.`

## Appendix B

**2.** Disk drive and keyboard.

**6.** Floppy and hard disks.

**12.** It varies. It starts at 256 or 512.

**16.** Keep it in a dust-free environment. Protect it against excessive heat and humidity. Provide a constant electrical current.

**21.** Every application program provides an editing feature so you can edit your mistakes. Or, in the worst case, you can retype your mistakes.

**26.** Priority of operations or precedence of operations refers to the order in which a computer handles calculations. The order is as follows:

- Expressions inside parentheses have the highest priority
- Exponentiation (raising to power) has the next highest priority
- Multiplication and division have the third highest priority
- Addition and subtraction have the fourth highest priority
- When there are two or more operations with the same priority, operations proceed from left to right

# Index